Understanding and Overcoming Learned H

Dedication

This book is dedicated to the partners of abusers who still suffer from the ravages of

learned helplessness and to those who have recovered from it.

Table of Contents

Chapter One

Introduction   Page 6

Chapter Two

The First Twelve Step Program   Page 44

Chapter Three

Journey through the Twelve Steps   Page 74

Chapter Four

Roots of Addiction   Page 95

Chapter Five

Step One   Page 183

Chapter Six

Step Two   Page 210

Chapter Seven

Step Three   Page 231

Chapter Eight

Step Four   Page 260

Chapter Nine

Step Five   Page 303

Chapter Ten

Step Six   Page 327

Chapter Eleven

Step Seven   Page 338

Chapter Twelve

Step Eight   Page 353

Chapter Thirteen

Step Nine   Page 371

Chapter Fourteen

Step Ten   Page 396

Chapter Fifteen

Step Eleven   Page 318

Chapter Sixteen

Step Twelve   Page 449

Chapter Seventeen

Conclusion   Page 468

References   Page 470

Acknowledgement

First and foremost, I wish to acknowledge and recognize my first sponsor who took a broken down, despondent, homeless drunk and addict and led him into the world of wellness. Second, I would like to acknowledge my family, friends, mentors, and all the people who stood by me as I stumbled through early recovery. Finally, I would like to acknowledge my friends and mentors who nurtured me and helped me mature to wellness, and now honor me for me knowledge and wisdom which in fact does not belong to me—it belongs to the thousands of sober men and women who got well using these principles, some of whom passed on the wisdom of the ages to me.

Chapter One

Introduction

When bad things happen, you would think that we would do whatever was necessary to change or escape the situation, but this is not necessarily the case. Research on what is known as "learned helplessness" has shown that when people feel like they have no control over what happens, they tend to simply give up and accept their fate.

What is Learned Helplessness?

Learned helplessness occurs when an animal or a human is repeatedly subjected to an aversive stimulus that they cannot escape from. Eventually, the animal or human will stop trying to avoid the stimulus and behave as if it is utterly helpless to change the situation. Even when opportunities to escape are presented, this learned helplessness will prevent any action.

Although the concept is strongly tied to animal psychology and behavior, it can also apply to many situations involving human beings. When people feel that they have no control over their situation, they may begin to behave in a helpless manner. This inaction can lead people to overlook opportunities for relief or change.

The Discovery of Learned Helplessness

The concept of learned helplessness was discovered accidentally by psychologists Martin Seligman and Steven F. Maier in 1967. They had initially observed helpless behavior in dogs that had been classically conditioned to expect an electrical shock after hearing a tone.

Later, the dogs were placed in a shuttle box that contained two chambers separated by a low barrier. A shuttle box is a scientific device used in animal learning experiments. The box is divided into two halves and the animal must move from one compartment to the other in order to get their reward or avoid an adversive stimulus. The floor of Seligman and Maier's, shuttle box was was electrified on one side, but not on the other. The dogs previously subjected to the classical conditioning made no attempts to escape, even though avoiding the shock simply involved jumping over a small barrier.

To investigate this phenomenon, the researchers devised another experiment. In this experiment, one group of dogs were strapped into a harnesses for a period of time and then released. The dogs in a second group were placed in the same harnesses, but were subjected to electrical shocks that could be avoided by pressing a panel with their noses. A third group received the same shocks as those in the second group, except the dogs in this group were not able to control the shock. For those dogs in the third group, the shocks seemed to be completely random and outside of their control.

The dogs were then placed in a shuttle box. Dogs from the first and second group quickly learned that jumping over the barrier eliminated the shock. However, those in the third group made no attempts to get away from the shocks. Due to their previous experience, they had developed a cognitive expectation that nothing they did could prevent or eliminate the shocks.

Learned Helplessness in People

The impact of learned helplessness has been demonstrated in different animal species, but its effects can also be seen in people. Consider one often-used example, where a child who performs poorly on math tests and assignments will quickly begin to feel that nothing they do will have any effect on their math performance. When later faced with any type of math-related task, the child may experience a sense of helplessness and will just stop trying.

Learned helplessness has also been associated with several different psychological disorders. Depression, anxiety, phobias, shyness, and loneliness can all be exacerbated by learned helplessness.

Likewise, for example, a woman who feels shy in social situations may eventually begin to feel that there is nothing she can do to overcome her symptoms. This sense that her symptoms are out of her direct control may lead her to stop trying to engage in social situations, thus making her shyness even more pronounced, leading to social isolation.

However, researchers have found that learned helplessness does not always extend across all settings and situations. A student who experiences learned helpless with regard to math class will not necessarily experience same helplessness when faced with performing calculations in the real world. In other cases, people may experience learned helplessness that extends across a wide variety of situations.

So, what explains why some people develop learned helplessness and others do not? Why is it specific to some situations, but more global in others? Many researchers believe that actions regarding something or explanatory styles play a role in determining how people are impacted by learned helplessness. This view suggests that an individual's characteristic style of acting on events helps determine whether or not they will develop learned helplessness.

A pessimistic style is associated with a greater likelihood of experiencing learned helplessness. People with this style tend to view negative events as being inescapable and unavoidable and tend to take personal responsibility for such negative events.

Learned Helplessness in Children

Learned helpless often originates in childhood, and unreliable, unresponsive, or unavailable caregivers often contribute to these feelings. Learned helplessness can begin very early in life. Children raised in institutionalized settings, for instance, often exhibit symptoms of helplessness even during infancy.

When children need help, but no one comes to their aid, they may be left feeling that they have no value or worth and nothing they do will change their situation. Repeated experiences that bolster these feelings of helplessness and hopelessness can result in growing into adulthood ultimately feeling that they are worthless and that there is nothing they can do to change their circumstance.

Some common symptoms of learned helplessness in children include:

- Low self-esteem
- Passiveness
- Poor motivation
- Gives up easily
- Lack of effort
- Frustration
- Procrastination
- Failure to ask for help

Learned helplessness can also result in anxiety, depression, or both. When children feel that they have had no control over events in their lives, they come to expect that future events will be just as uncontrollable. Because they believe that nothing they do will ever change the outcome of an event, children are often left thinking that they should not even bother trying.

Academic struggles can often lead to feelings of learned helplessness. A child who makes an effort to do well but still does poorly may end up feeling that he has no control over his grades or performance. Since nothing they do seems to make any difference, they will stop trying and their grades will suffer even more. Such problems can also affect other areas of the child's life. The child's poor performance in school can make them feel that nothing they do is right or useful, and so, they may lose the motivation to try in other areas of their life as well.

Learned Helplessness in Mental Health

Learned helplessness is thought to contribute to feelings of anxiety and may influence the onset, severity, and persistence of conditions such as Generalized Anxiety Disorder (GAD). When you experience chronic anxiety, you may eventually give up on finding relief because your anxious feelings seem unavoidable and untreatable, or you might engage in tension-relieving behaviors like rocking or hair pulling, as well as other obsessive compulsive tension-relieving behaviors such as running, exercising, risky activities, and chronic masturbation. Because of this, people who are experiencing mental health issues such as anxiety or depression may refuse medications or therapy that might help relieve their symptoms.

As people age, learned helplessness can become something of a vicious cycle. When encountering problems such anxiety or depression, people may feel that nothing can be done to ease their symptoms. People then fail to seek options that might help which then contributes to greater feelings of helplessness and anxiety, and might resort to suicide as a way out.

Learned helplessness can have a profound impact on mental health and well-being. People who experience learned helplessness are also likely to experience symptoms of depression, elevated stress levels, and less motivation to take care of their physical health.

Not everyone responds to experiences the same way. Some people are more likely to experience learned helplessness in the face of uncontrollable events, often due to biological and psychological factors. Children raised by helpless parents, for example, are also more likely to experience learned helplessness.

Learned Helplessness and Learned Restlessness

Overgeneralization of learned helplessness could encourage the assumption that problem-solving behavior such as voluntary escape or avoidance is always the most adaptive response to a threat. Clients in psychotherapy are often most threatened by their own unwanted responses, many of which normally elude voluntary self-control. Indeed, anxious efforts to avoid, escape, or otherwise control such responses sometimes have a self-defeating effect of producing them, as seen in such diverse conditions such as stuttering, insomnia, sexual dysfunction, and even some kinds of depression.

Such conditions have an experimental comparison in the persistence of punished escape or avoidant responses in what is known as vicious-circle learning. The persistence of ineffective coping behaviors is seen to be the opposite of learned helplessness, and is termed as "learned restlessness."

In contrast to learned helplessness, learned restlessness calls for a paradoxical treatment strategy of response prevention or instructed helplessness, whereby the client is persuaded to give up any deliberate escape or avoidance efforts, risking or accepting the feared stimuli.

As was outlined briefly above, the concept of "learned helplessness" is popular today in many circles, both clinically and experimentally. The concept was first used to describe the failure of some laboratory animals to escape or avoid shock, when given the opportunity, after previous exposure to inescapable shock in experiments done by Seligman and Maier in 1967.

The term has since been applied to the failure of human beings to seek, utilize, or learn problem-solving responses, as seen most dramatically in the depressed person who seems to have given up hope that effective voluntary control over important environmental events is possible.

The typical laboratory demonstration of learned helplessness utilized an experimental design in which two of three groups of dogs or other animals were first exposed to a series of shocks while confined in a harness or hammock. Test subjects in one of these groups were allowed to learn an instrumental escape response, whereas those in the second, yoked group had no instrumental control over the shock. Inexperienced subjects in the third group received no shock at this stage.

All animals were then given the opportunity to learn the usual escape or avoid response in a shuttle box. Those in the inexperienced and escape-conditioned groups readily learned to jump the barrier to safety, whereas many of those from the previously yoked group failed to learn the available response. The learned-helpless animals quickly ceased running about in the new situation and simply laid passively, whining quietly, as they received continued shocks. Even if they accidentally made an occasional escape response at first, they failed to repeat and learn this response.

This effect was by no means universal across all subjects or variations of procedure, but it does have some degree of validity across species and situations. With human subjects, exposure to aversive and uncontrollable noise has subsequently interfered with learning to control noise interfered with problem solving, while experience with insoluble discrimination problems likewise showed interference by uncontrolled noise.

Some naturally occurring forms of learned helplessness in humans can be of more direct clinical interest. In particular, Reactive Depression, a mood disorder triggered by a specific stressful event which can be anything that changes or threatens to change someone's everyday routine or expectations, has recently been interpreted as the outcome of a perception or belief that significant life events, both aversive and gratifying, are beyond the individual's control.

Hence, the familiar pattern in depression of giving up even when adaptive responses would seem to others to be available. Of course, some giving-up reactions are not as global or generalized as in depression. Take, for example, children who react to failure in an academic or achievement context by giving up further effort, thus feeding a vicious circle of under-achievement if not the broader pattern of depression.

The therapeutic implications derived from the learned helplessness have thus far been less than dramatic. Predictions that time and Electro-Convulsive Therapy (ECT) might both help in cases of learned helplessness and/or depression, although based on laboratory results, have not shown results. Perhaps more specific to the is the suggestion of forcibly exposing a victim of learned helplessness to successful control experiences, as when helpless dogs have been dragged across the shuttle box until they finally learn that they can escape shock on their own.

A more general suggestion is being proposed that early experiences with effective voluntary control over events might help immunize humans, as well as other animals, against later learned helplessness when various trauma are encountered.

Also of interest here is persuading children with learned helplessness to attribute their failures to their own correctable lack of effort, researchers were able to improve these children's overall performance by getting them to try harder. In contrast, a group of students with learned helpless who were simply given a steady diet of success still overreacted to later failure.

Already, the more general and popular statements that learned helplessness problem-solving behavior is always the most adaptive response to a threat are growing in popularity, but adaptive escape or avoidance responses are not always available. For some kinds of aversive events, they might be unavailable. In the that case, as in the inescapable-shock condition of learned helplessness experiments, emotional passivity is in fact the most adaptive course.

Researchers maintain that since feedback from the fear reaction is itself aversive to the organism, the persistence of learned fear reactions in unavoidable and inescapable pain situations would be biologically wasteful, if not downright self-punitive. Thus, the only adaptive response option available to a dog which is forced to receive a series of signaled or unsigned inescapable, unavoidable shocks is to relax, or to inhibit an aversive fear response. Researchers suggest that here too, attempts to avoid or otherwise control the aversive event instrumentally would be useless, if not counterproductive.

Of course, human beings are generally more able to control external sources of threat than are dogs administered inescapable shock in the laboratory; at least we like to hope so. Individuals might also hope to exercise voluntary control over their own physiological, emotional, cognitive, and behavioral responses since these become sources of threat or gratification in their own right.

Clients in psychotherapy, for example, often respond as much to their own unwanted responses as to external threats, and they seek to control and change themselves and others as much or more than external events, or as a means to achieve control over external events.

However, researchers suggest that voluntary self-controlling responses in particular are not always available or may have their own aversive consequences. The research in this area does not speak to this clinically important possibility, partly because their work is based on laboratory studies of the response to externally administered stimuli, and so, if problem-solving responses are sometimes not available, especially for purposes of voluntary self-control, then learned helplessness might indeed have its place as an adaptive reaction to uncontrollable events.

As a result, it is clearly necessary to place the concept of learned helplessness in a broader context by clarifying the circumstances in which it is an adaptive condition, not a pathological state, but in such circumstances we also find a maladaptive condition that is more or less directly opposed to learned helplessness.

It is certainly not the case that all clients in therapy present a pattern of learned helplessness. Many are actively searching for effective coping responses to deal with external or internal events. Indeed, some clients seem to exhibit not a giving-up syndrome, but a trying-too-hard syndrome, often in an effort to escape or avoid their own undesired reactions in certain situations—over-compensating versus under-compensating.

There are many common clinical patterns of unnecessary and maladaptive avoidance behaviors. Classic phobias follow this pattern. So do some drug dependence and social withdrawal problems. Consider, for example, the male client who avoids urinating in public restrooms for fear of being seen if he fails to perform, known as "shy penis." Here, of course, as with most phobias, the avoidance behavior may be successful in minimizing embarrassment or anxiety, and therefore, is protective. But this behavior is not only unnecessary, logically speaking, but also unpleasant or aversive in its own right.

On the other hand, in the case of chronic insomnia, the search for effective coping mechanisms might well continue even without notable success in escaping the feared event. Here, the individual's anxiety persists and feeds a self-exacerbating condition, but the individual almost never gives up and relaxes. A similar "exacerbation cycle" plays a prominent role in many other psychosomatic conditions, from angina pectoris to gastric ulcer. Likewise, stuttering provides another example where the individual's anxiety and even their very coping efforts maintain the speech difficulty.

The case of unnecessary avoidance responding in the laboratory is best known from demonstrations of the resistance of avoidance responding to normal extinction procedures. Just as the animal with learned helpless fails to learn that a coping response is now available, because it does not try hard enough to respond, the persistent avoider also fails to learn that such a response is no longer necessary, for this animal never gives up responding or tries not responding.

Less familiar, but even more clearly opposed to the learned helplessness model, are studies in which animals learn some response to escape or avoid shock but are later exposed to shock contingent upon that same response. Here, the original shock contingency is removed but coping responses are now punished instead. This is the paradigm of "vicious-circle learning," in which punished escape or avoidance responses are maintained by at least some subjects in a superstitious fashion, long after they have become counterproductive.

Here, the animal or human gets the worst of both worlds. They not only suffer the primary, punishing stimulation such as a shock, but their emotional arousal such as fear or frustration is maintained, instead of given up or inhibited as in learned helplessness. The animal or human in this position might even suffer pathological psychosomatic stress-related effects, such as ulcers, as a result.

In any case, the unusual persistence of punished avoidance behavior looks as strange to the observer who does not know the animal or the human's prior reinforcement history as does learned helpless behavior.

In a 1996 unpublished study, researchers observed that monkeys who first learned to avoid shock by lever pressing, but were later punished with shock for doing so, continued pressing the lever to shock themselves, and even when the shock was completely discontinued, the lever-pressing responses continued, even though they had now become objectively functionless, still produced painful consequences. As a result, the animals continued to punish themselves unnecessarily with shock intensities that they had previously worked hard to avoid. And so, anyone observing the needless self-injurious behavior of these animals without knowledge of their prior learning history would undoubtedly be baffled by their masochism.

Researchers have noted the parallel of vicious-circle learning with the learned helplessness pattern insofar as both involve trapping the animal or human in a change of environment that is not distinguished by the test subject. The animal or human that has learned helplessness fails to try when the situation now dictates that they should, and the animal or human that has learned to try often fails to give up when that becomes the more adaptive course.

The persistence of ineffective problem-solving behavior constitutes a variant of what has come to be known as "learned helplessness" called "learned restlessness." In these terms, an individual with learned restless is one who persists in futile, if not self-defeating attempts, to escape a feared event. Emotional arousal in the form of anxiety and/or frustration is naturally prominent in learned restlessness, just as low arousal and depression are emotional concomitants of learned helplessness. Literally, the individual with learned restlessness gets no rest, not even the rest of resignation.

The implications of "learned restlessness" also fit the clinical picture of many clients who in different ways are trying too hard to escape or avoid some aversive condition through voluntary, instrumental behavior. In such cases, some degree of learned helplessness might actually prove more adaptive in the long run.

Virtually every client comes to therapy seeking to escape or avoid some aversive condition. If the condition is not literally painful, as it is in many psychosomatic problems, it is psychologically distressing, as with anxiety problems, depression, insomnia, stuttering, sexual dysfunction, and many other difficulties. Occasionally, a presenting problem might be phrased in terms of positive goals to be achieved, although even here, a formulation of escape from the present, undesired condition could equally apply. The client might have come to feel more or less helpless insofar as they are now unable to control the aversive situation, but chances are they have previously tried several coping devices or responses, and seeking therapeutic help is another such response.

It seems unlikely that a professional helper would encourage this person to give up their search for help, or the search for an effective coping strategy. But if the therapist believed that a perfectly and permanently effective coping strategy of instrumental response was simply not available in this case, or that the problem was being maintained by the client's own emotional and instrumental reactions to the condition itself, then a strategy of encouraging the client to give up deliberate responding in this respect might seem more plausible.

Researchers have used an approach of this kind in their clinical work with psychosomatic pain patients. Researchers simply refused to focus their therapeutic efforts on pain complaints or pain relief per se, refocusing their patients' attention instead on formulating and working toward positive social, vocational, or avocational goals that did not in fact have to be contingent on prior pain relief. In a sense, this approach encouraged the patient to become less restless regarding his pain and less helpless regarding external sources of potential gratification.

This approach has much in common with "dereflection," discovered by Viktor Frankl in 1975, where a person is overly self-absorbed on an issue or attainment of a goal and by redirecting the attention, or dereflecting the attention away from the self, the person can become whole by thinking about others rather than themselves.

Viktor Frankl noticed a habit people had that he called: "hyperreflection," where you are preoccupied with how you look from an outside perspective as you are speaking or performing anything you are intent on "getting right," rendering the task you are engaged in impossible to perform.

The self-observation and self-preoccupation habit appears most acutely in the case of public speaking. With all eyes upon you, the tendency is to see yourself through their eyes as well, and then you will not be there for the audience because you have removed the focus from them and put it onto yourself.

Frankl's remedy for "hyperreflection" was "dereflection," where you take the focus off of yourself and reflect it instead on the task at hand, and so, lose yourself. You become present in the experience itself such as focus on your music; on your love for the other person; or on whatever you are doing and then, and so, through losing yourself, you find yourself. You actualize yourself only when the goal is not self-actualization and you are not thinking about yourself at all, but only about the value and meaning in the task at hand.

Here too, attention is refocused away from goals that often defy deliberate attainment, such as sexual fulfillment, in the belief that not trying so hard may be the surer path to such ends. Masters and Johnson's (1970) Sensate Focus Exercise also encourages sexually dysfunctional couples to temporarily give up their efforts to achieve orgasmic success or avoid failure while focusing on other aspects of sexual pleasure instead.

This might be a fairly obvious clinical course when the client is escaping or seeking to escape a condition that is intrinsically not so aversive as the client believes it to be. For instance, rational emotive therapists often deal with exaggerated social fears by using logical argument to undercut or "decatastrophize" them. Counter-productive efforts to avoid such experiences may then be given up. For example, the victim of "shy penis" mentioned above may be convinced that failure to perform at a urinal will meet with no great aversive consequences, and so, can be risked without the usual avoidance behavior.

Indeed, it might sometimes be appropriate to assure the client that they will experience their feared failure, at least for some time, and that they should learn to accept that eventuality with less anxiety or struggle. Reduced anticipatory anxiety may, of course, be a necessary step toward later being able to perform the desired response. A similar approach might be adopted toward insomnia and many other conditions where a giving up of all hope of voluntary control might undercut anticipatory anxiety and soon permit more normal, albeit "involuntary" functioning to occur. It is easy to see why explicit instruction in learned helplessness has rarely been attempted or even considered, but it would surely warrant further exploration.

A first guess would be to follow traditional voluntary/involuntary or central/autonomic distinctions. Adaptive control of the external environment is most often accomplished through muscular-skeletal responses under voluntary control. On the other hand, many internal, autonomically mediated functions are generally not under voluntary control, and certainly not under complete conscious or deliberate control. Thus, many emotional and psychophysiological problems, such as anxiety, depression, insomnia, tension headache, and sexual dysfunction, are aberrations of normally involuntary processes.

It might be argued that the solution to such problems lies in extending the individual's voluntary self-control to encompass them, using novel therapeutic means if necessary to do so. In many situations, deliberate relaxation is used as an antidote for anxiety, and so, an involuntary emotional reaction is supposedly displaced by voluntary physical responses. But not all clients can relax in this manner, perhaps especially if they try anxiously to do so, such as in the following example.

John was actively trying to relax. An electromyograph tom which he was connected constantly showed a high level of activity until he was told that he probably would never be able to learn to relax and should resign himself to the fact that he would always be tense. A few minutes later, John said: "Oh hell, I give up," at which time, the meter reading immediately dropped to a low level with so quickly that the therapist thought that the unit had malfunctioned. In the following sessions, John was successfully able to reduce his distress because he was not trying too hard to relax.

The trying-too-hard syndrome may also be found where complex motor coordination is required, as in athletic performance. This behavior is a mix of voluntary and involuntary responding, where some degree of effort is naturally required. However, as the finely coordinated muscle responses demanded by the game are learned, they become less deliberate and increasingly automatic. Then, like other involuntary behaviors, performance may suffer if it is made overly self-conscious or deliberate. Thus, beginners may be more likely to suffer problems of giving up, while pros may be more vulnerable to trying too hard.

Of more clinical relevance is the case of stuttering. Adult speech is a complex but largely automatic behavior that is naturally disrupted by an excess of intention or deliberation. Most stuttering conforms quite clearly to the learned-restlessness model, even if some stutterers exhibit learned helplessness or depressive features in other areas of adjustment. Their continued struggle to speak fluently or to avoid dysfluency maintains the vicious circle of disordered speech.

But the pattern is not so clear in cognitive or academic achievement problems. Researchers selected a group of young students identified as having learned helpless, such as being prone to give up in the face of failure and improved their performance by motivating them to try harder. Yet, some students failed through trying too hard, as seen in many older students with test anxiety or study problems. A given student's achievement problem may actually prove to be a rather complex mix or vicious cycle of trying too hard and giving up, or it may move from a stage of anxiety and maladaptive effort to a later burned-out stage of exhaustion and depression.

These examples highlight the clinical care that may be necessary if learned helpless re actions and learned restless reactions are to be differentiated and diagnosed correctly. But this task may be the most difficult where one pattern is superimposed upon another in a compounding of ingrown, self-exacerbating reactions to the initial difficulty. Conditions such as anxiety and depression are commonly viewed as relatively simple and unitary reactions to external events. For example, depression follows from the perception or belief that significant environmental events are independent of voluntary control. But as researchers acknowledge in passing, depression itself is an aversive condition that the individual may or may not try to escape.

Theoretically, the experience of depression might become the stimulus for either helpless or restless reactions. If the otherwise helpless and depressed individual is greatly ashamed or afraid of their depression, they may indeed cast about anxiously for relief from that condition. This is consistent with the observation that depression and anxiety are often entangled to different degrees. On the other hand, a person could conceivably get more depressed because they are depressed or more anxious because they are anxious and depressed. Researchers have offered theoretical models of how the compounding of anxiety occurs.

Secondary reactions to the condition itself help to explain why many anxiety and depression states seem so loosely connected to precipitating or controlling environmental events. Indeed, such reactions may be of no less importance than the initial reaction, since they can maintain or compound an otherwise relatively benign condition. Furthermore, the nature of these secondary reactions may dictate the point and direction of maximum therapeutic leverage, at least initially.

For example, take an individual who is anxious that they are depressed. A simple treatment to alleviate the individual's depression would tend to confirm the person's learned restless response to the depression per se. Perhaps more appropriate, at least at first, would be a paradoxical technique prescribing depression or otherwise undercutting the individual's anxious efforts to escape it. This strategy appears all the more reasonable if indeed much reactive depression tends to lift simply with time, as long as secondary reactions do not perpetuate it. Thus, even some depressed patients might benefit from learning increased helplessness, at least with regard to their depression.

Even where the clinical potential of giving up is apparent to the therapist in a given case, the biggest difficulty may lie in how to present this alternative to a client who is highly motivated to escape or otherwise control an unwanted condition. The clinician will certainly have to minimize the likelihood of the client angrily rejecting this course, or at the other extreme, overgeneralizing the hopelessness of the situation and giving in to a genuinely depressive reaction.

Here, another decision is critical: Should giving up be presented as a course of genuine resignation or as a more subtle way to try to improve the situation? This is the difference between "giving up trying" and "trying giving up," and most paradoxical treatments may be presented to the client in either light. Of course, the second formulation would generally be more palatable to the restless client. On the other hand, this does not really break the pattern of restless responding, since even a response of passivity may be attempted actively and deliberately as a coping device. Learned restlessness would tend to suggest that genuine resignation or resistance might often be more helpful than feigned resignation or resistance, but this critical point certainly requires clinical and experimental test.

Of course, the treatment strategy outlined here might also prove unpalatable to most clinicians, at least at first glance. Clinicians prefer to see and present themselves as helpers of the helpless and are unlikely to accept giving up, in themselves or their clients. But the temptation to always try to fulfill the client's search for a problem-solving device is not only built into the clinician's helping role; it is also reinforced by the growing behavioral emphasis on self-control technologies and treatments, some of which seek to extend the individual's voluntary control over processes which are normally involuntary.

Sometimes this is clearly possible and even the best course. But the implicit or explicit assumption that this is always possible and always the best course grows less from sound clinical observation than from a broader clinical and cultural view of voluntary effort and control as the solution to human problems. It is this broader bias that makes more and better coping the appealing goal for clients and clinicians alike and that also accounts, in part, for the immediate appeal of the learned-helplessness model and its therapeutic message that trying harder helps.

On the other hand, learned restlessness seems almost counterintuitive, at least to our work-oriented Western mind. In some Eastern traditions, especially Zen Buddhism, giving up is more readily recognized as an adaptive course in many situations. After all, even the ultimate goal of enlightenment is said to elude deliberate striving or deliberate non-striving. But hopefully some clients and clinicians can escape the trap of trying too hard, with regard to some of their personal and clinical objectives by selectively and appropriately giving up.

Experimental psychologists interested in learning have traditionally studied the behavior of animals and humans faced with rewards and punishments that the subject could control. So, in a typical instrumental learning experiment, the subject can either make some response or refrain from making it, and thereby influence the events around them. However, nature is not always so benign in its arrangement of the contingencies. Not only do we face events that we can control by our actions, but we also face many events about which we can do nothing at all. Such uncontrollable events can significantly debilitate organisms, and they produce passivity in the face of trauma; inability to learn that responding is effective; and produces emotional stress in animals, and possibly depression in man.

Regarding behavioral displays, when an experimentally inexperienced dog receives escape-avoidance training in a shuttle box, the following behavior typically occurs. At the onset of the first painful electric shock, the dog runs frantically about, defecating, urinating, and howling, until it accidentally scrambles over the barrier and escapes the shock. In the next trial, the dog, running and howling, crossed the barrier more quickly than in the preceding trail. This pattern continues until the dog learns to avoid shock altogether.

Researchers have found a striking difference between this pattern of behavior and that exhibited by dogs first given uncontrollable electric shocks in a Pavlovian hammock. This dog's first reactions to shock in the shuttle box were much the same as those of an inexperienced dog. However, in dramatic contrast to an inexperienced dog, a typical dog which had experienced uncontrollable shocks before avoidance training soon stopped running and howling and sat or laid, quietly whining, until shocks stopped. The dog did not cross the barrier and escape from shocks. Rather, it seemed to give up and passively accept the shocks. On succeeding trials, the dog continued to fail to make escape movements and took as much shock as the experimenter chose to give.

There was another peculiar characteristic of the behavior of dogs which had first experienced inescapable shock. These dogs occasionally jumped the barrier early in training and escape, but then reverted to taking the shocks, and they failed to learn that barrier-jumping produced a termination of the shocks. However, in inexperienced dogs, a successful escape response was a reliable predictor of future, short-term escape responses.

The escape-avoidance behavior of over 150 dogs which had received prior inescapable shocks was studied. Two-thirds of these dogs did not escape. The other third escaped and avoided in normal fashion. It is obvious that failure to escape is highly maladaptive since it means that the dog took 50 seconds of severe, pulsating shocks in each trial. In contrast, only 6% of experimentally inexperienced dogs failed to escape in the shuttle box. So, for any given dog, they either failed to escape on almost every trial or they learned normally.

We use the term: "learned helplessness" to describe the interference with adaptive responding produced by inescapable adverse stimuli and also as a shorthand to describe the process they we believe underlies the behavior. The phenomenon seems to be widespread, and has been reported by a number of investigators. Nor is it restricted to dogs. Deficits in problem-solving after experience with uncontrollable adverse stimuli has been shown in rats, cats, fish, mice, and humans.

The inability to control trauma not only disrupts escape in a variety of species, but also interferes with a range of adaptive behaviors. Rats that receive inescapable shocks initiate less pain-elicited aggression toward other rats; are slower to learn to swim out of a water maze as are mice; and are poorer at food-gathering behavior in adulthood when very hungry.

Situations involving uncontrollable events other than shock can produce effects which may be related to failure to escape shock. Escape deficits can be produced by passivity following defeat in fighting; trauma following defeat or restraint; and retardation in learning to bar press for food following uncontrollable food. In addition to impairing voluntary responding, uncontrollable shock produces more stress than controllable shock as measured by behavioral suppression, by defecation and conditioned, and by subjective report. Finally, more weight loss, anorexia, and whole brain norepinephrine depletion is found in rats experiencing uncontrollable as opposed to controllable shock.

Stocholm Syndrome

Stockholm syndrome is commonly linked to high profile kidnappings and hostage situations. Aside from famous crime cases, regular people may also develop this psychological condition in response to various types of trauma.

What is Stockholm Syndrome?

Stockholm syndrome is a psychological response and a form of learned helplessness. It occurs when hostages or abuse victims bond with their captors or abusers. This psychological connection develops over the course of the days, weeks, months, or even years of captivity or abuse. With this syndrome, hostages or abuse victims may come to sympathize with their captives. This is the opposite of the fear, terror, and disdain that might be expected from the victims in these situations.

Over the course of time, some victims come to develop positive feelings toward their captors. They may even begin to feel as if they share common goals and causes. The victim may begin to develop negative feelings toward the police or authorities. They may resent anyone who may be trying to help them escape from the dangerous situation they are in.

This paradox does not happen with every hostage or victim, and it is unclear why it occurs when it does. Many psychologists and medical professionals consider Stockholm syndrome a coping mechanism, or a way to help victims handle the trauma of a terrifying situation. Indeed, the history of the syndrome may help explain why that is.

What is the History of Stockholm Syndrome?

Episodes of what is known as Stockholm syndrome have likely occurred for many decades, even centuries. But it was not until 1973 that this response to entrapment or abuse came to be named. That is when two men held four people hostage for six days after a bank robbery in Stockholm, Sweden. After the hostages were released, they refused to testify against their captors and even began raising money for their defense.

25

After that, psychologists and mental health experts assigned the term "Stockholm syndrome" to the condition that occurs when hostages develop an emotional or psychological connection to the people who held them in captivity.

However, despite being well known, Stockholm syndrome is not recognized by the new edition of the *Diagnostic and Statistical Manual of Mental Disorders*. This manual is used by mental health experts and other specialists to diagnose mental health disorders.

What are the symptoms?

Stockholm syndrome is recognized by three distinct events or "symptoms."

Symptoms of Stockholm syndrome:

1. The victim develops positive feelings toward the person holding them captive or abusing them.
2. The victim develops negative feelings toward police, authority figures, or anyone who might be trying to help them get away from their captor. They may even refuse to cooperate against their captor.
3. The victim begins to perceive their captor's humanity and believe they have the same goals and values.

These feelings typically happen because of the emotional and highly charged situation that occurs during a hostage situation or abuse cycle.

For example, people who are kidnapped or taken hostage often feel threatened by their captor, but they are also highly reliant on them for survival. If the kidnapper or abuser shows them some kindness, they may begin to feel positive feelings toward their captor for this "compassion."

Over time, that perception begins to reshape and skew how they view the person keeping them hostage or abusing them.

Examples of Stockholm syndrome

Several famous kidnappings have resulted in high profile episodes of Stockholm syndrome including those listed below.

High Profile Cases

Patty Hearst

Perhaps most famously, the granddaughter of businessman and newspaper publisher William Randolph Hearst was kidnapped in 1974 by the Symbionese Liberation Army (SLA). During her captivity, she renounced her family, adopted a new name, and even joined the SLA in robbing banks. Later, Hearst was arrested, and she used Stockholm syndrome as a defense in her trial. That defense did not work, and she was sentenced to 35 years in prison, but was later pardoned.

Natascha Kampusch

In 1998, then 10-year-old Natascha was kidnapped and kept underground in a dark, insulated room. Her kidnapper, Wolfgang Přiklopil, held her captive for more than 8 years. During that time, he showed her kindness, but he also beat her and threatened to kill her. Natascha was able to escape, and Přiklopil committed suicide. News accounts at the time report Natascha "wept inconsolably."

Mary McElroy

In 1933, four men held 25-year-old Mary at gunpoint, chained her to walls in an abandoned farmhouse, and demanded ransom from her family. When she was released, she struggled to name her captors in their subsequent trial. She also publicly expressed sympathy for them.

Stockholm Syndrome in Today's Society

While Stockholm syndrome is commonly associated with a hostage or kidnapping situation, it can actually apply to several other circumstances and relationships. Stockholm syndrome may also arise in these situations:

Abusive Relationships

Research has shown that abused individuals may develop emotional attachments to their abuser. Sexual, physical, and emotional abuse, as well as incest, can last for years. Over this time, a person may develop positive feelings or sympathy for the person abusing them.

Child Abuse

Abusers frequently threaten their victims with harm, even death. Victims may try to avoid upsetting their abuser by being compliant. Abusers may also show kindness that could be perceived as a genuine feeling. This may further confuse the child and lead to them not understanding the negative nature of the relationship.

Sex Trafficking Trade

Individuals who are trafficked often rely on their abusers for necessities, like food and water. When the abusers provide that, the victim may begin to develop positive feelings toward their abuser. They may also resist cooperating with police for fear of retaliation or thinking they have to protect their abusers to protect themselves.

Sports Coaching

Being involved in sports is a great way for people to build skills and relationships. Unfortunately, some of those relationships may ultimately be negative. Harsh coaching techniques can even become abusive. The athlete may tell themselves their coach's behavior is for their own good, and this, according to a 2018 study, can ultimately become a form of Stockholm syndrome.

The Bottom Line

Stockholm syndrome is a coping strategy. Individuals who are abused or kidnapped may develop it. Fear or terror might be most common in these situations, but some individuals begin to develop positive feelings toward their captor or abuser. They may not want to work with or contact the police. They may even be hesitant to turn on their abuser or kidnapper.

Stockholm syndrome is not an official mental health diagnosis. Instead, it is thought to be a coping mechanism much like learned helplessness. Individuals who are abused or trafficked or who are the victims of incest or terror may develop it. Proper treatment can go a long way to helping with recovery.

In summary, experience with uncontrollable trauma typically has three basic effects: (1) animals become passive in the face of trauma, such as they are slower to initiate responses to alleviate trauma and may not respond at all; (2) animals are retarded at learning that their responses control trauma, such as if the animal makes a response which produces relief, they may have trouble "catching-on" to the response-relief contingency; and (3) animals show more stress when faced with trauma they cannot control than with equivalent controllable trauma.

This maladaptive behavior appears in a variety of species including man, and over a range of tasks which require voluntary responding.

Regarding its cause, it is commonly accepted that animals including humans can learn that responding controls rewards and punishments. We believe that animals are also sensitive to the independence of responding and reinforcers, and can learn that events are uncontrollable as well as controllable. The three main effects of uncontrollable trauma are explained by assuming the existence of such a form of learning:

Response Initiation

The probability that a subject will initiate responses to escape is lowered because part of the incentive for making such a response is the expectation that they will bring relief. If the subject has previously learned that their responses have no effect on trauma, this would defy such an expectation.

Delay of Learning

Learning that responding and adverse stimuli are independent variables that make it more difficult to learn that responding does produce relief, when the subject makes a response that actually terminates adverse stimuli. In general, if one has acquired a cognitive set in which "A" is irrelevant to "B," it will be harder for one to learn that "A" produces "B" when they do. In learned helplessness, this mechanism is responsible for the difficulty that helpless dogs and humans have in learning that responding produces relief, even after they respond and successfully turn off the adverse stimuli or trauma.

Emotional Stress

Learning that trauma is uncontrollable may produce more stress than learning that it is controllable. Thus, we have hypothesized that it is not trauma per se, but only uncontrollable trauma that produces failure to escape.

Researchers have tested and confirmed this hypothesis in several ways. They began by ruling out alternative hypotheses such as it is unlikely that the test subject has either become adapted, and therefore, not motivated enough to escape an adverse stimuli, or sensitized, and therefore, too disorganized to escape an adverse stimuli by pretreatment with an adverse stimuli; or for making the adverse stimuli very intense or very mild in the shuttle box so to did not reduce the phenomenon. Further, it is unlikely that the test subject has learned by explicit or superstitious reinforcement or by punishment during the application of inescapable adverse stimuli a motor response pattern that competed with barrier jumping in the shuttle box, for it occurs even if the dogs were temporarily paralyzed by with Curare and could make no overt motor responses during application of an adverse stimuli.

A Cure for Learned Helplessness

Only one treatment seems to cure learned helplessness. Researchers found that the dog does not try to escape because it expects that no response will produce a termination of shocks. By forcibly exposing the dog to the fact that responding produces results, this expectation can be changed. When "directive therapy" is used and helpless dogs are dragged with long leashes from on side of the shuttle box, across the barrier, to the other side, so that changing compartments terminates the shocks, all dogs eventually begin to respond on their own and their recovery from learned helplessness was complete and lasting. This finding has been successfully replicated in many experiments. This response is similar in humans. When humans are forced to see that responding produces results, their learned helplessness fades.

The behavior of animals during "leash pulling" is noteworthy. At the beginning of the procedure, a good deal of force had to be exerted to pull the dog across the barrier in the shuttle box, but less force was needed as training progressed. A stage is typically reached where a slight nudge of the leash would urge the dog into action. Finally, each dog initiated their own response, and thereafter, failure to escape was very rare. The initial problem seems to be one of "getting going." This is also true in humans.

Prevention

Dramatic successes in medicine have come more frequently from prevention than from treatment, and inoculation and immunization have saved many more lives than a cure has. Surprisingly, psychotherapy is almost exclusively limited to curative procedures, and preventative procedures rarely play an explicit role in therapy. In studies of dogs, researchers found that behavioral immunization provided an easy and effective means of preventing learned helplessness. Dogs that first received escapable shocks either in a shuttle box or in a hammock, and then in escapable shock in a hammock, learned later to escape and avoid the shuttle box, whereas dogs that received leashed inescapable shock failed to escape.

Other findings support the idea that experience in controlling trauma may protect organisms from the helplessness caused by inescapable trauma. Among dogs of unknown history, helplessness is rarely seen. Approximately two-thirds of dogs given inescapable shock became helpless, whereas one-third responded normally. Likewise, 6% of inexperienced dogs were helpless in the shuttle box without any prior experience with inescapable shock. Could it be possible that those dogs which did not become helpless even after inescapable shock had a pre-laboratory history of controllable trauma, whereas dogs who were helpless without any previous shock had experienced uncontrollable trauma before arriving at the lab?

To test this, researchers raised dogs from weaning in individual cages in the laboratory, and these dogs had very limited experience in controlling anything relative to dogs of unknown history. Such cage-reared dogs were more susceptible to helplessness. Although it took four sessions of inescapable shock to produce helplessness, one week later in dogs of unknown history, two sessions of inescapable shock in the hammock were sufficient to cause helplessness in the cage-reared dogs.

Regarding let us look at the dramatic findings on sudden death in wild rats. When wild rats are squeezed in the human hand until they stop struggling, then placed in a water tank, they drown almost immediately. Unlike non-squeezed rats which swim for 60 hours before drowning, these rats dive to the bottom and drown within 30 minutes. Sudden death is prevented by a technique which resembles our immunization procedure. If the experimenter holds the rat, then lets it go, holds it again and lets it go, sudden death does not occur. Further, if, after holding it, the experimenter puts the rat in the water, takes it out, puts it in again, and rescues it again, sudden death is prevented. These procedures, may provide the rat with a sense of control over trauma and thereby immunize against sudden death caused by inescapable trauma.

Depression

Since most of the investigations of uncontrollable trauma have used non-humans as test subjects, we can only speculate on the relationship of learned helplessness in animals to maladaptive behaviors in man. The phenomenon of human depression, particularly reactive depression, has a number of parallels to the phenomenon of learned helplessness. Like learned helplessness, depression is characterized by reduced response initiation as well as a "negative cognitive set" where an individual has difficulty in believing or learning that their own responses will succeed even when they do.

In a study of the symptoms of depression, a factor including feelings of hopelessness, helplessness, and worthlessness has been characterized as the essence of depression. It is also of interest that the norepinephrine depletion produced by uncontrollable adverse stimuli, also known as the catecholamine hypothesis of affective disorders which holds that norepinephrine depletion to be responsible for human depression.

Several researchers have postulated that learning and believing that one is helpless and hopeless is the central psychological cause of depression, and this articulates well with the origin of learned helplessness. Finally, successful psychotherapy in depression, like therapy for learned helplessness, may involve having the patient come to believe that they can be effective in controlling the events that are important to them, and recent evidence lends support to this view. However, a caveat is in order here, since most of the evidence for depression is largely anecdotal and selected, experimental tests on human subjects regarding the helplessness theory of depression are needed.

Learned Helplessness and Codependence

If you watch the TV program "Dancing with the Stars," you know what it takes to win the coveted Mirror Ball Trophy. As with any successful dancing collaboration, each partner is experienced with, and is acutely attuned to their partner's dance style and idiosyncratic moves.

To be successful on the dance floor, or to thoroughly enjoy the dance, the two partners need to be compatible on as many levels as possible, while knowing each other deeply and completely.

People with codependence dance well with people with narcissistic personality disorders or traits like addicts of all kinds, sociopaths, psychopaths, and abusers because their pathological personalities or "dance styles" fit together, like a hand in a glove. Almost instantly, they dance magnificently together because they are able to instinctively anticipate each other's moves. The choreography is effortless, as it feels like they have always danced together. Not only does each dancer instinctively and reflexively know their own role and stick to it, they do it like they have practiced it all their life. Dysfunctional compatibility is the engine that drives these dancers to the dancing championship finals.

People with codependence are drawn to pathological narcissists because they feel comfortable and familiar with a person who knows how to direct, control, and lead. The narcissistic dancer is simply the yin to their yang. Their giving, sacrificial, and passive codependence matches up perfectly with their partner's entitled, demanding, self-centered, and taking nature. Just because the codependent is the more passive of the two does not mean that they lack dancing mojo. Their dysfunctional agility and ability to predict their dancer partner's moves just by the subtlest of cues, makes her equally important to the illusionary grand prize both are feverishly seeking.

People with codependence expertly and adeptly predict and anticipate their pathologically narcissistic partner's every step, while still experiencing the dance as a passive, but positive, experience. Pathological narcissist dancers enjoy dancing with codependents because they are allowed to feel strong, secure, and in control. Dancing with their malleable partner is thrilling, as they direct the whole experience while believing that they are the only star on the dance floor.

34

The Codependent Dance

The "codependent dance" requires two people: the pleaser/fixer and the taker/controller. This inherently dysfunctional dance requires two opposite but distinctly balanced partners: a codependent and a narcissist. Codependent people, who are giving, sacrificing, and consumed with the needs and desires of others, do not know how to emotionally disconnect or avoid romantic relationships with individuals who are narcissistic—selfish, self-centered, controlling, and harmful. Codependent people habitually find themselves on a "dance floor" attracted to "dance partners" who perfectly match up to their uniquely passive, submissive, and acquiescent dance style.

As natural followers of their relationship dance, codependent people are passive and accommodating dance partners. Codependent people find narcissistic dance partners deeply appealing. They are perpetually attracted to their narcissistic partner's charm, boldness, confidence, and domineering personality. When codependent people and narcissists pair up, the dancing experience sizzles with excitement, at least in the beginning. After several dances, the enthralling dance experience predictably transforms into drama, conflict, and feelings of neglect and being trapped. Even with the chaos and discord, neither one dares end the partnership.

When a codependent person and narcissist come together in a relationship, their dance unfolds flawlessly. The narcissistic partner maintains the lead and the codependent follows. Their roles seem natural because they have been practicing them their whole lives, where the codependent reflexively gives up their power, and since the narcissist thrives on control and power, the dance is perfectly coordinated. No one gets their toes stepped on.

Typically, codependents give of themselves much more than their partners give back. So, they give and give, and their As "generous" but bitter dance partners, they seem to be stuck on the dance floor, always waiting for the "next dance," at which time they naïvely hope their narcissistic partner will finally understand their needs. Codependent people confuse caretaking and sacrifice with loyalty and love. Although they are proud of their unwavering dedication to

35

the person they love, they end up feeling unappreciated and used. Codependent people yearn to be loved, but because of their choice of dance partner, find their dreams unrealized. With the heartbreak of unfulfilled dreams, codependents silently and bitterly swallow their unhappiness.

Codependent people are essentially stuck in a pattern of giving and sacrificing, without the possibility of ever receiving the same from their partner. They pretend to enjoy the dance, but secretly harbor feelings of anger, bitterness, and sadness for not taking a more active role in their dance experience. They are convinced they will never find a dance partner who will love them for who they are, as opposed to what they can do for them. Their low self-esteem and pessimism manifests as a form of learned helplessness that ultimately keeps them on the dance floor with their narcissistic partner.

The narcissist dancer, like the codependent, is attracted to a partner who feels perfect to them: someone who lets them lead the dance, while making them feel powerful, competent, and appreciated. In other words, the narcissist feels most comfortable with a dancing companion who matches up with their self-absorbed and boldly selfish dance style. Narcissist dancers are able to maintain the direction of the dance because they always find partners who lack self-worth and confidence and have low self-esteem. With such a well-matched companion, they can control both the dancer and the dance.

Although all codependent dancers desire harmony and balance, they consistently sabotage themselves by choosing a partner who they are initially attracted to, but will ultimately resent. When given a chance to stop dancing with their narcissistic partner and comfortably sit the dance out until someone healthy comes along, they typically choose to continue their dysfunctional dance. They cannot leave their narcissistic partner because their lack of self-esteem and self-respect makes them feel like they can do no better. Being alone is the equivalent of feeling lonely, and loneliness is too painful to bear.

Without self-esteem or feelings of personal power, the codependent is incapable of choosing mutually giving and unconditionally loving partners. Their choice of a narcissistic dance partner is connected to their unconscious motivation to find a person who is familiar—someone reminiscent of their powerless and, perhaps, traumatic childhood.

Sadly, codependent people are children of parents who also flawlessly danced the dysfunctional codependent/narcissistic dance. Their fear of being alone, compulsion to control and fix at any cost, and comfort in their role as the martyr who is endlessly loving, devoted, and patient is an extension of their yearning to be loved, respected, and cared for as a child. Although codependents dream of dancing with an unconditionally loving and affirming partner, they submit to their dysfunctional destiny. Until they decide to heal the psychological wounds that ultimately compel them to dance with their narcissistic dance partners, they will be destined to maintain the steady beat and rhythm of their dysfunctional dance.

Through psychotherapy, and perhaps a twelve-step recovery program, codependent people can begin to recognize their dream to dance the grand dance of love, reciprocity, and mutuality is indeed possible. Through therapy and a change of lifestyle, they can build and repair their tattered self-esteem. The journey of healing and transformation will bring them feelings of personal power and efficacy that will foster a desire to finally dance with someone who is willing and capable of sharing the lead, communicating their movements, and pursuing a mutual loving rhythmic dance.

Can Learned Helplessness be Addictive?

Before we can make a case for learned helplessness as an addictive behavior, we must first define addiction, which is now referred to as Substance-Related and Addictive Disorders . The American Psychiatric Association defines addiction as a complex condition and a brain disease that is manifested by compulsive substance use despite harmful consequence. Operationally, experts utilize the *Diagnostic and Statistical Manual of Mental Disorders* (DSM) as a tool to unify diagnostic criteria in clinical and/or experimental design. The current version of this manual known as the DSM-5 includes a section for substance use disorders and non-substance-related disorders, and it incorporates eleven criteria for diagnosis. A patient must fulfill at least two of these criteria. In turn, these eleven criteria, by their characteristics, can be compiled into four broader groups:

Impaired Control

1. Use of larger amounts of a substance or behavior for a longer time than intended.
4. Craving
5. More time is spent looking for a substance or behavior, using a substance or doing a behavior, recovering from using a substance or doing a behavior, or dealing with consequences of using a substance or doing a behavior to excess.
6. Repeated attempts to quit or control substance or behavior misuse.

Social Impairment

1. Social and interpersonal problems related to substance or behavior misuse.
2. Major life roles are neglected.
3. Activities are given up for substance or behavior misuse.

Continued Use despite Risk

1. Using a substance or doing a behavior when it is hazardous to do so.
2. Physical and psychological problems related to misuse of a substance or a behavior.

Pharmacological Criteria

1. Tolerence.
2. Withdrawals.

Addiction

To understand learned helplessness as an addiction, it is helpful to explore a few facts about addiction in general. First of all, addictive substances and activities alter our mood by changing how we think and feel by changing the structure and function of our brains. The precise nature of the mood alteration can vary widely. Sometimes addictive substances and activities can alter our mood in ways we experience as pleasant or desirable, at least in the early stages of the addictive process. But they do not always make us feel better or "high." They may, in fact, make it difficult for us to feel anything at all. We might use addictive substances or activities so that we feel something; or we might use them so that we feel nothing at all.

Second, we can become physically addicted to a substance or activity itself; that is, our brains and bodies can become accustomed or dependent on the presence of a substance or an activity. As a result, we may require larger and larger doses of the substance or activity to get our desired level of mood alteration. This is called tolerance.

Third, if we are addicted to a substance or activity, our bodies and brains notice when the substance or activity is not present. This is called withdrawal. Addictions to alcohol, heroin, or barbiturates, for example, exhibit all these characteristics—mood alteration, tolerance, and withdrawal.

Even when a substance or activity itself is not addictive in the same sense as alcohol, heroin, barbiturates, or gambling, sex, or risk-taking, we can still become addicted to the mood alteration caused by use of the drug or activity. Marijuana, for example, is not thought to be addictive in the same sense as alcohol or heroin, but the mood alteration caused by its use can be very addictive. The fact that mood alteration can itself be addictive explains why people become addicted to gambling, sex, work, exercise, and many other things, even though no addictive substance is consumed.

In most of these cases, the body and brain produce its own addictive chemicals in response to our addictive behaviors. Finally, it is important to recognize that all addictions follow a similar cyclic process. The experience of addiction traps us in a cycle that looks something like this:

1. Preoccupation
2. Rituals and patterns of behavior
3. Using or acting out
4. Aftermath and consequences
5. Return to preoccupation

Let us briefly look at each element of this cycle.

Preoccupation Where Mood Alters Up

If you have been working for several months without any time off and you have a vacation scheduled for next month in a beautiful setting, you may find yourself daydreaming about how it looks and what you will be doing when you get there. In effect, you are borrowing pleasure from the future to get you through the now. This is not a bad thing. The ability to anticipate good things happening in the future is important. But suppose you are sitting in a counselor's office baring your soul and your counselor is thinking about their upcoming vacation. That kind of preoccupation is getting in the way of something important.

In the addictive process, a preoccupation with future use can do enormous damage to our relationships with others. Even before we actually use an addictive substance or act out in an obsessive compulsive way, we can experience mood alterations by anticipating the coming use or by grieving the absence of our drug of choice. Preoccupation about using can get in the way of important things, even before using takes place.

Rituals and Patterns of Behavior Where Mood Alters Up

Preoccupation leads eventually to what is often a ritualized set of pre-using or pre–acting-out behaviors. Ritualization simply means tending to do the same things in the same way. It refers to behaviors that we repeat over and over again before actually using or acting out which ramp our excitement or arousal. It can be as simple as having drinks with the same people at the same bar at the same time on the way home from work.

Like preoccupation, ritualization allows the addictive process to take more time. This is particularly true of addictions that do not involve consuming intoxicating substances. We can fill entire days, even weeks, with ritual preparations for acting out. The mood alteration that results from this ritualization can be as important to us as the acting out itself.

Using or Acting Out Where Mood Alters Up

Eventually, our pre-use rituals lead to their logical end point, and we engage in our addictive substance or activity. In this part of the cycle, we use our drug or activity of choice, we have another affair, we binge on ice cream, get into a codependent relationship with a wounded soul, or we do whatever we do to get the mood alteration we desire. The duration of the mood alteration resulting from using or acting out may be short, and it can be the briefest part of the whole cycle, but whether short or long, it leads to the same predictable consequences.

Aftermath Where Mood Alters Down

Eventually, we always find that using or acting out leads to acting in ways we would not have acted had we not been using or acting out. While "under the influence" of a substance or an activity, we act in ways that are inconsistent with our value system or we hurt people we care about, and as a result, we feel some combination of guilt, shame, remorse, or humiliation.

This phase of the cycle, known as the aftermath, is a low mood state or let down depression. It is a terrible, sad, and lonely place to be. Unfortunately, it sets up the "need" to return to the first step in the addictive cycle and start the whole mood-altering cycle all over again to escape the let down depression. We think that maybe the shame and fear we feel in the aftermath of using will go away if we just use again. This is usually not a conscious process. In any case, around and around we go. In this way, the low mood resulting from using leads us back to the mood elevation provided by the preoccupation stage.

Notice that every stage in the addictive cycle is mood altering, either up or down, even when we are not actually using. This is the reason that others experience no real comfort when we feel very bad about the consequences of our addiction and we promise not to use or act out anymore. They know that our feeling bad may just be part of the mood alteration cycle. Notice also that during the pre-using and using stages of the process our mood alters up, while during the post-using part of the process, our mood alters down and makes it "necessary,"even makes it a relief, to repeat the cycle.

Addiction never leads our soul to rest. It always leads to trying, trying harder and trying our hardest. It always leaves us tired, frustrated and depressed. Just like addiction to alcohol and drugs, the acting-out mood alters up, while the entire cycle mood alters down. The following less-than-comprehensive comparison illustrates the point:

The Alcoholic

The mood of the alcoholic alters up by drinking alcohol, whereas their mood alters down when they are not drinking alcohol or by simply thinking about the prospect of not drinking. The alcoholic chooses to be with people who have a relationship with alcohol similar to their own, but relationships with others often become a casualty. The alcoholic gravitates toward places that cater to, or are sympathetic to, or even encourage using behaviors such as a local bar or tavern.

The Obsessive Compulsive Codependent

The mood of the obsessive compulsive codependent alters up by engaging in activities related to getting into or maintaining codependent relationship with addicts, disabled, narcissistic, or abusive partners in a never-ending pattern of learned helplessness, whereas their mood alters down when they cannot get into or maintain these relationships. The obsessive compulsive codependent person chooses to be with people who have similar beliefs about codependent relationships as their own, but withdraws from friends and family members who do not have the same beliefs.

At its root, learned helplessness begins when our relationships stop being about the healthy relationships and becomes an attempt to moderate our moods with obsessive compulsive codependence instead. These behaviors seem to help us to control our mood, but that sense of control is only an illusion. We find over time that we need to engage in behaviors related to getting into codependent relationships more frequently or with more intensity in order to achieve the same alteration of our mood. And so, the pattern of learned helplessness evolves and takes over.

This is known as tolerance. Additionally, we experience depression, and a sense of meaninglessness or grief when we are not able for whatever reason to continue these behaviors. This is known as withdrawal.

Likewise, these behaviors also interfere with our ability to maintain healthy relationships or to function in life. The result is an exhausting, graceless, performance-oriented life that resembles living the god life but little.

Now that we have explored the idea that sugar can result in troublesome outcomes, next, we will explore sugar addiction, but first, let us explore the first twelve-step recovery program—Alcoholics Anonymous.

Chapter Two

The First Twelve Step Program—Alcoholics Anonymous

To understand a program of recovery and wellness, let us explore the first twelve-step recovery program—Alcoholic Anonymous. Alcoholics Anonymous is an informal fellowship of recovering alcoholics whose primary purpose is to help other alcoholics achieve sobriety and wellness. Alcoholics Anonymous advocates that alcohol addicts follow its twelve-step program and abstain from consuming alcohol in order to recover from alcohol addiction; and share their experience, strength, and hope with each other so that they might overcome their common problem.

Alcoholics Anonymous was the first Twelve-Step program and has become the model for over 55 recovery groups designed to help others overcome addictions and obsessions of all kinds and provide support for relatives and friends of people with various forms of addiction.

Early History of Alcoholic Anonymous

By 1934, a desperate alcoholic named Bill Wilson, also known as Bill W., had ruined his Wall Street career with his constant drunkenness. He was introduced to the idea of a "spiritual cure" by an old high school friend and drinking buddy, Ebby Thacher, also known as Ebby T., who had become a member of a fundamental Christian evangelical group, called the Oxford Group, and sobered up. However, Wilson returned to Towns Hospital for the fourth time in 1934 shortly after their historic visit.

Wilson was treated by Dr. William Silkworth who promoted a concept that the alcoholics had an allergy to alcohol and that it was not about a lack of will power. While in the hospital, Wilson reportedly underwent what he called a profound spiritual experience, although some contend that he experienced a drug-induced hallucination, that convinced him of the existence of a healing higher power, and he was able to stop drinking. Until then, Wilson was an agnostic, if not an atheist, who really had no use for God after his beloved girlfriend died suddenly shortly before he graduated from high school.

Wilson stopped drinking, sobered up, and never drank again, but he never achieved a true state of wellness. Wilson was an unrecovered sex addict who had numerous sexual acting out episodes throughout his adult life and cheated continuously on his wife throughout their marriage. Wilson was also a heavy coffee drinking and a heavy smoker. Wilson was heavily into LSD and the occult. After his spiritual experience, Wilson actively tried to sober up other drunks using an aggressive evangelistic preaching style but was unable to sober up anyone.

Wilson joined the Oxford Group, a Christian movement that had a following in Europe, China, Africa, Australia, Scandinavia and America in the 1920s and 30s that was founded by an American Lutheran pastor, Frank Buchman.

After a disastrous business trip to Akron, Ohio in 1935, Wilson felt the urge to drink again and so to stay sober, he sought out another alcoholic to help. Wilson was introduced to Dr. Robert Smith, also known as Dr. Bob Smith, a drunken physician. Wilson and Smith talked, and Smith also found sobriety through a face-to-face dialogue with another drunk.

As the result of Wilson and Smith's meeting, Alcoholics Anonymous' word-of-mouth program to help alcoholics was founded. By 1937, Wilson and Smith determined that they had reached out to 115 drunks and had helped 40 get sober, although 75 failed to get sober, a success rate of 53%, which is a remarkable feat even by today's standards. Two years later, with the first 40 sober alcoholics, Wilson expanded the program by writing a book entitled: *Alcoholics Anonymous,* subtitled: "The Story of How Many Thousands of Men and Women Have Recovered from Alcoholism," from which the new organization adopted as its name.

The book described a twelve-step program involving an admission of powerlessness, a moral inventory, asking for help from a Power greater than us, and making of direct amends. In 1941, book sales and membership increased after a radio interview and favorable articles in national magazines, particularly by Jack Alexander in *The Saturday Evening Post.*

By 1946, as the membership grew, confusion and disputes over group practices, finances, and publicity led Wilson to write the guidelines for non-coercive group management that eventually became known as the "Twelve Traditions." The "Twelve Traditions" guided how Alcoholics Anonymous groups function in the United States, and the "Twelve Concepts for World Service" guided how Alcoholics Anonymous is structured through the world.

Alcoholics Anonymous came of age at the 1955 International Convention of Alcoholics Anonymous in St. Louis when Bill Wilson formally turned over the control of Alcoholics Anonymous over to its General Service Board.

In this era, Alcoholics Anonymous also began its international expansion, and by 2017, the number of members in the United States was estimated at 1.2 million in over 56,000 Alcoholics Anonymous groups. Worldwide, there are approximately 2.1 million members of Alcoholics Anonymous in over 115,000 groups in over 180 countries.

In 2015, the World Health Organization estimated that there were about 240 million alcoholics in the world, and the National Institutes of Health estimated that there were between 12 and 17 million alcoholics in the United States.

As a result, Alcoholics Anonymous fellowship includes about 12% of the total population of alcoholics in the United States, and 1.5% of the world's population of alcoholics.

Regarding service work, a member who accepts a service position is known as a "trusted servant" with rotating and limited terms of office, typically lasting three months to one year. Additionally, each group is a self-governing entity where Alcoholics Anonymous World Services acts only as an advisor.

There are two principle operating bodies in Alcoholics Anonymous: The first is Alcoholics Anonymous World Services, Inc. which is housed in the General Service Office in New York City, where 79 workers keep in touch with local groups, with Alcoholics Anonymous groups in treatment and correctional facilities, with members and groups overseas, and with the thousands of outsiders who turn to Alcoholics Anonymous each year for information on the recovery program. Alcoholics Anonymous Conference approved literature is prepared, published, and distributed through this office.

Second, is Alcoholics Anonymous Grapevine, Inc., which publishes the *A.A. Grapevine*, the fellowship's monthly international journal. The magazine currently has a circulation of about 106,000 in the United States, Canada, and other countries. Alcoholics Anonymous Grapevine, Inc. also produces a selection of special items, principally cassette tapes and anthologies of magazine articles, which are spinoffs from the magazine.

The two operating entities are responsible to a board of trustees known as the General Service Board of Alcoholics Anonymous, of whom seven are "nonalcoholic friends" of the fellowship, and fourteen are members of Alcoholics Anonymous.

A General Service Conference, consisting of 93 delegates from Alcoholics Anonymous areas in the United States and Canada, and trustees, Alcoholics Anonymous World Services and Grapevine directors, and staff from the General Service Office and the Grapevine in New York, meets once a year and provides a link between the groups throughout the United States and Canada and the trustees who serve as custodians of Alcoholics Anonymous tradition and interpreters of policies affecting the fellowship as a whole.

At the local group level, formal organization is kept to a minimum. The group might have a small steering committee and a limited number of rotating officers known as "trusted servants" whose responsibilities include arranging meeting programs, providing refreshments, participating in regional Alcoholics Anonymous activities, and maintaining contact with the General Service Office.

Alcoholics Anonymous is served entirely by alcoholics, except for seven non-alcoholic friends of the fellowship out of 21 members of the Alcoholics Anonymous General Service Board and support staff.

Groups in Alcoholics Anonymous are self-supporting and are not charities. They have no dues or fees for membership. Groups rely on member donations, typically $1.00 each, collected at each meeting in the United States, to pay for expenses like room rental, refreshments, and literature. Visitors and new members are asked not to donate, and no one is turned away because they cannot pay.

Alcoholics Anonymous receives proceeds from books and literature sales amounting to over 7.7 million dollars each year, which constitutes more than 50% of the income for the General Service Office (GSO), which unlike individual groups, is not self-supporting and maintains a paid staff. It also maintains service centers which coordinate activities like printing material, responding to public inquiries, and organizing conferences. They are funded by local members and are responsible to the Alcoholics Anonymous groups they represent.

The Alcoholics Anonymous recovery program is based on an abstinence model. That is, not consuming alcohol in any form, working the Twelve Steps of Recovery, helping with duties and service work, and regular attendance at Alcoholics Anonymous meetings. Members are encouraged to ask their group for help in finding an experienced fellow alcoholic called a "sponsor" to help them work the Twelve Steps and follow the Alcoholics Anonymous program, ideally, one who has enjoyed sobriety for at least a year and who does not impose their personal views on the sponsee, but only teaches the suggested Alcoholics Anonymous program.

Anyone can attend "open meetings," although "closed meetings" are for alcoholics only, or those who feel they that might be alcoholics. There are groups for men only, groups for women only, groups for gay people, groups for those who speak other languages, and groups for professionals, such as doctors or lawyers.

Meeting formats vary between groups, and beginner meetings include a speech by the leader of the group about he or she came to Alcoholics Anonymous and what was learned, then a group discussion on topics related to alcoholism or the Alcoholics Anonymous is conducted.

The Beginning of Alcoholics Anonymous

In 1934, Bill Wilson came under the care of Dr. William D. Silkworth at Towns Hospital in New York City, where he reportedly experienced a profound spiritual experience that turned his life around.

Dr. Silkworth, "The little doctor who loved drunks," as Wilson later called him, introduced the basic concept of alcoholism as a disease composed of an obsession of the mind, coupled with an allergy of the body to Alcoholism Anonymous.

After Wilson's transforming experience at Towns Hospital, he left the hospital, and following Dr. Silkworth's counsel, went to work with other drunks. However, after several months of notable failures, Dr. Silkworth set Wilson down and set him straight. Dr. Silkworth gave him what he later called in *Alcoholics Anonymous Comes of Age: A Brief History of A. A.* (1957), "a great piece of advice," without which, Alcoholics Anonymous might never had been born.

Dr. Silkworth cautioned Wilson against preaching to or trying to convert them to the Oxford Group's precepts like absolute honesty. The doctor advised Wilson to discuss his own experiences with the obsession that condemned drunks to drink and the physical sensitivity or allergy of the body that caused them to go mad or die if they kept on drinking.

This advice set the stage for Wilson's meeting with Dr. Robert Smith, also known as Dr. Bob, a meeting in which Smith understood for the first time the medical facts of his own condition. That meeting, which Smith believed would be a fifteen-minute courtesy call, lasted all night and into the following day, and the miracle of one alcoholic talking to another that has since changed the lives of millions of suffering alcoholics was born.

Bill Wilson

Bill Wilson, also known as Bill W., was an alcoholic who had a promising career on Wall Street ruined by his drinking. He also failed to graduate from law school because he was too drunk to pick up his diploma, nearly wrecked his marriage, and was hospitalized for alcoholism three times in a year under the care of Dr. William Silkworth, yet he continued to drink.

When Ebby Thacher, Wilson's friend and mentor, visited him at his New York apartment, Wilson was astonished to find that his old drinking companion had sobered up through a spiritual experience. Until then, Wilson had struggled with the existence of God, but of his meeting with Thatcher, he wrote of what then seemed a novel idea. Thacher asked Wilson why he did not choose his own conception of God. Wilson stated that statement hit him hard. Wilson said it melted the icy intellectual mountain in whose shadow he had lived for years. Wilson claimed that he stood in the sunlight at last.

After attending his first Oxford Group meeting at the Calvary Mission, Wilson excitedly told his wife Lois about his spiritual transformation, yet the next day, he was drunk again, and eventually found himself back in Towns Hospital under Dr. Silkworth's care. Thacher visited Wilson at Towns Hospital and introduced him to the basic tenets of the Oxford Group and the book: *Varieties of Religious Experience* (1902) by the American psychologist and philosopher William James, which described experiences like Wilson's. While Wilson was lying in bed depressed and despairing, he allegedly cried out that he would do anything to free of his addiction and he demanded that if there was a God, He show Himself. Wilson then claimed that he had the sensation of a bright light, a feeling of ecstasy, and a new serenity that he had never known before. Wilson described his experience to Dr. Silkworth who told him not to discount it.

Upon his release from Towns Hospital on December 18, 1934, Wilson attended Oxford Group meetings at Calvary House in New York. There Wilson socialized after the meetings with other ex-drunks in the Oxford Group and became interested in learning how to help other alcoholics to achieve sobriety.

Dr. Robert Smith

Armed with his new-found spiritual ideas, Wilson spent the first half of 1935 trying to sober up other alcoholics but failed to bring any into sobriety. Dr. Silkworth advised Wilson to stop preaching and talk more about alcoholism as an allergy and an obsession that sets off an intense craving that no human power can resist that condemns alcoholics to go mad or die.

After a failed business venture in Akron, Ohio, in 1935, Wilson was tempted to drink and realized that he must talk to another drunk to stay sober. He phoned local ministers to ask if they knew of any alcoholics, and Norman Sheppard directed him to Oxford Group member Hennrietta Seiberling whose group had been trying to sober up a desperate alcoholic named Dr. Robert Smith, also known as Dr. Bob.

While a medical school student, Dr. Robert Smith had started drinking heavily and almost failed to graduate from medical school. He opened a medical practice and married, but his drinking put his practice and marriage in jeopardy. For seventeen years, Smith's daily routine was to stay sober until the afternoon, get drunk, sleep, then take sedatives (Barbiturates) to calm his morning jitters.

Seiberling convinced Smith to talk with Wilson, but Smith insisted that the meeting be limited to fifteen minutes. However, Smith was so impressed with Wilson's knowledge of alcoholism and ability to share from his own experience, their discussion lasted over six hours.

Smith became the first alcoholic Wilson brought into sobriety, and Smith's last drink was on June 10, 1935, a beer to steady his hand for surgery, which is considered by many to be the founding date of Alcoholics Anonymous.

The Influence of the Oxford Group on Alcoholics Anonymous

The Oxford Group, an evangelical Christian movement founded by Frank Buchman in the early 1900s, had a profound influence on the early development of Alcoholics Anonymous. Bill Wilson and Dr. Bob Smith both attended Oxford Group meetings to find help with their drinking, and it was members of the Oxford Group who brought them together in 1935. Members of the Akron Alcoholics Anonymous group were active in Oxford Group meetings, and once Wilson returned to New York, he was greatly influenced by Dr. Samuel Shoemaker of the Calvary Church, a leader of the Oxford Group in the United States, and one of the earliest and staunchest friends of Alcoholics Anonymous among the clergy.

Four basic Oxford Group principles became the foundation for Alcoholics Anonymous' Twelve Steps:

(1) Surrender to God through rigorous self-examination.

(2) Confession of character defects to another human being.

(3) Making restitution for harm done to others.

(4) Giving without thought of reward.

But more problematic for alcoholics were the "Four Absolutes:"

(1) Absolute honesty.

(2) Absolute unselfishness.

(3) Absolute purity.

(4) Absolute love.

Alcoholics Anonymous ultimately acknowledged that we seek spiritual progress rather than spiritual perfection, and that absolute values were hard to swallow for the members of Alcoholics Anonymous.

Members of Alcoholics Anonymous attended Oxford Group meetings regularly for the first two or three years of the fellowship, somewhat longer in Akron, but they broke away from the Oxford Group for several reasons. First, Frank Buchman was not particularly interested in helping drunks. Increasingly, he concentrated on socializing with the wealth and working with world leaders to bring about world peace. Secondly, the pioneers of Alcoholics Anonymous believed that the Oxford Group's evangelical approach would not work with alcoholics, many of whom were agnostic or atheists, and they had come up with the concept of "God as we understand Him," rather than a specifically Christian or religious approach.

Nevertheless, both Wilson and Smith had been enthusiastic members of Frank Buchman's Oxford Group, since it was the only available recovery program at the time, but the Oxford Group asked Wilson to leave and take his shabby alcoholics with him because Wilson was spending too much time with his alcoholic friends and not enough time following the dictates of Buchman. Still, Wilson and Smith believed in the tenets of the Oxford Group, and they formed their own independent group in 1935, called: *The Alcoholic Squadron of the Oxford Group.*

Bill Wilson's early, unsuccessful experience with exhorting drunks to get sober indicated a key truth: Alcoholics would respond to suggestion, but one could not tell them what to do. And finally, the members of Alcoholics Anonymous stressed the need for anonymity, rather than the Oxford Group's practice of working with prominent people.

The First Edition of the "Big Book"

Alcoholics Anonymous, subtitled: "The Story of How Many Thousands of Men and Women Have Recovered from Alcoholism," generally known as the "Big Book" because of the thickness of the paper used in the first edition was a 1939 basic text, described how to recover from alcoholism, primarily written by Bill Wilson. It is the originator of the groundbreaking "twelve-step method" widely used today to treat alcoholism and other forms addiction with a strong spiritual and social emphasis. Interestingly, the was called the "Big Book" because the thickness of the paper used in the first edition which made the book appear to be bigger than others books of similar size.

It is one of the best-selling books of all time, having sold over 30 million copies. In 2011, *Time* magazine placed the book on its list of the 100 best and most influential books ever written in English since the establishment of the magazine in 1923. In 2012, the Library of Congress designated it as one of 88 books that shaped America.

Bill Wilson. and Dr. Bob Smith began to work on how to best approach alcoholics and began trying to help men recover from alcoholism. The idea for the book developed at least as early as 1937 when Wilson and Smith realized their system had helped over 40 men stay sober for more than two years. But in Wilson's typical grandiose style, he proposed a lavish plan to write a book that was meant to carry their message far and wide; build hospitals all over the country to treat alcoholics; and to recruit, train, and send out hundreds of missionaries to find drunks and save them. But when Wilson's ideas were proposed to Smith and 40 sober alcoholics in Alcoholics Anonymous at the time, it did not go over well. Most of the 40 pioneers of Alcoholics Anonymous along with Smith distanced themselves from the project.

The "Big Book" was originally published in 1939 by Bill Wilson. The book serves as the basic text of Alcoholics Anonymous. There has been a series of reprints and revisions, as well as translations into dozens of languages. The second edition was published in 1955; the third edition was published in 1976; and the fourth edition was published in 2001. There have been no other editions published since, a span of 18 years, and none are planned. The book is published by Alcoholics Anonymous World Services, Inc. and is available through Alcoholics Anonymous offices and meetings, as well as through booksellers.

Initial fundraising efforts for the book failed after the new program idea was approved by Smith and a narrow majority of members, but in 1938, Wilson's brother-in-law, Leonard Strong, contacted Willard Richardson who arranged for a meeting with Leroy Chapman, an assistant of

John D. Rockefeller, Jr., a wealthy American financier and philanthropist who was a prominent member of the Rockefeller family.

Wilson envisioned receiving millions of dollars, but Rockefeller refused to give them any money, and said that money would spoil things. Instead, Rockefeller agreed to contribute $5,000 in $30 weekly installments for Wilson and Smith to use for personal expenses. Wilson was dejected and disappointed.

Later in 1940, Rockefeller held a dinner for Alcoholics Anonymous, which was presided over by his son, Nelson Rockefeller, and attended by wealthy New York bankers, as well as members of the newly-founded Alcoholics Anonymous. Wilson hoped the event would raise a lot of money for the new fellowship, but at the conclusion of the dinner, Rockefeller stated that Alcoholics Anonymous should be financially self-supporting, and that the power of Alcoholics Anonymous should lie in one man carrying the message of recovery to the next, not with financial reward, but only the goodwill of its supporters. This became the main abiding principle of Alcoholics Anonymous.

Although Wilson would later give Rockefeller credit for the idea of Alcoholics Anonymous being non-professional and self-supporting, he was initially disappointed with this position, and after the first Rockefeller fundraising attempt fell short, Wilson abandoned his plans for paid missionaries and treatment centers. Instead, Wilson formed a non-profit group called the *Alcoholic Foundation*, and decided to publish a book which would share his and Smith's personal experiences and what they did to stay sober, although Smith had little to do with the endeavor.

The Twelve Steps of Recovery

After the third and fourth chapters of the "Big Book" had been completed, Wilson decided that a summary of methods for overcoming alcoholism was needed to describe their word-of-mouth program. The basic program developed from the works of William James, Dr. William Silkworth, and the Oxford Group, and included six basic steps:

1. We admitted that we were licked, that we were powerless over alcohol.

2. We made a moral inventory of our defects or sins.

3. We confessed or shared out shortcomings with another person in confidence.

4. We made restitution to all those we had harmed by our drinking.

5. We tried to help other alcoholics, with no thought of reward in money or prestige.

6. We prayed to whatever God we thought there was for power to practice these precepts.

Wilson decided that the six steps needed to be broken down into smaller sections to make them easier to understand and accept.

By this time, Wilson was ready to write Chapter Five of the "Big Book," "How it Works." Wilson's wife Lois recalled that he was not feeling well, but the writing had to go on, so he took pad and pencil to bed with him. Wilson wondered how he could bring the program alive so that those reading this book could apply it to themselves and perhaps get well. He had to be very explicit. Wilson claimed that the Oxford Group principles that the Fellowship had been using were not definite enough, and that he had to broaden and deepen their implications. Wilson said he relaxed and asked for guidance, and when he had finished writing and reread what he had put down, he was quite pleased. The Twelve principles had developed—The Twelve Steps.

Wilson described the writing of the Twelve Steps of Recovery by saying that he finally got to the point that where he had to say what this book was all about and how this it works. Wilson claimed that he started with what had been a six-step program the idea came to him that he needed a definite statement of concrete principles that these drunks could not wiggle out of. Wilson claimed that there could not be any wiggling out of this deal at all and this six-step program had two big gaps which people could wiggled out of.

With contributions from other group members, including atheists who resisted religious material from the Oxford Group that could later result in controversy, by the fall of 1938, Wilson expanded the Six Steps to its final version of the Twelve Steps, which are detailed in chapter five of the "Big Book," called: "How it Works."

As a result, Alcoholics Anonymous was named after its primary text and guidebook *Alcoholics Anonymous*, also known as the "Big Book."

The Basis of the Twelve Steps

The basis of the Twelve Steps was based on the practices of the Oxford group which were:

1. Admission of personal defect (You have been defeated by sin).
2. Taking personal inventory (List your sins).
3. Confession of your sins to another person.
4. Making restitution of those one has harmed.
5. Helping others selflessly.
6. Praying to God for understanding and the power to put these precepts into practice.

Even though they were never written down, these were essentially the original principles that evolved into the twelve steps of Alcoholics Anonymous, years before their was a fellowship, or a Big Book, back when it was called the *Alcoholic Squadron of the Oxford Group*. These were the original "Six Steps" proposed by the early Alcoholics Anonymous program:

1. Complete deflation
2. Dependence and guidance for a Higher Power
3. Moral inventory
4. Confession
5. Restitution
6. Continued work with alcoholics

So, Wilson took the various practices and procedures of the Oxford Group and turned them into a Twelve Step program for Alcoholics Anonymous. The original Twelve Steps of Recovery he wrote were:

1. [we] Admitted we were powerless over alcohol—that our lives became unmanageable.

2. Came to believe that God could restore us to sanity.

3. Made a decision to turn our will and our lives to the care and direction of God.

4. Made a searching and fearless moral inventory of ourselves.

5. Admitted to God, to ourselves, and another human being the exact nature of our wrongs.

6. Were entirely will that God remove all these defects of character.

7. Humbly, on our knees, asked Him to remove our shortcomings—holding nothing back.

8. Made a list of all persons we had harmed, and became willing to make complete amends to them all.

9. Made direct amends to such people wherever possible, except when to do so would injure them or others.

10. Continued to take personal inventory and when we were wrong promptly admitted it.

11. Sought through prayer and meditation to improve contact with God, praying only for knowledge of His will for us and the power to carry that out.

12. Having had a spiritual experience as the result of this course of action, we tried to carry this message to others, especially alcoholics, and to practice these principles in all our affairs.

What was the importance of twelve steps? The meaning of the number: 12, which is considered a perfect number, is that it symoolizes God's power and authority, as well as serving as a perfect governmental foundation and it also symbolize completeness.

When Wilson presented his Twelve Steps of Recovery to 18 of the early members of the fellowship of Alcoholics Anonymous in New York, mostly agnostics and atheists, they promptly freaked out and howled in protest. They clearly foresaw Wilson's dogmatic religiosity was going to drive away many of the very alcoholics whom the program was supposed to help, and a loud shouting match ensued. Wilson was forced to back down and reluctantly toned down the language of his Twelve Steps somewhat. The word "God" in Step Two was replaced with "a Power greater than ourselves." The phrase "as we understand Him" was added after the word "God" in Step Three, and later in Step Eleven. Later, in the step Three, the phrase "turn our will and lives over to the care and direction of God" was changed to "turn our will and lives over to the care of God as we understood Him." The phrase in Step Seven, "on our knees" was removed.

The remainder of the Twelve Steps of Recovery were left unchanged, except for one giant concession. In the "Big Book," the Twelve Steps were preceded by a statement saying that these Steps were only "suggested as a program of recovery," instead of a must. Thus, began the watering down of the Twelve Steps and the original Alcoholics Anonymous program.

So, in the original First Edition of the "Big Book" written in 1939, the Twelve Steps were written as:

1. [We] Admitted we were powerless over alcohol—that our lives had become unmanageable.
2. Came to believe that a Power greater than ourselves could restore us to sanity.
3. Made a decision to turn our will and our lives to the care and direction of God as we understand Him.
4. Made a searching and fearless moral inventory of ourselves.
5. Admitted to God, to ourselves, and to another human being the exact nature of our wrongs.
6. Were entirely willing that God remove all these defects of character.
7. Humbly asked Him to remove our shortcomings—hold nothing back.

8. Made a list of all persons we had harmed, and became willing to make complete amends to them all.

9. Made direct amends to such people wherever possible, except when to do so would injure them or others.

10. Continued to take personal inventory and when we wrong promptly admitted it.

11. Sought through prayer and meditation to improve our contact with God, praying only for knowledge of His will for us and the power to care that out.

12. Having had a spiritual experience as the result of this course of action, we tried to carry this message to others, especially alcoholics, and to practice these principles in all our affairs.

The Twelve Steps of Recovery were further modified over the years to their present form as written above and have remained unaltered since. It should be noted that the original Alcoholics Anonymous program has become the foundation of over 55 other self-help programs that use Twelve Step of Recovery as their guide to wellness. These various programs simply change the word "alcohol" to what their affliction is, and recovery seems to work.

And so, in the Foreword of the Second Edition of the "Big Book," published in 1955, the forefathers and pioneers of Alcoholics Anonymous wrote that the spark that was to become the first Alcoholics Anonymous group was struck at Akron, Ohio, in June 1935, during a talk between a New York stockbroker named Bill Wilson and an Akron physician named Dr. Robert Smith. Six months earlier, Wilson had been relieved of his drinking obsession by a sudden spiritual experience, following a meeting with an alcoholic friend who had been in contact with the Oxford Groups of that day. He had also been helped by Dr. William Silkworth, a New York specialist in alcoholism, who is now seen as a medical saint by Alcoholics Anonymous, and whose story of the early days of our appears in the book. From this doctor, Wilson had learned the grave nature of alcohol addiction. Although he could not accept all the tenets of the Oxford Group, he was convinced of the need for moral inventory, confession of personal defects, restitution to those harmed, helpfulness to others, and the necessity of belief in and dependence upon God.

The forefathers and pioneers of Alcoholics Anonymous went on to say that prior to his journey to Akron, Wilson had worked hard with many alcoholics on the theory that only an alcoholic could help another alcoholic, but he had succeeded only in keeping himself sober himself. Wilson had gone to Akron on a business venture which had collapsed, leaving him greatly in fear that he might start drinking again. Wilson suddenly realized that in order to save himself he must carry his message to another alcoholic. That alcoholic turned out to be the Akron physician—Dr. Robert Smith, also known as Dr. Bob.

Furthermore, the forefathers and pioneers of Alcoholics Anonymous wrote that Smith had repeatedly tried many ways to resolve his alcoholic dilemma, and even though he was a deeply religious man, he failed. But when Wilson gave him Dr. Silkworth's description of alcoholism and its hopelessness, Smith began to pursue the malady with a willingness he had never been able to muster. Smith sobered and never drank again up to the moment of his death in 1950. This seemed to prove that one alcoholic could affect another as no non-alcoholic could. It also indicated that strenuous work, one alcoholic with another, was vital to permanent recovery.

In addition, the forefathers and pioneers of Alcoholics Anonymous told us that henceforth the two men set to work almost frantically upon alcoholics arriving in the wards of the Akron City Hospital. Their very first case, a desperate one, recovered immediately and become Alcoholics Anonymous number three. He never had another drink. This work in Akron continued through the summer of 1935. There were many failures, but there was an occasional heartening success. When Wilson returned to New York in the fall of 1935, the first Alcoholics Anonymous group had been formed in Akron, although no one realized it at the time.

Consequently, the fellowship of Alcoholics Anonymous was born when two hopeless drunks got together and saved a third hopeless drunk. As a result, the fellowship began to grow slowly. The second small group promptly took shape in New York, to be followed in 1937 with a third meeting in Cleveland.

And so, by the end of 1935, five people had recovered. By the end of 1936, 15 people had recovered. By the end of 1937, 40 people had recovered, and by the end of 1938, 100 people had recovered. Shortly after the publication of the "Big Book" in 1939, the number of recovered people swelled to 400.

Much of the growth between 1939 and 1940 took place in Cleveland, Ohio, as a result of a series of publications in the *Cleveland Plain Dealer* beginning in October 1939. By the end of 1940, the number of recovered people increased to 2,000.

The Fellowship gained national prominence with the publication of an article in the March 1941, issue of the *Saturday Evening Post*. By the end of 1941, 8,000 people had recovered. By 1950, the number of the recovered surged to 100,000 people, and this number doubled every 10 years until the late 1970s. Likewise, during this time, the fellowship enjoyed a 75% recovery rate.

However, in the late 1970s, the 28-Day program was developed by hospitals and insurance companies anxious to tap into the vast amount of federal funds available at the time. As a result, hospitals and insurance companies took over the primary treatment of alcoholics using a medical model and co-opting the Alcoholic Anonymous program of recovery. Consequently, the recovery rate of Alcoholics Anonymous slowed, stalled, and began to decline by the early 1990s. And so, by the end of the 1990s, the recovery rate had fallen to a dismal 5% or less. This meant that on any given day, less than 5% of those who came into the fellowship would be sober at the end of the year, and 50% would be out using again within a month.

Another factor that led to the steady decline in recovery rates was the demise of the wildly successful Twelve Step Classes in the late 1950s. The Twelve Step Classes were discontinued in the late 1950s as a result of the publication of the *Twelve Steps and Twelve*

Traditions, which essentially replaced the "Big Book," and *The Little Red Book*, and were replaced with Step Meetings and Beginners' Meetings in order to reach more desperate drunks, but with the desire to increase volume over quality, the face-to-face, on drunk talking to another that was the hallmark of the early fellowship began to disappear.

Furthermore, the forefathers and pioneers related an endorsement of the Fellowship of Alcoholics Anonymous by Dr. Silkworth. They wrote that as a psychiatrist directing a hospital for alcoholics, Dr. Silkworth appeared somewhat sentimental because he stood on the firing line, seeing the tragedies, the despairing wives, and the little children. Silkworth said let the solving of these problems become a part of your daily work, and even of your sleeping moments, and even the most cynical amongst us would not wonder that we have accepted and encouraged Alcoholics Anonymous movement. Silkworth said he feels that after we had found nothing that has contributed more to the rehabilitation of Alcoholics than the altruistic movement now growing up among them called Alcoholics Anonymous.

How did the fellowship get its name? The forefathers and pioneers of Alcoholics Anonymous wrote in the Foreword of the First Edition of the "Big Book" that it is important that Alcoholics Anonymous remain anonymous because the members were too few at that time to handle the overwhelming number of personal appeals which might result from the publication of the "Big Book." Being mostly business or professional folk, the early members could not well carry on their occupations in such an event. They wanted it understood that their alcoholic work is an avocation.

The forefathers and pioneers of Alcoholics Anonymous went on to say when writing or speaking publicly about alcoholism, the members were urged to omit their personal name, designating himself instead as "a member of Alcoholics Anonymous."

Furthermore, the forefathers also told us that Alcoholics Anonymous is not an organization in the conventional sense of the word. There are no fees or dues whatsoever. The only requirement for membership is an honest desire to stop drinking. They said Alcoholics

Anonymous is not allied with any faith, sect, or denomination, nor does it oppose anyone. The member said that they simply wish to be helpful to those who are afflicted.

Bill Wilson., co-founder of Alcoholics Anonymous, once said that the only purpose of a recovery group was to teach and practice the Twelve Steps of Recovery. In the beginning, the fellowship of Alcoholics Anonymous offered classes to take people through the Twelve Steps in one month and set them free. As a result, the original fellowship of Alcoholics Anonymous enjoyed a 75% to 93% success rate, which meant that 75% to 93% of the people who entered the fellowship got sober and stayed sober for a year or more, compared to less than 5% today. As a result, between the 1940s and the 1960s, thousands of alcoholics found the solution to alcoholism, as well as a new way of life free of alcohol in these Twelve Step classes.

And so, to get back to the kind of success rates the forefathers and pioneers of Alcoholics Anonymous enjoyed, I am going to lead you through the way the Twelve Steps of Recovery were done in the early days of Alcoholics Anonymous, so let us get started.

Moral Compass

Most people have a strong sense of morality including a sense of what is right and wrong; what one ought to do and not do; how others should be treated; and a sense of responsibility toward one's family, community, employer, and to society. However, about one in 25 people, roughly 4% or 5% of the population, seems to be missing this sense of morality. Such people are often termed as sociopathic, psychopathic, or antisocially disordered. Although the terms are not identical, they are similar enough for our purposes. This sociopathic part of the population will commonly develop addictions. Unfortunately, if someone in the other 99% of the population develops an addiction, they will begin to behave in a manner similar to a sociopath as their addiction progresses. In other words, they begin to lose their morality and integrity.

As addicted people, including obsessive compulsive codependence, gradually lose their moral compass, they begin to disrespect the rights and needs other people. They even mistreat the people that matter to them most. This begins by failing to meet certain responsibilities, commitments, or obligations. Examples of these failures might be failing to show up for things; becoming dishonest by failing to disclose information; or making excuses rather than making a sincere apology. These individuals develop a corrupted moral sense known as sociopath, and are known as sociopaths, and their most extreme form, are known as psychopaths.

This type of disregard will evolve into more obvious forms of disrespect and mistreatment as addiction progresses. This progression might include flat-out lying and deception; stealing from loved ones; and threatening these same people if their demands are not met. Unlike their sociopathic counterparts who lack a moral compass to begin with, people who once had a moral compass often experience tremendous feelings of guilt and self-loathing as they break their own moral code. Addiction can only relieve these feelings temporarily.

So, what is the difference between a sociopath and a psychopath? Sociopaths are often called psychopaths and vice versa, but there are differences between a psychopath and a sociopath. For example, psychopaths are far more likely to get in trouble with the law, whereas sociopaths are much more likely to blend in with society, and even though sociopaths and psychopaths do share some of the same traits, sociopathy or antisocial personality disorder is generally considered less severe than psychopathy. So, why is this important? Because all addicts, no matter what kind, all have traits of sociopathy. So, let us talk about sociopathy.

What is a Sociopath?

A sociopath is a person with antisocial personality disorder. Antisocial personality disorder is defined in the *Diagnostic and Statistical Manual of Mental Disorders* as a Cluster B personality disorder which are characterized as dramatic or emotional.

Sociopaths makes up approximately 3% to 5% of the general population. According to the American Psychiatric Association, about three out of 100 males are sociopaths. Approximately 70% of sociopaths who come from fatherless homes and 30% are born out of wedlock. As many as 15% to 25% of prison inmates show signs of being sociopaths.

Although sociopathy can only be diagnosed at the age of 18 or above, the following must be present before the age of 15 for the diagnosis:

- Repeated violations of the law

- Pervasive lying and deception

- Physical aggressiveness

- Reckless disregard for safety of self or others

- Consistent irresponsibility in work and family environments

- Lack of remorse

The Psychopath versus the Sociopath

Psychopathy can be thought of as a more severe form of sociopathy with more symptoms. Therefore, all psychopaths are sociopaths, but sociopaths are not necessarily psychopaths.

Additionally, approximately 93% of psychopaths are in the criminal justice system. It should be noted that all addicts, no matter what kind, have traits of sociopathy and fall on the narcissistic spectrum.

The Difference Between a Psychopath and Sociopath

Although the traits of each may seem similar, it is thought that sociopaths have a less severe form of lack of empathy and lack of guilt. It is thought that sociopaths may be able to form some deep bonds such as with family, whereas a psychopath cannot. Additionally, even though a sociopath would feel no guilt about hurting a stranger, they may feel guilt and remorse over hurting someone with which they share a bond if it serves them in some way. Likewise, it appears that some of the very antisocial behavior in sociopaths lessens over time while this cannot be said of psychopaths. Psychopaths appear to have no concern whatsoever of the consequences, whereas a sociopath may learn to avoid consequences over time by reducing antisocial behavior.

The psychopath is callous, yet charming. They will con and manipulate others with charisma and intimidation and can effectively mimic feelings to present as "normal" to society. The psychopath is organized in their criminal thinking and behavior, and can maintain good emotional and physical control, displaying little to no emotional or autonomic arousal, even under situations that most would find threatening or horrifying. The psychopath is keenly aware that what he or she is doing is wrong but does not care.

Conversely, the sociopath is less organized in their demeanor. They might be nervous, easily agitated, and quick to display anger. A sociopath is more likely to spontaneously act out in inappropriate ways without thinking through the consequences. Compared to the psychopath, the sociopath will not be able to move through society committing callous crimes as easily, as they can form attachments and often have normal temperaments.

Both psychopaths and sociopaths can commit horrific crimes, but a sociopath is less likely to commit them against those with whom there is a bond.

Regarding sociopathy and psychopathy, let us look at the profile of a psychopath. The common features of a psychopath are:

- Glibness and superficial charm

- Manipulative and conning

- They never recognize the rights of others and see their self-serving behaviors as permissible.

- They appear to be charming, yet are covertly hostile and domineering, seeing their victim as merely an instrument to be used.

- They may dominate and humiliate their victims.

- Grandiose sense of self

- Feels entitled to certain things as "their right."

- Pathological liar

- They have no problem lying coolly and easily and it is almost impossible for them to be truthful on a consistent basis.

- They can create, and get caught up in, a complex belief about their own powers and abilities.

- They are extremely convincing and even able to pass lie detector tests.

- Lack of remorse, shame, or guilt

- They have a deep-seated rage, which is split off and repressed, is at their core.

- They do not see others around them as people, but only as targets and opportunities.

- Instead of friends, they have victims and accomplices who end up as victims. To them, the end always justifies the means and they let nothing stand in their way.

- Shallow emotions

- When they show what seems to be warmth, joy, love and compassion it is more feigned than experienced and serves an ulterior motive.

- They are outraged by insignificant matters yet remaining unmoved and cold by what would upset a normal person. Since they are not genuine, neither are their promises.

- Incapacity for love

- Need for stimulation

- They live on the edge.

- Verbal outbursts and physical punishments are normal.

- Promiscuity and gambling are common.

- Callousness and lack of empathy

- They are unable to empathize with the pain of their victims, having only contempt for other people's feelings of distress and readily taking advantage of them.

- Poor behavioral control and have an impulsive nature.

- They exhibit rage and abuse, alternating with small expressions of love and approval which produces an addictive cycle for the abuser and the abused, as well as creating hopelessness in the victim.

- They believe that they are all-powerful, all-knowing, entitled to every wish, and they have no sense of personal boundaries and no concern for their impact on others. Early behavior problems and juvenile delinquency.

- They usually have a history of behavioral and academic difficulties, yet they get by conning others.

- They have problems making and keeping friends and they engage in aberrant behaviors such as cruelty to people or animals, stealing, etc.

- Irresponsible and unreliable

- They are not concerned about wrecking other peoples' lives and dreams.

- They are oblivious or indifferent to the devastation they cause.

- They do not accept blame themselves, but blame others, even for acts they obviously commit.

- Promiscuous sexual behavior and infidelity

- They often engage in promiscuity, child sexual abuse, rape, and sexual acting out of all sorts.

- Lack of realistic life plan and parasitic lifestyle

- They tend to move around a lot or make all-encompassing promises for the future, have a poor work ethic, but exploit others effectively.

- Criminal or entrepreneurial versatile

- They change their image as needed to avoid prosecution.

- They change their life story readily and frequently.

Other Related Qualities:

- Contemptuous of those who seek to understand them

- Does not perceive that anything is wrong with them

- Authoritarian

- Secretive

- Paranoia

- Only rarely in difficulty with the law, but seeks out situations where their tyrannical behavior will be tolerated, condoned, or admired

- Conventional appearance

- Goal of enslavement of their victim(s)

- Exercises despotic control over every aspect of the victim's life

- Has an emotional need to justify their crimes and therefore needs their victim's affirmation (respect, gratitude, and love)

- Ultimate goal is the creation of a willing victim

- Incapable of real human attachment to another

- Unable to feel remorse or guilt

- Extreme narcissism and grandiose

- May state readily that their goal is to rule the world

Keep in mind that difference between a sociopath and psychopath is a matter of degree because they are in same narcissistic spectrum. Sociopathy is a less severe form of psychopathy. Do you think you can spot one? Think again. In general, psychopaths are not the product of broken homes or the casualties of a materialistic society. Rather, they come from all walks of life and there is little evidence that their upbringing affects them. Elements of a psychopath's personality first become evident at a very early age, due to environmental factors. By the time that a person hits their late teens, the disorder is almost certainly permanent. Although many clinicians use the terms psychopath and sociopath interchangeably, a sociopath's criminal behavior is shaped by social forces and is the result of a dysfunctional environment.

Psychopaths have only a shallow range of emotions and lack a sense of guilt or shame. They often see themselves as victims, and lack remorse or the ability to empathize with others. Psychopaths play on the fact that most of us are trusting and forgiving people. The warning signs are always there, but it is just difficult to see them because once we trust someone, and so, our friendship becomes a blinder.

Even partners and lovers get taken for a ride by psychopaths. For a psychopath, a romantic relationship is just another opportunity to find a trusting partner who will buy into the lies. It is primarily why a psychopath rarely stays in a relationship for the long term, and often is involved with three or four partners at once. To a psychopath, everything about a relationship is a game. Consider the movie *Sliding Doors* (1998) to illustrate the point. In the film, the main character comes home early after just having been fired from her job. Only moments ago, her boyfriend had let another woman out the front door. But in a matter of minutes, he was the attentive and concerned boyfriend, taking her out to dinner and devoting the entire night to comforting her. All the while, he was planning to leave the next day on a trip with the other woman.

The boyfriend displays typical psychopathic characteristics because he falsely displays deep emotion toward the relationship. In reality, he is less concerned with his girlfriend's depression than with making sure she is clueless about the other woman's existence. In the romance department, psychopaths have an ability to gain your affection quickly, disarming you with words, intriguing you with grandiose plans. If they cheat, you will forgive them, and one day when they have gone too far, they will leave you with a broken heart and an empty wallet. By then, they will have a new player for their game.

The problem with their game is that we do not often play by their rules. Where we might occasionally tell a white lie, a psychopath's lying is compulsive. Most of us experience some degree of guilt about lying, preventing us from exhibiting such behavior on a regular basis. Psychopaths do not discriminate who they lie to or cheat on. There is no distinction between friend, family, or prey item they use, take advantage of, consume, or defeat.

No one wants to be the sucker, so how do we prevent ourselves from becoming close friends or getting into a relationship with a psychopath? It is almost impossible. Unfortunately, one way is to become more suspicious and less trusting of others. Our tendency is to forgive when we catch a loved one in a lie. Psychopaths play on this fact. However, we certainly are not advocating a world where if someone lies once or twice, you never speak to them again. What you can do is look at how often someone lies and how they react when caught. Psychopaths will lie over and over again, and where other people would sincerely apologize, a psychopath might apologize but will not stop.

Psychopaths also tend to switch jobs as frequently as they switch partners, mainly because they do not have the qualities to maintain a job for the long haul. Their performance is generally erratic, with chronic absences, misuse of company resources and failed commitments.

Often, they are not even qualified for the job and use fake credentials to get it. For instance, take a person who would get marketing jobs based on his image. He was a presentable and charming man who layered his conversations with educational and occupational references. But it becomes evident that the man did not have a clue what he was talking about and was unable to hold down the job.

How do you make sure you do not get fooled when you are hiring someone to baby-sit your child or for any other job? Hire based on reputation and not image. Check references thoroughly. Psychopaths tend to give vague and inconsistent replies. Of course, the best way to solve this problem would be to cure psychopaths of their condition. But there is no way to treat them. Their condition is pervasive and forever. Today's traditional methods of psychotherapy and drug treatments have failed to treat the psychopath. Therapy is more likely to work when an individual admits there is a problem and wants to change. The common problem with psychopaths is they do not see a problem with their behavior.

Psychopaths do not seek therapy willingly. Rather, they are pushed into it by a desperate relative or by a court order. To a psychopath, a therapist is just one more person who must be conned, and the psychopath plays the part right until the therapist is convinced of the psychopath's rehabilitation.

Even though we cannot treat psychopaths effectively with therapy, it does not mean that we cannot protect ourselves. The most important factor in keeping psychopaths at bay is to know your vulnerabilities. We need to realize our own potential and maximize our strengths so that our insecurities do not overcome us. Because a psychopath is a chameleon who becomes an image of what you have not done for yourself. Over time, their appearance of perfection will begin to crack, but by that time, you will have been emotionally and perhaps financially damaged. There comes a time when you realize there is no point in searching for answers; the only thing is to move on.

Chapter Three

Journey through the Twelve Steps

Our journey through the Twelve Steps of Recovery begins with some questions. First, are you a person who suffers from obsessive compulsive learned helplessness? Is your life unmanageable whether you engage in your obsessive compulsive learned helplessness or not? Do you want to find a design for living that is better than the one you had in the past? To what length are you willing to go to break your obsessive compulsive learned helplessness and live a new way of life?

Those who go back out and engage in their obsessive compulsive learned helplessness are usually the ones who cannot or will not commit themselves to a program of recovery and discovery that demands rigorous honesty with themselves and others. These are the ones who do not work the Twelve Steps of Recovery at all; the ones that stop working the Steps before they reach Step Four; the ones who quit after Step Eight; the so-called two-steppers who only work Step One and Twelve; the ones that allow pride in its many forms to get in the way of their recovery; or the ones who get distracted by relationships, excessive work, or engage in other addictions to escape.

Are you willing to work all twelve steps of recovery that this program requires for successful completion and a healthy outcome? How soon do you want to get well? If you answered to the affirmative to the questions above, let us get started.

First, let us look at three types of drinkers. Wait, you might think, what does drinking to excess have to do with obsessive compulsive learned helplessness? The answer is that these conditions all fall on the addiction spectrum and are the same whether you drink, use drugs, or engage in obsessive compulsive activities like gambling, sex, pornography, masturbating, eating, working, shopping, collecting, religion, or learned helplessness. And so, addiction is addiction, no matter whether you drink, use it, or do it. This of course includes obsessive compulsive learned helplessness.

The forefathers and pioneers wrote in the First Edition of the "Big Book," published in 1939, that moderate drinkers have little trouble in giving up liquor entirely if they have a good reason for it. They noted that they could take it or leave it alone.

The forefathers and pioneers went to say that the second type is the heavy drinker. They noted that regarding the heavy drinker, we have a certain type of hard drinker. He might have a drinking habit bad enough to gradually impair him physically and mentally, and it might cause him to die a few years before his time. They noted that if for a sufficiently strong reason, such as ill health, falling in love, change of environment, or the warning of a doctor, this man could also stop or moderate, although he might find it difficult and troublesome and might need medical attention.

The forefathers and pioneers explained that the third type is the alcoholic because they have lost the ability to choose and has lost the ability to control their drinking. Have you ever said that you were going to quit or tried to quit, but did not? Did you ever plan to drink just a few drinks, or a drug, or an activity, or getting into casual relationship but failed to control ho much you drank, used, did, or control your actions in a relationship?

So, let us compare different types of people who engage in obsessive compulsive learned helplessness. People who have moderate amounts of learned helplessness in their relationships with others have little trouble giving it up if they have a good reason for it. They occasionally misuse codependence, but they usually do not repeat the pattern.

The second type is the person who engages in obsessive compulsive learned helplessness heavily. Regarding a person who engages in obsessive compulsive learned helplessness heavily, here we have a certain type of hard user who seems to get overly involved in the use of codependence and learned helplessness in their relationships. They might have a habit or obsession bad enough to gradually impair them in their social life, home life, and work life, but if for a sufficiently good reason, this person can stop or moderate their use of learned helplessness, although they might find it difficult and troublesome and might need some professional help.

The third type is the person who is addicted to their obsessive compulsive codependent learned helplessness because they have lost the ability to choose and they have lost the ability to control their obsessive compulsive need to get into and maintain codependent relationships with wounded, resulting in a pervasive pattern of learned helplessness. Have you ever said that you were going to quit or tried to quit your addictive obsessive compulsive learned helplessness, but did or could not?

The true characteristics of the person addicted obsessive compulsive learned helplessness are: (1) they cannot stop their behavior permanently on their own as the moderate or heavily involved person can; (2) they cannot stop their obsessive compulsive learned helplessness and they cannot control what they will do or the consequences of their behavior once they engage in their obsessive compulsive learned helplessness; and (3) they demonstrate a "Jekyll-Hyde personality," where once they get engage in their obsessive compulsive learned helplessness, they became unrecognizable.

Like Dr. Jekyll and Mr. Hyde, where most of the time, this person is a nice quiet person, but once they get into a codependent relationship or a pattern of learned helplessness, they become obsessed with maintaining their codependent relationship and they turn into a monster; or one minute this person says they will never get into a relationship again and the next they are heading straight for another binge of codependence. And so, it is necessary that you examine your patterns of the use of learned helplessness and concede to your innermost self that you are not moderately or excessively involved in your use of learned helplessness, but you are addicted to obsessive compulsive learned helplessness.

The forefathers and pioneers of Alcoholics Anonymous described alcohol addict by saying you might start off moderately, but at some stage of your drinking, you begin to lose control of your drinking, once you start drinking.

In regard to obsessive compulsive learned helplessness, you might start off moderately, but at some stage in the progression of your condition, you begin to engage in your obsessive compulsive learned helplessness in a frightening downward spiral into destruction.

The forefathers and pioneers of Alcoholics Anonymous went on to say here is the person who is puzzling. They do absurd, incredibly tragic things when engaged in drinking binges. They are a real Dr. Jekyll and Mr. Hyde. They are seldom mildly intoxicated. They are always more or less insanely drunk. Their disposition while drunk does not resemble their normal nature. They might be one of the finest people in the world. Yet, let them get drunk, and they frequently become disgustingly, and even dangerously antisocial They have an amazing genius for getting drunk at exactly the wrong moment, particularly when some important decision must be made, or when engagements must be kept. They are often perfectly sensible, well-balanced, and competent in every other part of their life except for drinking, but in that respect, they are incredibly dishonest and selfish. They often possess excellent abilities, skills, and aptitudes, and have promising careers ahead of them. They use their gifts to build up a bright outlook for themselves and their family, and then pull the structure down on their head with a senseless series of binges. This is the person who goes to bed intoxicated convinced that they will not drinks again. Yet, the next day, they are searching madly for another drink.

Likewise, regarding a person engaged in a pervasive pattern of obsessive compulsive learned helplessness, here is a person who is puzzling. They do absurd, incredibly tragic things when engaged in their obsessive compulsive learned helplessness. They are a real Dr. Jekyll and Mr. Hyde. They are seldom moderately involved in their codependence or learned helplessness. They are always more or less insanely obsessed with getting into or maintaining a codependent relationship in an insane pattern of learned helplessness. Their disposition while engaged in their learned helplessness does not resemble their normal nature.

They might be one of the finest people in the world. Yet, let them get involved in a codependent relationship and they frequently become obsessively compulsively engaged in a codependent relationship with alcohol addict, drug addict, narcissistic personality, sociopath, or abuser in a crazy pattern of learned helplessness. They have an amazing genius for getting into a destructive bout of learned helplessness at exactly the wrong moment, particularly when some important decision must be made, or when engagements must be kept.

They are often perfectly sensible, well-balanced, and competent in every other part of their life except for relationships, but in this respect, they are incredibly dishonest and selfish. They often possess excellent abilities, skills, and aptitudes, and have promising careers ahead of them. They use their gifts to build up a bright outlook for themselves and their family, and then pull the structure down on their head by a senseless series of codependent relationship binges in their never-ending learned helplessness. This is the person who goes to bed convinced that they will never engage another codependent relationship binge again. Yet, the next day, they are obsessively compulsively engaged in another codependent relationship, thus starting the nightmare of learned helplessness all over again.

As matters grow worse, the person addicted to learned helplessness begins to use combinations of other high-intensity binges like drugs, alcohol, sex, exercise, or gambling to discharge their accumulating distress when they are not involved in sone kind of learned helplessness. Then comes the day when they simply cannot go on and they abruptly stop engaging in their binges of learned helplessness which throws them into a crisis. Perhaps, they go to a doctor who gives them a sedative to calm their distress, at which time, they begin to appear at counselor's offices and on psychiatric units.

If you have one or more of the 40 traits of an unmanageable life, you might be a real addict:

1. Do you have an obsessive compulsive need to get into or maintain codependent relationships to maintain your learned helplessness?

2. Do you avoid being alone or do you seek to be alone?

3. Do you lose time from work due to your obsessive compulsive need to get into a relationship with wounded souls to maintain your learned helplessness?

4. Are your binges of obsessive compulsive learned helplessness harming your family in any way?

5. Do you have cravings to get into or maintain obsessive compulsive codependent relationship to maintain your learned helplessness?

6. Do you get into obsessive compulsive codependent relationships to maintain your learned helplessness so you feel that you have value and worth?

7. Do you get irritable when you are not involved in an obsessive compulsive learned helplessness?

8. Does your obsessive compulsive need to get into and maintain your learned helplessness impact your family's welfare?

9. Have you harmed loved ones by your obsessive compulsive need to get into a codependent relationship to maintain your learned helplessness?

10. Has your obsessive compulsive need to get into a codependent relationship to maintain your learned helplessness changed your personality?

11. Do you suffer from body complaints when you are not involved in a codependent relationship to maintain your learned helplessness?

12. Are you restless when you are not involved in getting into a codependent relationship to maintain your learned helplessness?

13. Do have difficulty sleeping when you are not involved in getting into a codependent relationship to maintain your learned helplessness?

14. Are you becoming more impulsive in getting into a codependent relationship to maintain your learned helplessness?

15. Do have less control since you started getting involved in getting into a codependent relationship to maintain your learned helplessness?

16. Has your desire to begin or complete new things decreased since you began getting into a codependent relationship to maintain your learned helplessness?

17. Has your ambition to achieve greater things decreased since you began getting into a codependent relationship to maintain your learned helplessness?

18. Do you lack energy to pursue your goals since you began getting into a codependent relationship to maintain your learned helplessness?

19. Do you in get into codependent relationships and maintain your learned helplessness to achieve a sense social competence?

20. Do you get into codependent relationships and maintain your learned helplessness to get yourself out of a depression?

21. Do you get into codependent relationships and maintain your learned helplessness to relieve marked feelings of inadequacy?

22. Has your sexual potency suffered since you started getting into codependent relationships to maintain your learned helplessness?

23. Do you show marked dislike for or hatred toward others since you started getting into codependent relationships to maintain your learned helplessness?

24. Has your jealousy increased since you started getting into codependent relationships to maintain your learned helplessness?

25. Do you show marked moodiness when not involved in getting into codependent relationships to maintain your learned helplessness?

26. Has your performance at work been impacted since you started getting into codependent relationships to maintain your learned helplessness?

27. Has your need to get into codependent relationships to maintain your learned helplessness made you more insensitive?

28. Are you harder to get along with since you started getting into codependent relationships to maintain your learned helplessness?

29. Do you hang around with lesser people or lesser environments since you started getting into codependent relationships to maintain your learned helplessness?

30. Is engaging in codependent relationships to maintain your learned helplessness endangering your health?

31. Is engaging in codependent relationships to maintain your learned helplessness affecting your peace of mind?

32. Is engaging in codependent relationships to maintain your learned helplessness making your home life unhappy?

33. Is engaging in codependent relationships to maintain your learned helplessness jeopardizing your business, job, or career?

34. Is engaging in codependent relationships to maintain your learned helplessness harming your reputation?

35. Is engaging in codependent relationships to maintain your learned helplessness disturbing the peace and harmony of your life?

36. Have you ever had a partial or complete loss of memory while in or after engaging in a codependent relationships to maintain your learned helplessness?

37. Have you ever experienced an inability to concentrate when in or after engaging in codependent relationships to maintain your learned helplessness?

38. Have you ever felt remorse after engaging in codependent relationships to maintain your learned helplessness?

39. Has a physician or counselor ever treated you for your learned helplessness condition?

40. Have you ever been hospitalized in a crisis unit as a consequence of your obsessive compulsive learned helplessness?

The forefathers and pioneers of Alcoholics Anonymous tell us in the Foreword of the First Edition of the "Big Book" written in 1939 that the purpose of the book is to show others how they recovered from addiction.

They wrote that we of Alcoholics Anonymous are more than one hundred men and women who have recovered from a seemingly hopeless state of mind and body. To show other addicts precisely how we have recovered is the main purpose of this book.

This was a revolutionary statement because until the fellowship of Alcoholics Anonymous was founded in 1935 and the "Big Book" was written in 1939, there was little hope for addicts. Now, anyone who is willing to follow the directions of this simple program of recovery, and many like it, can recover from this dreaded disorder.

The forefathers and pioneers of Alcoholics Anonymous gave us a message of hope. They wrote they had discovered a common solution. They had found a way out on which they could all absolutely agree, and upon which they could join in brotherly and harmonious action. This was the great news this book carried to those who suffer from addiction—there was a cure.

The forefathers and pioneers of Alcoholics Anonymous went on to tell us that there is a solution. Almost none of us like the self-searching, the leveling of pride, and the confession of shortcomings which this process requires for success. But we see that it really works in others, and we have come to believe in the hopelessness and futility of the life we had been living. When we are approached by those in whom the problem has been solved, there is nothing left for us do but to pick up the simple kit of survival tools laid at our feet. We have found much of heaven and we have been rocketed into a fourth dimension of existence of which we had not even dreamed.

Furthermore, the forefathers and pioneers of Alcoholics Anonymous explained that there is no middle ground for those who suffer from addiction. We are either going to be consumed by it or find a spiritual solution and be spared. Half measures availed us nothing. We stood at the turning point. The forefathers and pioneers explained that if you are seriously addicted, there is no middle-of-the-road solution. The forefathers and pioneers were in a position where life was becoming impossible, and if they passed into the region from which there was no return through human aid, and so, they had but three alternatives: (1) sober up, (2) get covered up, or (3) get locked up.

For example, the forefathers and pioneers of Alcoholics Anonymous related a story about a prominent American businessman, Rowland Hazard., who was a chronic alcoholic, and the prominent Psychiatrist Dr. Carl Jung. They wrote that Hazard, an American businessman, had ability, good sense, and high moral character, but for years, he floundered from one hospital to the next. The forefathers and pioneers wrote that Hazard had consulted the best-known American psychiatrists, but then went to Europe, placing himself in the care of the celebrated physician and psychiatrist, Dr. Carl Jung, who treated him. The forefathers and pioneers went on to say that although experience had made Hazard skeptical, he finished his treatment with unusual confidence.

The forefathers and pioneers wrote that his physical and mental conditions were unusually good, and above all, Hazard believed he had acquired such a profound knowledge of the inner workings of his mind and its hidden mechanics that relapse was unthinkable. Nevertheless, the forefathers reported that he was drunk within a short time. More baffling still, Hazard could give himself no satisfactory explanation for his fall. The forefathers and pioneers noted that Hazard returned to Jung, whom he admired, and asked him point-blank why he could not recover. Hazard wished above all things to regain control of his drinking, although he seemed quite rational and well-balanced in other aspects of his life. Yet, it seemed that he had no control whatever over alcohol.

The forefathers and pioneers went on to tell us that Hazard begged the doctor to tell him the whole truth, and he got it. The forefathers and pioneers stated that in the doctor's judgment Hazard was utterly hopeless, and that he could never regain his position in society, and he would have to place himself under lock and key or hire a bodyguard if he expected to live long. The forefathers and pioneers stated that Jung told Hazard that he had the mind of a chronic alcoholic, and that he had never seen one single case recover where that state of mind existed to the extent that it did in Hazard. The forefathers and pioneers noted that Hazard felt as though the gates of hell had just slammed shut on him.

The forefathers and pioneers continued by saying that Hazard asked if there were any exceptions. They noted that Jung said yes there was. Jung explained that exceptions to cases such as Hazard's had been occurring since early times. The forefathers and pioneers noted that Jung explained that here and there, occasionally, alcoholics have had what was called a "vital spiritual experience." The forefathers and pioneers stated that Jung claimed that these occurrences are phenomena, and they appeared to be huge emotional displacements. Jung went on to say that ideas, emotions, and attitudes which were once the guiding forces of the lives of alcoholics were suddenly cast to one side, and a completely new set of conceptions and motives begin to dominate them.

The forefathers and pioneers of Alcoholics Anonymous explained that most of us have been unwilling to admit we are real addicts, and no one likes to think they are bodily and mentally different from their fellows. Therefore, it is not surprising that our careers of getting into destructive obsessive compulsive codependent relationship binges have been characterized by countless vain attempts to prove that we can act like normal people. The idea that somehow, someday we can control and enjoy our relationships like others is the great obsession of every obsessive compulsive codependent person or relationship addict. The forefathers and pioneers noted that the persistence of this illusion is astonishing, and we may pursue it to the gates of insanity.

Furthermore, the forefathers and pioneers of Alcoholics Anonymous discussed our loss of control and the lengths we go to act normally. They noted that addicts are men and women who have lost the ability to control their behavior. We know that for most real obsessive compulsive codependent or relationship addicts, few ever recover control of their ability to engage in healthy relationships wisely without some kind of help. All of us have felt at times that we were regaining control, but such intervals, usually brief, were inevitably followed by still less control and more serious consequences, which led in time to pitiful and incomprehensible demoralization. We must be convinced that we are in the grip of a progressive condition. Without help, we, we get worse, never better.

The forefathers and pioneers of Alcoholics Anonymous went on to say that we are like people who have lost their legs. We will never grow new ones, but with a program of recovery and transformation, a miracle happens—we grow new legs. Neither does there appear to be any kind drug or treatment that will make a person who engages obsessive compulsive learned helplessness engage in relationships in wise and healthy ways, but there is a cure—the Twelve Step of Recovery program. We have tried every imaginable remedy. In some instances, there has been a brief respite from our addiction, followed always by a still worse relapses. Physicians who are familiar with addiction agree there is no such thing as making a normal healthy person out of a person with an obsessive compulsive need to get into codependent relationships with wounded souls to maintain their learned helplessness. Science may one day accomplish this, but it has not done so far, but there is one tried and true way out—the Twelve Steps of Recovery.

Furthermore, the forefathers and pioneers of Alcoholics Anonymous wrote that despite all we can say, many who are alcoholics or addicts, including those who engage in obsessive compulsive codependent relationships with wounded souls to maintain their learned helplessness, are not going to believe they are addicts and will try in so many ways to prove that they are not. By every form of self-deception, they will try to prove themselves to be an exception to the rule—a non-addict. If anyone who is showing an inability to control their obsessive compulsive need to get into codependent relationships with wounded souls to maintain their learned helplessness could do an about-face and act like a normal person, our hats are off to them. Heaven knows, we have tried hard enough and long enough to act like other people.

Additionally, here are some of the methods we have tried: engaging in casual relationships; limiting the amount time we are in a relationship; never being alone; always being alone; never inviting dates into our homes; always inviting our dates to our homes; never going to a public place with a date; always going to a public place with a date; swearing off relationships forever, with or without a solemn oath; working out more; reading more inspirational books; or going to a counselor. We can add to this list ad infinitum.

The forefathers and pioneers of Alcoholics Anonymous made a provocative statement regarding controlled use. They wrote that we do not like to pronounce anyone as an addict, but you could quickly diagnose yourself. Step over to the nearest barroom and try some controlled drinking. Try to drink and stop abruptly. Try it more than once. It will not take long for you to decide, if you are honest with yourself about it. It might be worth a bad case of jitters if you get a full knowledge of your condition.

Likewise, regarding your obsessive compulsive learned helplessness, just try to getting involved with a potential partner. Try it more than once. It will not take long for you to decide, if you are honest with yourself about it, to realize that you are a person with obsessive compulsive learned helplessness, and once you engage in some kind of obsessive compulsive codependent behavior with a wounded soul, you will have very tough time staying away from your learned helplessness without severe emotional distress.

The forefathers and pioneers went on to say although there is no way of proving it, they believed that early in their addiction careers most of them could have stopped. But the difficulty was that few of them could stay stopped. Mark Twain, who was a very heavy cigar smoker, once said that quitting smoking was the easiest thing he ever did; he did it a thousand times.

For example, the forefathers and pioneers of Alcoholics Anonymous told us of a man of 30 who was doing a great deal of spree drinking. He was very nervous in the morning after these bouts and quieted himself with more liquor. He was ambitious to succeed in business but saw that he would get nowhere if he continued to drink. Once he started, he had no control whatever. He made up his mind that until he had been successful in business and had retied, he would not touch another drop. An exceptional man, he remained dry for 25 years and retired at the age of 55, after a successful business career. Then he fell victim to a belief which practically every alcoholic has—his long period of sobriety and self-discipline had qualified him to drink as other men. In two months, he was in a hospital, puzzled and humiliated. He tried to regulate his drinking for a while, making several trips to the hospital in the meantime. Then, gathering all his forces, he attempted to stop altogether and found he could not. Every means of solving his problems which money could buy was at his disposal. Every attempt failed. Although a robust man at retirement, he went to pieces quickly and was dead within four years.

This frightening scenario is not uncommon in addicts of all kinds and is known as progression. It is important that you realize your illness progresses whether you engage in your obsessive compulsive learned helplessness or not, as demonstrated above, and if you engage in another obsessive compulsive binge of learned helplessness, it will be as if you never stopped. Consequently, disability will likely follow in a short time.

The forefathers and pioneers of Alcoholics Anonymous went on to describe the addict and tell us what it would take to recover. They said when you honestly want to, you likely found that you could not quit entirely, or when engaging in your obsessive compulsive learned helplessness, you had little control over the intensity of your use, you are probably a person with obsessive compulsive learned helplessness. If that be the case, you might be suffering from an illness which only a mental and spiritual transformation will conquer.

But the concept that once an addict, always an addict has raised a very contentious argument over whether an addict can be cured of their addiction. Unfortunately, this issue has been confused by contradicting statements in the "Big Book" and people in twelve-step programs, and by the treatment industry as a whole. Bill Wilson, co-founder of Alcoholics Anonymous, said it clearly enough by saying that the Lord had been so wonderful to him by "curing" him of this terrible affliction, that he just wanted to keep talking about it and telling people.

Likewise, Dr. Robert Smith, co-founder of Alcoholics Anonymous, also stated it plainly enough by saying that there was a man named Bill Wilson who had experienced many years of frightful drinking, who had had most all the drunkard's experiences known to man, but who had been "cured" by the very means he had been trying to employ—that is to say the spiritual approach.

An article in the *A.A. Grapevine*, Alcoholics Anonymous' monthly newsletter, said that Smith once told Wilson that they had better round up some drunks to work on. Smith phoned the nurse in charge of admissions at Akron City Hospital and told her how he and another drunk from New York City had a cure for alcoholism.

Alcoholics Anonymous Number Three, attorney Bill Dotson, echoed Wilson's cure statement by saying that the sentence uttered by Wilson: "The Lord has been so wonderful to me, curing me of this terrible affliction, that I just want to keep telling people about it," had been a sort of golden text for the Alcoholics Anonymous program and for him.

Frank Amos, who was to become an Alcoholics Anonymous Trustee, set forth these facts in his report to John D. Rockefeller, Jr. on his investigation of "Akron cure" said that Dr. Howard S., general practitioner at Cuyahoga Falls Hospital, said that one of his patients had been an alcoholic and had been cured by Smith and his friends' and the Christian technique prescribed. So, according to the forefathers and pioneers of Alcoholics Anonymous, they believed that a cure was not only possible, it was likely.

The forefathers and pioneers of Alcoholics Anonymous went on to say that addicts who were reasonably mentally well and in other ways genuinely wanted to be cured of their addiction were the type with whom the founders and pioneers had achieved their great success. On the other hand, addicts who were mentally ill, or who were sociopaths, or stubbornly held on to their old ideas had proven to be very difficult problems, and so far, the percentage of cures has been very low in these cases.

The biography of Bill Wilson's physician William D. Silkworth written by Dale Mitchel shows the heart of the early Alcoholics Anonymous' reliance on God. Mitchel wrote that Silkworth had not been given the appropriate credit for his position on a spiritual conversion, particularly as it might relate to true Christian benefits. It was Silkworth who used the term: "The Great Physician" to explain the need in recovery for a relationship with Jesus Christ. In the formation of Alcoholics Anonymous, Wilson initially insisted on references to God and Jesus, as well as the Great Physician. Silkworth, a medical doctor, challenged the addict with a spiritual conversion and a relationship with God as part of a program of recovery. His approach with Bill Wilson was no different. Wilson and Smith believed reliance on the Creator was a necessity.

Regarding Wilson, consider these telling statements about his decision for Christ and the importance of turning to God for help. During his third visit to Towns Hospital, Wilson had a discussion with Dr. Silkworth on the subject of the "Great Physician." In fact, Wilson himself wrote that he had thought about this discussion before he decided to check himself into Towns for the last time, at the urging of his wife and his brother-in-law.

In his autobiography, Wilson wrote that he remembered saying to himself that he would do anything at all and if there be a "Great Physician," he should call on him.

Before his final trip to Towns Hospital, Wilson, like his friend Ebby Thacher, had gone to the altar at the Calvary Rescue Mission and made a decision for Jesus Christ. He said Ebby had told him that he had done all right and had given my life to God and wrote of his later conversion experience at Towns by saying that he was sure he had been born again.

Then, at Towns Hospital, Wilson said he cried out: "If there be a God, let him show himself." Wilson said that the effect was instant and electric. Wilson stated that suddenly his room blazed with an indescribably white light and he was seized with an ecstasy beyond description. Wilson said he became acutely conscious of a presence which seemed like a veritable sea of living spirit which he thought must be the great reality of God. Wilson claimed that he thanked the God who had given me a glimpse of His Absolute Self, and this great and sudden gift of grace had always been his.

Dr. Silkworth informed Wilson that he had some kind of conversion experience. Wilson commented: "God comes to most men gradually, but His impact on me was sudden and profound."

Interestingly, in a conversion experience seemingly identical to that of Wilson's grandfather Willie in East Dorset, Wilson, like his grandfather Willie, was cured and never drank again.

Regarding Dr. Bob Smith, he was not struck with a "white light" conversion experience but had been converted years before as a youngster in St. Johnsbury, Vermont. To overcome his alcoholism, he joined a tiny group recovered drunks on the carpet of the home of T. Henry Williams in Akron and prayed for deliverance. The miraculous cure came in the unexpected visit, call, and presence of Bill Wilson at Henrietta Seiberling's Gate Lodge where the two men met, exchanged stories, and soon were on their way to founding Alcoholics Anonymous in Akron on June 10, 1935.

Smith did not hold back about God or a cure for addiction. At City Hospital, newcomers in the early Alcoholics Anonymous program were asked the primary question: "Do you believe in God?," and there was only one acceptable answer. Of course, the only correct answer was "yes." If the prospective candidate said "no," he was disqualified and left to his demise. Later, the prospective candidate was taken upstairs in a private prayer ceremony where, with several "elders" praying over him, he knelt, made a decision for Christ, asked God to take alcohol out of his life, and prayed for the strength and guidance to live according to cardinal Christian principles.

Of the original founders and pioneers who went to any lengths to work the Akron Program of Recovery and established and maintained their relationship and fellowship with a God of their understanding, over 50% were permanently cured. Again, Smith was clear about the reason. He wrote: "Your Heavenly Father will never let you down!"

There is no doubt that the early Akron Alcoholics Anonymous was a fundamentalist Christian organization with a requirement of a "real surrender" ceremony that confirmed acceptance of Jesus Christ which as a required and essential part of the Akron recovery program that was necessary to belong to the Akron fellowship, and so, newcomers had to make a "real surrender."

This was akin to the altar call at rescue missions or the confession of Christ with other believers in churches and other revival gatherings, except that it was a very small, private ceremony which took place upstairs and away from the regular meeting. Four Alcoholics Anonymous old-timers—Ed Andy from Lorain, Ohio; J. D. Holmes from Indiana; Clarence Snyder from Cleveland; and Larry Bauer in Akron—all independently verified orally and in writing that the Akron surrenders required acceptance of Jesus Christ as Lord and Savior.

Those conversions took place at the regular Wednesday meeting upstairs in the manner described in *James 5:15-16*. Kneeling, with "elders" at his side, the newcomer accepted Christ, and with the prayer partners, asked God to take alcohol out of his life and to help, guide him, and strengthen him to live by cardinal Christian teachings such as those in the Oxford Group's Four Absolutes—Honesty, Purity, Unselfishness, and Love

It should be noted that there is a distinct difference between sobriety, abstinence, and wellness or mental, emotional, emotional, physical, and spiritual well-being. Abstinence is not recovery—it is the prerequisite for recovery. Sobriety is an outstanding achievement that should not be minimized, but if you want to go beyond just sobriety or abstinence and strive for and achieve wellness, you need to do the inner work to know and let go of your fears, inadequacies, inferiorities, and insecurities that lie at the core of your addiction and makes your life unhappy and unmanageable. In other words, your obsessive compulsive learned helplessness is a side show to the real problem, and there will be no happiness, joy, or prosperity until you discover, let go, and put away what lies at the core of your defects of character—the nature of your wrongs.

Now that you know what you must do in order to recover from your obsessive compulsive learned helplessness, you must undergo a life-changing mental, emotional, physical, and spiritual transformation. It should be noted that your obsessive compulsive learned helplessness can be a disabling condition, but it is curable.

Prior to Alcoholics Anonymous, most alcohol addicts died drunk, were locked up in jails or insane asylums, or became homeless bums. Similarly, being a person with obsessive compulsive learned helplessness who gets into and maintains an obsessive compulsive relationship with some rather unsavory characters like alcohol addicts, drug addicts, narcissistic characters, sociopaths, and abusers to maintain your learned helplessness often results in physical and emotional injury, homelessness, unemployment, chronic health problems, and sometimes death.

The forefathers and pioneers of Alcoholics Anonymous tell us of our options. They wrote that if you believe that you are an atheist or agnostic such an experience might seem impossible, but to continue on your present path means disaster, especially if you are a person with obsessive compulsive learned helplessness of the hopeless variety. To be doomed to be a person with obsessive compulsive learned helplessness in an endless series of unhealthy relationship binges and to live in a perpetual pattern of ever more destructive binges is not an easy alternative to face.

So, regardless of what your beliefs are, a spiritual experience, awakening of the spirit, or epiphany is not only possible, it is guaranteed, if you keep an open mind and work the Twelve Steps of Recovery as prescribed by the original forefathers and pioneers of Alcoholics Anonymous. Furthermore, those who have agnostic or atheist beliefs, the forefathers and pioneers of Alcoholics Anonymous tell us that no matter what your present beliefs are, there is hope for you. They wrote that it is not so difficult. At first, some of us tried to avoid the issue all together, hoping against all hope that we were not a person with a real case of obsessive compulsive learned helplessness. But after a while, we had to face the fact that we must find a spiritual basis of life or else. Perhaps it is going to be that way with you. But cheer up, even though something like half of the original fellowship of Alcoholics Anonymous were atheists or agnostics, their experience shows us that you need not be concerned.

It is indeed amazing that a newcomer could enter the fellowship Alcoholics Anonymous without any specific spiritual beliefs, or for that matter, without any spiritual beliefs whatsoever and recover from addiction. All a person needs is an open mind and a willingness to believe that this program can work for them. The Twelve Steps of Recovery have changed this writer's life and the lives of millions of other addicts of all kinds. This program will change your life too, if you honestly want to recover from this affliction, get well, and are willing to do what is necessary to get there.

The forefathers and pioneers of Alcoholics Anonymous tell us about the spiritual experience. They wrote that lack of power was their dilemma. They had to find a Power by which they could live, and it had to be a Power greater than themselves. But where and how do we to find this Power? Well, that is exactly what this book is about. Its main object is to enable you to find a Power greater than you which will help you solve your problem—your obsessive compulsive learned helplessness and what drives it.

The forefathers and pioneers of Alcoholics Anonymous asked us to develop our own concept of God, whatever we conceive that to be. In other words, they want us to find a God of our own understanding or a Power greater than us. They wrote that much to their relief, they discovered that they did not need to consider another person's conception of God. Our own conception, however inadequate, is enough to make the approach and to affect a contact with Him. As soon as we admitted the possible existence of a Creative Intelligence, a Spirit of the Universe underlying the totality of things, we began to be possessed of a new sense of power and direction, provided we took other simple steps. We found that this Power does not make terms too hard for those who seek Him. To us, the Realm of Spirit is broad, roomy, and all-inclusive; never exclusive or forbidding to those who earnestly seek Him.

The forefathers and pioneers of Alcoholics Anonymous tell us that we must take some actions, which will lead us to our Creator and guide us to the Realm of the Spirit. They tell us that we will change from being self-centered to being other-centered, and our lives will change from being material to being spiritual. Although Alcoholics Anonymous is derived from a fundamentalist evangelical religious program, the Oxford Group, you are free to call this Power anything you wish, as long as it is a Power greater than you.

The forefathers and pioneers of Alcoholics Anonymous used many different names for this Power, including: Creative Intelligence, Universal Mind, Spirit of the Universe, Creator, Higher Consciousness, or Great Reality, among others.

Therefore, the forefathers and pioneers of Alcoholics Anonymous maintained that in order to recover from addiction, we must find a Power greater than ourselves and join this Power, but where do we find this Power? The forefathers and pioneers of Alcoholics Anonymous tell us that if we do not believe this, we are fooling ourselves, for deep down in every man, woman, and child is the fundamental idea of a Power greater than us, no matter what we choose to call it. It might be obscured by calamity, pomp, or worship of other things, but in some form or other it is there. For faith in a Power greater than us, and miraculous demonstrations of that Power in human lives are facts as old as man himself.

The forefathers and pioneers of Alcoholics Anonymous went on to say that they finally saw that faith in a Power greater than them was a part of their make-up, just as much as the feeling they had for a friend. Sometimes we had to search fearlessly, but this Power was there. This Power was as much a fact as we were. We are part of it, and it is part of us. We found the "Great Reality" deep down within us. In the last analysis, it is only there that it might be found.

These are revolutionary concepts. Let us summarize them. First, the forefathers and pioneers of Alcoholics Anonymous tell us they found a way to free themselves from the bondage of addiction. Second, they tell us the solution is a Power greater than ourselves. Third, they tell us where to find this Power--inside each of us. Now that you know where to find this Power, much of the rest of this book is devoted to the question of how to find this it.

Chapter Four

The Roots of Addiction

Let us now explore the nearly universal forces and experiences that lie underneath and drive addictions of all kinds, including obsessive compulsive learned helplessness.

Social Incompetence

In recent years, researchers have discovered that social incompetence has become a major factor in driving people into addictions of all kinds. Mastering social, emotional, and cognitive skills and behaviors is needed to succeed as a competent member of society, but many of us never developed such social competence, leaving us feeling inadequate, inferior, and insecure, resulting in an overwhelming drive to hide, compensate for, or escape from these intense feelings of incompetence. These often become the roots of our addictions. It should be noted that addictions of all kinds are an illness of escape.

Social competence refers to the social, emotional, cognitive skills, and behaviors that children, teens, and adults need for successful social inclusion. Despite this simple definition, social competence can be an elusive concept because the skills and behaviors required for healthy social development and inclusion vary with the age and with the demands of situations we experience. For instance, a socially competent preschool child behaves in a much different manner than a socially competent adolescent. Equally, the same behaviors such as aggression and shyness have different implications for social inclusion depending upon the age of the child and the social context in which the behaviors occur.

A child's social competence depends upon several factors including the child's social skills, social awareness, and confidence. The term: "Social skill" is used to describe a child's knowledge of and ability to use a variety of social behaviors that are appropriate to a given interpersonal situation and that are acceptable to others in any given situation. The capacity to inhibit selfish, impulsive, or negative social behavior is also a reflection of a child's social competence. The term: "Emotional Intelligence" refers to a child's ability to understand other people's emotions; perceive subtle social cues; read complex social situations; react appropriately in social situations; and demonstrate insight about other people's motivations and goals. Children who have a wide range of social skills and who are socially aware and perceptive are more likely to be socially competent. Social competence is the broader term used to describe a child's social effectiveness; that is, a child's ability to establish and maintain high quality and mutually satisfying relationships with others and to avoid negative treatment or victimization by others.

In addition to social skills and emotional intelligence, factors such as the child's confidence or level of social anxiety can affect their social competence. Social competence can also be affected by the context in which the child interacts and the extent to which there is a good match between the child's skills, interests, and abilities and those of the other children in their social environment. For example, a quiet and studious boy might appear socially incompetent in a peer group full of boisterous athletes but might do just fine in a group who shares his interest in quiet games or computers.

Importance of Social Competence

Although parents are the primary source of social and emotional support for children during the first few years of life, in later years, especially during adolescence, peers begin to play a more significant, complementary, and unique role in promoting a child's social-emotional development. Increasing with age, peers rather than parents become a child's preferred companions, providing important sources of entertainment and support. In the context of peer interactions, young children engage in fantasy play that allows them to assume different roles; learn to take another person's perspective; and develop an understanding of the social rules of their particular culture.

In addition, relationships with peers typically involve more give-and-take than relationships with adults which provides an opportunity for the development of social competencies such as cooperation and negotiation. During adolescence, peer relations become very important. A key developmental task of adolescence is the formation of an identity which is the sense of the kind of person they are and the kind of person they want to be. Adolescents try on different social roles as they interact with their peers, and their peers serve as a social stepping stones as adolescents move away from emotional dependence on their parents and toward autonomous functioning as an adult. In many ways, childhood peer relations serve as a training ground for future interpersonal relations, providing children with opportunities to learn about reciprocity and intimacy. These skills determine effective interpersonal relations in adult life, including relations with co-workers and with romantic partners.

When children experience serious difficulties with peer relations, the development of social competency is impaired. Rejection or victimization by peers in the form of bullying and teasing might become a source of significant stress to a developing child, contributing to feelings of loneliness and worthlessness. In addition, peer rejection can escalate into a negative developmental spiral. When children with poor social skills are rejected, they are often excluded from positive interactions with peers that are critical for the learning of social skills.

Rejected children typically have fewer play partners and friends than do accepted children. Observations of rejected children reveal that they spend more time playing alone and interacting in smaller groups than their more popular peers. In addition, companions of rejected children tend to be younger in age and more unpopular than the companions of accepted children. Exclusion from a peer group can deprive rejected children of opportunities to develop adaptive social behaviors. As a result, deficits in social competence of rejected children might increase over time, along with feelings of social anxiety and inadequacy, inferiority, and insecurity.

Deficits in Social Competence and Peer Rejection

Many children experience difficulties getting along with their peers at some point during their youth. Sometimes, these problems are short-lived, and for some children, the effects of being left out or teased by classmates are transitory. However, for other children being ignored or rejected by peers might become a lasting problem that has lifelong consequences, such as a dislike for school, poor self-esteem, social withdrawal, difficulties with adult relationships, and all kinds of addiction issues.

Extensive research has been undertaken to try to understand why some children experience serious, long-lasting difficulties with peer relations. To explore factors leading to peer difficulties, researchers typically employ a quantitative method for measuring social relationships to identify children who are or are not successful with their peers. In this method, children in a classroom or group setting are asked to identify children who they like most and those who they like least. Children who receive many positive nominations such as being liked the most and fewer negative nominations such as being liked the least are classified as "popular;" those who receive fewer positive and fewer negative nominations are described as "neglected," and those who receive fewer positive and many negative nominations are classified as "rejected."

Evidence compiled from studies using child interviews, direct observations, and teacher ratings suggest that "popular" children exhibit high levels of social competence where they are seen as friendly, cooperative, and engage readily in conversation. Peers describe them as helpful, nice, understanding, and attractive. Popular socially competent children consider other children's perspectives, sustain their attention to the play task, and are able to stay calm in situations where there is conflict. Likewise, they are agreeable and have good problem-solving skills. Socially competent children are also sensitive to play etiquette. They enter a group using diplomatic strategies such as asking permission to join in. They uphold standards of equity and show good sportsmanship, making them good companions and friendly play partners.

Children who have problems making friends are those who are either "neglected" or "rejected," and often show deficits in social skills. One of the most common reasons for peer social problems are behaviors that annoy other children. Children, like adults, do not like behavior that is bossy, selfish, or disruptive. To them, it is simply not fun to play with someone who does not share or does not follow the rules. Sometimes children who have learning problems or attention problems have trouble making and keeping friends because they find it hard to understand and follow the rules.

Children who get angry easily or lose their temper when things do not go their way also have a hard time getting along with others. Children who are rejected by peers often have difficulty focusing their attention and controlling their behavior. They show high rates of non-compliance, interference with others, or aggression such as teasing or fighting. Peers describe rejected classmates as disruptive, short-tempered, unattractive, and likely to start fights and to get in trouble with a teacher or authority figure.

But not all aggressive children are rejected by their peers. Children are particularly likely to become rejected if they show conduct problems such as disruptive, hyperactive, or disagreeable behaviors in addition to physical aggression. Socially competent children who are aggressive tend to use aggression in a way that is accepted by peers such as fighting back when provoked, whereas the aggressive acts of rejected children include tantrums, verbal insults, cheating, or tattling. In addition, aggressive children are more likely to be rejected if they are hyperactive, immature, or lack in positive social skills.

Children can also have friendship problems because they are very shy or feel uncomfortable or unsure of themselves around others. Sometimes children are ignored or teased by classmates because they are perceived as being different which sets them apart from other children. When children are shy and ignored by classmates and are classified as neglected, it does not necessarily indicate a deficit in social competence. Many neglected children have friendships outside of the classroom setting, and so, their neglected status is simply a reflection of their quietness and low profile in the classroom.

Developmentally, peer neglect is not a stable classification, as many neglected children often develop more confidence as they move into social situations with more familiar or more compatible peers. However, some shy children are highly anxious socially, and very uncomfortable around peers in many situations. Shy, passive children who are actively disliked and rejected by classmates are often teased and victimized by others. These children often have deficits in core areas of social competence that have a negative impact on their social development. For example, many of these children are emotionally dependent on adults, and are immature in their social behavior. They are often inattentive, moody, depressed, or emotionally volatile, which makes it difficult for them to sustain positive play interactions with others.

The long-term consequences of sustained peer rejection can be quite server. Often, deficits in social competence and peer rejection overlap with other emotional and behavioral problems, such as attention deficit, aggression, and depression. The importance of social competence and satisfying social relations is life-long and enduing. Studies of adults reveal that friendship is a critical source of social support that protects us against the negative effects of life stress. People with few friends are at higher risk for depression and anxiety.

Peer rejection in childhood predicts a variety of difficulties in later life, including school problems, mental health disorders, and antisocial behavior. In fact, one study of peer rejection showed it to be a more sensitive predictor of later mental health problems than school records, achievement, IQ scores, or teacher ratings.

It appears that positive peer relations play a very important role in supporting the process of healthy social and emotional development. Challenging peer relations are associated with both simultaneous and future maladjustment of children, and therefore warrant serious attention from parents and professionals working with these children. When assessing the possible factors that contribute to a child's social difficulties and when planning remedial interventions, it is important to understand the developmental processes associated with social competence and peer relations.

Developmental Changes and Social Competence

The important markers of social competence are remarkably consistent across the developmental periods of the preschool years, middle childhood, and adolescence. Across these developmental periods, prosocial skills such as friendly and cooperative behaviors and self-control skills such as anger management, negotiation skills, and problem-solving skills are crucial parts of social competence. Additionally, developmental changes occur in the structure and quality of peer interactions which affect the complexity of skills that contribute to social competence. As children grow, their preferences for play change, and the thinking and language skills that provide a foundation for social competence also evolve. As a result, the kinds of interactions that children have with peers change both qualitatively and quantitatively during development.

The ways in which children spend their time together changes with development. During the preschool years, social competence involves the ability to separate from parents and engage with peers in shared play activities, particularly fantasy play. As preschool children are just learning to coordinate their social behavior, their interactions are often short and marked by frequent squabbles. As a result, their friendships are less stable than at later developmental stages. In addition, aggressive play is common, particularly among boys.

By elementary school, children begin to develop an interest in sports, structured board games, and group games with complex rules. Being able to understand and follow game rules and being able to handle competition in appropriate ways such as being a good sport become important skills for social competence. At this age, children play primarily in same-sex groups of friends and expect more stability in their friendships. As a result, loyalty and dependability become important qualities of good friends.

During preadolescent and early adolescent years, communication including social media, calling each other on the phone, texting each other, and hanging out become a major focus for peer interactions. At this age, social competence involves the willingness and ability to share thoughts and feelings with one another, especially for girls. When adolescent friends squabble, their conflicts typically center around issues such as gossiping, disclosing secrets, loyalty issues, and perceived betrayal. It is at this stage that friends and romantic partners consistently rival parents as the teen's primary sources of intimacy and social support.

In addition to developmental changes in the content and focus of peer relations, development brings on changes in the structure of peer relations. During the preschool and early elementary school years, children are primarily focused on group acceptance and having companions to spend time with and play with. However, during the middle to late elementary school years, children begin to distinguish regular friends from best friends. The establishment of close, best friendships is an important developmental milestone at this age, so in addition to gaining acceptance from a group of peers, one of the hallmarks of social competence is the ability to form and maintain satisfying close friendships.

Many of the positive characteristics that promote popularity in childhood such as cooperativeness, friendliness, and consideration for others also promote the development of and the maintaining of close friendships. Friendships emerge when children share similar activities and interests, and when they develop positive and mutual bonds between each other.

Group acceptance and close friendships follow different timetables and serve different developmental functions. During the early elementary years, the need for group acceptance emerges filling a need for belonging, and the need for close friends emerges in preadolescence years to meet newfound needs for affection, alliance, and intimacy outside the family. Crucial features of close friendships are reciprocity and similarity, mutual intimacy, and social support.

A third major shift in the complexity of peer relations involves the changing role of cliques and peer groups. Grade school children seem to have little conception of peer groups. For example, when fifth graders were interviewed and asked about groups at their school, a typical reply was: "what do you mean, reading groups?" In contrast, by the eighth grade, children have distinct ideas about groups at their school, responding to this question with labels such as populars, jocks, geeks, nerds, floaters, good-alts, normals, stoners, emos, goths, gamers, and loners.

The recognition of cliques and specific peer groups as organizational structures of a larger peer group usually emerges during early adolescence. In part, the understanding of cliques reflects a cognitive advance, as children in adolescence begin to use more formal operational thinking to consider abstract ideas such as "cliques" and apply them to their thinking about their peers. In part, the growth of cliques in the organizational structure of peer groups reflects the structure of American schools, which typically transition from small elementary schools to large middle schools around sixth or seventh grade.

The change in the school context has a large impact on the nature of the peer group, as the typical middle school peer group involves a very large and diverse group of peers. In the context of this large group, children associate with smaller networks of familiar classmates. Typically, the grouping into friendship networks takes place in the form of shared interests, activities, and attitudes. Children in the same friendship networks influence each other in matters of dress, behavior, and language, leading to identifiable characteristics of group members that become the basis for group labels such as jocks, nerds, or geeks.

From an emotional standpoint, adolescents are focused on developing a sense of themselves and in sorting out how their identities fit or do not fit with the expectations of others and the social roles available to them. As a link to identity formation, adolescents become keenly aware of group peer norms and increasingly seek to associate with peers and use peer standards to evaluate their own and other's social behavior. Whereas in elementary school, peer status referred to their state of acceptance or rejection from their classroom group, but by adolescence, their peer status is complicated by the nature of the various groups that they might seek, where they might attain or be refused membership status. In other words, in addition to finding friends, adolescents often worry about their place in the larger social structure of cliques and crowds.

As a result, the increased level of social awareness and self-consciousness that accompanies the advanced social reasoning of adolescence and the increased importance that adolescents place on peer acceptance might reinforce the impact of perceived peer rejection on their emotional adjustment and concept of self. Social shunning or self-imposed isolation might also become a more important determinant of peer rejection during adolescence than at younger ages.

At all ages, the treatment a child receives from their peers might influence his or her social competence. Once rejected by peers, disliked children often find themselves excluded from peer activities and exposed to shunning, or more severely to bullying and teasing by peers. Peers might develop negatively biased attitudes and expectations of rejected children and treat these children differently with more aggression and hostility than with their well-accepted peers.

Children who are particularly stressed by the academic demands of school, such as those rejected children with attention deficits or hyperactive behaviors, might be at increased risk for negative interactions with teachers and peers. Over time, teachers tend to become less positive and less conditional in their reactions to these problematic students, which decreases their effectiveness at managing social behavior.

During preadolescent and later adolescent years, the combination of shunning from conventional peer groups and the evolution of peer group cliques and crowds can be problematic for rejected children. That is, adolescents who feel pushed out of the conventional peer groups might begin to affiliate with defiant peers or those who using drugs and alcohol. As cliques of deviant groups form in adolescence, these groups might begin to exert a strong influence on their members, shaping their attitudes and social behaviors; thus, increasing the likelihood of future antisocial and deviant behavior.

In adolescence, youth tend to turn to their peer groups for guidance in matters of dress code, social behavior, social attitudes, and identity formation. In peer networks containing many members who exhibit high rates of aggression, group norms are likely to be accepting of aggression. Thereafter, although affiliations with deviant peers might provide companionship and support, the cost of such affiliations might be great in terms of their negative influence such as exhibiting antisocial behavior and attitudes. Preadolescent children who form friendships with antisocial peers appear to be at heightened risk for later antisocial behavior, including delinquency, drug use, and dropping out of school.

Family Contribution to Social Competence

Because the family is the primary context for social development, there are many ways in which family interaction patterns might help or hinder the development of a child's social competence. Some researchers have speculated that the origins of social competence can be found in infancy in the quality of the parent-child attachment. Studies have shown that babies whose parents are consistent and sensitive in their responses to the infant's distress are less irritable, less anxious, and better emotionally regulated. In contrast, parents who are inconsistent or insensitive to their infant's signals of distress are more likely to be anxious, irritable, and difficult to soothe. Likewise, these children learn both to model their parents' insensitivity and to rely on intrusive, demanding behavior in order to get attention. As they grow up, these children generalize these socially incompetent behaviors to their peer interactions, resulting in peer rejection.

As children get older, family interaction styles and the ways in which parents' discipline them might play a primary role in the development of non-compliant or aggressive behavior in children. In families where parents are extremely demanding and use inconsistent, harsh, and punitive discipline strategies, family interaction patterns are frequently characterized by conflict, and children often exhibit behavior problems. When children generalize the aggressive and oppositional behavior that they have learned in the home to their interactions with peers, other children often reject them. Indeed, research has revealed that aggressive behavior is the common link between harsh, inconsistent discipline and rejection by peers.

In contrast, parents of more socially competent children are typically more positive and less demanding with their children than parents of less competent children. In addition, parents of popular children set good examples by modeling appropriate social interactions, and assist their children by arranging opportunities for peer interaction, carefully supervising these experiences, and providing helpful feedback about conflict resolution and making friends.

Child Characteristics and Social Competence

In addition to family interaction patterns and various aspects of the parent-child relationship, a child's own thoughts, feelings, and attitudes might influence their social behavior. Research has revealed that many rejected children make impulsive, inaccurate, and incomplete judgments about how to behave in social situations and are lacking in social problem-solving skills. They often make numerous errors in processing social information, including misinterpreting other people's motives and behavior; setting social goals for themselves that are unrealistic or inappropriate; and making poor decisions about their own conduct in social situations, often blaming others.

For example, aggressive children are more likely to interpret an accidental push or bump by another peer as intentionally hostile and respond in an aggressive way. Similarly, socially incompetent children are often more interested in getting even with other peers for perceived injustices than they are in finding positive solutions to social problems. As a result, they expect that aggressive, coercive strategies will lead to a desired outcome.

Many children who are rejected by peers have lower self-esteem, feel lonelier, and are more dissatisfied with their social situations than popular more socially competent children. These feelings inferiority and inadequacy can cause them to give up and avoid social situations, which can in turn can make their peer interaction problems worse. Interestingly, not all rejected children feel badly about their social difficulties. Studies have shown that aggressive-rejected children tend to blame outside factors for their peer problems and are less likely to express distress, whereas withdrawn-rejected children often blame their problems on themselves.

Four Steps to Social Competence

Another factor that is common in addicts of all kinds is social competence. Initially known as the "four stages for learning any new skill," the Four States of Competence was a learning model originally introduced by Noel Burch, an employee of Gordon Training International. First drafted in the 1970s, this "conscious competence" learning model is described as the psychological states that are involved in transforming skill incompetence to competence or outright mastery.

Background

The Four States of Competence is a model that describes the process by which we learn a new skill. It shows that humans are originally oblivious of their incompetence. Once they are aware of their incompetence, they try to develop a skill that they can utilize along the way. As time progresses, this acquired skill is effectively used without conscious contemplation. It is in this stage when a human develops mastery, also known as "unconscious incompetence."

The Four States of Competence was patterned after Erikson's Four Stages of Learning. It is sometimes likened to a Johari Window. However, it deals with self-awareness, whereas the four states of competence cover the learning process.

The Johari Window

The Johari window is a technique used to help people better understand their relationship with themselves and others, which was created by two psychologists: Joseph Luft (1916–2014) and Harrington Ingham (1916–1995) in 1955. It is used primarily in self-help groups and corporate settings as a heuristic exercise. Luft and Ingham called their Johari Window model "Johari" after combining their first names, Joe and Harry.

The Johari Window was composed of four panes:

- The upper right pane is the Arena where traits were known to the self and to others

- The upper left pane is Blind Spot where traits were not known to the self but know to others

- The lower right pane is the Façade where traits are not known to others but known to the self

- The lower left pain is the Unknown where traits are not known to the self or to others

During the exercise, subjects are given a list of 56 adjectives used as possible descriptions of themselves out of which they need to pick some that they feel describe their own personality. The subject's peers are then given the same list, and each pick equal number of adjectives that describe the subject. These very adjectives are then inserted into a grid.

The philosopher Charles Handy called this concept the "Johari House with four rooms." Room 1 is the part of ourselves that we see and others see. Room 2 is the aspects that others see but we are not aware of. Room 4 is the most mysterious room in that the unconscious or subconscious part of us is seen by neither ourselves nor others. Room 3 is our private space, which we know but keep hiding from others.

The four quadrant of the Johari Window include:

The Open or Arena

Adjectives that are selected by both the participant and his or her peers are placed into the Open or Arena quadrant. This quadrant represents traits of the subjects that both they themselves and their peers are aware of.

The Hidden or Façade

Adjectives selected only by subjects, but not by any of their peers, are placed into the Hidden or Façade quadrant, representing information about them their peers are unaware of. It is then up to the subject to disclose this information or not.

The Blind

Adjectives that are not selected by subjects but only by their peers are placed into the Blind Spot quadrant. These represent information that the subject is not aware of, but others are, and they can decide whether and how to inform the individual about these "blind spots."

The Unknown

Adjectives that were not selected by either subjects or their peers remain in the Unknown quadrant, representing the participant's behaviors or motives that were not recognized by anyone participating. This may be because they do not apply or because there is collective ignorance of the existence of these traits.

A Johari window consists of the following 56 adjectives used as possible descriptions of the participant:

- able
- accepting
- adaptable
- bold
- brave
- calm
- caring
- cheerful
- clever
- complex
- confident
- dependable
- dignified
- empathetic
- energetic
- extroverted
- friendly
- giving
- happy

- helpful
- idealistic
- independent
- ingenious
- intelligent
- introverted
- kind
- knowledgeable
- logical
- loving
- mature
- modest
- nervous
- observant
- organized
- patient
- powerful
- proud
- quiet

- reflective
- relaxed
- religious
- responsive
- searching
- self-assertive
- self-conscious
- sensible
- sentimental
- shy
- silly
- spontaneous
- sympathetic
- tense
- trustworthy
- warm
- wise
- witty

The Journey of Competence

The journey from not knowing to competence is detailed in the following steps:

Stage 1: Unconsciously Incompetent

"I don't know what I don't know."

Before we undertake an activity that is novel to us, we trudge through the state of "unconscious incompetence." During this stage, we lack the skills, knowledge, and capacity to do a certain a certain skill.

The stage of unconscious incompetence can linger for years. In order to learn a new skill, it is important for us to recognize our inability in order to perform a skill perfectly. The burden of becoming informed about our incompetence lies with us and an expert in said skill who can teach us.

An example of unconscious incompetence is this: you are in your yoga class and the instructor asks you to execute the "Lord of the Dance" pose. You try to do it but you look like an octopus failing out of a tree but you continue with it anyway because you do not know that you are doing it all wrong. The instructor then tells you that you are executing the pose incorrectly. The acknowledgement of this mistake then paves the way for the second stage of competence, which s Consciously Incompetent.

Stage 2: Consciously Incompetent

"I know what I don't know."

The second stage of proficiency, the phase of "conscious incompetence" starts when we develop conscious awareness of the things you do not know. In this state, we plant ourselves with hopes and aspirations.

Most view stage 2 as the most uncomfortable phase, because we recognize the fact that we are a failure in a certain activity. The only difference it has with stage 1 is that we do not pursue the thing we "suck at." Shame and acknowledgement of our shortcomings can be attributed to this.

Although this can be embarrassing, the acknowledgement of our incompetence prods us to move and train, so we can be competent at it, eventually.

Just like stage 1, we might linger in stage 2 for a prolonged period of time. The duration of our stay in the conscious incompetence stage depends on our learning determination, as well as the acceptance and acknowledgment of our incompetence.

The most important hallmark of this stage is our ability to perceive and recognize the keys to competency—ones that are exhibited by other more capable individuals.

Continuing with the example of stage 1, we know we have reached the stage of unconscious incompetence when we see ourselves in the mirror and realize that we have been doing the pose wrong. Because we are conscious of our wrongdoings, we try to undertake measures that can help improve our pose.

Stage 3: Consciously Competent

"I grow and know and it starts to show."

Slowly taking over the role of the master, an individual lodged in the third stage begins the adventure towards utmost competency. A consciously competent individual dedicates him or herself in the improvement of a skill by undertaking repeated practice, participation, and formal training of the said skill.

The development of competence is faster than the development of consciousness, as we grow and know, it starts to show.

Proceeding with the example above, we know we have arrived at stage 3 or "conscious competence" when we engage in activities that will help us perfect the pose. This can include practicing at home, watching video streams of yoga, or spending more time at yoga class.

Stage 4: Unconsciously Competent or Mastery

"I simply go because of what I know."

As we build experience and expertise, we reach the stage of "unconscious competence" where we do not have to think about the activity, and we are very good at it.

Unlike the first two stages, the journey to unconscious competence does not take a lot of time. It happens quickly with constant practice. However, we can go in and out of unconscious competence, depending on our mastery of skills.

As an unconsciously competent person, we are summoned because of what you know. We deem it to "feel right," that is why we go ahead with the activity. We prove to be good at it without exerting too much effort.

Back to our example: Unconscious competence or mastery means that we have finally reached the pinnacle of the skill. Thanks to our dedication in learning and perfecting the yoga pose, we can finally do it without much thinking or contemplation. We can accomplish the "Lord of the Dance Pose" perfectly, and because we do not have to dwell too much when performing this pose, we just continue with the skill because it feels good and right.

The Four Steps of Social Competence Related to Addiction

As shown above, there are four psychological stages associated with learning a new skill. It is easy to apply the principles of these stages to the levels of transformation that takes place in recovery. Not just recovery from addiction, but also recovery from self-sabotaging thoughts and behaviors associated with obsessive and negative thinking.

When it comes to addiction the progression of transformation starts with denial or a stage known as "unconscious incompetence." Eventually, the process evolves to having a "spiritual awakening" in the "conscious competence" stage of learning how to live clean and sober.

There is a level beyond the God Consciousness of a Spiritual Awakening. There is an unconscious state of competence that equates to being on autopilot in God's world. This degree of vigilance requires a willingness to join our will with that of God's will, but this takes a great amount of effort until it takes no effort at all.

The word "unconscious" in this context means: Awake, but not aware. Competence equates to manageability over our life.

Remember, these four levels of transformation apply to many facets of the human experience.

The Four Levels of Transformation:

1 - Unconscious Incompetence

2 - Conscious Incompetence

3 - Conscious Competence

4 - Unconscious Competence

Level 1—Unconscious Incompetence

The definition of "unconscious incompetence" is the human state in which there is something wrong with us, and we are not consciously aware of its existence. Usually, this is the result of denial. Untreated addicts and alcoholics in the midst of chaos fall into this level.

Our lives are truly unmanageable, and we do not even know it. Denial is the mind's defense mechanism that prevents us from feeling the pain associated with reality and truth.

If we ask a person if alcohol or drugs are affecting the quality of their life, they will most likely answer "no," and follow-up with statements like:" it's my spouse that has a problem," or "my job sucks." Likewise, if you ask them: "Why are you doing this?," you might hear: "I don't know."

Some forms of Denial related to Unconscious Incompetence include:

Avoidance - "there is nothing wrong"

Deflection - blame others

Reflection - blame the accuser

Minimizing - "I'm not that bad"

Rationalization- "If you were me..."

Uniqueness - "I am different"

Eventually, the consequences of denial, "unconscious incompetence," becomes too devastating and the person becomes conscious of their problem. However, a person with a true dual-diagnosis or a personality disorder like narcissistic personality disorder or sociopathy might have a more difficult time becoming honest enough to get past this stage.

To enable movement into the next level, people might experience moments of clarity. However, these people are not ready to take action; they are simply no longer oblivious to the problem.

Level 2—Conscious Incompetence

This is the initial conscious awareness that some facets of our life have become unmanageable. Not possessing true clarity now, we are still behaving incompetently. It is the recognition of being lost in the woods without a clue of which direction to walk.

This is when the negative consequences of our behavior really start to surface. Our incompetence issues start to arise, along with loss of self-esteem and integrity. The downward slide seems to pick up momentum once we climb on the addiction elevator for ride to the bottom.

The elevator going down usually looks something like this:

Ground Floor—Extreme lows and highs.

Our selfishness speaks first and loudly. Planning the next high or cleaning up the wreckage of the last intoxicating event takes priority over living in the present.

1st Floor Down—Family Problems

Our family members know there is a problem with us. It has become the proverbial elephant in the room. Once the family recognizes the problem, they will usually take one of two courses of action - neither are correct:

1. They do nothing hoping that the problem will just go away. They fear discussing the elephant in the room.

2. They nag, which always makes things worse. It causes more stress with the abuser and adds on the already low self-esteem. In order to numb this pain, the abuser will drink or use.

They have not a clue how to deal with the person becoming insane right in front of their eyes. The person abusing alcohol and/or drugs or engaging in behaviors is now conscious that there is a problem at home, although most will rarely admit that they are the source.

2nd Floor Down—Problems with Friends

Healthy friends distance themselves from the addict and the unhealthy friends are attracted to the addict. The addicted person seeks "lesser people" to associate with or they totally isolate. Healthy acquaintances want nothing to do with them.

3rd Floor Down—Financial Problems

It is expensive to be addicted. The cost of the alcohol, drugs, and behaviors alone should be alarming. The cost of missed opportunities also comes into play. The poor financial decisions due to the compulsive behaviors, result in financial turmoil. The cost of legal consequences soon arises for most.

4th Floor Down—Legal Problems

Speeding tickets, stop sign violations, reckless driving, driving under the influence, accidents, and criminal charges for crimes committed under the influence or in the search of their drug or behavior of choice repeatedly place addicted people in front of a judge.

Throw in some domestic violence and trespassing and even the previously squeaky-clean citizen might find themselves making trips to the courthouse.

5th Floor Down—Career Problems

This is the turning point for many, especially people who worked hard to get their career. Addicted people tend to be good at faking it. So, for many of them, it takes a legal problem to jeopardize a person's career. Despite an active company Employee Assistance Program, EAP, addicts tend to avoid "those people" at all cost. But after an arrest and facing the loss of a career, those EAP people became one of the addict's favorite resources.

6th Floor Down—Jails and Institutions

These fine facilities are full of people with "untreated" or "unwilling to be treated" alcohol addiction, drug addiction, or behavioral addictions. For some, this loss of freedom is worse than death.

7th Floor Down—Death

One way to get to the addict is to have them picture themselves in their casket and to think about what would be said at their funeral. Another way is to the addict write their obituary.

A bout with "conscious incompetence" usually brings the addict to believe they were hopeless, and they would die an addict. Their blind uniqueness tells them that: "No rehab would work for me" and "AA is for losers!" Many addicts truly believe that they just cannot stop. Many die rather than move on to the next phase. A person might be stuck on this level for a long time. The old saying applies: "The choices are being locked up, covered up, or sobered up."

Level 3 - Conscious Competence

Becoming aware that we have choices is instrumental in "conscious competence." We recognize the need for change, and we become consciously aware that we are not alone on life's journey. We find satisfaction in helping others. We take responsibility for our thoughts and actions.

People experiencing conscious competence are not only aware of their addictions; they remind themselves every day of their addictions. People new to a twelve-step program and people completing treatment who have become honest, open-minded, and willing are firmly planted in this stage.

Many of these folks love how they feel with their newfound appreciation for life. Certain promises start to come true usually between completing Step -4 and Step -9 of the twelve steps.

The Promises can be found on page 83-84, of the book: *Alcoholics Anonymous* and say that if we are painstaking about this phase of our development, we will be amazed before we are half way through. We are going to know a new freedom and a new happiness. We will not regret the past nor wish to shut the door on it. We will comprehend the word serenity and we will know peace. No matter how far down the scale we have gone, we will see how our experience can benefit others. That feeling of uselessness and self-pity will disappear. We will lose interest in selfish things and gain interest in our fellows. Self-seeking will slip away. Our whole attitude and outlook upon life will change. Fear of people and of economic insecurity will leave us. We will intuitively know how to handle situations which used to baffle us. We will suddenly realize that God is doing for us what we could not do for ourselves.

These promises are integral in recognizing the results of our commitment to sobriety and wellness. However, there is still plenty of room for growth after the promises start coming true.

Nevertheless, one of the complaints posed by mental health and substance abuse professionals as well as people in recovery about twelve-step recovery programs is that after achieving long-term sobriety, many twelve-steppers tend to dwell on how sick they are, not on how well they are. This criticism has some merit.

Some people in recovery might be permanently stuck in this phase of their development. But that is not entirely a bad thing. It beats living as an active addict. On the other hand, others continue to move forward in their recovery, and they are able to achieve social competence, gain self-worth and value, and maintain humility.

An example of being stuck at this phase is when a person with over 20 years of sobriety states they are still powerless over alcohol. They seem to be comfortable living in the problem, instead of the solution. There is a tendency to place too much emphasis on "drunk-a-logs" and on how pitifully sick they are, as opposed to how well they have become living in the solution and in wellness.

People who stall in "conscious competence" make recovery more work than necessary. They truly believe they are still living in the throes of Step 1 – powerless over their addiction and their lives are unmanageable. They often argue that the first step implies that we never recover from being powerless. This is simply not true because we are all-powerful; otherwise, how do people get sober.

There are many great teachers in twelve-step programs. Newcomers should not be drawn to those who claim they know the answers, but instead, be drawn to those seeking truth. The truth-seekers tend to read, pray, meditate, journal, and practice wellness more than others. Rather, whether they know it or not, they aspire to become unconsciously competent.

Level 4—Unconscious Competence

Every person achieving "unconscious competence" spends a great deal of time in the "conscious competence" phase. We can only find ourselves in Level 4 by experiencing the repetition of new values, principles, and virtues required in Level 3 to maintain sobriety and wellness. Like miracles, unconscious competence comes to us; we do not go to it.

As stated in the introduction of this article: there is an unconscious state of competence that means we are on autopilot in God's world. This degree of vigilance and practice requires a willingness to join our will with that of God's will, but this takes a great amount of effort until it takes no effort at all.

People who live their lives in the flow of doing what is right, without consciously thinking about it, experience "unconscious competence." For these people prayer, mediation, and being of service is all part of daily life. The reward is in the service. They tend not to take things personally nor do they cave in to the weight of their selfishness. This is spiritual recovery in the highest form.

Living life on this level might be the result of any of the following:

- Having had a Spiritual Awakening as a result of the twelve steps

- A profound spiritual experience such as a "near death" experience

- A massive shift in personal values

- Remission from a terminal disease

- Years of living clean and sober in wellness

The person who has thoroughly experienced the twelve-steps and has had a "spiritual awakening" referred to in Step 12, will most likely agree with the premises that today, alcohol and drugs have no power in their life, in fact, they rarely think of drinking or using. They have a God of their understanding, the fellowship of a Twelve-Step program, and they work daily on the maintenance of their spiritual well-being. They are "unconsciously competent" about avoiding people, places, and things that are not on their spiritual path. They no longer allow their pride to challenge God's will for them by accepting only One Voice to speak to them.

They recognize steps like these are simplified ways for humans to digest God's will slowly. God's accomplishments are not gradual, nor do they ever change. With God, time is meaningless because it is eternal.

As half-measures avail us nothing when it comes to recovery from addiction, half-measures also avail us nothing when it comes to willingness of accepting God's will for us. Intuitively knowing how to handle situations that used to baffle us, correlates to the state of "unconscious competence" discussed here.

In might not sound like it, nevertheless we are very present in the moment when experiencing "unconscious competence." This is because our minds are free of the fear and anxiety created by our misuses of pride.

How Does this Relate to Addiction and Recovery?

Social competence is a complex, multi-dimensional concept consisting of social skills; emotional skills, such as emotion regulation; cognitive skills, such as fund of information; processing, acquisition, and perspective; and behavioral skills, such as conversation skills, prosocial behavior, as well as motivational and expectancy skill sets, such as moral development and self-efficacy needed for successful social adaptation and integration. Social competence also reflects having an ability to take another person's perspective into consideration concerning a situation, learning from past experiences, and applying that learning to the changes in social interactions. Social competence is the foundation upon which our expectations for future interactions with others is built, and upon which individuals develop perceptions about their own behavior. Often, the concept of social competence frequently encompasses additional concepts such as social skills, social communication, and interpersonal communication.

Past and current research explores the understanding of how and why social competence is important in healthy social development. The study of social competence began in the early twentieth century. A noteworthy discovery was that social competence was related to future mental health, which fueled research on how children interact with their peers and function in social situations. As research developed, different definitions and measurement techniques developed to suit these new findings.

In the 1930s, researchers began investigating peer groups and how children's characteristics affected their positions within their peer groups. In the 1950s and 1960s, research established that children's social competence was related to problems in school settings as well as maladaptive outcomes in adulthood. Research on social competence expanded greatly, as increasing amounts of evidence demonstrated the importance of social interactions.

As a result, researchers began to view social competence in terms of problem-solving skills and strategies in social situations, and as a result, social competence was conceptualized in terms of effective social functioning and information processing. In the 1970s and 1980s, research began focusing on the impact of children's behavior on relationships, which influenced the study of the effectiveness of teaching children social skills that were age, gender, and context specific.

In an effort to determine and explain why some children were not exhibiting social skills in some interactions, many researchers devised social information processing models to explain what happens in social interactions. These models concentrated on factors in interactions such as behavior; how people judge each other; and how they respond to social cues. They also focused on how people select social goals; decide on the best response to a situation; and acting on the chosen response. These studies often looked at the relationship between social cognition and social competence.

In the mid-1980s, prominent researchers of social competence identified three sub-domains of social competence: (1) adaptive behavior; (2) social skills; and (3) peer acceptance, which are often used to assess social competence. Research during this time often focused on children who were not displaying healthy social skills in efforts to identify and help these children who were potentially at risk for long-term negative outcomes due to their poor social interactions. Researchers proposed that these children could have one of four deficits: (1) skill deficits, in which they did not have the knowledge or cognitive abilities to carry out certain behaviors; (2) performance deficits; (3) self-control skill deficits, and (4) self-control performance deficits, in which they had excessive anxiety or impulsivity that prohibited proper execution of the behaviors or skills they knew and understood.

Despite all the developments and changes in the area of social competence throughout the twentieth century, there was still a general lack of agreement about the definition and measurement of social competence. The definitions of the 1980s were less ambiguous than previous definitions, but they often did not acknowledge factors like age, situation, and specific skill understood in the complex concept of social competence.

Factors that Contribute to Social Competence

Temperament

Temperament is an idea that describes a person's biological response to their environment. Issues such as the ability to be soothed, sociability, and arousal make up this concept. Most often sociability contributes to the development of social competence.

Attachment

Social experiences are built on the foundation of the parent–child relationships and are important in the later development of social skills and behaviors. Attachment of an infant to a caregiver is important for the development of later social skills and behaviors that develop social competence. Attachment helps the infant learn that the world is safe, predictable, and trustworthy; whereas, if attachment is incomplete, the infant learns that the world is unpredictable and cruel.

Researchers described four types of attachment styles in infancy: (1) secure; (2) anxious–avoidant; (3) anxious–resistant; and (4) disorganized-disoriented. The foundation of the attachment bond between the child and parent allows the child to venture out from his or her mother as a way to try new experiences and develop new interactions. Children with secure attachment styles tend to show higher levels of social competence relative to children with insecure attachment such as anxious–avoidant, anxious–resistant, and disorganized-disoriented.

Parenting Style

Parents are the primary source of social and emotional development in infancy, early childhood, and middle childhood, and late childhood. The parent's socialization practices influence whether their child will develop social competence or not. Parenting style captures two very important elements of parenting: (1) parental warmth and responsiveness; and (2) parental control and demanding. Parental responsiveness such as warmth or support refer to the extent to which parents intentionally foster individuality, self-regulation, and self-assertion by being attuned, supportive, and agreeable to a children's special needs and demands. Parental demanding such as behavioral control refers to the claims that parents make on children to become integrated into the family by their demands for maturity, over-supervision, discipline, and how they confront a child who disobeys.

Categorizing parents according to whether they have high or low on parental demanding and responsiveness creates a sorting of four parenting styles: (1) indulgent/permissive; (2) authoritarian; (3) authoritative, and (4) indifferent/uninvolved. Each of these parenting styles reflects patterns of parental values, practices, and behaviors, along with a distinct balance of responsiveness and demanding.

Parenting styles contribute to a child's well-being in the areas of social competence, academic performance, psychosocial development, and problem behavior. Research based on parent interviews, child reports, and parent observations consistently found that children and adolescents whose parents were authoritative rated themselves and were rated by objective measures as being more socially competent than those whose parents were not authoritative. Children and adolescents whose parents were uninvolved performed most poorly in all areas. Other factors that contribute to social competence included teacher relationships, peer groups, neighborhood involvement, and community involvement.

Attachment and Socialization

The belief that child-parent attachment plays an important role in social development seems to occupy center stage in most contemporary theories of childhood socialization. The origins of this belief are traceable to Freud's emphasis on the significance of the infant-mother attachment for virtually all aspects of subsequent personality development. Its durability over subsequent decades has been sustained by the wealth of empirical data linking attachment to a wide range of socialization outcomes in both childhood and adulthood.

Included in these are patterns of social competence; prosocial behavior; antisocial behavior; and behavior problems in early childhood. In addition, major longitudinal studies of delinquent and criminal behavior have consistently documented links between family factors and subsequent antisocial behavior. Prominent among these have been parental characteristics such as lack of warmth, poor supervision, inconsistency, and poor child-rearing practices; factors that have been demonstrated in more recent studies associated with anxious child-parent attachment.

Ironically, the mechanisms of emotional dependence and defensive identification proposed by Freud to explain the association between attachment and socialization have largely been invalidated by modern empirical research. Furthermore, they have not been replaced in more recent attachment theories by alternative explanatory concepts.

Researchers have long been interested in the association between attachment and antisocial behavior, and their theories provide us with a rich source of speculation about attachment and socialization. Likewise, most researchers accept the basic idea that children unwittingly identify with the sense of modeling themselves after their parents in the normal course of human development. Nonetheless, attachment theory posits no formal mechanisms through which the child-parent attachment might explain the emergence of antisocial behavior, but researchers continue to search of an explanation.

The primary aim of researchers and behaviorists is to rekindle an interest in child-parent attachment as a powerful and perhaps decisive factor in the socialization process. They address themselves in considerable detail to the role of attachment in both psychodynamic and more contemporary social learning and cognition views of socialization. The emphasis of investigation is on the limitations of each in accounting for the emergence and stability of prosocial and antisocial behavior within individuals. Second, researchers employ a social influence perspective to integrate the best features of each model into a single theoretical framework that emphasizes the role of child-parent attachment.

The Links of Secure Attachment

We know from existing research that characteristics of caregiver behavior that seem to produce secure child-parent attachment include availability; patience; consistency; contingent responsiveness; facilitation; cooperation rather than interference with the infant's ongoing behavior; and the maintenance of a positive climate for interaction. We also know also when early parent-child interactions have been harmonious, the child develops a secure attachment relationship and a wide range of socially valued and predictive outcomes. Included among these are personal attributes such as self-esteem; social competence; self-control; empathy; ego-resilience; and positive affect.

Securely attached children have also been found to be more reciprocal such as sharing; mastering successful verbal requests; mastering social initiation; and shared laughter in their interactions with other peers, as well as more attentive, sociable, cooperative, and compliant with adults than are anxiously attached children. As a result, secure child-parent attachment is associated not only with multiple characteristics of personal competence, but also with behavioral patterns that very much reflect a generalized pro-social orientation toward others.

Research during the past decade has contributed greatly to our understanding of the knowledge that children acquire skills and abilities in the context of secure attachment relationships. However, it is not clear why these accomplishments are so characteristically associated with subsequent prosocial versus antisocial behavior outcomes. Perhaps more accurately said, it has been deceptively easy to assume that these outcomes follow "naturally" from secure attachment relationships, without asking ourselves why. In fact, a little exploration reveals that there is nothing at all obvious or self-evident about the link between prosocial and antisocial behavior outcomes.

It is well known that the most troublesome antisocial children, delinquents, and adult criminals are often among the most knowledgeable in terms of how to evaluate and behave in social situations, as well as how to anticipate accurately the likely responses of others. Yet, these skills are employed in the service of antisocial, rather than prosocial behavior. And so, although these characteristics are obviously necessary in the act of pro-social behavior, they are by no means adequate to explain its emergence and continuity within individuals. Neither are we any closer to an understanding of prosocial motivation by knowing that a child is securely attached to his or her parents. There are certainly good reasons to expect prosocial behavior toward attachment figures from these children, but how and why this generalizes across individuals, situations, and time remains an important unanswered question.

Child-Parent Attachment During Infancy

Beginning in the first year of life, the quality of the child-parent attachment develops and is maintained through mutual attentiveness to and cooperation with signals between the parent and the child. In early infancy, these signals are necessarily immediate, specific, situational, and non-verbal, although they are often vocal. However, as the child develops and acquires new abilities, there is a corresponding increase in the dimensions of and demands on the relationship for both parent and child. Ultimately, the relationship evolves into what researchers termed a "goal-corrected partnership" in which the child becomes increasingly aware of the parent's goals, and his or her strategies for accomplishing them. This awareness is then reflected in the child's enhanced ability to organize and coordinate his or her own experience with the goals, expectations, and demands of his or her parent.

So, let us look at what this process looks like. From birth to about 7 weeks the infant has no real preference for their caregiver. From 7 weeks to about 7 months, the infant begins to develop attachment with their primary and secondary caregivers, usually mom and dad. From 7 months to about 14 months, the child develops a strong attachment to their caregivers but also develops separation anxiety and stranger anxiety. From 14 months to about 24 months, the child begins to develop strong mutual attachments other significant people in the child's life. At about 24 months, the child begins the first separation-individuation phase of development known as "the terrible twos."

Maintaining cooperative interaction with the parent gradually requires attentiveness to less immediate, more general, and increasingly more verbal signals and cues. At the same time, it requires the parent to be more sensitive to the child's capabilities and needs for organization; a readiness and ability to adopt new strategies that facilitate the child's assimilation of and/or accommodation of novel socialization demands; and the continued maintenance of a positive affective climate.

Within the context of a secure relationship, parents gradually and consistently escalate their expectations, monitoring carefully the child's ability to recognize, interpret, and respond to their demands. As a result, whatever stressors these changes in the relationship might bring are minimized by the parent. As a result, the child continues to benefit and suffer minimally from the relationship as its demands and dimensions expand.

It is within the context of this interaction that the child also develops the powerful affective bond with parents that Freud emphasized so strongly as the prototype of all future love relationships. Researchers preserved this notion and its implications by discussing attachment in terms of "working models." These metaphors refer to both the child's and parent's systems of expectations, beliefs, feelings, and attitudes about themselves, each other, and the world, based on their previous experiences.

The child, according to this view, constructs an initial working model of the parent consistent with his or her history of interactive experiences with this person. For the securely attached child, this model will typically be characterized by positive feelings toward attachment figures, and the expectation that they will be reliable, sensitive, responsive, and available in times of need. Additionally, because this working model is the child's first well-formulated model of human relationships, it will also influence his or her initial expectations about sibling, peer, and other adult relationships in the future. In addition, because the child's working models of self and parents are initially closely intertwined, a history of successful participation in a secure attachment relationship will also produce perceptions of competence and self-esteem in the child.

Similarly, when early child-parent interactions have been harmonious, the parents will develop an equally positive working model of the child. And because this working model is also constructed from an interaction history, parents of a securely attached child will develop positive expectations about the future. Most notably, these expectations will reflect confidence about the abilities, cooperativeness, trustworthiness, and the future socializability of the child. On the other hand, if early child-parent interactions have not been harmonious, parents might be less likely to provide facilitating, cooperative, affectively positive, and age-appropriate rearing experiences for that child in the future.

It should be clear from this perspective that the period of child-parent attachment provides parents with a set of more or less optimal socialization conditions, where the child during this period is virtually insulated from exposure to dramatically different and/or potentially conflicting and inconsistent rule systems. Consequently, parents are in a powerful position to organize the child's experiences around a coherent and consistent set of rules and principles. They are therefore in a unique position to shape the child's initial models of him or herself, other people, and the world at large.

When these advantages of the child-parent attachment period have been used judiciously by sensitive and facilitating parents, the predictable outcome is the child's development of a secure attachments. We believe that the seeds of prosocial motivation are very much present within the context of secure relationships. It would be an overstatement to characterize the child as having made a conscious commitment to prosocial commerce at this point.

Nevertheless, there is a limited although important sense in which the securely attached child is already behaviorally committed by virtue of his or her active participation in the establishment and maintenance of an inherently prosocial child-parent attachment. The child's prosocial motivation or disposition to continue organizing his or her experience around prosocial themes stems from and is maintained by the powerful reinforcing value of the rules and principles that define the prosocial system through which the child has benefited. It is through the child-parent attachment itself, beyond discrete events within that system, that the child experiences the world and others in it as coherent, reliable, worthy of engaging, and secure. Equally important, it is the child-parent attachment itself that renders the child's world an orderly and predictable place through its guidelines and principles for future action.

Birth Order Traits

Personality Traits of the Firstborn

Simply by being a first child, a firstborn will naturally be raised with a mixture of instinct and trial-and-error. This often causes parents to become by-the-book caregivers who are extremely attentive, stringent with rules, and overly neurotic about the trivial. This, in turn, might cause the child to become a perfectionist, always striving to please their parents.

Firstborns bask in their parents' presence, which may explain why they sometimes act like mini-adults. They are also diligent and want to excel at everything they do. As the leader of the pack, firstborns often tend to be:

- Reliable

- Conscientious

- Structured

- Cautious

- Controlling

- Achievers

Strengths of the Firstborn

The firstborn is often used to being the center of attention because they have mom and dad to themselves before siblings arrive. Many parents spend more time reading and explaining things to firstborns. It is not as easy when other kids come into the picture. That undivided attention may have a lot to do with why firstborns tend to be overachievers. In addition to usually scoring higher on IQ tests and generally getting more education than their brothers and sisters, firstborns tend to out-earn their siblings.

Challenges of the Firstborn

Success comes with a price: Firstborns tend to be type A personalities who never cut themselves any slack. They often have an intense fear of failure, so nothing they accomplish feels good enough, and because they dread making a misstep, oldest kids tend to stick to the strait and narrow. They are typically inflexible. They do not like change and are hesitant to step out of their comfort zone.

In addition, because firstborns are often given a lot of responsibility at home, whether it is helping with chores or watching over younger siblings, they can be quick to take charge and can be bossy when they do. That burden can lead to excess stress for a child who already feels pressure to be perfect.

Personality Traits of the Middle Child

If the couple decides to have a second child, they might raise their second-born with less of an iron fist due to their previous experience. They might also be less attentive since there are other children in their lives. Therefore, the middle child is often a people-pleaser due to the lack of attention he gets in comparison to his older sibling and younger sibling.

The middle child often feels left out and a sense of: 'Well, I'm not the oldest. I'm not the youngest. Who am I?" This sort of hierarchical floundering leads middle children to make their mark among their peers, since parental attention is usually devoted to the beloved firstborn or baby of the family. What is more, middle children are the toughest to pin down because they play off their older sibling.

In general, middle children tend to possess the following birth order personality traits:

- People-pleasers
- Somewhat rebellious
- Thrives on friendships
- Has large social circle
- Peacemaker

Strengths of the Middle Child

Middle-borns are go-with-the-flow types, where once a younger sibling arrives, they must learn how to constantly negotiate and compromise in order to "fit in" with everyone. Not surprisingly, middle kids score higher in agreeableness than their older and younger siblings.

Because they receive less attention at home, middle-borns tend to forge stronger bonds with friends and be less tethered to their family than their brothers and sisters. They are usually the first of their siblings to take a trip with another family or to want to sleep at a friend's house.

Challenges of the Middle Child

Middle kids once lived as the baby of the family, until they were dethroned by a new sibling. Unfortunately, they are often acutely aware that they do not get as much parental attention as their "trailblazing" older sibling or the beloved youngest, and they feel like their needs and wants are ignored. Middle kids are in a difficult position in a family because they think they are not valued, It is easy for them to be left out and get lost in the shuffle. And there is some validity to their complaint. A survey by TheBabyWebsite.com, a British parenting resource, found that one-third of parents with three children admit to giving their middle child far less attention than they give the other two.

Personality Traits of the Youngest Child

Youngest children tend to be the most free-spirited due to their parents' increasingly laissez-faire attitude towards parenting the second or third, or fourth, or fifth... children. The baby of the family tends to have the following birth order traits:

- Fun-loving
- Uncomplicated
- Manipulative
- Outgoing
- Attention-seeker
- Self-centered

Strengths of the Youngest Child

Last-borns generally are not the strongest or the smartest in the room, so they develop their own ways of winning attention. They are natural charmers with an outgoing, social personality. No surprise then that many famous actors and comedians are the baby of the family, or that they score higher in "agreeableness" on personality tests than firstborns.

Last-borns also make a play for the spotlight with their adventurousness. Free-spirited last-borns are more open to unconventional experiences and taking physical risks than their siblings and research has shown that they're more likely to play sports like football and soccer than their older siblings, who preferred activities like track and tennis.

Challenges of the Youngest Child

Last-borns are known for feeling that "nothing I do is important." And so, none of their accomplishments seem original. Their siblings have already learned to talk, read, and ride a bike. So, parents react with less spontaneous joy at their accomplishments and may even wonder: 'Why can't he catch on faster?'"

Last-borns also learn to use their role as the baby to manipulate others in order to get their way. They are the least likely to be disciplined. Parents often coddle the littlest when it comes to chores and rules, failing to hold them to the same standards as their siblings.

Personality Traits of the Only Child

Being an only child or being born with an age speed of more than 10 years is a unique position. Without any siblings to compete with, the only child monopolizes their parents' attention and resources, not just for a short period of time like a firstborn, but forever. In effect, this makes an only child something like a "super-firstborn," where only children have the privilege and the burden of having all their parents' support and expectations on their shoulders. Thus, only children tend to be:

- Mature for their age
- Perfectionists
- Conscientious
- Diligent
- Leaders

Adverse Childhood Experiences

An adverse childhood experience (ACE) describes a traumatic experience in a person's life occurring before the age of 18 that the person remembers as an adult. There are nine ACEs including:

- Physical abuse

- Sexual abuse

- Emotional abuse

- Mental illness of a household member

- Problematic drinking or alcoholism of a household member

- Illegal street or prescription drug use by a household member

- Divorce or separation of a parent

- Domestic violence towards a parent

- Incarceration of a household member

First, a bit of background might help you figure this out. The CDC's Adverse Childhood Experiences Study (ACE Study) uncovered a stunning link between childhood trauma and the chronic diseases people develop as adults, as well as social and emotional problems. This includes heart disease, lung cancer, diabetes and many autoimmune diseases, as well as depression, violence, being a victim of violence, and suicide.

The first research results were published in 1998, followed by 57 other publications through 2011. They showed that childhood trauma was very common, even in employed white middle-class, college-educated people with great health insurance. It showed that there was a direct link between childhood trauma and adult onset of chronic disease, as well as depression, suicide, being violent and a victim of violence. The study showed that more types of trauma increased the risk of health, social and emotional problems. Likewise, the study showed that people usually experience more than one type of trauma; rarely is it only sex abuse or only verbal abuse.

The study showed that two-thirds of the 17,000 people in the ACE Study had an ACE score of at least one and 87% of those had more than one. Eighteen states have done their own ACE surveys and their results are like the CDC's ACE Study.

The study's researchers came up with an ACE score to explain a person's risk for chronic disease. Think of it as a cholesterol score for childhood toxic stress. You get one point for each type of trauma. The higher your ACE score, the higher your risk of health and social problems. Of course, other types of trauma exist that could contribute to an ACE score, so it is conceivable that people could have ACE scores higher than 10; however, the ACE Study measured only ten types.

As your ACE score increases, so does the risk for disease, social, and emotional problems. With an ACE score of 4 or more, things start getting serious. The likelihood of chronic pulmonary lung disease increases 390%; hepatitis, 240%; depression 460%; and the likelihood of suicide increases 1,220%.

By the way, if you think that the ACE Study is yet another government funded study involving inner-city poor people of color, take note: The study's participants were 17,000 mostly white, middle, and upper-middle class college-educated people from San Diego with good jobs and great health care. They all belonged to the Kaiser Permanente health maintenance organization.

At the same time that the ACE Study was being done, parallel research on the brains of children found that toxic stress physically damages a child's developing brain. This was determined by a group of neuroscientists and pediatricians, at Harvard University, Rockefeller University, and the Child Trauma Academy.

When children are overloaded with stress hormones, they are in flight, fright or freeze mode. They cannot learn in school. They often have difficulty trusting adults or developing healthy relationships with peers and often do not fit in and become loners. To relieve their anxiety, depression, guilt, shame, and/or inability to focus, they turn to easily available biochemical solutions—nicotine, alcohol, marijuana, methamphetamine, or activities in which they can escape their problems such as high-risk sports, sexual acting out, and work, or over-achieving.

Using drugs or overeating or engaging in risky behavior leads to consequences as a direct result of this behavior. For example, smoking can lead to COPD (Chronic Obstructive Pulmonary Disease) or lung cancer. Overeating can lead to obesity and diabetes. In addition, there is increasing research that shows that severe and chronic stress leads to bodily systems producing an inflammatory response that leads to disease.

The ACE score is a measure of cumulative exposure to adverse childhood conditions. Exposure to any single ACE condition is counted as one point. If a person experienced none of the conditions in childhood, the ACE score is zero. Points are then totaled for a final ACE score. It is important to note that the ACE score does not capture the frequency or severity of any given ACE in a person's life, focusing instead on the number of ACE conditions experienced. In addition, the ACE conditions used in the ACE survey reflect only a select list of experiences.

Many studies have examined the relationship between ACEs and a variety of known risk factors for disease, disability, and early mortality. The Division of Violence Prevention at the Centers for Disease Control and Prevention (CDC), in partnership with Kaiser Permanente, conducted a landmark ACE study from 1995 to 1997 with more than 17,000 participants. The study found that ACEs are common. For example, 28% of study participants reported physical abuse and 21% reported sexual abuse. Many also reported experiencing a divorce or parental separation or having a parent with a mental and/or substance use disorder.

The study found that ACEs cluster. Almost 40% of the Kaiser sample reported two or more ACEs and 12.5% experienced four or more. Because ACEs cluster, many subsequent studies now look at the cumulative effects of ACEs rather than the individual effects of each.

Likewise, the study found that ACEs have a dose-response relationship with many health problems. As researchers followed participants over time, they discovered that a person's cumulative ACEs score has a strong, graded relationship to numerous health, social, and behavioral problems throughout their lifespan, including substance use disorders. Furthermore, many problems related to ACEs tend to be comorbid or co-occurring.

Research has demonstrated a strong relationship between ACEs, substance use disorders, and behavioral problems. When children are exposed to chronic stressful events, their neurodevelopment can be disrupted. As a result, the child's cognitive functioning or ability to cope with negative or disruptive emotions may be impaired. Over time, and often during adolescence, the child might adopt negative coping mechanisms, such as substance use or self-harm. Eventually, these unhealthy coping mechanisms can contribute to disease, disability, and social problems, as well as premature mortality.

What is an Addiction?

When we hear the word "addiction," many images come to mind. We see the falling-down drunk; we see a woman who sells her body in exchange for a "fix;" we see a permanently disabled teen in a wheelchair because of a drunk-driving crash; we read about a famous entertainer who died of an overdose; we see another whose sensational sex scandals are splashed across the tabloids; we see a person who's life has been destroyed by a serious of religious binges or death in a cult like the People's Temple or the Branch Dividians; we see a person who obsessively compulsively binges on sugar products, weighs 600 pounds, and who is bed bound and cannot walk; and we see a person engaging a disastrous series of obsessive compulsive codependent relationships with addicts, narcissistic characters, sociopaths, and abusers to maintain their rearmed helplessness that results in intimate partner violence, gaslighting, physical and emotional abuse, complex post-traumatic stress disorder, homelessness, financial problems, health problems, death, or suicide.

Most of us know a friend or family member whose lives have been devastated by addiction. We all know that addiction is a serious problem. But behind this widely-held agreement, there are many disagreements and questions. What is addiction? How big is the addiction problem? How does addiction differ from experimentation, misbehavior, or bad habits? What causes addiction? How does one overcome it? How successful is addiction treatment? How should society respond to individuals with addiction? What should governments do about addiction? Is addiction mostly a modern problem? Is the addiction problem getting worse?

The term "addiction" comes from the Latin word: *addĭctus* meaning to assign by decree, made over, bound, or devoted. It is the past participle of *addĭcere* meaning to assign, to make over by sale or auction, to award, to appoint, to ascribe, to hand over, surrender, to enslave, to devote, to sentence, or condemn. In Roman Law, *addict* meant to deliver or hand over a person or thing formally in accordance with a judicial decision.

Furthermore, the word addiction emerged from the Latin word: *addico* meaning a judge, especially the praetor, who awarded a debtor as a slave to his creditor. In a more general sense, it means to give oneself up to slavery. The word *addico* is a compound word build of *ad* (to, towards, at) and *dico* (say, affirm, tell). According to Roman law, an *addictio* was a person who was enslaved through a judicial procedure. In the time of the Roman Empire, when a debtor could not repay his debts, creditors could recover their losses using a legal procedure known as *addĭcere*. In this procedure, if proven that the debtor lacked the means to repay, the praetor, or justice, could turn the debtor over to the creditor as a slave until the debt was paid.

Today, the term *addict* is used to describe a person who is bonded or enslaved by a substance; an activity that is pleasurable or stimulating, or getting into and maintaining an obsessive compulsive codependent relationship. It is notable that the word *addiction*, used today to describe repeated consumption of alcohol, use of drugs, or obsession with food, sex, gambling, sugar, or people is derived from a Latin word which expresses the slavery or bondage of a person.

For centuries, the word "addiction" meant being "given over" or being devoted to something. However, the nineteenth century temperance and anti-opium movements used it in a more restrictive way, linking "addiction" to drugs, illness, excessive illegal or immoral behaviors, and to withdrawal symptoms and tolerance. Both the traditional and restrictive meanings survived into the present. In the ensuing uncertainty about its meaning, some authorities now wish to replace the word *addiction* with substitute terms like *drug dependence* or *substance abuse*. But the term *addiction* is too valuable to discard. Its traditional sense designates the profoundly important, albeit sometimes harmful, capacity of people to become "given over" to drugs or behaviors. On the other hand, the restrictive meaning refers only to a special case, which is defined arbitrarily and inconsistently. It is outmoded because of these problems.

And so, addiction can mean many things to many people. For our purpose, we will define addiction as follows:

Addiction is the repeated involvement with a substance or activity, despite the substantial harm it now causes, because that involvement was and may continue to be pleasurable and/or valuable.

The reader should not confuse this definition of addiction with other related terms. Although similar, this definition of addiction should not be confused with the diagnostic criteria for a category of disorders known as "Substance-Related and Addictive Disorders" in the *Diagnostic and Statistical Manual of Mental Disorders*, Edition 5 (DSM-5, APA, 2013).

There are four key parts to this definition of addiction:

1. Addiction includes both substances and activities such as alcohol, drugs, food and sugar, stimulating behaviors like sex and gambling, and people.

2. Addiction leads to substantial harm.

3. Addiction is repeated involvement despite substantial harm.

4. Addiction continues because it was, or is, pleasurable and/or valuable.

Now let us examine each part of this definition of addiction in greater detail. Please note that definition of addiction includes both substances and activities.

Here, we will discuss the first part of the definition: people might become addicted to substances, activities, or people. Substance addiction includes any substance that is taken into the body. This might include street drugs, alcohol, nicotine, food, or sugar products, and prescription medications when used improperly. An activity addictions include activities such as gambling, sex, the Internet, gaming, pornography, shopping, work, food addiction, sugar addiction, religious addiction, and obsessive compulsive codependence or people addiction. Obsessive compulsive codependence or people addiction is described as unhealthy dependent relationships on unhealthy people.

Sometimes these are called "process addictions." Notice that it is quite possible to live a full and satisfying life without using any of these substances or activities to excess. However, there are also substances and activities that are essential to our very survival but even these things can become addictions. For instance, obese people often describe food as a type of addictive substance, but clearly no one can live without food. Other people describe religious activities with a dependence, intensity, or fanaticism so deep and damaging that their religious obsession could be described as an addictive activity. Other people describe romantic relationships with a dependence so deep and damaging that their relationship could be described as an addictive activity.

Obviously, many people engage in these substances and activities at various times in their lives, but most do not develop any significant problems or difficulties. This leads to the question: At what point does an activity or substance use become an addiction? The rest of our definition will help you to answer this question: Where is the line between behaving badly and addiction?

Definition of Addiction Includes Substantial Harm

In this section, we will discuss the second part of the definition: substantial harm. The most commonly agreed upon part of any definition of addiction is that it leads to substantial harm. Addiction harms not only the person with the addiction, but also everyone else around them. When distinguishing between "bad behavior" and addiction, the primary consideration is: Has the behavior caused substantial harm?

In other words, what are the negative consequences of this behavior? If a person buys two beers at a bar every week, even very expensive beer, it probably will not create a financial disaster. They might not be able to afford going out to lunch with their co-workers. It is just a choice they are willing to make. They have not sacrificed too much. On the other hand, if they buy twenty beers a night, every night, that might create a substantial financial burden. They might not even be able to afford their groceries, much less lunch with their co-workers. The odds are good that they might not be able to keep their job either.

Similarly, depending upon your own personal values, occasionally looking at porn probably does not cause substantial harm to most people. But if someone begins to prefer porn over human contact or cannot enjoy sex without porn and starts to spend half of their income on purchasing porn, they start to meet the criteria for substantial harm.

Likewise, occasionally consuming sugar of some kind probably does not cause substantial harm to most people. But if someone begins to obsessively and compulsively engage in sugar binges to the exclusion of other meaningful life activities, they likely meet the criteria for substantial harm.

Additionally, occasionally getting into a dependent relationship of some kind probably does not cause substantial harm to most people. But if someone begins to obsessively and compulsively engage in getting into and maintaining unhealthy relationships with abusive partners to the exclusion of other meaningful life activities, they likely meet the criteria for substantial harm.

One way to understand "substantial harm" is to consider the harmful consequences of the activity or substance use. Let us call these consequences costs. Some costs are obvious. They arise directly from the substance or activity itself. There are also other, less-obvious costs. These occur because of the preoccupation with the addiction. Direct costs might be unique to the specific substance or activity itself such as if you snort enough cocaine you will damage your nose. If you drink enough alcohol, you will damage your liver and digestive system. If you watch porn all day and masturbate excessively, you will lose interest in real sexual partners and suffer from a sex addiction-induced erectile dysfunction, or at worst, a fractured penis. If you shoot up enough heroin, you will damage your veins and get Hepatitis C. If you gamble too much, you will lose a great deal of money or get beat up by a bookie because you did not pay your gambling debts. If you engage in enough obsessive compulsive sugar binges, you could become obese, or develop diabetes, pancreatitis, liver problems, circulatory problems, which could result in amputation of extremities or death. Or if you get into obsessive compulsive codependent relationships with unhealthy characters like addicts, narcissistic people, sociopaths, or with abusive partners to the exclusion of other other health y people or meaningful life activities

Some direct costs universally apply to most addictions, such as declining health, damage to interpersonal relationships, and diminishing financial resources. But the less-obvious, indirect costs arise solely from the preoccupation with addiction. Eventually, an addiction becomes so central in a person's life that it consumes all their time, energy, and preoccupies their thoughts, and the addict throws away everything they ever valued—family, friends, wealth, and health, and spiral into an ever-decaying slide into nothingness.

Sometimes individuals affected by addiction do not see, cannot see, or will not see that their involvement with a substance or activity has resulted in substantial harm. Therefore, they might "deny" they have addiction. Nevertheless, if they must deny they have an addiction; they probably have one. Of course, this "denial" makes perfect sense because substantial harm is a defining characteristic of addiction. Without it, there is no addiction.

However, to other people these individuals seem indifferent to the harm their addiction has caused. In response to this apparent lack of concern, these individuals are often told they are "in denial." This statement implies a form of dishonesty. We have never found accusations of this sort to be helpful. Denial is psychological human defense strategy where a person refuses to accept a reality, fact, acting as if the painful event, thought, or feeling did not exist. It is considered one of the most primitive of the defense mechanisms because it is characteristic of early childhood development.

A more useful approach is to recognize that many individuals are simply unaware of the total costs associated with their addiction because of their own selfishness. This recognition leads to a non-judgmental approach that encourages an honest and accurate appraisal of these costs. This helps people recognize the substantial harm caused by remaining involved in an obsessive compulsive relationship with an abuser.

Next, we will discuss the third part of the definition: repeated involvement despite substantial harm. You could experience significant negative consequences ("substantial harm") from substance use or an activity, but you probably would not label your behavior an addiction unless it happened regularly. For instance, the first time someone gets drunk, they might have serious car crash. We would probably not label this person an alcoholic, even though "substantial harm" has occurred. Or, let us imagine that your son, age 28, gets drunk at his younger sister's wedding. He throws up on the wedding cake and he calls his sister a whore. He drops Aunt Sally on the floor while dancing with her, and next, he proceeds to pass out on the dance floor. For the five years before this wedding day debacle, he consumed no more than 1-2 drinks per day, a few times a month. Are you ready to call him an alcoholic? Probably not. Are you upset? Yes, you would be very upset! It becomes evident that addiction refers to a repeated behavior despite negative consequences.

Ordinarily, once the costs of an enjoyable behavior pile up, people will begin to naturally restrict or quit that behavior. This is another fact that distinguishes addictive behavior from mere "bad behavior." Many people temporarily indulge in pleasurable activities that we might term as "bad behavior." These might include drinking, drugging, indiscriminate sex, gambling, excessive consumption of entertainment, overeating, people addiction, or learned helplessness.

All addictions begin in this rather normal way of pursuing pleasure or relief. The problem of addiction does not develop because of these pleasurable activities. Addiction becomes evident when someone seems to be unable to limit or stop these obsessive compulsive activities. They seemingly demonstrate a "loss of control." As a result, the problem of addiction is not that someone enjoys these activities; the problem of addiction is that they cannot seem to stop it.

Imagine that someone goes gambling for the first time. Win or lose, it is fun. Sometimes it is very fun and not too much money gets spent. The experience is affordable, relative to that person's income. What is the harm in that? Now let us imagine that same person goes to a casino again, planning to spend $100, just as they did the first time. However, this time they keep getting credit card cash advances for much more than they can afford. By the end of the evening, they blew their entire paycheck. They might feel a lot of remorse and regret about what happened. Most people would not wish to repeat that experience, and thankfully most do not. However, people who develop addiction will repeat that experience over and over and return to the casino, spending more than they can afford. This occurs despite the commitments to themselves or to others to "never to do that again." This quality of addiction bears further explanation.

Likewise, imagine that someone who eats a box of donuts for the first time. It is stimulating and tastes good. The experience is rewarding. What is the harm in that? Now let us imagine that same person goes to the bakery to get another box of donuts, just as they did the first time. However, this time they over-spend and get caught up in a binge and they buy and consume three boxes of donuts and a pint of ice cream. By the end of the month, they realize they are eating three boxes of donuts and three pints of ice cream per day. They might feel a lot of remorse and regret about what happened. Most people would not wish to repeat that experience, and thankfully most do not. However, people who develop addiction will repeat this experience over and over and binge over and over, until they they weigh 400 pounds and have a 52 inch wast. This occurs despite all the commitments to themselves or to others to "never to do that again." This quality of addiction bears further explanation.

As a person's addiction progresses or gets worse, they feel "out-of-control" or "powerless" over their behavior. Despite their best intentions to remain in control of their behavior, there are repeated episodes with more negative consequences. Sometimes the person is aware of this reduced control. Other times, they might deceive themselves about how easy it would be to quit "anytime I want to." Ultimately, everyone must make their own decision about whether to change a particular behavior. But, the requirements for making changes to our behavior are frequently under-estimated. They often require a great deal more effort and determination than someone realizes.

Family and friends are less easily deceived. These episodes of reduced control are more obvious to other people. Unfortunately, the addict is the last to see their addictive behavior. Family and friends often wonder: "Well since you seem to believe you can control this behavior, why don't you?!" A person in relationships with someone who is developing an addiction can often feel betrayed. Their loved one seems so different. Their "choices" seem to be incompatible with their usual goals, commitments, and values.

But in the case of obsessive compulsive codependence learned helplessness, as the person with this condition progresses, the individual seeks more codependent relationships with unhealthy people causing them to engage in a set of obsessive compulsive behaviors that they have difficulty stopping or moderating ignorer to maintain their learned helplessness. But as the person who suffers from obsessive compulsive learned helplessness avoids or escapes their distress, they feel that they are worthless and have no value, and so, they again seek more and codependence relationships with unhealthy people to feel better, thus maintaining their learned helplessness.

If a close friend or family member attempts to address this pattern by saying something like: "Don't you realize you have a major problem and you need help?!," the result is more likely to erupt into a major argument than a major change of behavior. People with addiction problems are rather adept at turning the tables and blaming others such as: "I wouldn't have to find another partner if you were here for me."

Instead of admitting a problem exists, a person who is developing an addiction might deny the existence of any problems. On the other hand, they might suggest that their "complaining" partner exaggerated the problem, or even caused the problem. It is often difficult to determine whether people genuinely believe these ideas or are simply unwilling to face the frightening thought that they might have a problem.

In some cases, there might be sincere regret followed by a promise to change. After enough broken promises to change, promises are no longer believable. Family and friends settle into expecting the worst and trying to live with it. Alternatively, they might actively express their legitimate anger and frustration. The arguments and tension can be severe.

The Definition of Addiction Includes Pleasure and/or Value

Let us discuss the fourth part of the definition: pleasure and/or value. You might begin to wonder why the addict begins using or doing in the first place. Why would someone want to do something that brings about harm to them and others? The answer is deceivingly simple: because at first it was pleasurable and it was valuable to them. It did something for them. The addicted person might find it "valuable" because it reduced stress or tension. Maybe it provided a temporary escape from dismal circumstances or sheer boredom. Perhaps it helped to briefly relieve depression. In fact, people are genetically predisposed to repeat things that are rewarding or bring about pleasure as this ensures our very survival. Without this genetic predisposition, we would not eat or reproduce.

Notice our definition includes the concept that the substance or activity might no longer be pleasurable and/or valuable. In fact, over time many addictions become very unpleasant. Despite this fact, what usually remains pleasurable, valuable, and rewarding is the release from the powerful cravings that develop. Sometimes this is called cravings-use-pleasure-rest cycle.

How do You Know if You Have an Addiction?

If you find yourself wondering if you might have an addiction, the following descriptions might be a good starting point for you. These descriptions will help you to evaluate the harmful costs of the activity or substance use that concerns you. In addition to your own evaluation, try to imagine how others might rate you on these behaviors. You do not need to develop a precisely correct description of the costs of your addiction. However, it is important to recognize whether these costs are beginning to cause you substantial harm. If so, then perhaps it is time to do something about the behavior that concerns you. Later, we will talk about various approaches to self-help and treatment for addiction.

The emotional costs of addiction include living with daily feelings of fear, anger, sadness, shame, guilt, paranoia, loss of pleasure, boredom, emotional instability, self-loathing (disgust with oneself), loneliness, isolation, and feelings worthlessness. The frequency and magnitude of these negative feelings can contribute to the development of an additional mental health disorder. Addictions regularly co-occur with other psychiatric disorders.

The social costs of addiction include disruption or damage to important relationships; decreased ability or interest in forming meaningful connections with others; and limiting one's social sphere to other unhealthy, addicted people.

The physical and health costs of addiction include poor general health; poor personal hygiene; lowered energy and endurance; diminished enjoyment of sex or sexual dysfunction; poor sleep; damage to organ systems; and damaging the health of an unborn child with certain types of substance use.

The intellectual costs of addiction include loss of creative pursuits; decreased ability to solve problems; and poor memory.

The work and productivity costs of addiction include decreased productivity in all aspects of life; missing important deadlines and failing to meet obligations; impaired ability to safely operate tools and equipment including driving; and lost time due to accidents arising from being impaired, such as falling and breaking a leg.

The financial costs of addiction include money spent on the addiction itself; money spent dealing with the consequences of addiction such as healthcare costs and legal costs.

The legal costs of addiction include direct legal costs due to direct involvement with an illegal system such as arrests or incarceration; and indirect legal costs because of what someone did while engaging in their addiction such as DUI, bar fights, domestic violence, and divorce; or did not do such as failing to care for children properly.

The lost time due to addiction includes sacrificing time spent in meaningful, life enriching activities in order to engage in addictive behaviors. Meaningful, life-enriching activities are of two basic types: (1) love or time spent in relationships with others, and (2) work or time spent being productive including employment, learning, working on personal projects, volunteering, or helping others. However, time is a limited resource. When time is increasingly spent pursuing an addiction, it limits the amount of time available to devote to these other two basic human activities.

First, is the diminished personal integrity due to addiction. Most people have a strong sense of morality. This includes a sense of what is right and wrong; what one ought to do and not do; how others should be treated; and a sense of responsibility toward one's family, community, employer, and to society. However, about one in 25 people, roughly 4% or 5% of the population, seems to be missing this sense of morality. Such people are often termed as sociopathic, psychopathic, or antisocially disordered. Although the terms are not identical, they are similar enough for our purposes. This sociopathic part of the population will commonly develop addictions. Unfortunately, if someone in the other 99% of the population develops an addiction, they will begin to behave in a manner similar to a sociopath as their addiction progresses. In other words, they begin to lose their morality and integrity.

As addicted people gradually lose their moral compass, they begin to disrespect the rights and needs of other people. They even mistreat the people that matter to them the most. This begins by failing to meet certain responsibilities, commitments, or obligations. Examples of these failures might be failing to show up for things; becoming dishonest by failing to disclose information; or making excuses rather than making a sincere apology.

This type of disregard will evolve into more obvious forms of disrespect and mistreatment as addiction progresses. This progression might include flat-out lying and deception; stealing from loved ones; and threatening these same people if their demands are not met. Unlike their sociopathic counterparts who lack a moral compass to begin with, people who once had a moral compass often experience tremendous feelings of guilt and self-loathing as they break their own moral code. Addiction can only relieve these feelings temporarily.

So, what is the difference between a sociopath and a psychopath? Sociopaths are often called psychopaths and vice versa, but there are differences between a psychopath and a sociopath. For example, psychopaths are far more likely to get in trouble with the law, whereas sociopaths are much more likely to blend in with society, and even though sociopaths and psychopaths do share some of the same traits, sociopathy or antisocial personality disorder is generally considered less severe than psychopathy. So, why is this important? Because all addicts, no matter what kind, all have traits of sociopathy.

Brain Plasticity

The human brain has historically been a mysterious thing. For many years, it was thought that the brain completed its development early in childhood and then sat there fixed and unchanging, vulnerable to damage from which it could not heal. But then an opera singer with Multiple Sclerosis regains her voice; a blind man teaches himself to see again; a man with Parkinson's disease cures his symptoms by walking; and addict overcomes his addiction.

Research has now discovered that the brain is not fixed and unchanging but is a flexible organ with the ability conform itself to behavior, reorganize itself to accommodate change, and compensate for damage. The brain is inventive, responsive, and through careful modulation, is full of promise.

The Ever-Changing Brain

As you think new thoughts, practice new skills, and participate in new behaviors, new neural pathways form. As these thoughts and behaviors are repeated, the pathways grow stronger, new habits emerge, and the brain is rewired to invite the use of these new pathways.

Like a well-worn forest trail that we walk every day, we know them by feel where the memory of their twists and turns are imprinted on us, sewn into our consciousness. Meanwhile, the pathways we no longer use weaken and become impassable and hostile in comparison to our more popular open pathways.

The plastic nature of our brain, or neuroplasticity, opens a world of potential for people to optimize their minds through improved cognitive function, memory, language skills, and guard against age-related decline. It also gives us a new way of conceptualizing addiction, and the promise of treatment possibilities to guide addicts to recovery using the innate resources of their own brains.

Addiction as a Brain Disorder

For years, debate has raged between the schools of thought that frame addiction as a choice versus addiction as a disease. But through an understanding of the brain as an adaptable organ, we can reach a more sophisticated model, describing addiction as a reorientation of the brain that creates new neural pathways and perpetuates addictive behavior.

Rather than an arbitrary choice, the addict's brain has remapped itself to make the feeding of their addiction the most natural course of action. When a person indulges in addictive behavior, their brain is flooded with a powerful highly rewarding chemical known as dopamine. Dopamine release is not the only highly rewarding, it also increases our ability to learn and teaches our brain to remember how this happened, so we can feel this way again.

As the behavior is performed again and again, the level of dopamine release decreases and new extremes must be reached to the same desired effect. Eventually, tolerance build up to such a point that the addictive behavior no longer provides pleasure at all, but merely provides an avoidance of much feared withdrawal. But even in the face of diminishing rewards, the neural pathways beg for the repetition of the desired behavior, and so the brain has now adapted for addiction.

The Power of Neuroplasticity

Although neuroplasticity might be a culprit in the creation of addiction, it also holds the key to recovery. By harnessing the moldability of the brain and abandoning the neural connections fed by addictive behaviors, new pathways can be formed through the development of healthy behaviors and though processes. Through carefully created treatment plans, people suffering from addiction can be released from its grip and move toward stability, insight and self-awareness.

The Journey Toward Recovery

By embracing the potential of neuroplasticity and integrating neural modulation into therapeutic practice, addiction treatment programs can harness the healing powers of the brain and relieve suffering. This nuanced understanding of the brain offers new hope the millions of people suffering from addiction as we forge new paths to lasting sobriety and wellness.

The Biology of Addiction and Recovery

So, how do people get addicted anyway? The recent contributions of science and medicine during the past 50 to 60 years have greatly advanced our understanding of addiction. We are beginning to understand biological forces that affect behavior in both humans and animals. Addiction is easier to understand when we consider that our biology programs us to pursue pleasure. However, we are not slaves to our biology. The unrestrained pursuit of pleasure represents a type of developmental immaturity as depicted in the classic story of Peter Pan. We can understand this by using a Bio-Psycho-Social-Spiritual model to explain this. The psycho-social-spiritual portion of the Bio-Psycho-Social-Spiritual model influences whether we mature beyond our biological limitations.

Here, we will explore the biological forces that drive addiction. In subsequent sections, we will discuss the psychological, social, and the spiritual portions of the Bio-psycho-social-spiritual model.

Until recently, people with addictive disorders were viewed as selfish, weak-willed, morally corrupt folks, who seemed to behave badly without regard for themselves or others. However, in the past 30 years, this perspective has begun to change. People with addictive problems will tell you, willpower is not enough in that it can help you stop, but it is not very effective at helping you stay stopped. As we will soon see, our biological make-up explains why this is so.

Furthermore, advancements in neurobiological research have changed the way we view addiction. Addiction is no longer limited to problematic substance use. We now know that certain activities can also be addictive such as eating, sex, gambling, gaming, and codependence or people addiction. This is because addiction is a problem of brain functioning. We become addicted to the chemicals our brain releases and to the people, places, and activities related to the addiction. As a result, addiction is a problem of brain functioning and our genetics greatly determine this.

The American Society of Addictions Medicine (ASAM), the nation's largest professional society of addiction physicians, is dedicated to treating and preventing addiction. ASAM released a new definition of addiction in August 2011. It stated that genetics account for about

50% of the likelihood that someone will develop an addiction This ASAM definition of addiction describes addiction as a "chronic disease of the brain."

Nevertheless, it remains controversial whether we should reduce addiction to a "chronic disease of the brain." Yet, there is strong evidence to suggest that there is a genetic component to addiction. Clearly, addiction does not develop merely because someone is weak-willed. Addicted people do not choose their genetics. Therefore, they do not control whether they are at risk for developing an addiction.

However, we are not slaves to our biology and biology does not completely drive our behavior. People are certainly capable of choosing recovery over addiction. This makes addictive disorders very similar to other diseases and disorders. Many health problems require lifestyle changes to restore us to health. For instance, people with diabetes must regularly check their blood sugar levels and count carbohydrates. People with heart disease must choose a healthier diet and an exercise program. Obviously, these folks did not choose to have these health challenges. However, but they most certainly do choose how to handle them. The same is true for people with addictions.

How Does Addiction Affect the Brain?

The brain is the most dynamic and complex organ in our body. The brain's proper functioning ensures our very survival. When our brain functions well, we are constantly adapting to our environment. Ironically, it is the brain's ability to be so adaptive that contributes to the formation of addictions of all kinds, including alcohol addiction. Addictions of all kinds cause changes to the brain in at least four fundamental ways:

1. Addiction causes changes to the brain's natural balance (homeostasis)

2. Addiction alters brain chemistry

3. Addiction changes the brain's communication patterns

4. Addiction causes changes to brain structures and their functioning

Addictions of all kinds interfere with an important biological process called *homeostasis*. Scientists consider the human body a biological system. All biological systems attempt to maintain a "normal" balance, known as homeostasis. The brain functions as the overseer of this balance. It makes various adjustments to maintain a balanced, well-functioning, biological system. Each person's normal balance is individually determined. Alcohol abuse, drug abuse, and activity addictions lead to changes in this normal balance.

Chronic over-stimulation of the brain like that which occurs in addictions of all kinds interfere with the maintenance of this balance (homeostasis). When the brain has difficulty maintaining homeostatic balance, the wonderfully adaptive brain adjusts. It does this by creating a new balanced set-point. The creation of a new balance is called *allostasis*.

These concepts are easier to understand if we use an example more familiar to most people. Suppose you gain ten pounds. At first, you will just keep trying to fit into your clothing. However, tight clothing is uncomfortable. At some point, you must adapt to the change in your body size. You will eventually acknowledge you need to buy larger clothing. Once you buy larger clothing, you are more comfortable. You have come to accept that your clothing size is now size "Large," whereas before it was size "Medium." In effect, you changed your "homeostatic balance" from size Medium to size Large. Having reset your size to "Large," you are now more comfortable. Keep in mind, if you lose those ten pounds to achieve greater health, you will again have to readjust your clothing size. So, even though you are now healthier, you still must make an unpleasant and costly adjustment—buying all new clothes in a smaller size. This is very similar to the unpleasant adjustment the brain must go through when people try to give up their addiction. Although this is a positive change, we will be uncomfortable while the brain readjustments itself. This process is called allostasis.

Ironically, the brain's wonderful ability to be so adaptive through allostasis causes significant changes to the brain's functioning. These changes account for many behaviors associated with addiction such as: (1) the powerful need to obtain alcohol, drugs, or continue harmful activities despite the harm to self or loved ones; (2) the difficulty of quitting an addictive alcohol use, drug use, or activities, and (3) the obsessive, all-consuming nature of alcohol, drug, or behavioral addictions become so all-consuming that little else in life matters. This is because alcohol, drug, and behavioral addiction caused the brain's balance to change to accommodate the addiction. Once changed, the brain requires the addictive substance like alcohol or drugs or activities in order to maintain this new homeostatic balance.

Addiction Changes Our Brain Chemistry

Most everyone recognizes that good communication is important. Communication is the key to well-running human systems whether the system is a group of family members or a group of people who work together. Our bodies are no different. Without good communication, our bodies do not function well. Not surprisingly, our brains are responsible for this communication. To understand addiction's effect on brain chemistry, we must first understand how this communication system works.

Our five senses—sight, sound, taste, touch, and smell—gather and transmit information about our environment to the most primitive part of our brain known as a *limbic system* also known as the reactive brain. Our brains must then process and analyze this information. Although the brain takes in and analyzes an extraordinary amount of information, it relies on a rather simple electrochemical process for communication.

The brain's communication system permits specific areas of the brain to rapidly interact with other brain regions. The brain achieves this communication through a vast, interconnected, network of specialized cells called neurons. Our brains have about over 80 billion neurons and about 100-500 trillion neuronal connections. These neuronal connections form the foundation for an electro-chemical communication system.

The brain is composed of many different regions or sections. Each of these regions serves a different function. Therefore, these different regions of the brain must have a way to communicate with each other. In particular, the brain must communicate with, and coordinate, all the body's systems:

Integumentary System (skin, hair, and nails)	Lymphatic System
	Respiratory System
Muscular System	Endocrine System
Skeletal System	Digestive System
Circulatory System	Urinary System
Nervous System	Reproductive System

This is like how individual players on a sports team must communicate with each other to coordinate their actions together as a team. As a result, the brain's communication system is essential to our health, well-being, and overall functioning. Conversely, when this communication system is altered, it negatively affects us.

This brain's communication system is constantly changing and adapting. These qualities allow us to learn, remember, and adjust to our changing circumstances. Various drugs including alcohol and prescribed medications, as well as certain stimulating behaviors, can alter the brain's communication system. It makes sense that anything that alters the brain's communication system will alter the way the brain functions. We need to understand how this communication system works so we can understand some of the defining characteristics of addiction. These include cravings, withdrawals, compulsions, and the continued use of addictive substances and activities despite harmful consequences.

The neuron is the primary unit of communication within the brain. A single neuron is extremely tiny, and was said, scientists estimate that there are over 80 billion neurons in the human brain. Imagine just how complex and distinct our brain is from the person next to you. As you know, good communication is a two-way street: We both listen (receive information) and we speak (send information). The same is true of the brain's communication system. Neurons can both send and receive communication signals. The *dendrite* is the portion of a neuron that typically receives information from other neurons (listens), and the *axon* is portion of the neuron that sends out information to other neurons (speaks).

When humans communicate with each other, we typically use words and gestures. But the different parts of the brain communicate with each other using electrical-chemical signals. Neurons use electrical pulses to send their communication signals along a neural pathway. These electrical impulses are called action potentials. When a neuron fires, the action potential travels down the neuron's axon where it ends. At the end of the axon is the axon terminal or pre-synapse. In this area, special chemical messengers called neurotransmitters and neuromodulators lay in wait. These are stored in specialized capsules called vesicles. The action potential causes the release of these chemical messengers into an open space between one neuron's axon and the next neurons' dendrites. This open space is the synaptic cleft. At the other side of the synaptic cleft is the post synapse that is formed by the dendrites of connecting neurons. In the post synapse, there are special receptors that receive the neurotransmitters.

Receptors and neurotransmitters function in a way that is like a key that fits into a keyhole. Receptors are like keyholes and neurotransmitters are like the keys. When neurotransmitters fit into the receptors it is called binding. Once a neurotransmitter is bound to a receptor, the key turns the lock. Once the lock opens, it communicates with the receiving neuron's dendrites. In the post synapse, there might be many different receptors. However, a particular neurotransmitter might be able to fit into or bind to several different receptor types. This is like the way a single key can open several different locks. The particular receptor type determines the type of signal that is transmitted. As a result, the receptor type is often more critical to the communication than the particular neurotransmitter.

It might be easiest to visualize this communication as a single chain of events: First, a neuron sends an electrical impulse (action potential) down the axon. Next, the electrical impulse causes chemicals (neurotransmitters and neuromodulators) to be released into the space between two neurons. Then these chemicals can signal the next neuron to send an electrical impulse and so on. This electro-chemical process forms the brain's communication system.

Addiction Changes the Brain's Communication Pathways

Previously, we described the brain's electro-chemical communication system. This communication system sends information through a vast network of interconnecting neurons. Overtime, the brain develops a preferred or standard pathway to send signals between neurons (neural pathways). Until recently, we thought the brain's neural pathways had completely formed by the time we reached adulthood. However, because of new scientific developments, we now know the brain is much more dynamic than we thought. The human brain continues to create new neurons and form neural pathways throughout our entire lifespan. As a result, neurons are dynamic cells that are constantly adapting to changing circumstances. If something damages a person's brain such as a stroke or injury, the neurons can make new communication route around the damaged area. This ability is known as neural plasticity.

Scientists found that neuroplasticity regulates learning processes and helps us to adapt to our surroundings. As early as 1949, the neuroscientist Donald Hebb claimed that neurons that frequently fire together form stronger linkages. In other words, "neurons that fire together, wire together." This is known as Hebb's Law. This is one of the earliest descriptions of what we now call neuroplasticity.

To better understand neuroplasticity, an analogy might be helpful. Our brains' form neural pathways in a way that is like the formation of a well-traveled hiking trail. The more we travel a path, the faster, easier, and more familiar that path becomes. As we travel it more and more, it becomes wider, smoother, and easier to travel. It becomes a preferred route. The same is true of neural pathways in our brain. Overtime, the brain forms familiar neural pathways these become habitual routes. If a familiar route is blocked, the brain eventually forges a new route.

Let us continue with our analogy. Suppose you walk through the woods each day to visit a friend. You use the same trail each time. One day, as you travel along your familiar path, you discover a huge tree has fallen over and it is blocking your path. You will need to forge a new path to go around the tree. At first, this new path will be narrow, difficult, and slow. It might even be uncomfortable. But overtime, it will become a well-worn, comfortable path and it will be just as easy as the original path.

New neural pathways are formed as addiction develops. This is because addiction chemically altered the brain's communication system. When we take that drug away, the brain must again form new neural pathways. Just as when we had to forge a new trail in the woods, this is initially uncomfortable. Neuroplasticity explains why the initial period of recovery is difficult and uncomfortable. But we know from our hiking trail example, this difficulty is only temporary.

This information is very helpful to know when attempting recovery. We can be successful if we preserve through this brief, uncomfortable period. Remember, it was difficult and uncomfortable to forge a new pathway around a fallen tree. The same is true for the initial period of recovery. It can be difficult and uncomfortable while these new neural pathways are forming. If a recovering person does not give up during this initial period of discomfort, new neural pathways will form that support recovery. These new pathways will become more established and better developed over time. As they do, recovery becomes easier and more comfortable. But it should be noted that it takes from 12 to 18 months of conscious effort to develop and cement these new neural pathways into a consistent long-term way of behaving and life-long diligence to keep them strong.

We have emphasized the adaptive, dynamic qualities of our brains ensure our survival. Unfortunately, the brain's ability to be so adaptive is also at the root of addiction. The brain adapts to the strong effects of addictive drugs and activities. When it does, changes occur in the brain regions associated with reward, memory and emotion, decision-making, and stress regulation. These changes to our brain make the repeated use of addictive substances or activities very compelling.

The good news is that our brains' neuroplasticity allows us to correct these changes. Therefore, although addiction leads to structural and functional changes in the brain, we can learn new coping skills that change the structure and function of our brains back to normal. The brain's plasticity allows these new coping skills to be imprinted.

Addiction Changes Brain Structure and Functioning

The brain is composed of many different regions and structures. The brain's communication system permits these various regions and structures to coordinate their activities. Each of these different regions and structures serves different purposes. Addictions can alter these regions and structures. Subsequently, addictions of all kinds including alcohol can alter the way brain regions function. Here, we discuss the regions and structures that are affected by the addictive process. We will review the brain's role in commonly observed problems associated with addiction: (1) Impaired decision-making, impulsivity, and compulsivity; (2) alcohol, drug, or behavior-seeking and cravings; (3) habit formation, craving, withdrawal effects, and relapse triggers; and (4) stress regulation and withdrawal.

Addiction is a process that coordinates the transition from impulsive to compulsive behavior. Impulsivity occurs during the early stages of addiction. During this phase, people impulsively act on powerful urges to experience the pleasure of their addiction whatever it might be. Anxiety is not associated with the urges during these early stages. Instead, addiction reflects acting on impulsive desire to receive immediate pleasure from the alcohol, drug, or activity. People are not considering the future consequences.

As addiction progresses, a shift begins to occur. At this point, the compulsive aspect of addiction takes hold. When this shift occurs, people are no longer pursuing their addiction solely for pleasure. The compulsions compel them to participate in their addiction to relieve anxious, uncomfortable feelings. These might arise at the mere thought of stopping the addiction for any reason such as supply shortages or lack of opportunity. At this later compulsive stage, pleasure comes in the form of relief from these anxious, uncomfortable feelings. As a result, despite the negative consequences of addiction, the addictive behavior continues in a compulsive manner.

Another way to describe the prefrontal cortex is to think of it as a braking system. The prefrontal cortex acts as the brain's brakes. It sends out signals to inhibit particular behaviors or actions. When addiction damages this brain area, it limits the brain's ability to control other behavioral systems as well. Imagine how difficult it would be to operate a car without brakes. At this point, we might say the brain is high-jacked by the addiction. The prefrontal cortex also projects to other brain regions associated with addictive problems. These include the reward system; memory and emotion; and stress regulation centers of the brain. Therefore, damage to the prefrontal cortex might further interfere with the functioning of these other brain regions as well.

Although addiction damages the brain's brakes, the prefrontal cortex, this is not to say there is a complete loss of control. We are not slaves to our biology. We have a tremendous amount of control over our actions. So, even when are led to believe that we are powerless over our addiction or people, places, and things; this is untrue. This is true even when impulsive and compulsive forces are operating. This recognition is vitally important if someone wishes to recover from addiction. When a person consciously decides that the costs of addiction far outweigh its benefits, they become motivated and able stop. This allows them to actively counter the effects of addiction on the frontal cortex and other brain regions.

Unfortunately, people's addictions limit their ability to use rationale thought. This is due in part to the damage to the prefrontal cortex. They might incorrectly tally the costs and benefits of their addiction; over-estimating its benefits, while minimizing its costs. The addict is often told: "You're in denial." This is incorrect. When people use this phrase, they are applying it improperly. Denial refers to a psychological defense, or justification for a negative behavior. This is quite different than a loss of rational brain functioning that occurs with addiction. This is where addiction treatment professionals can be very helpful. They can guide addicted persons to make an accurate assessment of the costs and benefits. This more accurate assessment often leads to the motivation to change. Once someone decides it is time to change, they have taken the first step toward recovery.

The addiction process relies on learning and memory to drive the addiction cycle forward. Addiction alters the system. However, people can learn how counteract these changes. There are specific techniques that people can learn to oppose powerful urges. As people become more skillful, the wonderfully adaptive brain adjusts and corrections. This in turn leads to lasting recovery from addiction.

As drug use or addictive activity increases, the involvement of various brain regions associated with our emotional state also increases. The brain region most often associated with our emotional state is the Amygdalae. Scientists think this brain region plays an important role in addiction because of its association with emotions and stress.

The amygdalae are a pair of almond-shaped masses located deep within the temporal lobes of the brain which are responsible for the response and memory of emotions, especially fear. We all have both "good" memories and "bad" memories about various events in our lives. What makes a memory "good" as opposed to "bad" are the emotional states that occurred during those events. When the brain forms these memories, it stores the memory of the event along with the emotions or emotional energy that accompanied it. When we smell the sea air, feel the ocean breeze, or hear the seagulls, we have a pleasant memory and emotional experience. This is because these things have been repeatedly associated with relaxing and enjoyable times. The memory of the sea is stored along with a pleasant emotional state. So, we can merely think of the sea, without actually being there, and we will experience a pleasant emotional state.

Likewise, an addicted person might only need see, hear, feel, taste, or think about something that reminds them of their addiction and they will experience an intense urge to use that is tied to the intense feeling of pleasure related to the addiction event. The memory of engaging in the addiction is stored with a pleasant emotional state. As a result, the pleasing memories of engaging with an addiction can lead to repeating those behaviors and forming a habit.

Emotional memory has another role in the development of addiction, called *Cue Anticipation*. Cue anticipation refers to environmental cues that can initiate or elevate craving. Cravings often lead to relapse. For this reason, these cues are often called relapse triggers. Therefore, a successful recovery plan will include a strategy for coping with cues or relapse triggers.

These environmental cues or relapse triggers can be anything that is associated with the addiction. It could be a certain time of day, a place, a person, or an activity. For instance, suppose a man is addicted to pornography. He usually gets online after his wife goes to bed. The mere act of his wife getting ready to go to bed serves as a cue that prompts powerful cravings. Later, even his own anticipation of his wife going to bed will serve as a powerful cue.

The Amygdalae's role in emotional memory is responsible for these cues taking root. The brain forms an association between pleasant memories of drug use or addictive activities, and the cues. The more a person repeats this cycle, the more it strengthens the emotional memory circuits associated with these cues. Eventually, this leads to a complete pre-occupation with the addiction.

So far, we have been discussing the role of the Amygdala and positive emotional memories. The brain might also form an association between unpleasant emotions and a memory or forming a "bad" memory. These negative emotional memories play an important role in withdrawal. The negative emotional memory of anxiety becomes associated with the physical signs of withdrawal. As withdrawal begins, the symptoms trigger an unpleasant emotional memory. This increases the negative experience of withdrawal. Withdrawal avoidance by returning to the addiction often becomes the cornerstone of the addiction in the later stages. As a result, in the earlier stages of addiction, the pleasurable experience of the drug motivates a repetition of that behavior. In the later stages, relief of withdrawal symptoms such as physical and/or emotional discomfort achieves pleasure. This pleasurable relief from withdrawal symptoms continues to motivate the repetition of that behavior.

Stress Regulation and Withdrawal

Addiction affects another area of the brain called the hypothalamus. The hypothalamus has many duties. It controls body temperature, hunger, thirst, and sleep. The hypothalamus also plays a key role in our response to stress. Stress regulation is highly relevant to our understanding of addiction because stress or tension drives addiction. When an individual experiences stress, the hypothalamus releases chemicals called hormones. These hormones allow the brain and the body to respond to that stress. Unlike neurotransmitters which are chemicals limited to the brain hormones travel throughout the body through the blood system. Therefore, hormones can exert an effect on other body systems as well. When these chemical hormones operate in the brain, we refer to them as neuromodulators. These hormones or neuromodulators can act just like neurotransmitters in the brain. Like neurotransmitters, they have their own receptors associated with them.

Stress is a well-known relapse trigger. It can prompt powerful cravings in addicted people. Many of us know someone who tried to quit smoking but ultimately relapsed when they became "stressed out." Unfortunately, during the initial period of recovery withdrawal symptoms create stress. This creates an unfortunate cycle. Stress prompts addictive use, whereas efforts to discontinue use produce stress or tension. During withdrawal, these stress hormones are elevated. Even though stress levels are high, the brain's anti-stress neuromodulators appear to decrease, as do dopamine and serotonin in the nucleus accumbens. This suggests that withdrawal affected the reward system as evidenced by decreasing dopamine and serotonin. At the same time, withdrawal activates the stress and anxiety systems. This double punch heightens the negative experience of withdrawal. This prompts people to seek relief via the addictive substance or activity—relapse.

In summary, the neurotransmitter pathways associated with the amygdalae and the hypothalamus play a crucial role in sustaining the addiction process. This occurs thorough:

1. The negative emotional memory that is associated with alcohol, drug, or activity withdrawal.

2. The positive emotional memory that is associated with alcohol, drug, or activity cues.

3. The disruption that occurs to stress regulation.

4. The pleasurable relief from withdrawal symptoms that occurs by resuming alcohol use, drug use, or addictive activities.

The Body Keeps the Score

When your senses become obscured, you no longer feel fully alive, but if you have a comfortable connection with your own inner sensations, you will feel in charge of your body, your feelings, and your self.

William James stated in his revolutionary 1884 theory of how our bodies affect our feelings that a purely disembodied human emotion is a nonentity. Two generations later, Rilke wrote in a beautiful letter of advice to a young woman that he was not one of those who neglected the body in order to make it a sacrificial offering for the soul, since the soul would thoroughly dislike being served in such a fashion. Yet, in the nearly 140 years since, we have made little progress on making sense of, much less making use, of the inseparable interchange between our physical body and our psycho-emotional interior landscape that we call our soul or self.

Nowhere is this relationship more essential, yet more endangered, than in our healing from trauma, and no one has provided a more illuminating, sympathetic, and constructive approach to healing than Boston-based Dutch psychiatrist and pioneering PTSD researcher Bessel van der Kolk. In his landmark book: *The Body Keeps the Score: Brain, Mind, and Body in the Healing of Trauma*, published in 2014, he explored the extreme disconnect from the body that so many people with a history of trauma and neglect experience and the most fertile path to recovery by drawing on his own work and a wealth of other research in three main areas of study: neuroscience, which deals with how mental processes function in the brain; developmental psychopathology, which is concerned with how painful experiences impact the development of our mind and brain; and interpersonal neurobiology, which examines how our own behavior affects the psycho-emotional and neurobiological states of those who are close to us.

Van der Kolk noted that trauma affects not only those who have suffered it, but also those who are connected to them, especially those who love them. Van der Kolk said that you do not have to be a combat soldier, or a firefighter, or a police officer to witness trauma. Trauma happens to us, our friends, our families, and our neighbors. Research by the Centers for Disease Control and Prevention has shown that about 20% of Americans were sexually molested as a child; about 25% were beaten by a parent to the point of leaving a mark on their body; and over 30% of couples engages in physical violence on others and on each other. A quarter of us grew up with alcoholic parents or relatives, and over 12% witnessed our mother being beaten or hit.

It takes a tremendous amount of energy to keep functioning while carrying the memories of trauma and terror, and the shame of utter weakness and vulnerability.

In trauma survivors, Van der Kolk noted that the parts of the brain that have evolved to monitor for danger remain over-activated, where even the slightest sign of danger or threat, real or perceived, can trigger an acute stress response accompanied by intense unpleasant emotions and overwhelming sensations of anxiety and distress. Such post-traumatic reactions make it difficult for survivors to connect with other people, since closeness often triggers a sense of danger, and yet, the very thing we have come to dread the most after experiencing trauma—close contact with other people—is also the very thing we need the most in order to regain psycho-emotional wellness and healing.

Van der Kolk noted that being able to feel safe with other people is probably the single most important aspect of mental health. Safe connections are fundamental to meaningful and satisfying lives.

This is why we have evolved a refined mechanism for detecting danger—we are incredibly attuned to even the slightest, subtlest emotional shifts in those around us, and even if we do not always heed these intuitive perceptions, we can read other people's friendliness or hostility on the basis of such imperceptible cues as facial expressions and body language. But one of the most destructive effects of trauma is that it disrupts our ability to accurately read others, rendering the trauma survivor either less able to detect danger; more likely to misperceive danger where there is none; or not react to a threat when there is one.

Paradoxically, what normalizes and repairs our ability to read danger and safety correctly is human connection. Van der Kolk stated that social connection is not the same as merely being in the presence of others. The critical issue is reciprocity, where being truly heard and seen by the people around us, where we feel that we are held in someone else's mind and heart.

For our bodies to calm down, heal, and grow, we need a deep-down feeling of safety. No doctor can write a prescription for friendship and love—these are complex and sometimes difficult capacities to achieve. You do not need a history of trauma to feel self-conscious and even panicked at a party with strangers, but trauma can turn the whole world into a frightening gathering of aliens.

Beginning to adequately address trauma requires a cultural shift away from the disease model on which twentieth century psychology and psychiatry were built. That model has seeded a number of cultural deformities that affect everything from our longtime denial of the relationship between stress and physical illness to the way we make sense of our romantic failures. Trauma and its psychological consequences are not mental diseases, but are adaptations.

Van der Kolk stated that the brain-disease model overlooks four fundamental truths: (1) our capacity to destroy one another is matched by our capacity to love and heal one another, and so, restoring relationships and community is central to restoring well-being; (2) language gives us the power to change ourselves and others by communicating our experiences, helping us to define what we know and who we are, and finding a common sense of meaning; (3) our ability to regulate our own physiology, including some of the so-called involuntary functions of the body and brain, through such basic activities as breathing, moving, and touching; and (4) our ability to change social conditions to create environments in which children and adults can feel safe and where we can thrive.

When we ignore these most perfect dimensions of humanity, we deprive people of ways to love, to heal from trauma, and restore our and their autonomy. Being a patient, rather than a participant in our healing process, separates suffering people from their community and alienates them from an inner sense of self.

Van der Kolk asserted that the most essential aspect of healing is learning to fully inhabit our inner sense of self in all of its dimensions, not only emotional and psychological, but bodily, as well, which are inseparable from one another. Van der Kolk explained that the natural state of mammals is to be on guard or vigilant. However, in order to feel emotionally close to another human being, our defense system must be temporarily shut down. In order to play, mate, and nurture our young, our brain needs to turn off its natural vigilance.

Many traumatized individuals are too hyper-vigilant to enjoy the ordinary pleasures that life has to offer, whereas others are too numb or shut-down to absorb new experiences or to be alert to signs of real danger.

Many people feel safe as long as they can limit their social contact to superficial conversations, but actual physical contact can trigger intense distress reactions. However achieving any sort of deep intimacy such as a close embrace, sleeping with a mate, or sex requires allowing ourselves to experience immobilization without fear. It is especially challenging for traumatized people to know when they are actually safe and to be able to activate their defenses when they are in danger.

Van der Kolk argued that this requires having experiences that can restore a sense of physical safety. One place where our culture fails, is in integrating this physical aspect with our psycho-emotional infrastructure of experience—a failure that spans from our clinical methods of treating trauma to our education system. More than half a century ago, Aldous Huxley wrote beautifully about the need for an integrated mind-body system in our education systems. Van der Kolk noted that education tends to engage the cognitive capacities of the mind, rather than the bodily-emotional engagement system, which makes for a totally incomplete model of human experience.

In a sobering statement, Van der Kolk wrote that despite the well-documented effects of anger, fear, and anxiety on the ability to reason, many educational programs continue to ignore the need to engage the safety system of the brain before trying to promote new ways of thinking. The last things that should be cut from school schedules are chorus, physical education, recess, and anything else involving movement, play, and joyful engagement. When children are oppositional, defensive, numbed out, shut down. or enraged, it is also important to recognize that such bad behavior may repeat action patterns that were established to survive serious threats, even if they are intensely upsetting.

For instance, with an eye to heightening counterpoints like a karate program for rape survivors and a theater program in Boston's inner-city schools, Van der Kolk considered the reasons and the urgency for engaging the body in the healing process because the body keeps the score. If the memory of trauma is encoded in the body in heartbreaking and gut-wrenching emotions; in autoimmune disorders and skeletal/muscular problems; and if mind, brain, and body communication is the royal road to emotion regulation, this demands a radical shift in our assumptions.

Drawing on his work with patients who have survived a variety of traumatic experiences, from plane crashes to rape to torture, Van der Kolk considered the great challenge of those of us living with trauma: When our senses become muted, we no longer feel fully alive.

In response to the trauma, and in coping with the dread that persists long afterward, these patients have learned to shut down their brain areas that transmit the body feelings and emotions that accompany and define terror.

Yet, in everyday life, those same brain areas are responsible for registering the entire range of human emotion and sensations that form the foundation of our self-awareness, and our sense of who we are. What we witnessed is a tragic adaptation where in an effort to shut off these terrifying memories and emotions, they also mute our capacity to feel fully alive and to be fully connected and integrated with others.

Although this dissociation from the body is an adaptive response to trauma, the troublesome day-to-day anguish comes from the reliving or triggering of these remembered responses by stimuli that do not warrant such responses.

Van der Kolk examined the interior machinery of the brain at play during trauma. The elementary self system in the brain stem and limbic system is significantly activated when people are faced with the threat of annihilation, real or perceived, which results in an overwhelming sense of fear or terror accompanied by intense physiological arousal. To people who are reliving a trauma, nothing makes sense, and so, they are trapped in a forever, inescapable life-or-death situation, seen as a state of paralyzing fear or blind rage. The mind and body are constantly aroused, as if they are always in imminent danger. They startle in response to the slightest noise and are acutely frustrated by the smallest irritation. Their sleep is chronically disturbed with nightmares and night terrors, so they in a constant state of fatigue. This in turn can trigger desperate attempts to shut those feelings down by freezing, dissociation, or using alcohol and drugs suppress their distressing feelings.

In a passage similar to the philosopher Martha Nussbaum's writings on the relationship between action and victimhood, Van der Kolk added that action starts with what scientists call "interoception," which is our awareness of our subtle sensory, body-based feelings, where the greater that awareness, the greater our potential to control our lives.

Knowing what we feel is the first step to knowing why we feel that way. If we are aware of the constant changes in our inner and outer environment, we can mobilize to manage them. Van der Kolk noted that one of the most damaging effects of trauma is that it disrupts our ability to know what we feel; that is, to trust our own perceptions, and this mistrust makes us misperceive threats where none exist. This, in turn, creates an antagonistic relationship with our own bodies, which produces an excess of toxic energy that the body now has to find a way to get rid of.

Van der Kolk explained that if you have a comfortable connection with your inner sensations and if you can trust them to give you accurate information, you will feel in charge of your body, your feelings, and your self.

However, traumatized people chronically feel unsafe inside their own bodies, where the past is alive in the form of gnawing interior anxiety, distress, and discomfort. Their bodies are constantly bombarded by visceral warning signs, and in an attempt to control these processes, traumatized people often become expert at ignoring their perceptions and in numbing awareness of what is happening inside, as well as what is happening in the environment outside them, and so, they learn to hide from themselves and the outside world.

The more people try to push away and ignore internal warning signs, the more likely they are to take over and leave them bewildered, confused, and ashamed. People who cannot comfortably notice what is going on inside become vulnerable to respond to any sensory shift either by shutting down or by going into a panic, and so, they develop a fear of fear itself.

The experience of fear derives from primitive responses to threat where escape is thwarted in some way. People's lives will be held hostage to fear until that visceral experience changes or is altered. Self-regulation depends on having a friendly relationship with our body. Without it, we have to rely on external regulations such as from medication, drugs like alcohol, constant reassurance, compulsive compliance with the wishes of others, people addiction, and learned helplessness.

In its most extreme form, this lack of internal regulation leads to re-traumatizing experiences. Because traumatized people often have trouble sensing what is going on in their bodies and accurately perceiving what is happening in their environment, they lack an ability to respond well to frustration. They either react to stress by becoming "spaced out" or they respond with excessive anger. Whatever their response is, they often cannot tell what is upsetting them. This failure to be in touch with their bodies contributes to their well-documented lack of self-protection and high rates of revictimization and also to their remarkable difficulties feeling pleasure, sensuality, connection with others, and having a sense of meaning or purpose in their lives. One step further down on the ladder to self-oblivion is depersonalization, which is losing your sense of yourself.

What then can we do to regain power and control over our very selves? Pointing to decades of research with trauma survivors, Van der Kolk argued that it begins with befriending our bodies and our sensory interiority.

Trauma victims cannot recover until they become familiar with and befriend the sensations in their bodies. Being frightened means that you live in a body and a mind that is always on guard. Angry people live in angry bodies and angry minds. The bodies of child-abuse victims are tense and defensive until they find a way to relax and feel safe. In order to change, people need to become aware of their sensations and the way that their bodies interact with the world around them.

Physical self-awareness is the first step in releasing the tyranny of the past. In a sentiment similar to Schopenhauer's "The Hedgehog's Dilemma," sometimes called "The Porcupine's Dilemma," which is a metaphor about the challenges of human intimacy that describes a situation in which a group of hedgehogs seek to move close to each other to share heat during cold weather, but they must remain apart because they cannot avoid hurting each other with their sharp spines. Although they all share the intention of a reciprocal closeness, this cannot occur, for reasons they cannot avoid—they would injure each other with their sharp spines.

Van der Kolk wrote that the most natural way for human beings to calm themselves when they are distressed is by clinging to another person. This means that patients who have been physically or sexually violated face a dilemma: They desperately crave touch while simultaneously being terrified of body contact.

The mind needs to be reeducated to feel physical sensations, and the body needs to be helped to tolerate and enjoy the comforts of touch. Individuals who lack emotional awareness are able, with much practice, to connect their physical sensations to psychological events. Then they can slowly reconnect with themselves.

Van der Kolk noted that how we respond to trauma, is to a large extent conditioned by our formative relationships with our caretakers, or parents, whose task is to help us establish a secure base. Essential to this is the notion of attunement between a parent and a child, mediated by the body, where the subtlest of physical interactions in which the caretaker mirrors and meets the baby's needs, making the infant feel attended to and understood.

Attunement is the foundation of secure attachment, which is in turn the framework of our psycho-emotional health later in life. Van der Kolk noted that a secure attachment combined with the cultivation of competency builds an internal locus of control, the key factor in healthy coping throughout life. Securely attached children learn what makes them feel good. They discover what makes them and others feel bad, and they acquire a sense of control, where their actions can change how they feel and how others respond.

Securely attached children learn the difference between situations they can control and situations where they need help. They learn that they can play an active role when faced with difficult situations.

In contrast, children with histories of abuse and neglect learn that their terror, pleading, and crying does not register with their caregivers. Nothing they can do or say stops the beating or brings attention or help. In effect, they are being conditioned to give up when they face challenges later in life—the grounds for learned helplessness.

With an eye to the work of psychoanalyst Donald Winnicott, who pioneered the study of attachment and the notion that attunement between a mother and an infant lays the foundation for the child's sense of self later in life, Van der Kolk summarized these findings by noting that if a mother cannot meet her baby's needs, the baby learns to become the mother's idea of what the baby is. Having to discount its own inner sensations, and trying to adjust to its caregiver's needs, means the child perceives that something is wrong with them as a being, somehow fundamentally flawed. Children who lack physical attunement are vulnerable to shutting down the direct feedback from their bodies, the seat of pleasure, purpose, and direction in our lives.

The need for attachment never lessens. Most human beings simply cannot tolerate being disengaged from others for any length of time, and therefore, become possessive and clingy. People who cannot connect through work, friendships, or family usually find other ways of bonding, as through illnesses, lawsuits, or family feuds. Anything is preferable to that intolerable sense of irrelevance and alienation.

Although we cannot prevent most traumatic experiences from happening, having a solid formative foundation can make healing much easier. But what are those of us without a secure attachment to do? Pointing to his mindfulness-based work with trauma survivors, Van der Kolk offered an assuring direction by saying that no one can "treat" a war, or abuse, or rape, or molestation, or any other horrendous event, for that matter. What has happened cannot be undone because it has already happened. But what can be dealt with are the imprints of the trauma on the body, mind, and soul. The crushing sensations in your chest that you may label as anxiety or depression; the fear of losing control; always being on alert for danger or rejection; the self-loathing; the nightmares and flashbacks; the fog that keeps you from staying on task and from engaging fully in what you are doing; and being unable to fully open your heart to another human being are the result of this inner conflict.

Van der Kolk maintained that the crucial point is that trauma robs us of what he called: "self-leadership" —the sense of having control over ourselves and being in charge of our own experience. Therefore, the path to recovery is paved with the active rebuilding of that sense.

Van der Kolk noted that the challenge of recovery is to reestablish ownership of your body, mind, and soul or self. This means feeling free to know what you know and to feel what you feel without becoming overwhelmed, enraged, ashamed, or collapsed.

For most people this involves: (1) finding a way to become calm and focused; (2) learning to maintain that calm in response to images, thoughts, sounds, or physical sensations that remind you of the past; (3) finding a way to be fully alive in the present and engaged with the people around you; and (4) not having to keep secrets from yourself, including secrets about the ways that you have managed to survive.

One of the paradoxical necessities of the recovery process is the need to revisit the trauma without becoming so overwhelmed by sensations as to be re-traumatized by it. Van der Kolk maintained that the way to accomplish this is by learning to be present with these overwhelming emotions and their sensorial counterparts in the body. In other word, to at one with them.

Van der Kolk wrote that traumatized people live with seemingly unbearable sensations. They feel heartbroken and suffer from intolerable sensations in the pit of their stomach or tightness in their chest. Yet, avoiding feeling these sensations in our bodies increases our vulnerability to being overwhelmed by them.

Traumatized people are often afraid of feeling. It is not so much the perpetrators, who hopefully, are no longer around to hurt them, but their own physical sensations that now are the enemy. Apprehension about being hijacked by uncomfortable sensations keeps the body frozen and the mind shut off. Even though the trauma is a thing of the past, the emotional brain keeps generating sensations, as if the trauma is happening again and again, that make the sufferer feel scared and helpless. It is not surprising that so many trauma survivors are compulsive eaters and drinkers, fear making love, and avoid many social activities, and so, their sensory world is largely off limits.

Another paradox of healing is that although contact and connection are often terrifying to the traumatized, social support and a sense of community are the foundation upon which a health relationship with our own feelings and sensations is built.

Half a century after Dorothy Day's assertion that "we have all known the long loneliness and we have learned that the only solution is love and that love comes with community," Van der Kolk noted that all of us, but especially children, need confidence that others will know, affirm, and cherish us. Without that, we cannot develop a sense of control that will enable us to assert: "This is what I believe in; this is what I stand for; this is what I will devote myself to."

As long as we feel safely held in the hearts and minds of the people who love us, we will climb mountains and cross deserts and go forth and do great things. Children and adults will do anything for people they trust and whose opinion they value. But if we feel abandoned, worthless, or invisible, nothing seems to matter. Fear destroys curiosity and playfulness. In order to have a healthy society, we must raise children who can safely play and learn. There can be no growth without curiosity and no adaptability without being able to explore, through trial and error, who you are and what matters to you.

The Good News: The Brain Also Helps to Reverse Addiction

There is no question that addiction wreaks havoc on the brain. Addiction causes significant chemical, structural, and molecular changes that quite literally hijack the brain. However, treatment can reverse or counteract these effects. Additionally, as the recovery process proceeds, the brain continues to heal.

It is true that many changes occur in the brain after addiction takes hold. But we must also remember that the brain is a dynamic and ever-changing system. Changes to the brain's neural circuits, chemistry, function, and structures powerfully drive the addiction forward. However, a strong motivation to change, can just as powerfully counter these changes. People can learn new coping skills. They can practice behavioral modification techniques. These efforts will counter those damaging changes. Professional assistance can be enormously helpful as someone learns to overcome addiction's effect on the brain.

Abstinence from addictive substances or activities can lead to a reversal of many physical changes that occurred during addiction. Combination therapies such as medications with psychotherapy help the recovery process by managing the physiological effects of addiction and withdrawal. Cognitive-behavioral treatments work to mend and repair the psychological impact of addiction, but there is no substitute for the inner work necessary to identify and clear the forces and experiences that drive our addiction and the conscious repeating of new values, principles, and virtues necessary to change the structure, function, and neural pathways in the brain long enough to make them permanent.

It should be clear that the brain is really quite amazing. It has the capacity to control its own physiology and is highly adaptive. Each behavioral step we make forward has a beneficial physiological effect on the brain. A sincere effort to change behavior is a powerful tool that mends the damaged brain.

When we change our behavior, and find healthy outlets for satisfying cravings, we correct damaged brain function. These positive changes form new memory and behavioral circuits in the brain that strengthen and reinforce recovery efforts. Yes, the brain has changed because of the addictive process. Nevertheless, even people with severe addiction problems can succeed in overcoming their addictions, and many do so without any outside help. Motivation is the key.

Recovery from Addiction: Psychology of Motivation and Change

We have been talked a great deal about how people become addicted. We also talked about the changes that people need to make in order to recover from addition. However, it should be rather obvious that if it were just a simple matter of wanting to change, we suspect most addicted persons would be no longer be addicted. Recent research in the study of addiction has revealed that a primary component of recovery from addiction is motivation. So, where does the motivation for change ultimately come from? Perhaps the best answer we have comes from a study of individuals who recovered on their own, without any outside help without rehabs or twelve-step support groups such as Alcoholics Anonymous or Narcotics Anonymous. Studies of these folks suggest that self-change occurred when they decided the costs of their addiction outweighed its benefits. Stated differently, they recognized that they would lose something of great value if they continued engaging in their addictions. In other words, "Enough is enough!" People also needed a second ingredient: The belief that change was possible.

To achieve satisfaction with our lives, we must develop a sense of meaning and purpose, and we must know what we want, and how to obtain it. Oftentimes, there are competing and conflicting priorities. Nonetheless, we must make choices that optimize our life satisfaction. We give up some things in order to gain something else. Addiction recovery appears to be no different. Addiction and recovery are competing priorities, so we cannot have both. Many times, people feel conflicted about giving up their addiction. This is certainly understandable. People can strengthen their motivation to change. They do this by carefully evaluating the pros and cons of change in the form of recovery versus no change resulting a continuation of their addiction leading to ruin. As we will see here, this is exactly what people do who recover on their own. They weigh out the costs and benefits of their addiction, and they decide they will change because continuing simply is not worth the price. In other words, they work Steps One, Two, and Three of Twelve Step recovery, just as the forefathers of Alcoholics Anonymous or Narcotics Anonymous did.

Having decided to change, we need to figure out how to make that change happen. Some people have no difficulty figuring out they need to change and how to do it. These people recover without any outside assistance. For others, the decision to change is difficult, whereas the "how to" part is quite simple. This is Step Four of Twelve Step Recovery. These individuals might benefit from some guidance that helps them to accurately weigh the costs and benefits of their addiction. As we mentioned above, addiction disrupts our rational thought and judgment. Therefore, people sometimes have difficulty making an accurate appraisal. This does not mean they are "in denial." It simply means that they might benefit from some outside guidance. Motivational Interviewing might be a beneficial tool to help these folks. For other people, both tasks are challenging. The decision to change is a hard one and so is the "how to" accomplish change. These individuals will greatly benefit from professional and/or non-professional help.

But no two people are alike. Some people need no help to change, recover, and get well, whereas others need help in making the decision to change; but once decided, they need little further assistance. Still other people have difficulty with both the decision to change, and how to make that change occur. Addictions treatment should be fluid and flexible enough to match the specific needs of each person. Nevertheless, when a decision is made to change, the process of change is begun, no matter how that change happens, it takes about 30 days to make a change and it takes 12 to 18 months of conscious effort to that change permanent. So, no matter how change happens, people in recovery have to the time. Otherwise, the new behaviors extinguish very quickly, and we return to our old ways—relapse.

Now, let us move on to working the Twelve Steps of Recovery.

Chapter Five

Step One

We admitted that we were powerless over our obsessive compulsive learned helplessness; that our lives are unmanageable.

The Chinese philosopher Laozi once said: "A journey of a thousand miles begins with a single step," and so it is with the twelve steps of recovery from obsessive compulsive learned helplessness. The First Step is the beginning of the recovery process. Therefore, the healing begins here, but we cannot go any further until we have worked this Step thoroughly and honestly.

In the early stages of recovery, some people feel their way through the First Step by intuition; whereas others choose to work Step One in a more systematic fashion. But reasons for formally working Step One vary from person to person. It might be that you are new to this idea of discovery and recovery, and you have just fought and lost an exhausting battle with your obsessive compulsive learned helplessness.

It might be that you have been around awhile, but you have discovered that your distress has become active again in some other area of your life, such as drugs, alcohol, food, sex, pornography, searching for love, working, exercising, pain-seeking, cutting, hoarding, collecting, risk-taking, or shopping, forcing you to face your powerlessness and the unmanageability of your life once again. Often growth is motivated by pain or a crisis; so, it might be time to work the Steps thoroughly, beginning our journey to wellness.

Whatever the case, it is time to do some healing work, and engage in some specific activity that will help us find freedom from our distress, whatever form it is currently taking. My hope is that you will internalize the principles of Step One, to deepen your wellness, to make the principles of acceptance, humility, willingness, honesty, and open-mindedness a fundamental part of who you are.

First, you must arrive at a point of surrender. There are many ways to do this. For some of us, the road we traveled getting to the First Step was more than enough to convince us that unconditional surrender to the pursuit of wellness was our only option. Whereas others start this process even though they were not entirely convinced that they were powerless over their obsessive compulsive learned helplessness, or that they have really hit an emotional or spiritual bottom. Only in working the First Step do we truly come to realize that we are powerless over our obsessive compulsive learned helplessness, and that we have hit a bottom, and that we must surrender to this inescapable fact. Otherwise, the trauma-drama continues.

Before we begin working the First Step, we must stop all behaviors or activities associated with our obsessive compulsive learned helplessness whatever it takes. If you are new to the world of discovery, recovery, and wellness; and your First Step is primarily about looking at the effects of obsessive compulsive learned helplessness, you must regain your power and begin to manage your own life more effectively. If you have been away from the insanity of your obsessive compulsive learned helplessness for a while, your First Step might be more about your powerlessness over some other behavior that has made your life unmanageable, which is not at all uncommon, and you might need to find a way to stop the behavior so that your surrender is not clouded by your distorted thinking.

Denial

Denial a psychological defense mechanism in which confrontation with a personal problem or with an unpleasant reality is avoided by denying the existence of the problem or reality. Denial is the part of your condition that blocks that fact that you have a problem from your awareness. When you are in denial, you are unable or unwilling to see the reality of your condition and what impact it is having on you and others around you. Consequently, you naturally and instinctively refuse to acknowledge its effect. You tend to project the distress within you on to others by blaming them, or citing unreasonable expectations of families, friends, and employers. You compare yourself with others whose behaviors seem worse than your own. You might blame and condemn a person for their addiction, while ignoring or down-playing your own. Or you take on many of the characteristics of your abuser. If you have been around the world of wellness for some time, you might compare the current manifestation of your powerlessness, rationalizing that nothing you do today could possibly be as bad as that other person's addiction.

One of the easiest ways to tell that you are in denial is when you find yourself giving plausible, but untrue reasons or excuses for your behavior.

Answer the following questions:

- Have you given plausible, but untrue reasons or justifications for your behavior?
- What have they been?
- Have you compulsively acted on an obsession, and then acted as if you had actually planned to act that way?
- When were those times?
- How have you blamed other people for your behavior?

- How have you compared your insane cycle of obsessive compulsive learned helplessness with others who suffer from obsessive compulsive learned helplessness?

- Is your powerlessness over your obsessive compulsive learned helplessness "bad enough" if you do not compare it to anyone else's?

- Are you comparing the current manifestation of your behavior to the way your life was before?

- Are you plagued by the idea that you should have known better?

- Have you been thinking that you have enough information about your condition to get your behavior under control before it gets out of hand?

- Are you avoiding action because you are afraid you will feel shame when you face the results of your obsessive compulsive learned helplessness?

- Are you avoiding action because you are worried about what others might think?

Hitting Bottom: Despair and Isolation

Our powerlessness over our obsessive compulsive learned helplessness brings us to a place where we can no longer deny the nature of our problem. All the lies, rationalizations, and illusions fall away as we stand face-to-face with what our lives have become. We realize that we have been living without hope. We find that we have become friendless or so completely disconnected that our relationships are but a sham, a parody of love and intimacy. Although it might seem that all is lost when we find ourselves in this state, the truth is that we must pass through this place before we can embark upon our journey of discovery.

Answer the following questions:

- What crisis brought you to this point?

- What situation led you to formally work Step One?

- When did you first recognize that your powerlessness over obsessive compulsive learned helplessness was a problem?

- Did you try to correct it?
- If so, how?
- If not, why not?

Powerlessness

The first part of this Step refers your powerlessness over your obsessive compulsive learned helplessness when you engage in it. Powerless over your obsessive compulsive learned helplessness means that you have less power over your relationships; what you do when you are in these relationships to maintain your learned helplessness; and what you do after you end a codependent relationship. But it does not mean that you are totally powerless over all people or life events. To the contrary, you are a powerful being who has been designed perfectly and commanded by your Creator or a Power greater than you to have control or dominion over your life and your world.

The truth is that you were powerful enough to come up with a protective strategy to protect yourself from a real or imaginary threat by developing a normal and natural adaptive process, namely your obsessive compulsive learned helplessness, and so, what is your obsessive compulsive learned helplessness doing for you; not what it is doing to you. So, the primary question is: How can you be so competent in most areas of your life but be a total train wreck in areas that involve relationships?

But an admission that your obsessive compulsive learned helplessness has defeated you is essential in order to recover from this condition that has the earmarks of an addiction. Obsessive compulsive learned helplessness has beat you, so now it is time to beat it. The forefathers and pioneers of Alcoholics Anonymous devoted 51 pages in the Alcoholics Anonymous text, known as the "Big Book," to the surrender process, which is to admit your powerlessness over your obsessive compulsive learned helplessness.

The forefathers and pioneers of Alcoholics Anonymous begin by describing the physical and mental symptoms of alcohol addiction which, of course, applies equally to obsessive compulsive learned helplessness, as well as all addictions. The physical and mental aspects of addiction are thoroughly described by the forefathers and pioneers of Alcoholics Anonymous in the chapter of the "Big Book" entitled: "The Doctor's Opinion." It should be noted that much of this chapter is based on two letters written in the late 1930s by Dr. William Silkworth, a physician at Towns Hospital in New York City, who treated Bill Wilson, co-founder of Alcoholics Anonymous. In the late 1930s, very little was known about addiction to alcohol and drugs, and even less on other addictions like obsessive compulsive learned helplessness, but much of what Dr. Silkworth wrote is still very relevant and true today.

The forefather sand pioneers of Alcoholics Anonymous related how Dr. Silkworth described how Bill Wilson, co-founder of Alcoholics Anonymous, a once respected Wall Street stock broker and analyst, who had lost everything due to his drinking, recovered from alcoholism in 1934. They wrote that in late 1934, Silkworth attended Wilson who, although he had been a competent businessman of good earning capacity, was an alcoholic of a type Silkworth had come to regard as hopeless.

Dr. Silkworth went on to say that in the course of Wilson's fourth treatment, he acquired certain ideas concerning a possible means of recovery. As part of his rehabilitation, he commenced to present his ideas to other alcoholics, impressing upon them that they must do likewise with still others. This has become the basis of a rapidly growing fellowship of these men and their families. This man and over a hundred others appear to have recovered from alcoholism. Dr. Silkworth concluded by saying that he personally knew scores of cases who were of the type with whom other methods had failed completely.

Dr. Silkworth had been treating alcoholics for years at Towns Hospital with some success. Wilson was just another typical hopeless alcoholic, but on his fourth trip to the hospital in 1934, he discovered the solution to alcoholism with the help of a friend, Ebby Thacher, and went on to found the Alcoholics Anonymous program in 1935 with the help of Dr. Robert Smith, an Akron physician.

One important thing Wilson found was that in order to stay sober, he had to work with other alcoholics. He also learned that alcoholism was a physical disorder, as well as a mental illness, which only a spiritual reordering could overcome.

The forefathers and pioneers of Alcoholics Anonymous endorsed Dr. Silkworth's hypothesis on the physical and mental aspects of addiction. They wrote that the physician who, at their request, gave them a letter, that expanded on his views on addiction. In that statement, Silkworth confirmed what those who had been suffering the devastation of alcohol addiction believed: the mind and body of the alcoholic is quite as abnormal compared to normal drinkers. It did not satisfy the forefathers and pioneers to be told that they could not control their drinking just because they were somehow flawed; that they were in full-flight from reality; or they were outright mental defectives. In our belief, any description of the alcoholic that leaves out these mental and physical factors is incomplete.

The forefathers and pioneers of Alcoholics Anonymous went on to relate Dr. Silkworth's theory. They wrote that they believed that the action of alcohol and drugs, as well as activities like sugar addiction on these chronic addicts was a manifestation of an allergy, and that the phenomenon of craving was limited to this class of drinkers, drug users, those who engage in stimulating activities like sex, or those who engage in obsessive compulsive learned helplessness, and never occurred in the average temperate drinkers, drug users, those who engage in healthy relationships with healthy people.

These types can never safely use alcohol, drugs, engage in excessive stimulating activities, or engage in any form of obsessive compulsive learned helplessness in any form at all. Once they form such a habit to feel better and they found that they could not break it, and once they had lost control over their use and became reliant on it, their problems piled up on them and their condition become astonishingly difficult to solve.

The forefathers and pioneers of Alcoholics Anonymous went on to say that men and women drink, use drugs, engage in stimulating activities, or engage in obsessive compulsive learned helplessness essentially because they like the effect produced by their "drug of choice," whether it drugs, alcohol, stimulating behaviors, or engaging in their obsessive compulsive learned helplessness—it helps them escape from whatever is tormenting them. The sensation of escape is so elusive that, although they admit that it is injurious, they cannot differentiate the true from the false after a time.

To them, their addicted life style seems normal to them. They are restless, irritable, and discontented unless they can again experience the sense of ease and comfort which comes from engaging in their obsessive compulsive learned helplessness. After they have succumbed to their desire again, as so many do, the phenomenon of craving develops, and they pass through the well-known stages of a binge, emerging remorseful with a firm resolution not to repeat their behavior again. This is repeated over and over, and unless this person experiences an entire psychic change, there is very little hope of they will recovery.

Nevertheless, the forefathers and pioneers of Alcoholics Anonymous understood Dr. Silkworth's difficulty in proposing a theory that addiction was an allergy. Silkworth wrote that doctors have realized for a long time that some form of moral psychology was of urgent importance to alcohol addicts, drug addicts, stimulating activity addicts, and this who suffer fro obsessive compulsive learned helplessness and its application presented difficulties beyond their conception. What with our ultra-modern standards and our scientific approach to everything, we are perhaps not well equipped to apply the powers of good that lie outside our synthetic knowledge.

The forefathers and pioneers of Alcoholics Anonymous went on to say that the doctor's theory that we have an allergy to alcohol, drugs, stimulating activities, and obsessive compulsive learned helplessness is interesting. The forefathers and pioneers noted that as laymen, their opinion as to its soundness might of course mean little. But as ex-addicts, we can say that

Silkworth's explanation makes good sense. It helps explain many things that that can not otherwise be accounted for.

Alcohol addiction, drug addiction, stimulating activity addiction, and obsessive compulsive learned helplessness appear to be a multi-faceted disorders that is made up of an allergy, a brain disorder, and a thinking disorder. The first part of this disorder is physical. If you are an alcohol addict, drug addict, stimulating activity addict, or a person who engages in obsessive compulsive learned helplessness, you are physiological and psychologically dependent on a substance, behavior, or person in order to function "normally," and therefore, become dependent on these external things where you become powerless over them when you start drinking it, using it, or doing it.

Are you allergic to a food or medicine, or is there something that you hate to eat? What effect does it have on you? Have you ever knowingly, deliberately used that food or medicine since you learned that you were allergic to it? What effect did your last obsessive compulsive learned helplessness have on you? Did you get into an obsessive compulsive codependent relationships again and again to maintain your learned helplessness, even after learning that you were allergic to it?

So, why can you control using foods and medications that you are allergic to, but you cannot do the same with your obsessive compulsive learned helplessness? The truth is that you do have control over it until you do it.

Regarding alcohol, the answer lies in how alcohol is broken down in the body. There is a phenomenon called craving that is caused by a chemical called *acetone*, which is one of the chemicals produced when alcohol is broken down in the body, primarily by the liver. In addition, *acetaldehyde*, which is related to formaldehyde, a chemical solution used to embalm people, diacetic acid (vinegar), water, sugar in the form of carbohydrates, and Carbon Dioxide (CO_2) are also produced in this process.

It should be noted that acetone and acetaldehyde are powerful poisons that build up to toxic levels in the bloodstream and cause flushed faces, headaches, and extreme nausea.

In 80% of the population, these symptoms pass quickly and are gone when the alcohol is out of the body, usually within a few hours. However, in alcoholics, the acetone stays around longer because in alcoholics, liver and pancreas function is at about one-third to one-tenth of the normal rate of normal people; varying as we get older. Because the acetone stays in the body longer, anxiety increases, producing a craving for more alcohol to moderate the anxiety produced in the body.

It should be noted that once you start drinking, you set up the condition of craving, which produces more anxiety, so you take another drink. Consequently, you now have twice as much craving and anxiety, so you take another drink to reduce your anxiety and feel better, and now you have three times as much craving and anxiety, and so on.

Let us take a closer look at this abnormal physical reaction to alcohol. Alcohol is a powerful poison, which the body rejects as a poison. The normal response to drinking alcohol is to have one or two drinks and then stop when the person is relaxed, but the reaction of the alcoholic is much different. For the alcoholic, one or two drinks are just a warm-up. The forefathers and pioneers of Alcoholic Anonymous stated that Dr. Silkworth found that alcoholics have one symptom in common: they could not start drinking without developing the phenomenon of craving. This phenomenon differentiates these people and sets them apart as a distinct group of drinkers. It has never been, by any treatment with which we are familiar, permanently eradicated. The only relief we have to suggest is entire abstinence.

Regarding drugs, the answer lies in how drugs are broken down in the body. There is a phenomenon called craving that is caused by a normal adaptation process in the brain that adapts to the presence of drugs and demands more drugs to maintain balance or homeostasis.

For most of the population, these urges to use pass quickly and are gone when the drugs are out of the body, usually within a few hours or days. However, in drug addicts, the chemicals in the brain that produce urges stay around longer, and so, the brain shuts off receptor sites in the brain, which cause powerful urges to use more drugs to maintain homeostasis.

It should be noted that once you start using drugs, you set up the condition of craving, which produces more anxiety or distress in the body, so you use more drugs. Consequently, you now have twice as much craving and anxiety, so you use again to reduce your anxiety and feel better, and now you have three times as much craving and anxiety, and so on.

Regarding your obsessive compulsive learned helplessness, the answer lies in how you manage anxiety or distress in the body. Like, alcohol and drugs, there is a phenomenon called craving that is caused by a normal adaptation process in the brain that adapts to the presence of certain stimulating behaviors and demands more of these behaviors to maintain balance or homeostasis.

For most of the population, the arousal and urge to engage in these behaviors passes quickly and are gone when we cease the behavior, usually within a few hours, but for the addict, anxiety and arousal remain at high levels, then suddenly drop off. This in turn produces a "let down depression" that produces a strong urge to engage a stimulating behavior like obsessive compulsive learned helplessness to bring you back to an aroused state and maintain homeostasis. Likewise, in stimulating activities like obsessive compulsive learned helplessness, the chemicals in the brain that produce urges stay around longer, and so, the brain shuts off receptor sites, which cause powerful urges to use more of theses behaviors to maintain homeostasis.

It should be noted that once you start engaging in these behaviors, you set up the condition of craving, which produces more anxiety or distress in the body, so you engage in more stimulating activities setting up a vicious feedback loop that drives your obsessive compulsive learned helplessness. Consequently, you now have twice as much craving and anxiety, so you use again to reduce your anxiety and feel better, and now you have three times as much craving and anxiety, and so on.

The forefathers and pioneers of Alcoholics Anonymous, as well as modern twelve-step programs and the addiction treatment industry, have adopted a belief that an addict, no matter what kind, can never drink, use drugs, engage in stimulating activities, or get into dependent relationships like a "normal" people can without dire consequences.

However, there is a second aspect to addiction that often confounds recovery. Abstinence might work if addictions of all kinds were just only a physical illness, but Dr. Silkworth found that addiction has a mental component as well.

In addition to the normal physical reaction described above, we have a mental obsession. Our unconscious minds tell us that we are okay, even as our addiction is bringing us closer and closer to powerlessness and instability. Sooner or later, some of us return to our addiction of choice despite our best efforts. What we are finding is that addiction is not the problem; the problem is the problem. As a result, an addict can sober up easily enough, but if they do not undo the forces that lie under and drive their addiction; they will always return to it, consequently confounding themselves and those around them.

The forefathers and pioneers of Alcoholics Anonymous noted that Silkworth observed that men and women drink essentially because they like the effect produced by alcohol—escape. This is true with all addictions. To the alcohol addict, their alcoholic life seems the only normal one. To the drug addict, their drug addicted life seems normal to them. Likewise, to the obsessive compulsive codependent person or relationship addict, their life seems perfectly normal to them. But they are restless, irritable, discontented, and distressed by the forces that lie under their addiction, and unless they can again experience the sense of escape and comfort by engaging in their obsessive compulsive codependence or relationship addiction, they will remain tormented by their distress.

Furthermore, the forefathers and pioneers of Alcoholics Anonymous described how this mental obsession kills so many alcohol and drug addicts and disrupts the lives of other addicts. They wrote that it is not surprising that our drinking careers have been characterized by countless vain attempts to prove we could drink like other people. The idea that somehow, someday we will control and enjoy our drinking like other normal drinkers is the great obsession of every abnormal drinker. The persistence of this illusion is astonishing. Many of us pursue it to the gates of insanity or death. Likewise, this is true of all addicts including people with obsessive compulsive learned helplessness. Stopping is not the problem; it is staying stopped. Likewise, this is common in all addictions including obsessive compulsive learned helplessness.

The forefathers and pioneers of Alcoholics Anonymous went on to emphasize that once the forces that drive our addiction are let loose and we consume alcohol, use drugs, engage in stimulating activities, or get into another mutually dependent relationship with an alcohol addict, drug addict, narcissistic person, or abuser to maintain their learned helplessness, the mental obsession to consume more alcohol and drugs; engage in more stimulating activities; or getting into another mutually dependent relationship with an alcohol addict, drug addict, narcissistic person, or abuser overpowers us, no matter how strong our willpower or our conviction is; and most of us cannot stop drinking, using drugs, doing stimulating activities, or getting into another codependent relationship once we start.

The forefathers and pioneers of Alcoholics Anonymous wrote that for those who are unable to drink moderately, the question is how to stop altogether. Of course this holds true for all kinds of addiction including obsessive compulsive learned helplessness. We are assuming, of course, that you want to stop your obsessive compulsive learned helplessness. Whether such a person can quit upon a non-spiritual basis depends upon the extent to which the they have already lost the power to choose whether they will use again or not. Many of us feel that we have plenty of character. There is a tremendous urge to cease our addiction forever, but yet, we found we could stop for short periods, but we could not stay stopped. Something kept driving us back into the darkness of addiction. This is the baffling feature of addiction as we know it—this utter inability to leave it alone, no matter how great the necessity or the wish.

And so, if our minds did not deceive us and tell us that it was okay to drink, use drugs, engage in excessive stimulating activities, or engage in an obsessive compulsive codependent relationships with another wounded soul to maintain our learned helplessness, we would never trigger the physical craving for more and more of these powerful addictive processes because we have an abnormal reaction of the body and an obsession of the mind, which dooms us to a miserable life, unless we change something.

The forefathers and pioneers of Alcoholics Anonymous stated that Dr. Silkworth wrote that after they have succumbed to the desire again, as so many do, and the phenomenon of craving develops, they pass through the well-known stages of addiction, emerging remorseful, with a firm resolution not to use again. This pattern is repeated over and over, and unless this person can experience an entire psychic change there is very little hope for their recovery.

Therefore, a prominent doctor in the field of alcoholism said that the medical community can not really help us, and have proven this many times by their inability cure this terrible malady. This best they can ever do is moderate it and treat the symptoms of the condition, but that is not a cure, it is a bandaid. Our only hope was a discovery of a new of life free addiction and the forces that drove us there in the first place.

In order to understand more about the physical and mental aspects of addiction, as well as a solution, which is essential for recovery and wellness, we need to explore Bill Wilson's story —co-founder of Alcoholics Anonymous.

As stated previously, Bill Wilson was a successful Wall Street stockbroker in New York City. In few short years, he lost everything, became unemployed, and a hopeless drunk. Yet, some people have difficulty relating to Wilson's story because he was such a low-bottom, hopeless drunk who continued to use alcohol long after it had become a problem.

The forefathers and pioneers of Alcoholics Anonymous described Wilson's progression into terminal-stage alcoholism and his admission that alcohol had become his master and beat him in the chapter of the "Big Book:" "Bill's Story."

Wilson wrote that no words could describe the loneliness and despair he found in his biter morass of self-pity. He said that quicksand stretched around him in all directions. He said he had met my match. He said he had been overwhelmed and alcohol was his master.

But Wilson could not stop drinking on this admission alone. In late 1934, an old high school friend, Ebby Thacher, visited Wilson. Wilson was drunk, but his old friend had been sober for several months. When Wilson asked Thacher how he stopped drinking, Thacher told Wilson that he got religion.

Wilson was shocked but let Thacher continue because according to Wilson, his gin would last longer than Thacher's preaching.

Thacher went on to explain to Wilson that he has found a group of people who rely upon a Power greater than themselves and who live based on the Guidance they receive from this Power. In 1934, this was known as the Oxford Group. In 1938, it became known as the Moral Rearmament.

It should be pointed out that the Oxford Group was a life-changing fellowship that saved thousands of alcoholics that was to become the foundation for the future Alcoholics Anonymous, which used Four Spiritual Activities.

These are:

1. Surrender

2. Sharing and witnessing

3. Restitution

4. Quiet Time and Guidance

As a result of their meeting, Thacher provided Wilson with the Oxford Group solution, and for the first time, Wilson understood that he could change his life by surrendering himself to a God of his understanding. Wilson made this surrender, but soon after, he was drunk again. Wilson checked into Towns Hospital in New York City, and there, under the care of Dr. Silkworth, was physically withdrawn from alcohol for the fourth time in a year.

While Wilson was recovering, he applied and practiced the Four Spiritual Activities of the Oxford Groups. The forefather sand pioneers of Alcoholics Anonymous tell us that Wilson made a complete surrender. In the chapter: "Bill's Story:" the forefathers and pioneers noted that Wilson wrote that there he humbly offered himself to God, as he then understood Him, to do with him as He would. Wilson said he placed himself unreservedly under His care and direction.

Wilson then shared his character defects with Thacher. Wilson wrote that he ruthlessly faced his sins and became willing to have his newfound Power, a God of his understanding, take them away. Wilson said Thacher visited him and fully acquainted him with his problems and deficiencies.

It should be noted that according to the Oxford Group, a sin was anything that separated us from God or from each other. They believed that selfishness was the cause. Therefore, we free ourselves from sin by joining our will with the will of the God of our understanding.

Then Wilson agreed to make restitution to those he had harmed, which was an important part of moving away from the problem of relying on self-will or selfishness toward the solution of casting aside selfishness and joining our will with that of the God of our understanding.

Wilson wrote that he made a list of people he had harmed or toward those he felt resentment. Wilson said he expressed his entire willingness to approach these individuals and admitting his wrongs. Wilson said he was never critical of them and set out to right all such matters to the utmost of his ability.

Wilson also practiced Quiet Time and Guidance. According to the Oxford Group, these activities were essential for establishing a two-way communication with the Spirit of the Universe.

Wilson wrote that he tested his thinking by the new God-consciousness within him and common sense would become a common sense. He said he would sit quietly when in doubt, asking only for direction and strength to meet his.

Furthermore, the forefathers and pioneers of Alcoholics Anonymous stated that Thacher explained to Wilson the necessity of witnessing to others. Wilson wrote that it was an imperative to work with others. Wilson said faith without works was dead and noted how appallingly true this was for the alcoholic. Wilson said that for if an alcoholic failed to perfect and enlarge his spiritual life through work and self-sacrifice for others, he could not survive the certain trials and low spots ahead. Wilson observed that if he did not work, he would surely drink again, and if drank, he would surely die, and so, then faith would be dead indeed.

When Wilson took the actions prescribed by the Oxford Group and had a sudden powerful spiritual experience or awakening, he experienced the fundamental psychic change that Dr. Silkworth talked about in "The Doctor's Opinion" in the book: *Alcoholics Anonymous*.

Wilson wrote that these were revolutionary and drastic proposals, but the moment he fully accepted them, the effect was electric. He said there was a sense of victory, followed by such a peace and serenity he had never known. He said that he felt lifted, as through the great clean wind of a mountain top blew through and through. Wilson said God comes to most men gradually, but His impact on him was sudden and profound.

Wilson's life was changed forever, and he never drank again, but it should be noted that although Wilson wrote the Twelve Steps of Recovery, he never really worked them; he worked the *Four Spiritual Activities* of the Oxford Group. Consequently, Wilson never the achieved the level of wellness most others in Alcoholics Anonymous achieved. He was and remained an unreformed and unrestrained sex addict who engaged many sexual acting out episodes before and after his time in Alcoholics Anonymous. Wilson cheated on wife continuously and was a notorious womanizer. Wilson was a heavy coffee drinker; a heavy smoker; was heavily into LSD; and he was into the occult.

Can you concede to your innermost self that you are powerless over your obsessive compulsive learned helplessness? Note here, that addiction in any form has no power over you unless you do it.

The second part of our disorder is related to brain chemistry and brain function and structure. When you engage in your obsessive compulsive learned helplessness for long enough, the function and structure of your brain is dramatically changed, and you become dependent on the behavior to function "normally" or to maintain a status quo or homeostasis. So, when you suddenly stop your obsessive compulsive learned helplessness, you began to experience withdrawal symptoms including anxiety, jitteriness, irritability, nausea, restlessness, headaches, insomnia, dehydration, and emotional reactivity, because these behaviors interfere with the production and release of chemicals in your brain that effect electrical activity, which control your judgment, movement, senses, breathing, heart rate, temperature control, fluid retention, and how you experience pleasure.

It should be noted that one you cease your obsessive compulsive learned helplessness, abnormalities in your brain persist for months causing feelings of discomfort or anxiety which can trigger a desire to relieve these feelings with the only means that you know works for you— engaging in your obsessive compulsive learned helplessness. Nevertheless, once your brain function and structure is altered, it remains altered for as long as you allow it to remain so. So, in other words, once you have introduced these behaviors into your brain in enough quantity and intensity and trained the brain and body to use the effects of these behaviors to moderate your distress, your brain adapts to their presence, and becomes dependent on it to moderate distress and maintain status quo or homeostasis.

However, when you engage in your obsessive compulsive learned helplessness, your brain reacts by demanding more obsessive compulsive codependent relationships with wounded souls in order to function "normally" and maintain your learned helplessness, which causes craving, accompanied by withdrawal symptoms when you are not engaging in your obsessive compulsive learned helplessness, a reaction to the loss of stimulation, known as Post-Intoxication Syndrome or hangover.

But this is not a permanent condition. Current science shows that the brain is plastic, and so, although it can be transformed into an addicted brain, it can be transformed back into a well brain. So, the idea that you have a fatal incurable disease that you will never recover from is a myth. The fact is that as the forefathers and pioneers of alcoholics Anonymous well knew. So, the truth is you can be cured.

Can you concede to your innermost self that you have dramatically altered your brain function and structure, which has caused you to engage in your obsessive compulsive learned helplessness.

The third part of our disorder is a thinking problem. In fact, most literature on addiction suggests that it is the major problem. To begin with, you have a mental defense against most things or people that cause you anxiety or distress, which is part of your self-preservation and survival instincts. In the case of obsessive compulsive learned helplessness, this defense is particularly strong because you have become sensitized to anxiety and distress when you engage in too much obsessive compulsive learned helplessness, you will avoid it all costs. Consequently, you keep going back to your obsessive compulsive learned helplessness to maintain your it, even after experiencing many negative and sometimes painful consequences as result of it.

Do you know why? The answer lies in the structure of the mind. We have three parts of our mind: (1) the conscious part, which is the aware and awake state of our being, and (2) the subconscious, which is the working memory between the conscious mind and the unconscious mind; and (3) the unconscious part which is the state of our being which is beneath our awareness. It should be noted that even though we have no conscious awareness of this, it still dramatically influences our thinking, beliefs, and behavior.

For example, your unconscious mind might say: "I want to eat a pint of ice cream because it makes me feel better," but if you resist, you begin experiencing tension or distress, which the body considers a threat, so your unconscious mind deals with the threat by compelling you to engage in your obsessive compulsive learned helplessness to escape. Therefore, the unconscious often has much more influence over your behavior than your conscious mind, but what results is complex.

Another example is: a person in his 50s was stung numerous times when he was a child by wasps jumps in panic when a fly buzzes by his ear. Is it normal for him to jump when a fly buzzes by his ear? Yes. Does he understand why he jumps? No, because somewhere in his unconscious mind and body (body memories) is a record of the pain he experienced long ago, which is beneath his awareness in his unconscious. Yet, it still causes him to react in a defensive way when a stimulus occurs that reminds him of the original attack. Nevertheless, it should be noted that even when he becomes consciously aware of why he jumps, he will continue react the same way, until he understands why he responds so through working through the original incident.

What lies in your unconscious mind? You might think that you would not know because it is beneath your level of awareness, but what lies here has a profound effect on your behavior. It should be noted that in your unconscious is stored a memory of every repressed thought, idea, emotion, experience, belief, value, attitude, trauma, and hurt you have ever experienced, and those, not our conscious mind, determine how you really think, feel, believe, and behave.

Therefore, if you are going to stop being self-destructive and reacting to your distress, hurt, pain, and anger, as well as those memories in your unconscious mind that make you restless, irritable, and discontented, by escaping from them by getting into recurrent obsessive compulsive codependent relationships, you should understand what is in your unconscious by examining your behavior in the here and now, not the past.

Let us review. The main problem seems to be that there are memories, beliefs, and rules in your unconscious mind, which you do not even know are there because they are beneath your awareness, but really do influence your behavior, the way you think, the beliefs you have, and the emotions you experience.

For instance, a person with obsessive compulsive learned helplessness might say using their conscious mind: "I don't want to get into a codependent relationship with an addict again because I always loose," but their unconscious mind has a record of all those times when they were so irritable, restless, and discontented when they were not getting involved in a codependent relationship with and addict, narcissistic person, sociopath, or abuser caused by their hurt feelings, pain, boredom, anger, resentment, and bitterness. Consequently, the mind and body cause significant craving or urges to engage in some kind of obsessive compulsive obsessive compulsive learned helplessness to discharge the pent up distress, and so, you act out on your urge, even when your conscious mind realizes that avoiding these behaviors has stopped working and is now becoming a problem. However, your unconscious mind is driven by a different motive—to feel better.

As people who are powerless over their obsessive compulsive learned helplessness, we react to the word "powerless" in a variety of ways. Some of us recognize that a more accurate description of our situation simply could not exist, and we readily admit our powerlessness with a sense of relief. Whereas others might recoil at the word, connecting it with weakness or believing that it indicates a character defect or deficiency. Understanding powerlessness, and how admitting that you are powerlessness over your obsessive compulsive learned helplessness is essential to your recovery, will help you get over any negative feelings you might have about the concept.

We are powerless when the driving force in our life is beyond our control. Your powerlessness over your obsessive compulsive learned helplessness certainly qualifies as such an irresistible, sometimes uncontrollable, driving force. You cannot moderate or control your need to engage in your obsessive compulsive learned helplessness, as well as other compulsive behaviors, even when they are causing you to lose the things that matter most to you. And so, you cannot stop, even when to continue would surely result in irreparable mental, emotional, physical, social, and economic damage. Remember: once your condition sets upon you; no human power can resist it—it takes over.

As a result, you find yourself doing things that you would never do if you were not engaging in your obsessive compulsive learned helplessness; things that make you shudder with shame when you think of them. You might even decide that you really do want to get into some kind of obsessive compulsive learned helplessness, but you realize that you are simply unable to stop even when the opportunity presents itself because other forces are driving your overwhelming desire to escape.

You might have tried to stop your incessant need to engage in your obsessive compulsive learned helplessness, perhaps with some success, for a period of time without a program of wellness, only to find that your untreated condition eventually took you right back to where you were before.

In order to work the First Step, you need to prove to yourself on a deep level that you are truly powerless over our obsessive compulsive codependence or relationship addiction.

Answer the following questions:

- Over what, exactly, are you powerless?
- Have done you things in as a result of your need to engage in obsessive compulsive learned helplessness that you would never do in recovery and wellness?
- What were they?
- What things have you done to maintain your obsessive compulsive learned helplessness that went completely against all your beliefs and values?
- How does your personality change when you engage in your obsessive compulsive learned helplessness?

- Do you become arrogant? Self-centered? Mean-tempered? Passive to the point where you cannot protect yourself? Manipulative? Whiny?

- Do you manipulate other people to maintain your obsessive compulsive learned helplessness?

- If so, How?

- Have you tried to end your obsessive compulsive learned helplessness, but found that you could not?

- What were these times like?

- How has your behavior caused you to hurt yourself or others?

Unmanageability

The second part of the First Step relates to unmanageability. Unmanageability describes a state in which your life is crazy and out of control, which leads to overwhelming feelings unhappiness, anger, frustration, and sadness. Unmanageability also means that you do crazy, unpredictable things whether you engaged in your obsessive compulsive learned helplessness or not, as your life spirals out of control.

Was your life unmanageable because you engaged in your obsessive compulsive learned helplessness? Consequently, did you use your obsessive compulsive learned helplessness to relieve your anxiety or tension caused by your hurt, pain, anger, and distress, but subsequently lost your ability to control your obsessive compulsive learned helplessness? This is an important question to answer because it goes to the core of your problem.

It should be noted how Step One was written by the forefathers and pioneers of Alcoholics Anonymous. Please note that there is no "and" between the two phases in Step One. If the forefathers and pioneers of Alcoholics Anonymous had intended to say that your life was unmanageable because of your addiction, in your case, your obsessive compulsive learned helplessness, they probably would have put an "and" between the two phases, instead of a semi-colon.

Also note that First Step is written in the past tense. What does this mean? It means, as far as the forefathers and pioneers of Alcoholics Anonymous were concerned, they were no longer powerless over their addiction because they had stopped drinking, and so, alcohol no longer had power over them. The same thing is true for obsessive compulsive learned helplessness. You are no longer powerless over your addiction because you stopped engaging in your obsessive compulsive learned helplessness, and so, it no longer has power over you, and cannot have power over you unless you pick it up again.

The unmanageability of our lives stems from four core areas that underlie all forms of our unmanageability: lack of power, lack of praise, lack of pleasure, and lack of safety. And so, if we have any one or combination of these, we will try to overcompensate for these "holes on our soul" out of self-preservation, leading to all sorts of confounding behaviors which lead to an unmanageable life.

The First Step asks you to admit two things: one, that you are powerless over your obsessive compulsive learned helplessness; and two, that your life has become unmanageable. Actually, you would be hard pressed to admit one without the other. Your unmanageability is the outward evidence of our powerlessness over your obsessive compulsive learned helplessness.

There are two general types of unmanageability: outward unmanageability, which is the kind that can be seen by others; and inner, or personal, unmanageability. Outward unmanageability is obviously identified by powerlessness over your obsessive compulsive learned helplessness and the problems related to it. Some of us have never been unable to sustain any kind of relationship for more than a few months because of our obsessive compulsive need to be involved in other activities such as our obsessive compulsive learned helplessness, whereas some of us have been cut off from our families, and they have asked us never to contact them again.

Inner or personal unmanageability is often identified by unhealthy or untrue beliefs about ourselves—the world we live in and the people in our lives. We might believe we are worthless, whereas, on the other hand, we might believe that the world revolves around us—not just that it should, but that it does. We might believe that it is not really our job to take care of ourselves; someone else should do that for us. We might believe that the responsibilities the average person takes on as a matter of course are just too large a burden for us to bear. We might over or under react to events in our lives. Emotional volatility is often one of the most obvious ways in which we can identify personal unmanageability.

Answer the following questions:

- What does unmanageability mean to you?
- Have you ever minimized your obsessive compulsive learned helplessness?
- Have you ever done anything you could have been arrested for?
- What have those things been?
- What trouble have you had at work or school because of your need to engage in your obsessive compulsive learned helplessness?
- What trouble have you had with your family as a result of your obsessive compulsive learned helplessness?
- What trouble have you had with your friends as a result of your obsessive compulsive learned helplessness?
- Do you insist on having your own way?
- What effect has your insistence had on your relationships?
- Do you consider the needs of others?
- What effect has your lack of consideration had on your relationships?
- Do you accept responsibility for your life and your actions?
- Are you able to carry out your daily responsibilities without becoming overwhelmed? How has this affected your life?

- Do you fall apart the minute things do not go according to plan?

- How has this affected your life?

- Do you treat every challenge as a personal insult?

- How has this affected your life?

- Do you maintain a crisis mentality, responding to every situation with panic?

- How has this affected your life?

- Do you ignore signs that something might be seriously wrong with your health or with your children, thinking things will work out somehow?

- Describe.

- When in real danger, have you ever been either indifferent to that danger or somehow unable to protect yourself?

- Describe.

- Have you ever harmed someone as a result of your obsessive compulsive learned helplessness?

- Describe.

- Do you have temper tantrums or react to your feelings in other ways that lower your self-respect or sense of dignity?

- Describe.

- Did you take drugs, act out sexually, gamble, or engage in risky activities to change or suppress your feelings?

- What were you trying to change or suppress?

In order to answer these questions, you must look at your childhood, adolescence, and young adult years to determine whether your unmanageability began early in your life and discover the circumstances that led to the condition of unmanageability that led you to out of control desire to engage in your obsessive compulsive learned helplessness to relieve your anxiety in order to define the problem. It should be noted that your obsessive compulsive learned helplessness is not the problem; the problem is the problem. The forefathers and pioneers of Alcoholics Anonymous tell us exactly what we must do to admit that we were powerless over our addiction; that are lives had become unmanageable.

They write that we learned that we had to fully concede to our innermost selves that we were addicts. This is the first step in recovery. The delusion that we are like other people, or presently may be, must be smashed.

In order to smash the delusion that you are not an addict, I am going to ask you to answer a simple question: Are you ready to concede to your innermost self that you are powerless over your obsessive compulsive learned helplessness? In other words, are you a person with obsessive compulsive learned helplessness? If you are not convinced that you are a person with obsessive compulsive learned helplessness, or you believe that your life is not unmanageable, this program is obviously not for you. Throw this book away and your misery will be cheerfully refunded. Nonetheless, you should know that even though you might be here by mistake, would it not be better to be in a recovery fellowship by mistake, or be outside it living a miserable existence in a never ending string of obsessive compulsive codependent relationships to maintain your learned helplessness?

In conclusion, as you repeatedly failed to control your obsessive compulsive desire to engage in obsessive compulsive learned helplessness trying over and over unsuccessfully to master our environment with our dysfunctional thinking and beliefs, your unconscious mind keeps telling you a lie: it will be different this time, you will enjoy it this time, and you can control it this time. This is the insanity of your disorder. Of course, you believe the lies, and as with the fly mentioned above, you react to your unconscious mind, even though consciously you are aware of the serious consequences of your obsessive compulsive learned helplessness.

Can you admit to your innermost self that you have done insane things in the past, whether you were engaging in your obsessive compulsive learned helplessness or not? Can you admit to your innermost self that you have made some decisions that were probably not in your best interest and that you were unhealthy in mind, body, and soul, which was likely driven by your unconscious desire to avoid anxiety or distress?

The operative principle behind Step One is Honesty. If you cannot get honest about the scope of your problem; and that problem is not your obsessive compulsive learned helplessness, it is what underlies and drive the problem, and get honest about making a sincere effort to resolve these underlying problems, you will not succeed. The definition of honesty is: the absence of the intention to deceive.

~

Chapter Six

Step Two

Came to believe that a Power greater than ourselves could restore us to sanity.

The forefathers and pioneers of Alcoholics Anonymous give us an excellent overview of the recovery process. They wrote that for we have been only mentally and physically ill, but our soul has been sick. When this malady of the soul is overcome, we straighten out mentally and physically. Therefore, our goal is to correct the malady of the soul that has cut us off from the God of our understanding or a Power greater than us and has doomed us, until now, to a living Hell. If you are soul sick, how do you overcome it?

Furthermore, the forefathers and pioneers of Alcoholics Anonymous tell us how it works. They wrote that rarely have we seen a person fail who has thoroughly followed our path. Those who do not recover are people who cannot or will not completely give themselves to this simple program, usually men and women who are constitutionally incapable of being honest with themselves. They are such unfortunates. They are not at fault; they seem to have been that way. They are naturally incapable of grasping and developing a manner of living which demands rigorous honesty. Their chances are less than average. Likewise, there are those who suffer from grave emotional and mental disorders, but many of them do recover if they have the capacity to be honest.

Our stories disclose in a general way what we used to like, what happened, and what we are like now. If you have decided that you want what we have and are willing to go to any length to get it, then you are ready to take certain steps. At some of these we balked. We thought we could find an easier, softer way. But we could not. With all the earnestness at our command, we beg of you to be fearless and thorough from the very start.

Some of us have tried to hold on to our old ideas and the result was nil until we let go absolutely. Remember that we deal with alcohol—cunning, baffling, and powerful. Without help it is too much for us. But there is One who has all power—that One God. May you find Him now. Half measures availed us nothing. We stood at the turning point. We asked His protection and care with complete abandon. Many exclaimed: "What an order! I couldn't go through with it." Do not be discouraged. No one among us has been able to maintain anything like perfect adherence to these principles. We are not saints. The point is, that we are willing to grow along spiritual lines. The principles we have set down are guides to progress. We claim spiritual progress rather than spiritual perfection.

Our description of the alcoholic; the chapter to the agnostic; and our personal adventures before and after makes clear three pertinent ideas: (1) that we were alcoholic and could not manage our own lives; (2) that probably no human power could have relieved our alcoholism; and (3) that God could and would if He were sought. Although this was written for alcohol addiction, it applies equally to all addictions, including obsessive compulsive codependence or relationship addiction.

The forefathers and pioneers of Alcoholics Anonymous tell us we need to experience a psychic change, an epiphany, a spiritual awakening. The forefathers and pioneers stated that Dr. Silkworth described the effect of this change on the alcoholic by saying that on the other hand, and strange as this might seem to those who do not understand, once a psychic change has occurred, the very same person who seemed to be doomed and who had so many problems he despaired of ever solved them, suddenly finds himself easily able to control his desire for alcohol, the only effort necessary being that required to follow a few simple rules.

What are these simple rules? They are trust in a God of your understanding or a Power greater than you; clean house; adopt a new set of values, principles, and virtues; practice these everyone, every day, everywhere; make restitution; and help others. Therefore, if we follow these guidelines, we will receive the ultimate reward—a spiritual awakening, peace and serenity, and a freedom for addiction and what sent us into addiction in the first place.

Now that you have admitted that you are a person with obsessive compulsive learned helplessness, let us look at what you have to do to recover and get well. The forefathers and pioneers of Alcoholics Anonymous tell us that if a mere code of morals or a better philosophy of life were enough to overcome alcohol addiction, or any addiction for that matter, many of us would have recovered long ago. But we found that such codes and philosophies did not save us, no matter how hard we try. We could wish to be moral and we could wish to be philosophically comforted. In fact, we could wish these things with all our might, but the needed power was not there. Our human resources, marshaled by our human will alone, are not enough to free us from the ravages of addiction.

And so, just a desire to be moral and ethical was not enough. We needed something else. We needed moral guidance and we needed to act. What is it going to take for us to find this Higher Power that the forefathers speak of? The answer lies in Appendix II of the "Big Book."

The forefathers and pioneers wrote emphatically that any addict capable of honesty facing their problems in the light of their experience can get well. We can only be defeated by an attitude of intolerance or belligerent denial. We find that no one need have difficulty with the spirituality of this program. Willingness, honesty, and open mindedness are the essentials of recovery.

The forefathers and pioneers of Alcoholics Anonymous tell us that it is our arrogance and shortsightedness that keeps us in the darkness of addiction and blocks us from the sunshine of the spirit. Bill Wilson, co-founder of Alcoholics Anonymous, had a great deal of difficulty accepting this spiritual solution to alcoholism because he was an agnostic who believed in a pragmatic, materialistic, and secular scientific approach to life, and became quite distressed when Ebby Thacher started talking to him about God.

Wilson wrote that despite the living example of his friend, there remained in him vestiges of his prejudice toward God. As an agnostic, if not a self-serving atheist, Wilson said that word "God" still aroused a certain antipathy within him. Wilson said that when the thought was expressed that there might be a God personal to him, this feeling was intensified. Wilson said he did not like the idea. He said he grasp such conceptions as Creative Intelligence, Universal Mind, or Spirit of Nature but he resisted the thought of a Czar of the Heavens; however, loving He might be.

Then according to the founders and pioneers of Alcoholics Anonymous, Ebby Thacher presented Wilson with a revolutionary concept. Wilson wrote that Thacher suggested what then seemed a novel idea. Wilson said his friend asked him: "Why don't you choose your own conception of God?" Wilson said that statement hit him hard. Wilson said it melted the icy intellectual mountain in whose shadow he had lived for so many years. Wilson claimed that he stood in the sunlight of a great spirit at last and It was only a matter of being willing to believe in a Power greater than himself. Wilson said he realized that nothing more was required of him than to make his new beginning. Wilson claimed that he saw that growth could start from that point. Upon a foundation of complete willingness, he might build what he saw in his friend Thacher.

This is how Wilson started his spiritual journey to a God of his understanding and lasting sobriety. Unfortunately, he never found wellness because although he did stop drinking, Wilson was truly free of his addictions, his abstinence from alcohol all began with his willingness to believe. Now, let us examine how the forefathers and pioneers of Alcoholics Anonymous describe their concept of God.

They asked us to set aside our contempt for spiritual principles and consider our own concept of a God of our understanding, whatever we conceive that to be. We begin to realize that just might be some validity to the Alcoholics Anonymous spiritual solution to alcoholism. They wrote that they found that as soon as they were able to lay aside prejudice and express even a willingness to believe in a Power greater than themselves, they commenced to get results, even though it was impossible for any of them to fully define or comprehend that Power.

As a result, the forefathers and pioneers of Alcoholics Anonymous tell us it is impossible to define God. So, we must stop trying to comprehend God, whatever we conceive that to be, with our minds and start accepting this Power with our hearts. They wrote that when we speak of God, we mean a God of your own understanding or a Power greater than you. This also applies to other spiritual expressions that you find in the "Big Book" of Alcoholics Anonymous, published in 1939. Do not let any prejudice you might have against spiritual terms deter you from honestly asking yourself what they mean to you. At the start, this was all we needed to commence spiritual growth, to affect our first conscious relation with God, as we understood Him. Afterward, we found ourselves accepting many things which then seemed entirely out of reach. That was growth, but if we wished to grow, we had to begin somewhere. So, we used our own conceptions, however limited it was.

However, sometimes we must take our lives to the very brink of disaster and look squarely in the eyes of death before we are willing to acknowledge the presence of a Power greater than us. But there is hope even for even the most stubborn amongst us. The forefathers and pioneers of Alcoholic Anonymous tell us that most of us eventually become teachable, despite our stubbornness. They wrote that faced with destruction, we soon become as open minded on spiritual matters as we had tried to be on other questions. In this respect, our addiction was a great persuader. It finally beat us into a state of reasonableness. Sometimes this is a tedious process. I hope no one else will be prejudiced for as long as some of us were.

Furthermore, the forefathers and pioneers made a powerful case for the existence of a Power greater than us. They wrote that when we saw others solve their problems by a simple reliance upon the principles and virtues of a righteous life and the Spirit of the Universe, we had to stop doubting this Power. Our ideas did not work, but the idea of a Power greater than us of our own understanding did.

The forefathers and pioneers of Alcoholics Anonymous tell that we must decide. We must decide whether we believe in a Creator, a Spirit of the Universe, Higher Power, Higher Consciousness, or a God of our understanding or not. They wrote that when we became addicts, crushed by a self-imposed crisis that we could not postpone or evade, we had to fearlessly face the proposition that either God as we understand Him is everything or He is nothing. This Power either is or is not. What was our choice to be?

The insanity referenced in Step Two refers to three areas of concern. First, it refers to the mistaken belief that you can engage in healthy relationships like normal people can in the full knowledge that when you do so, you cannot stop your obsessive compulsive learned helplessness, what you do while you are engaged in it, or predict the consequences of your actions. Consequently, not being able to realize the unconscious drives that underlie your behavior, you repeatedly engage in your obsessive compulsive learned helplessness over and over in a vain attempt to relieve your unacceptable anxiety and distress.

George Bernard Shaw once wrote: "The earth is the insane asylum of the universe." Pick up any newspaper or listen to any news broadcast, and the first thing that becomes apparent is that this world and the people in it are often not quite right, which means that many people, not just addicts, are somehow flawed. You might bristle at the thought that someone might accuse you of being flawed or dysfunctional, but perhaps you should look at your own behavior. It is true that our society has put people in insane asylums because they had irrational ideas or engaged in behaviors that were self-destructive, which could have been dangerous to themselves and others.

But is it true that you have consciously affirmed that you do not want to engage in more obsessive compulsive learned helplessness, but often have done just the opposite? So, is it clear that your thinking and behavior meets the classification of insanity? It is also obvious that you could not do anything about your crazy behavior because you are totally powerless, hopeless, and insane in the presence your obsessive compulsive desire to engage in learned helplessness, as evidenced by the fact that you have a brain that is dependent on it to feel normal and you have a thinking disorder.

Second, the insanity referenced in the Second Step refers to the opposite of wellness or wholeness. In order to function well, you need to be mentally, emotionally, physically, and spiritually balanced. But it should be noted that you cannot regain wellness if you never had it. In this case, you would have to discover wellness and wholeness by adopting a new set of values and principles that would promote healthy living.

Third, the insanity referred in the Second Step refers to the mistaken idea that you can use things on the outside of you to fix things on the inside of you. It simply does not work.

Furthermore, Step Two tells us that there is some mysterious power that millions of addicts before you, who are just like you, have found, which can help you stop believing the self-deception that you can be like normal folk some day and live a normal healthy life, and overcome the dysfunctional beliefs, perceptions, thoughts, and behaviors that made your life unmanageable even when you were not engaging in your obsessive compulsive learned helplessness. We are also told that this Power can restore you to sanity, which means wholeness or wellness, so that you can react sanely and normally to the stressors of life.

It should be noted that this miracle or epiphany happens automatically by the time you complete Step Four and if you have been diligent in rooting out the underlying causes of your life problems. The Power we speak of manifests itself in the form of sanity, or the wholeness of mind, body, soul, and emotions. More importantly, the Power you seek is the wisdom of God in the form of your own internal guidance system, which could guide you away from your insane, dysfunctional behavior, and lead you to sane, non-self-destructive way of life when you reconnect with it.

Can you admit that you have done some insane things when you are engaged in your sugar addiction, and under the influence of your dysfunctional thinking and beliefs, even when you were not engaged in them, that were harmful to yourself and others?

Can you concede to your innermost self that you are caught up in your obsessive compulsive learned helplessness; that your brain chemistry is seriously altered; and you have been living under the influence of a set of dysfunctional rules and beliefs that is in conflict with your own God-given integral values system, which leads to anxiety and distress, which subsequently lead to your obsessive compulsive learned helplessness?

Can you concede that an unmanageable life is an insane way to live? Can you believe that you need some power, other than your own selfish will, to help you detach from your resentment and bitterness, modify your dysfunctional thinking and behavior, and subsequently be relieved from the ravages of your obsessive compulsive learned helplessness?

Now, it is time to choose. The forefathers and pioneers of Alcoholics Anonymous give us some good orderly direction. They wrote that we needed to ask ourselves but one short question: Do you now believe, or are you even willing to believe, that there is a Power greater than you? As soon as you can say that you believe, or you are willing to believe, you are on your way to wellness. It has been repeatedly proven among us that upon this simple cornerstone a wonderfully effective spiritual structure could be built.

The Second Step poses a question that only the most egotistical, cynical addict would dare to question or ignore. Can you concede to your innermost self that there is some power in the universe that is greater than you?

Are you entirely willing to try to tap into a power that has saved millions from insane thinking and behavior, and come up with a new design for living that will result in a happy, manageable, and productive life?

The operative principle of Step Two is Hope. In order to engage in a course of recovery from addiction, you must have hope of success. If there is no hope, why try? Perhaps you have failed on our own, so how about enlisting some help? A way to instill hope is to realize that recovery is not a question of ability; after all, there are millions of people in recovery, but rather of persistence and application.

Whereas Step One strips us of our illusions about our powerlessness over our obsessive compulsive learned helplessness; Step Two gives us a vision and a hope for wellness. The Step Two tells us that what we found out about our powerlessness over our obsessive compulsive learned helplessness in the First Step is not the end of the story. Likewise, Step Two tells us that the pain and insanity with which we have been living is unnecessary. These torments can be relieved, and in time, you will learn to live without them through working the Twelve Steps of Recovery.

The Second Step fills the void we feel when we have finished Step One. As you approach Step Two; you will begin to consider that there just might be a Power greater than you—a Power capable of healing your hurt, calming your confusion, and restoring you to wellness.

Many people who are new to the program are puzzled by this step's implication that we have been insane. From acknowledging your powerlessness to admitting your "insanity" seems like an awfully large leap. However, after being around a program of recovery for a while, you might began to understand what this step is really all about. We find that our insanity is defined as: "repeating the same mistakes, expecting different results." We can certainly relate to that. After all, how many times have you tried to get away with something you had have never gotten away with before, each time telling yourself: "It will be different this time."

As you live the principles of this Step, you will soon discover how deep your insanity actually runs and you often find that it just scratches the surface. Some of us resisted this step because we thought it required us to be religious. Nothing could be further from the truth. There is absolutely nothing, in this journey to wellness that requires you to be religious or believe in anything religious. The idea that anyone might join us, regardless of their religion or lack of religion is fiercely defended by twelve-step fellowships. Members of twelve-step fellowships strive to be inclusive in this regard and do not tolerate anything that compromises the unconditional right of all people to develop their own individual understanding of a Power greater than themselves or not. This is a restoration of our spirit; not a religious program.

The beauty of the Second Step is revealed when we begin to think about what "a God of our understanding" could be. We are encouraged to choose a Power that is loving, caring, and most importantly, able to restore us to wellness.

The Second Step does not say: "We came to believe in a Power greater than ourselves." It says: "We came to believe that a Power greater than ourselves could restore us to sanity." The emphasis is not on who or what this Power is, but on what this Power can do for us. As we continue to work this Step, we discover that no matter how long our wellness has gone on and how far our insanity has progressed; there is no limit to the ability of a Power greater than ourselves to restore our sanity or wellness.

Hope

The hope we get from working Step Two replaces the desperation with which we came into to recovery and wellness. Every time we followed what we thought would be a path out of our powerlessness over our obsessive compulsive learned helplessness, whether it was medicine, counseling, or psychiatry, we found that they only took us so far, but none of these was enough for us. As we ran out of options and exhausted our resources, we wondered if we would ever find a solution to our dilemma, if there were anything in the world that might work. In fact, we might have been slightly suspicious when we first came into the world of wellness, wondering if this was just another method that would not work, or that would not work well enough for us to make a difference.

However, something remarkable occurred to us as we proceeded. There are other people who are powerless over their obsessive compulsive learned helplessness out there who lived just as we did, and as people who were powerless over their obsessive compulsive learned helplessness in recovery and wellness, they were free of their obsessive compulsive learned helplessness. We believed in them, and we knew somehow, we could trust them. They know the insane world of obsessive compulsive learned helplessness; not just the obsession with codependent relationships, but the despair of their powerlessness. These recovered and well people who were once powerless over their obsessive compulsive learned helplessness and knew these places as well as we do because they had been there themselves.

Our hope is renewed throughout our discovery and wellness. Each time something new is revealed to us about our affliction, the pain of that realization is accompanied by a surge of hope. No matter how painful the process of demolishing our denial might be, something else is being restored in its place within us. Even if we do not feel like we believe in anything, we begin to believe that we can be restored to wellness, even in the most hopeless times.

Answer the following question:

- What do you have hope for today?

Insanity

If you have any doubts about the need for a renewal of sanity or wellness in your life, you are going to have trouble with this Step. Reviewing your First Step should help you if you are having doubts. Now is the time to take a good look at your insanity.

Answer the following questions:

- Do you believe you can control your obsessive compulsive learned helplessness to escape your distress?
- What were some of your experiences with this, and how were your efforts unsuccessful?
- What things did you do that you can hardly believe you did when you look back at them?

- Did you put yourself in dangerous situations?

- Did you behave in ways of which you are now ashamed?

- What were those situations like?

- Did you make insane decisions as a result of your powerlessness over your obsessive compulsive learned helplessness?

- Did you quit jobs, leave friendships and other relationships, or give up on achieving other goals for no reason other than that those things that interfered with your wellness?

- Did you ever harm yourself or someone else in your mad dash to engage in another bout of obsessive compulsive learned helplessness to feel better?

Insanity is a loss of our perspective and our sense of proportion. For example, you might think that your personal problems are more important than anyone else's. In fact, you might not even be able to consider other people's needs at all. Small problems become major catastrophes. Your life has gotten out of balance. Some obvious examples of insane thinking is the belief that you can stay free of your obsessive compulsive learned helplessness on your own, or the belief that your powerlessness over your obsessive compulsive learned helplessness was your only problem and that everything is just fine now because you have stopped it. In the world of recovery, insanity is often described as the belief that we can take something outside us, such as alcohol, drugs, power, sex, food, or relationships to fix what is wrong inside of us, such as our traumas, fears, inadequacies, inferiorities, and insecurities.

Answer the following questions:

- How have you over-compensated or under-compensated for your perceived shortcomings?

- How has your life been out of balance?

- In what ways does your insanity tell you that things outside of yourself can make you whole or solve all your problems? Consuming alcohol to excess? Using drugs? Compulsive gambling, eating, or sex? Obsessive compulsive learned helplessness?

- Is part of your insanity the belief that the symptom of your powerlessness over your obsessive compulsive learned helplessness is your only problem?

If you have been free of your obsessive compulsive codependence or relationship addiction for a while, you might find that a whole new level of denial is making it difficult to see the insanity in your life. Just as you did in the beginning of your road to wellness, you need to become familiar with the ways in which you have been insane. Many of us have found that our understanding of insanity goes further than the definition of insanity. We make the same mistakes over and over again, even when we are fully aware of what the results will be. Perhaps we are hurting so bad that we do not care about the consequences, or we figure that acting on an obsession will somehow be worth the price.

Answer the following questions:

- When you have acted on your obsessive compulsive learned helplessness, even though you knew what the results would be, what were you feeling and thinking beforehand?

- What made you go ahead?

Coming to Believe

The discussion above provided several reasons why you might have trouble with this Step. There might be others. It is important for you to identify and overcome any barriers that could prevent you from coming to believe.

Answer the following questions:

- Do you have any fears about coming to believe?

- What are they?

- Do you have any other barriers that make it difficult for me to believe?

- What are they?

- What does the phrase, "We came to believe...," mean to you?

As people who are powerless over our obsessive compulsive learned helplessness, we are prone to wanting everything to happen instantly. But it is important to remember that Step Two is a process, not an event. Most of us do not just wake up one day and know that a Power greater than ourselves can restore us to sanity. We gradually grow into this belief. Still, we do not have to just sit back and wait for our belief to grow on its own; we can help it along.

Answer the following questions:

- Have you ever believed in anything for which you did not have tangible evidence?

- What was that experience like?

- What experiences have you heard from other people recovering from their powerlessness over their obsessive compulsive learned helplessness about the process of coming to believe?

- Have you tried any of them in your life?

- In what do you believe?

- How has your belief grown since you have been in wellness?

A Power Greater Than Ourselves

Each one us comes to recovery with a whole history of life experiences. That history will determine to a large measure the kind of understanding we develop of a Power greater than ourselves or a God of our understanding. In this Step, you do not have to have a lot of specific ideas about the nature or identity of this Higher Power. That sort of understanding will come later. The kind of understanding of a Higher Power that is most important to find in the Second Step is an understanding that can help you. We are not concerned here with theological elegance or doctrinal adherence; we just want something that works.

How powerful does a Power greater than you have to be? The answer to that question is simple. Your powerlessness over your obsessive compulsive learned helplessness is a negative power, without a doubt, greater than you are. It has caused you to abandon and disown your loved ones; it has overwhelmed your maternal needs to have and raise children; it has replaced your need for a meaningful career; and it has overwhelmed your needs for emotional, physical, and financial security. Your powerlessness over your obsessive compulsive learned helplessness has led you down a path of insanity and caused you to act differently than you wanted to behave. You need something to combat that, something at least as powerful as your condition.

Answer the following questions:

- Do you have problems accepting that there is a Power greater than you in the universe?
- What are some things that are more powerful than you are?
- Can a Power greater than yourself help you get well and stay well?
- How?
- Can a Power greater than you are help you recover?
- How?

Some of us might have a very clear idea about the nature of a Power greater than us, and there is absolutely nothing wrong with that. In fact, Step Two is the point at which many of us begin to form our first practical ideas about a Power greater than us, if we have not done so already. Many people who are powerless over their obsessive compulsive learned helplessness have found it helpful to identify what a Power greater than them is not before identifying what it is. In looking at what a Power greater than us can do for us might help us begin to discover more about this Power.

There are many understandings of a Power greater than us that we can develop. We can think of it as the power of sound spiritual principles that all religions uphold as moral excellence, God, Jesus Christ, "Good Orderly Direction," or anything else of which we can conceive of, as long as it is loving and caring and more powerful than we are or our condition. As a matter of fact, you do not have to have any understanding at all of a Power greater than you to be able to use this Power to stay clean and seek wellness.

Answer the following questions:

- What evidence do you have that a Power greater than you is working in your life?
- What are the characteristics that this Power has?
- What are the characteristics that this Power does not have?

Restoration to Wellness

The term "restoration" is defined as changing to a point of previous healthy functioning where engaging in healthy relationships is a normal part of our lives. We find that just as our insanity was evident in our loss of perspective and sense of proportion, so we can see sanity or wellness in our lives when we begin developing a perspective that allows us to make better decisions and allows us to act on our environment, instead of reacting to it. We find that we have choices about how to act. We begin to have the maturity and wisdom to slow down and consider all aspects of a situation before acting.

Naturally, our lives will change. Most of us have no trouble identifying the stability and wellness in our lives when we compare our healthy behaviors in long-term wellness today with our early days in the world of recovery and discovery with just a separation from our unhealthy codependence on relationships. All of this is a process, and our need for a restoration to wellness will change over time.

When you are new in a program of recovery and discovery, being restored to sanity or wellness probably means not having put up with the insanity of your obsessive compulsive learned helplessness anymore; when that happens, perhaps some of the insanity that is directly and most obviously tied to your own behavior will stop. You will cease your selfish behavior and you will cease putting yourself in certain degrading situations that serve no purpose but your own selfish need to avoid the sum of all human fears for you—real or perceived rejection, loss or lack of attachment, abandonment, being engulfed or possessed.

If you have been in the world of recovery and discovery for some time, you might find that you have no trouble believing in a God of your understanding or a Power greater than you that can help you stay centered, but you might not have considered what a restoration to wellness means to you beyond just separation from your obsessive compulsive learned helplessness. As you grow in your recovery, it is very important that your idea of the meaning of sanity or wellness also grows with it.

Answer the following questions:

- What are some things you consider examples of wellness?
- What changes in your thinking and behavior are necessary for your restoration to wellness?
- In what areas of your life do you need wellness now?
- How is restoration a process?
- How will working the rest of the Steps help you in your restoration to wellness?
- How has sanity already been restored to you in your recovery?

Some of us might have unrealistic expectations about being restored to wellness. You might think that you will never engage in your obsessive compulsive learned helplessness again or that as soon as you start to work this Step, you will behave perfectly all the time and have no more trouble with obsessions, emotional turmoil, or imbalance in your life. This description might seem extreme, but if you find yourself disappointed with your personal growth in recovery or the amount of time it takes to be restored to wellness, you might recognize some of your beliefs in this description.

Most of us have found that we gain the most serenity by letting go of any expectations we might have about how our recovery is progressing.

Answer the following questions:

* What expectations do you have about being restored to sanity?
* Are they realistic, or unrealistic?
* Are your realistic expectations about how your recovery is progressing being met or not?
* Do you understand that discovery and wellness happen over time, not overnight?

Finding ourselves able to act sanely, even once, in a situation with which we were never able to deal successfully before is evidence of sanity and wellness and a real triumph.

Answer the following questions:

* Have you had any experiences like that in your recovery?
* What were they?

Spiritual Principles

In the Second Step, we will focus on open-mindedness, willingness, faith, trust, and humility. The principle of open-mindedness that we find in the Second Step arises from the understanding that we cannot reach wellness alone; that we need help. It continues with opening our minds to believing that help is possible for us. It does not matter whether you have any idea of how this Power greater than you is going to help you; just that you believe that it is possible.

Answer the following questions:

- Why is having a closed mind harmful to your wellness?
- How are you demonstrating open-mindedness in your life today?
- In what ways has your life changed since you have been in wellness?
- Do you believe more change is possible?

Practicing the principle of willingness in the Second Step might begin simply. At first, you might just go to twelve-step meetings for people who suffer from obsessive compulsive learned helplessness and listen to other people who suffer from obsessive compulsive learned helplessness share about their experiences with this Step. Then you might begin applying what you hear to your own discovery. Of course, you can ask your mentor to guide you.

Answer the following questions:

- What are you willing to do to be restored to wellness?
- Is there something you are now willing to do that you were previously unwilling to do?
- What is it?

You cannot just sit back and wait to feel a sense of faith when working Step Two. You must work at it. One of the suggestions that worked for many of us is to "act as if" we had faith. This does not mean that we should be dishonest with ourselves. You do not need to lie to others about where you are with this Step. You are not doing this to sound good or look good. "Acting as if" simply means living as though you believe that what you hope for will happen until it does.

In the Second Step, this would mean living as though you expect to be restored to wellness. There are a variety of ways this might work in our individual lives. Many members suggest that we can begin "acting as if" by going to meetings regularly and taking direction from our sponsor.

Answer the following questions:

- What actions have you been taking that demonstrates your faith?
- How has your faith grown?
- Have you been able to make plans, having faith that your condition is not going to get in the way?

Practicing the principle of trust may require overcoming a sense of fear about the process of being restored to wellness. Even if you have been sober only for a short time, you have probably already experienced some emotional pain as you have grown in wellness. You might be afraid that there will be more pain or discomfort. In one sense, you are right about this; there will be more pain and discomfort, but you cannot grow without it. However, none of it will be more than you can bear, and none of it has to be borne alone.

If you can develop your sense of trust in the process of recovery, discovery, and wellness and in a Power greater than you, you can walk through the painful times that may lie ahead. You will know that what is waiting you on the other side will be more than just superficial happiness, but a fundamental transformation that will make your lives more satisfying on a deeper level.

Answer the following questions:

- What fears do you have that are getting in the way of your trust?
- What do you need to do to let go of these fears?
- What actions are you taking that demonstrate your trust in the process of recovery?

A Power Greater Than You

The principle of humility springs from your acknowledgment that there is a Power greater than you. It is a tremendous struggle for most of us to stop relying on our own selfish thinking and begin to ask for help, but when we do, we have begun to practice the principle of humility found in the Second Step.

Answer the following questions:

- Have you sought help from a Power greater than you today?
- How?
- Have you sought help from your sponsor, gone to twelve-step meetings, and reached out to other people who are recovering from powerless over their obsessive compulsive learned helplessness?
- What were the results?

Moving On

As we get ready to go on to Step Three, you will want to take a look at what you have gained by working Step Two. Writing about your understanding of each step as you prepare to move on helps you internalize the spiritual principles connected to it.

Answer the following questions:

- What actions can you take that will help you along in the process of coming to believe?
- What are you doing to work on overcoming any unrealistic expectations you might have about being restored to sanity?
- What is your understanding of Step Two?
- How has your prior knowledge and experience affected your work on this step?

As you move on to Step Three, a sense of hope is probably arising within your spirit. Even if you are not new to the world of wellness, you have just reinforced your knowledge that recovery, growth, and change are not just possible, but inevitable when you make the effort to work the Steps and get out of the way. You can see the possibility of relief from the particular brand of insanity in which you have most recently been gripped by your powerlessness over your obsessive compulsive learned helplessness. You likely have already begun to experience some freedom and you are beginning to be released from the blind pursuit of your insanity.

You have explored your insanity and have started to trust a Power greater than you to relieve you rom having to continue the same path. You are beginning to be freed from our illusions. You no longer must struggle to keep your powerlessness over your obsessive compulsive learned helplessness a secret or isolate yourself to hide our insanity. You have seen how a program of recovery has worked for others, and you have discovered that it is beginning to work for you as well. Through your newfound faith, you begin to achieve the willingness to move into action and work Step Three.

❧

Chapter Seven

Step Three

Made a decision to turn our will and our lives over to the care of God, as we understood Him.

The forefathers and pioneers of Alcoholics Anonymous began this Step by stating that being convinced, we were at Step Three. What are we convinced of? Having done Step Two, we have come to believe that a Power greater than ourselves could restore us to sanity or wellness.

Now, you must decide to put this Power to work. In other words, you must get out of the way and let the God of your understanding or a Power greater than you direct your life.

The forefathers and pioneers of Alcoholics Anonymous discuss self-will and the will of a God of your understanding or a Power greater than you, explaining that we are like actors trying to control every detail of a play. They wrote that the first requirement is that we be convinced that any life run on selfish will can hardly be a success. On that basis, we are almost always in collision with something or somebody, even though our motives are good. Most people try to live by self-propulsion. Each person is like an actor who wants to run the whole show, and is forever trying to arrange the lights, the ballet, the scenery, and the rest of the players in his own way to serve his own selfish needs or wants.

Does this sound like an addict? We always seem to be trying to prove to everyone that they would be better off if they did things our way. It is this selfish, self-centered behavior that has gotten us into trouble. In addition, the forefathers and pioneers of Alcoholics Anonymous tell us that we need to take responsibility for our selfishness and ask the God of our understanding or a Power greater than us to remove this shortcoming. They wrote that selfishness is the root of our troubles. Driven by a hundred forms of fear, self-delusion, self-seeking, and self-pity, we step on the toes of our fellows and they retaliate. Sometimes they hurt us, seemingly without provocation, but we invariably find that at some time in the past, we have made decisions based on self which later placed us in a position to be hurt.

The forefathers and pioneers of Alcoholics Anonymous went on to say that our troubles are basically of our own making. They arise out of us, and the addict is an extreme example of self-will run riot, although we usually do not think so. Above all, we addicts must be rid of this selfishness. Let it be known that the God of your understanding or a Power greater than you makes that possible if you get out of the way. There often seems no way of entirely getting rid of self without His aid and our action.

The forefathers and pioneers of Alcoholics Anonymous tell us what we must do is rid ourselves of selfishness. They wrote that this is the how and why of it. First, we had to quit playing "God." It does not work for us to be in control of everything and everyone. Next, we decided that hereafter in this drama called life, the God of our understanding or a Power greater than us was going to be our Director and we will join Him. He is the Principal; we are His agents. He is the Father, and we are His children. Most good ideas are simple, and this concept is the keystone of the new and triumphant arch through which we now pass to freedom. When we sincerely take such a position, all sorts of remarkable things followed. We have a new Employer. Being all powerful, He provides us with what we need, not necessarily what we want, if we keep close to Him, stay out of his way, and perform His work well.

Contrary to what you might believe, the whole world does not revolve around you, and once you get your stuff out of the way, step aside, and put the God of your understanding or a Power greater than you in the center of your world with you, you will be amazed at how much better your life will become. In other words, when your selfish self is in charge, you drive the God of your understanding or a Power greater than you from you. To get well, you must join your will with the will of a God of your understanding or a Power greater than you; thus, bringing the God of your understanding or a Power greater than you back to you and joining together on your mission to wellness. So, now you know your place in the Universe, and you have become aware of the presence of a God of your understanding or a Power greater than you.

The forefathers and pioneers of Alcoholics Anonymous explain this awareness by telling us that established such a footing, we became less and less interested in ourselves and our selfish little plans and designs, and more and more, we became interested in seeing what we could contribute to life and others. As we feel new power flow in, as we enjoyed peace of mind, as we discover we could face life successfully, and as we become conscious of His presence, we began to lose our fear of today, tomorrow, and the hereafter. We are reborn as the children of our Creator.

It should be noted that the Step Three written in the First Edition of the "Big Book," published in 1939, is written somewhat differently than in later editions. It stated: "Made a decision to turn our will and lives over to the care and direction of God."

Please note that you are not turning your will and your life over to the care of a light bulb, a tree, a telephone pole, to Ralph, or to a group of people. Have no doubt about it; if someone turns their life over to the care of a tree, they probably has a mental disorder that might be beyond the scope and knowledge of Alcoholics Anonymous.

Regarding turning your will and life over to a group, many groups of people, especially twelve step recovery groups, are not very functional and tend to operate on a characteristic known as "Group Think." Group Think occurs when a group takes on the beliefs of its leader. So, turning your will and life over to the care and direction of a group of people leads to just another form of powerlessness called dependence—exactly what the forefathers and pioneers of Alcoholics Anonymous were determined to break.

Let it be known, the name of the power you seek is a Power greater than you, as you believe Him or It or it to be. This Power might be known as the Spirit of the Universe, Higher Consciousness, Higher Power, the Creator, Creative Intelligence, Universal Mind, Great Spirit, or the Great Reality, God, Jehovah, Yahweh, Jesus, Mohamed, Buddha, among others. This Power is all about us and speaks to us from our own divinely-given internal guidance system or spirit.

This idea might bother you if you were raised with the negative concept of an angry, vengeful, dogmatic, and punishing Judeo-Christian God; were raised as agnostic or atheist; or have rejected God because you blame Him for the wrongs of others did to you, or your own misadventures.

Yet, we are told that we must find a new, positive conception of a God of our understanding or a Power greater than us who is kind, forgiving, available to us, and merciful if we are going to discover peace and serenity. So, the opposite of a self-destructive and insane way of life is a spiritual life of peace and serenity. Therefore, the definition of a spiritual person is a person who has clear, right, and logical thinking.

Furthermore, we should discuss spiritual living, which is a sane and responsible way of life. But before we do this, we need to clear up a few misconceptions about what spiritual living is all about.

First, it is not about living a religious life. Although living a religious way of life is perfectly acceptable and might be preferred because this way of life gives us order and purpose and could be most powerful and restorative because it gives a sense of connection with others and a sense of significance necessary for a good life. Remember: the opposite of addiction is not sobriety; it is connections or the attachment to healthy others.

Secondly, those of us who have recovered from obsessive compulsive learned helplessness are miracles of recovered healthy mental and emotional health, not miracles of spiritual health, because your spirit, created by the Power of the Universe, whatever you conceive that to be, is the only part you have that is untouched by your insanity and dysfunction.

You have seen that the process of recovery is a deliverance from obsessive compulsive sugar use, and liberation from the conflict and insanity of a life produced by a value system that was imposed on you by your parents and society, which is not compatible with your own internal guidance system or spirit. So, you now possess the power to break the chains these thoughts and people have over you, and cease doing the insane things you did in the past driven out of resentment and bitterness. You have seen that breaking these chains will set you free to accept a Power greater than yourself and live a life of peace and serenity free of internal conflict, fear, and resentment.

Nevertheless, we are told that there is nothing incompatible between a spiritual existence and a life of sane and happy usefulness. However, we are not trying to turn anyone into a saint because we are human—fallible and prone to making mistakes.

To the contrary, we proclaim that we are not saints and never shall be in this lifetime. Yet, we have not had anywhere near the degree of stability in our lives that we would like. Consequently, we suffered anxiety or tension from emotional pain, hurt, uselessness, and unmanageability from our own internal conflict, which subsequently led to our misuse of sugar or sugar products and subsequent unmanageability and dysfunction to relieve our intolerable tension.

However, it should be noted that normal, spiritually-minded people typically demonstrate a degree of stability, happiness, and serenity, but the conflict between your integral value system and the one that was imposed on you by your parents and the environment that you were raised in caused you go through an insane, stressful life driven by your own self-will and selfish self. Yet, it should be noted that people who have a value systems that is compatible do not seem to suffer from the internal conflict seen in people from dysfunctional families; do not seem to suffer from the out-of-control behaviors like our obsessive compulsive learned helplessness to avoid tension or anxiety; and tend to be at peace with themselves and their world.

For 200,000 years, modern man has survived quite well in a dangerous world by living in accordance with their own internal guidance system, which is composed of survival instincts; defense strategies; instinctual drives; innate beliefs; values, and virtues; our relationship ideal; and our ideal life rules.

But in order to become a happy, successful, and sane human being, you must join your human will with that of a God of your understanding or a Power greater than you and connect it with your internal guidance system. This task is accomplished by resolving your resentments and conflicts with others; monitoring your selfish self; overcoming your fears, inferiorities, inadequacies, and insecurities; and clearing the wreckage of your past and getting out of the way. This opens us to the directions that lead to a successful life guided from the power of a God as you understand Him or a Power greater than you.

In addition, we are told that whether we engage in religious addiction or not, we are not able to manage our lives and we cannot meet the demands of daily life because our internal conflicts overwhelm us with tension, anxiety, bitterness, and resentment. Consequently, this leads us to our obsessive compulsive behaviors. Why?

The answer lies in the fact that you are running your life on a set of beliefs, values, and virtues that were imposed on you by your parents, which are not compatible with your innate, integral value system. Your values, beliefs, and virtues are held deep in your unconscious mind in a place known as the soul, the psyche, or the self. It should be noted that it is not about a desire to become perfect, or living a glum, austere way of life. Nevertheless, if you have an internal conflict, you will likely to engage in obsessive compulsive codependence or relationship addiction again in order to habitually relieve your tension and distress, resulting in powerless and destructive behavior.

Therefore, you will either find guidance from a God of your understanding or a Power greater than you to help you moderate your thinking and behavior, or you will be doomed to live the same miserable life you have lived so far. Henceforth, if you cannot resolve the forces that distress you and start responding to life with your own internal guidance system, which you have either ignored or that has been displaced by an alien value system, you will likely engage in your obsessive compulsive codependence or relationship addiction again and again to sooth your accumulating tension and distress. Furthermore, this matter is complicated in that you are haunted by and driven by hidden traumatic memories to escape from your distress whether you are engaging in obsessive compulsive learned helplessness or not.

We are told that twelve-step fellowships have freed millions of people from the insanity of addictions of all kinds by guiding them through the Twelve Steps of Recovery. People, who were once thought to be hopeless by themselves, their families, and others, can be restored to wellness. They can also be rewarded with the promised freedom from the effects of this cunning, baffling, and powerful disorder, if they work the Steps thoroughly and honestly.

However, there seems to be two groups that have great difficulty with recovery from the insanity of addiction: (1) those who are so stubbornly self-destructive that they refuse to work the Twelve Steps of Recovery, and (2) those who cannot or will not be honest with themselves. They seem to be in denial and cannot see a different view of things usually because of their bitterness and resentments.

Nonetheless, even though we encourage them to see their part in their past problems, they cannot or will not see their part in it, and often blame everyone else for their situation. Yet, millions of so-called hopeless addicts of all kinds have been relieved from their mental and physical malady; have had a spiritual awakening as the result of working these Steps; and have uncovering their own innate value system or internal guidance and walked free.

Furthermore, recovery seldom fails unless people do not work the Steps or are constitutionally incapable of being honest with themselves. Even people with co-occurring severe mental disorders can recover too, if they can be honest about what the problem really is.

Regarding atheists and agnostics, they too can recover if they can get in touch with the concept of a Higher Consciousness, Higher Power, Universal Mind, Wise Mind, or Creative Intelligence. Contrary to some beliefs, we do not have sick spirits because our spirit is the only part of us that is untouched by our dysfunction. We have a soul sickness.

The soul malady we suffer from is more like a muscle that has shrunk and grown useless due to disuse. Each of us has a spirit or Devine spark and a soul inside us that usually guides us through life. Additionally, this soul contains a set of innate values, beliefs, standards, and ideals that was placed in us when we were created.

It should be noted that you would not send a child to the store without guidance or directions. Likewise, God or the Spirit of the Universe would not send you here to navigate this world without guidance, but just as an unused muscle weakens, so does your innate internal guidance system.

As a result, if your innate value system conflicts with your imposed value system, then tension and distress will be produced, which is usually dealt with by some kind of defensive strategy or avoidant behavior, such as engaging in your obsessive compulsive learned helplessness to relieve anxiety or distress.

So, the Twelve Steps of Recovery give you a way to tap into your internal guidance system that has been lying under your imposed belief system and the wreckage of your past. Our experience proves this point beyond doubt. You could not stop engaging in your obsessive compulsive learned helplessness, even though your conscious mind says you are going to because many of your confounding behaviors, thoughts, and beliefs are in your unconscious mind, and therefore, are unavailable to your conscious mind or awareness, and as a result, you betray all your promised to quit angering and alienating all those around you.

However, dysfunction is not the exclusive domain of addicts. From a wider perspective, we can see dysfunction and insanity throughout our society, not just amongst addicts. Research has found that 96% of all families are to some degree "dysfunctional," where the system by which the family interacts is distorted by the addictions and compulsions of one or more members, and so, ignores the needs of each individual. It is the "don't trust, don't feel" rules in such families that lead the children into self-destructive patterns. It seems that most people think they come from a dysfunctional family.

Yet, we do not judge another person's insanity, nor do we get angry about it. We simply observe it, so we can remain vigilant, watching out for the return of our own misuse of pride and selfish destructive behavior. It can return with a vengeance when our selfish self returns to misguide us, rather than allowing us to be guided by our own internal value system. Why?

It is because our innate internal guidance system represents or our internal guidance system through which the will of the God of our understanding or a Power greater than us for us is shown and motivates us toward happiness, joy, and prosperity, whereas our selfish self drives us to the gates of insanity or death fueled by our own internal conflict, resentment, and fear.

Let us examine our human will. Our human will is the faculty of the mind that selects at the moment of decision a desire among the various desires present. It itself does not refer to any particular desire, but rather to the mechanism responsible for choosing from among our desires. In philosophy, the human will is important as it is one of the parts of the mind, along with reason and understanding. It is considered central to the field of ethics because of its role in enabling deliberate action and it is the ability to control our thoughts and actions in order to achieve what we want to do.

Let us also examine what was left out of Step Three by the man that wrote it, Bill W., that might help make this clearer. What Step Three meant to the forefathers and pioneers of Alcoholics Anonymous and what Bill Wilson could not have known because of his own extreme selfishness was: "We made a decision to join our will with that of God," instead of what he wrote: "Made a decision to turn our will and our lives over to the care and direction of God as we understood Him." The truth is that we do not and cannot surrender our human will or our lives to anyone or anything because these were gifted to us by our Creator and cannot be given away.

The reason Bill Wilson could not understand this concept was that he suffered from what is known as narcissistic personality disorder which is characterized by a need for leadership or authority; superiority; arrogance; self-absorbed; self-admiration; exploitative; and entitlement. People like Wilson with this disorder typically display:

- An obvious self-focus in interpersonal exchanges

- Problems in sustaining satisfying relationships

- A lack of psychological awareness

- Difficulty with empathy

- Problems distinguishing the self from others

- Hypersensitivity to any insults or imagined insults

- Vulnerability to shame rather than guilt

- Arrogant body language

- Flattery towards people who admire and affirm them

- Detesting those who do not admire them

- Using other people without considering the cost of doing so

- Pretending to be more important than they actually are

- Bragging and exaggerating their achievements

- Claiming to be an "expert" at many things

- Inability to view the world from the perspective of other people

- Denial of remorse and gratitude

The forefathers and pioneers of Alcoholics Anonymous realized that our human will was gifted to us by our Creator and could not be surrendered, and they realized that they had to surrender their selfish self, not their own human will.

So, the real problem is that you have been living a life run by your selfish self to avoid unacceptable anxiety or distress. That is, the unconscious desire to engage in destructive behaviors like obsessive compulsive learned helplessness to avoid anxiety or tension, even though your conscious rational mind tells you it is wrong, instead of following your own innate desire toward happiness, joyousness, and prosperity.

The traits of an unmanageable life, like those mentioned above, are really the traits of a poorly managed life because it is your destructive selfish self that has run amok. You have forgotten the notion of your healthy human will was gifted to you by the God of your understanding or a Power greater than you. You proved that you have no free human will when you got up this morning and your conscious mind said you would never engage in your obsessive compulsive learned helplessness again, but you did it again anyway. So, how is a life run on an innate internal guidance system, which represents your own human will coupled with the will the God of our understanding or a Power greater than you different from a life run by your selfish self? The following should help explain it:

God's Coupled with our Will	Our Destructive Selfish Self
1. Harm no one.	1. Harm people by lowering them to my level.
2. Be humble.	2. Feel important.
3. Let me be the judge.	3. Criticize and judge all.
4. Let me be in control.	4. Let me control everyone and everything.
5. Love all.	5. Fear everyone.
6. Serve all.	6. Use all.
7. Be still.	7. Be in motion.
8. You already have everything you need.	8. You do not have enough of everything and never will.
9. I will guide you—follow me.	9. I want to lead.
10. I will provide for you.	10. I will provide for myself.
11. I will change you.	11. I hate change.
12. I know everything	12. I need to know everything.

Since there is only our human will and the will the God of your understanding or a Power greater than you to motivate you, which of the two would you think was driving you when you acted out on your obsessive compulsive learned helplessness?

In review, your selfish self leads to fear, resentment, and insanity, whereas when your innate internal guidance system which is part of the the God of your understanding or a Power greater than you is joined with that of this Power, you will be lead to peace and serenity. It should be pointed out that within you is a perfect spirit or Universal Mind that represents God's Will or the Will of the Universe, or Nature which is untouched by your dysfunction.

However, as stated previously, you also have an external or imposed guidance system, which represents the values of parents, members of the clergy, teachers, other adults, our society, and our culture as a whole that was laid upon your internal value system in your unconscious mind over your life. This external guidance system is not present at birth. It is imposed on your unconscious mind as a set of rules, beliefs, and standards through rewards and punishments, which are often in conflict with your innate values, beliefs, standards, and ideals.

As a result, these imposed beliefs make you do things and feel things that you might not like, which consequently lead to rebelliousness, defiance, family conflict, and discord. This is called the selfish self or self-will run amok.

For instance, since our society is a "can't ever get enough" kind of society, this message is imprinted in our unconscious mind. Therefore, a person who is driven by selfishness will can never be happy. This internalized message also trains you to believe in the Principle of Scarcity, which states that you will not have enough, or you are not good enough. This causes you to either be crushed by raging insecurity or poor self-esteem or become obsessively driven to get more and more of everything.

Therefore, in working Step Three, you are admitting three things: (1) you have tried to manage your life with a value system that is not yours and it is not working; (2) you have an alien value system within you that is in conflict with your own innate God-given value system; and (3) your selfish self has resulted in a terrible mess of your own making and the only rational way to undue it is to cast aside your alien value system, reclaim your own innate value system, and join your will that of a God of your understanding or a Power greater than you as directed through your own internal guidance system.

So, the Step Three question is this: Are you willing to do Steps Four through Nine in order to seek new management in your life that will rid you of your selfish self that has run amok; rid you of your insane, destructive behaviors; and rid you of your unmanageable life?

Having done Step Three, realize that you can manage your life with the direction and guidance the God of your understanding or a Power greater than you, and you will know peace, serenity, and prosperity, no matter how far down the road of addiction you have gone.

Realize that you and this Power can handle life's problems together if you will get out of the way.

Realize that this Power will never abandon you, as people in your life have, and will do so again. Did it ever occur to you that perhaps He left you alone in the crucible of your resentment and bitterness until you decided to surrender and call on Him after having been insanely self-destructive and hurting yourself and others long enough?

Realize that the God of your understanding or a Power greater than you can and will take away your insane behavior that has brought you so much pain when you clear the wreckage of your past and get out of the way. He forgives you and loves you, as you stumble through life, even if you do not believe in Him.

You have seen that whether you are engaging in your obsessive compulsive codependence or relationship addiction or not; you do not have the power to change your need to get rid of your distress; your brain disorder; or your thinking disorder. You have seen that your troubles are not from your obsessive compulsive learned helplessness, but are from the loud roaring conflict inside that has caused you to try to run the show yourself and use ever-increasing amounts of obsessive compulsive learned helplessness to quiet your anxiety and distress. Can you think of anything worse than living another 20, 30, or 40 years feeling the hurt, pain, anger, and stress of your unmanageable life? Now, that you have completed Step Three, let us look at how the founder affirmed their decision with the following prayer:

Dear God,

I am sorry about the mess I have made of my life. I want to turn away from all the wrong things I have ever done and all the wrong things I have ever been. Please forgive me for it all. I know You have the power to change my life and could turn me into a winner. Thank You, God for getting my attention long enough to interest me in trying it Your way.

God, please take over the management of my life and everything about me. I am making this conscious decision to turn my will and my life over to Your care and I am asking You to please take over all parts of my life.

Please, God, move into my heart. However, You do it, is Your business, but make Yourself real inside me and fill my awful emptiness. Fill me with Your love and Holy Spirit and make me know Your will for me. And now, God, help Yourself to me and keep on doing it. I am not sure I want You to but do it anyhow.

I rejoice that I am now a part of Your people, that my uncertainty is gone forever, and that You now have control of my will and life. Thank you and praise Your name. Amen

The operative principle of Step Three is Faith. Faith is defined as: the confidence in what we hope for and assurance about what we do not see. This stage of action is to begin to employ the recovery skills you are learning. You can seek help, but it is also necessary to utilize it. Your job is to become willing to do the right thing. A simple way to view the "next right thing" is do not engage in your behavior. Have faith that recovery will work.

You have worked Steps One and Two and you have begun the process of surrender. Likewise, you have demonstrated your willingness to try something new. This has charged you with a strong sense of hope. But if you do not translate your hope into action right now, it will fade away, and you will end up right back where you started. The action you need to take is working Step Three.

The central action in Step Three is deciding. But the idea of making that decision might terrify you, especially when you look at what you are deciding to do in this Step. Deciding any decision is something most of us have not done in a long time. Mostly, we have had our decisions made for us by our powerlessness over our obsessive compulsive learned helplessness or just by default because we did not want the responsibility of deciding anything for ourselves, least we be wrong. When we add to this the concept of joining our human will to something that most of us do not understand at this point, we might just think this whole thing is beyond us and start looking for a shortcut or a softer easier way to work our programs of recovery. These thoughts are dangerous, for when we take shortcuts in our program of recovery, we short circuit our wellness.

The Third Step decision might be too big to make in one leap for many of us. Your fears of the Third Step, and the dangerous thinking to which these fears lead, can be eased by breaking this step down into a series of smaller, separate steps. The Third Step is just one more step of the path to recovery from your addiction. Making the Third Step decision does not necessarily mean that you must suddenly, completely change everything about the way we live your life. That will come in time. Fundamental changes in your life happen gradually as you work on your recovery, and all such changes require your participation. You do not have to be afraid that this step will do something to you that you are not ready for or would not like.

It is significant that this Step suggests we join our will with that of the God of our understanding or a Power greater than us. These words are particularly important. By working the Third Step, you are allowing someone or something to care for you, not control you or conduct your life for you. This Step does not suggest that you become a mindless robots with no ability to live your own life, nor does it allow those of us who find such irresponsibility attractive to indulge such an urge.

Instead, you are making a simple decision to change direction, to stop rebelling at the natural and logical flow of events in your life, and to stop wearing yourself out trying to make everything happen as if you oversee the world. You are accepting that a Power greater than you will do a better job of caring for you and your life than you have. You are furthering the spiritual process of discovery and wellness by beginning to explore what you understand the word "God" to mean to you as an individual.

In this Step, each one of us will have to come to some conclusions about what we think the God of our understanding or a Power greater than us means. Your understanding does not have to be complex or even complete. It does not have to be like anyone else's. You may discover that you are very sure what the God of your understanding or a Power greater than you is not, but not what this Power is, but that is okay. The only thing that is essential is that you begin a search that will allow you to further your understanding as your process of discovery continues. Your concept of God will grow as you grow in your wellness. Working the Third Step will help you discover what works best for you.

Deciding to Decide

As we have already discussed, many of us might find ourselves unnerved by the thought of making a big decision. You might feel intimidated or overwhelmed. You might fear the results or the implied commitment. You might think it is a once-and-for-all action and fear that you would not do it right or could have to do it over again. However, the decision to turn your will and life over to the care of the God of your understanding is one you can make repeatedly, daily if need be. In fact, you are likely to find that you must make this decision regularly, or risk losing your recovery because of complacency.

It is essential that you involve your heart and spirit in this decision. Although the word "decision" sounds like something that takes place mostly in the mind, you need to do the work necessary to go beyond an intellectual understanding and internalize this choice.

Answer the following questions:

- Why is deciding central to working this Step?
- Can you make this decision just for today?
- Do you have any fears or reservations about it?
- What are they?

You need to realize that deciding without following it up with some kind of action is meaningless. For example, you can decide one morning to go somewhere and then sit down and not leave your home for the rest of that day. Doing so would render your earlier decision meaningless, no more significant than any random thought you might have.

Answer the following questions:

- What action have you taken to follow through on your decision?
- What areas of your life are difficult for you to turn over?
- Why is it important that you turn them over anyway?

Self-Will or Selfish Self

Step Three is critical because you have acted on your self-will or selfish self for too long, abusing your right to make choices and decisions. So, what exactly is self-will? Sometimes it is total withdrawal and isolation, where you end up living a very lonely existence; whereas sometimes, you live a life of excess and running amok. Sometimes self-will causes us to act to the exclusion of any considerations other than what you want. You ignore the needs and feelings of others. You barrel through life, stampeding over anyone who questions your right to do whatever you want. You become a tornado, storming through the lives of family, friends, and even strangers, totally unconscious of the path of destruction you have left behind. If circumstances are not to your liking, you try to change them by any means necessary to achieve your selfish aims. You try to get your way at all costs. You are so busy aggressively pursuing your impulses that you completely lose touch with your conscience and with a God of our understanding or a Power greater than us.

To work this step, you need to identify the ways in which you have acted on your selfish self.

Answer the following questions:

- How have you acted on your selfishness?

- What were your motives?

- How has acting on your selfishness affected your life?

- How has your selfishness affected others?

Surrendering your selfish self does not mean that you cannot pursue goals or try to make changes in your lives and the world. It does not mean you have to passively accept injustices to yourself or to other people for whom you love or are responsible for. You need to differentiate between destructive selfishness and constructive action.

Answer the following questions:

- Will pursuing your goals harm anyone?
- How?
- In the pursuit of what you want, is it likely that you will end up doing something that adversely affects yourself or others?
- Will you have to compromise any of your principles to achieve this goal?
- Will you have to be dishonest, cruel, or disloyal?

If you are new to a program of recovery and just beginning to work Step Three, you will probably end up wondering what the will the God of your understanding or a Power greater than you is for you, thinking that this Step asks you to find this out. You do not formally focus your attention on seeking knowledge of the will the God of your understanding or a Power greater than you for you until the Eleventh Step, but you do begin the process that will lead you to that point in Step Three. Most people in early recovery have a spiritual awakening of epiphany where of this between Step Four and Five.

A spiritual awakening is difficult to define with one word or phrase because it is different for everyone who experiences it, but there are some clear signs that you have had a personal and spiritual transformation in recovery. For example, you may portray some or all of the following characteristics:

A Clear Attitude Change

When you first started recovery, you were angry, defiant, uncooperative, and unwilling to change. Today, you are quick to admit when you are wrong; you calmly accept criticisms, both good and bad; and you are eager to share helpful advice with others. It is clear by your actions that your attitude has changed.

Personality Change

You have stopped labeling yourself as an addict, and instead, you have embraced your humor, unique musical abilities, and your ability to listen well. Your body language has morphed from stances that are closed off and rigid to ones that are open and relaxed.

Improved Outlook On Life Has Changed

Your perception of yourself and the world around you has completely changed. You recognize that you have received a second chance at life and you are eager to make the most of it. You accept both the good and the bad things, knowing that you will be able to handle whatever life throws your way without relying on obsessive compulsive learned helplessness keep you afloat.

Increased Ability to Share and Feel Emotions

Before you got sober, you were unable to admit your feelings and emotions to yourself, let alone anyone else. In sobriety, you discovered the power of feeling, expressing, and sharing those emotions and how working through them improved the overall quality of your life.

Overall Improved Well-being

In your addiction, you felt numb, anxious, and depressed all the time. Now you feel alive, fulfilled, full of purpose, and energetic, despite what is going on around you in the world.

God's will for you is something you will gradually come to know as you work these steps. At this point, you can come to some very simple conclusions about the will of a God of your understanding or a Power greater than you that will serve you well for the time being. It is the will of the God of your understanding or a Power greater than you for you to get well.

Answer the following questions:

- Describe the times when your will has not been enough.
- What is the difference between your will and the will the God of your understanding or a Power greater than you?

At some point in your discovery and wellness, you might find that you have somehow shifted from trying to align your will with the will the God of your understanding or a Power greater than you to running on self-will. This happens so slowly and subtly that you hardly even notice. It seems as though you are especially vulnerable to selfishness when things are going well. You cross the fine line that divides humble and honest pursuit of goals from subtle manipulation and forced results. You find yourself going just a little too far in a discussion to convince someone that you are right. You find yourself holding on to something just a little too long. You suddenly realize that you have not contacted your mentor in quite a while. You feel a quiet, almost tangible discomfort that will alert you to this subtle shift away from recovery, if you will listen.

Answer the following questions:

- Have there been times in your recovery when you have found yourself subtly taking back your selfish will?

- What alerted you?

- What have you done to recommit yourself to the Third Step?

The God of Your Understanding or a Power Greater than You

Before we delve deeply into the process of joining your will with that of a God of your understanding or a Power greater than you, you should work on overcoming any negative beliefs or unproductive preconceptions you might have about the word "God."

Answer the following questions:

- Does the word "God," or even the concept itself, make you uncomfortable?

- What is the source of your discomfort?

- Have you ever believed that God caused horrible things to happen to you or as punishing you?

- What were those things?

You should choose a God of our understanding or a Power greater than you that is loving and caring and greater than you. These simple guidelines can encompass as many understandings of this Power as there are people on earth. They do not exclude anyone. If you understand the word "God" to mean the power of a program of wellness, these guidelines fit. If you understand the word "God" to mean the spiritual principles of wellness, these guidelines fit. If you understand the word "God" to mean a personal power or being with whom you can communicate, these guidelines fit. It is essential that you begin exploring and developing your understanding. Your sponsor or mentor can help immeasurably in this process.

Answer the following questions:

- What is your understanding of a Power greater than you today?

- How is this Power working in your life?

As important as it is to figure out what the God of your understanding or a Power greater than you is to you, it is more important that you develop a relationship with whatever you understand this Power to be. You can do this in a variety of ways. First, you need to somehow communicate with the God of your understanding or a Power greater than you. Some of us call this prayer, and some might call it other things. This communication does not have to be formal, or even verbal.

Second, you need to be open to communication from the God of your understanding or a Power greater than you whatever you choose it to be. This might be done by paying attention to how you feel, your reactions, and what is going on inside and around you. Or you might have a personal routine that helps you connect with a Power greater than yourself. It might be that the God of your understanding or a Power greater than you speaks to you or helps you see the right thing to do through other significant people in your lives.

Third, you need to allow yourself to have feelings about the God of your understanding or a Power greater than you. You might get angry. You might feel love. You might feel frightened. You might feel grateful. It is okay to share the entire range of human emotions with this Power whatever you conceive it to be. This allows you to feel closer to this Power upon which you rely and helps develop your trust in that Power.

Answer the following questions:

- How do you communicate with the God of your understanding or a Power greater than you?
- How does the God of your understanding or a Power greater than you communicate with you?
- What feelings do you have about the God of your understanding or a Power greater than you?

As many of us stay sober for some time, we work on developing an understanding of the God of our understanding or a Power greater than us. Our growing understanding reflects our experiences. We mature into an understanding of God that gives us peace and serenity. We trust the God of our understanding or a Power greater than us and we are optimistic about life. We begin to feel that our lives are touched by something beyond our comprehension, and we are glad and grateful that this is so.

Then one day, something happens that challenges everything you believe about the God of your understanding or makes you doubt the existence of that Power altogether. It might be a death or an injustice, or a loss. Whatever it is, it leaves you feeling as though you have been kicked in the stomach. You just cannot understand it.

Times like these are when you need of a God of your understanding or a Power greater than you the most, although you probably find yourself instinctively drawing away. Your grasp the God of your understanding or a Power greater than you is about to undergo a dramatic change. You need to keep reaching out to a God of your understanding or a Power greater than you, asking for acceptance if not understanding. You need to ask for strength to go on. Eventually you will reestablish your relationship with this Power, although probably on different terms.

Answer the following questions:

- Are you struggling with changing beliefs about the nature of a God of your understanding or a Power greater than you?
- Is your current concept of a God of our understanding or a Power greater than us still working for you?
- How might it need to change?

As your understanding of a God of your understanding or Power greater than you grows and evolves, you will find that you will react differently to what goes on in your life. You might find yourself able to courageously face situations that used to strike fear in your heart. You might deal with frustrations more gracefully. You might find yourself able to pause and think about a situation before acting. You will probably be calmer, less compulsive, and abler to see beyond the immediacy of the moment.

Surrendering Your Selfish Self

The order in which you prepare to join your will with that of the God of your understanding or a Power greater than you is significant. First, we get our selfish self out of the way; then we gradually join our will with that of the God of our understanding or a Power greater than us. It seems that it is easier for us to grasp the destructive nature of our selfish self and see that it must be pushed aside and surrendered; consequently, it is usually the first to go. Harder for us to grasp is the need to surrender our selfish will or control over people and things.

For us to be comfortable with allowing the God of our understanding or a Power greater than us to care for us, we will have to develop trust. You might have no trouble surrendering your need to engage in obsessive compulsive codependence or relationship addiction, but you want to remain in control of the rest of your life. You might trust the God of your understanding or a Power greater than you to care for your work life, but not your relationships with our significant others. You might trust the God of your understanding to care for your partner, but not your children. You might trust the God of your understanding with your safety, but not your finances.

Many of us have trouble letting go completely. We think we trust a God of our understanding with certain areas of our lives, but immediately take back control the first time we get scared or things are not going the way we think they should. It is necessary for us to examine our progress in turning it over.

Answer the following questions:

- What does "to the care of" mean to you?

- What does it mean for you to surrender your selfish will and join your will to that of the God of your understanding?

- How might your life be changed if you make the decision to surrender your selfish self and join your will to that of the God of your understanding or a Power greater than You?

- How do you allow the God of your understanding or a Power greater than you to work in your life?

- How does the God of your understanding or a Power greater than you care for you and your life?

- Have there been times when you have been unable to let go and trust the God of your understanding or a Power greater than you to care for the outcome of a particular situation? Describe.

- Have there been times when you have been able to let go and trust the God of your understanding or a Power greater than you for the outcome? Describe.

To move your selfish self out of the way and join your human will to that of a God of your understanding or a Power greater than you, you must take action. Many of us find that it works best for us to make some formal declaration on a regular basis. You might want to use the following example: "Take my selfish will, guide me in my recovery, and show me how you wish me to live." This seems to capture the essence of Step Three for many of us. However, you can certainly feel free to find your own words, or to find a more informal way of acting. Many of us believe that every day we are not engaging in obsessive compulsive learned helplessness, we are taking practical action on our decision to join our will with that of a God of our understanding or a Power greater than us.

Answer the following questions:

- How do you act to make this joining happen?

- Are there any words you say regularly?

- What are they?

Spiritual Principles

In considering the spiritual principles intrinsic to Step Three, we will focus first on surrender and willingness. Then we will look at how hope translates into faith and trust. Faith is being sure of what we hope for and certain of what we do not see.

Finally, we will see how the principle of commitment is feed to the Third Step. Practicing the principle of surrender is easy for us when everything is going along as we would like; well, so we think. Actually, when things are going smoothly, it is more likely that we are being lulled into a belief that we are in charge, which does not require much "surrender." Keeping the principle of surrendering your selfish self is essential, even when things are going well.

Answer the following questions:

- What are you doing to reinforce your decision to join your will with that of a God of your understanding or a Power greater than you?

- How does the Third Step allow you to build on the surrender you have developed in Steps One and Two?

We usually feel most willing immediately following surrender. Willingness often comes in the wake of despair or a struggle for control. We can practice the principle of willingness, before it becomes necessary and possibly save ourselves some pain.

Answer the following questions:

- In what ways have you demonstrated willingness in your discovery and wellness so far?

- Are you fighting anything in your wellness?

- What do you think would happen if you became willing to let wellness prevail in that area of your life?

There is a spiritual progression from hope to faith to trust in the Third Step. As you begin Step Three, you carry with you a sense of hope that was born in you as you worked the Second Step. Hope springs from the knowledge that your life is full of possibilities. There are no hard certainties yet, just the first whispers of anticipation that you just might be able to fulfill your heart's deepest desires. Lingering doubts fade as hope becomes faith. Faith propels you forward into action, where you actually do the work that those who you have faith in are telling you is necessary if you are to achieve wellness. In the Third Step, faith gives you the capacity to decide and carry that decision into action. Trust comes into play after faith has been applied. You have probably made significant progress toward fulfilling your goals; now you have evidence that you can influence the course of your lives through taking positive action.

Answer the following questions:

- How have hope, faith, and trust become positive forces in your life?
- What further action can you take to apply the principles of hope, faith, and trust in your program of wellness?
- What evidence do you have that you can trust confidently in your wellness?

The principle of commitment is the culmination of the spiritual process of Step Three. Making the decision to surrender and join your will with the will of the God of your understanding repeatedly, even when your decision does not seem to be having any positive effect, is what this step is all about. You can practice the spiritual principle of commitment by reaffirming your decision on a regular basis and by continuing to take action that gives your decision substance and meaning-for instance, working the rest of the steps.

Answer the following questions:

- What have you done recently that demonstrates your commitment to wellness and to working a program?
- Have you taken a service position?
- Have you agreed to sponsor another person recovering from obsessive compulsive c learned helplessness?
- Have you continued to go to twelve-step meetings no matter how you feel about them?
- Have you continued to work with your sponsor even after they told you an unpleasant truth or gave you some direction you did not want to follow?
- Did you follow that direction?

Moving On

As you get ready to go on to Step Four, you will want to take a look at what you have gained by working Step Three. Writing about your understanding of each Step as you prepare to move on helps you internalize the spiritual principles connected to it.

Answer the following questions:

- Do you have any reservations about your decision to surrender your selfish self and join your will with that of a God of your understanding or a Power greater than you?
- Do you feel that you are now ready to take this major step?
- How does your surrender in the First Step help you in the Third Step?
- What action do you plan to take to follow through on your decision?
- How does working the remainder of the Steps fit into this?

We end our work on Step Three with an increase in our level of freedom. If we have been thorough with this Step, we are profoundly relieved to realize that the world will go along just fine without our intervention. The responsibility of running everything is a huge burden, and we are happy to lay it down. We might feel comforted that a loving Power as we understand Him is caring for our us, letting us know in subtle ways, and sometimes in not so subtle ways, that the path we are on is the right one. We have seen our old ideas for what they were, and we are willing to let go of them and allow change to happen in our lives. We might even find that we are willing to take some risks we never had the courage to take before, because we are secure in the knowledge of this Power's ability to care for us and direct us.

Some people pause before making major decisions and ground themselves in their own spirituality. We look to the source of our strength, invite a God of your understanding or a Power greater than you to work in our lives, and move forward once we are sure we are on the right track. Now we need to take another step along the path of recovery, a step that makes our Third Step decision real. It is time to make a searching and fearless moral inventory of ourselves.

Chapter Eight

Step Four

Made a searching and fearless moral inventory of ourselves.

The forefathers and pioneers of Alcoholics Anonymous began this Step by comparing a personal inventory with a business inventory. They wrote that we started upon a personal inventory. This was Step Four. They explained that a business that takes no regular inventories usually goes broke. They observed that taking a commercial inventory is a fact-finding and fact-facing process. It is an effort to discover the truth about what is happening with the business.

The object is to disclose damaged or unsalable goods and to get rid of them promptly and without regret.

Therefore, if a business is failing, it needs new management, and the first thing a manager must do is to take an inventory of the businesses' assets and liabilities to see what has been causing the trouble. He must look at the company's books, its accounts payable, its accounts receivable, it human resources, its salable inventory on hand, and its equipment.

Remember that your sugar addiction is not causing your troubles because many people stop acting out on their obsessive compulsive learned helplessness, but their lives are still miserable and unmanageable. Remember that your obsessive compulsive learned helplessness is not the problem; the problems is the problem, so to get well, you get into the core of the problem, not chase symptoms around. And so, you must find out what you have, what you need to keep, and what you need to get rid of. Keep in mind: in the inventory, you are not looking for all your wrongs. Instead, you are looking for what is good and admirable about you, along with the nature of your wrongs that resulted in your defects and excesses of that are truly causing your troubles.

Perhaps, we should define what defect of character and shortcomings are. A fault, failing, weakness, flaw, and inadequacy are all synonyms for the word defect. Character refers to the mental and moral qualities of an individual. Therefore, the ever-present phrase in the recovery world "defects of character" implies moral and psychological flaws and failings in an individual. A shortcoming is a fault or failure to meet a certain standard, typically in a person's character.

The forefathers and pioneers of Alcoholics Anonymous told us that we launched out on a course of vigorous action, the first step of which is a personal housecleaning, which many of us had never attempted. Although our decision was a vital and crucial step, it could have little permanent effect unless at once followed by a strenuous effort to face, and to be rid of, the things in ourselves that have been blocking us.

It should be noted that the forefathers and pioneers of Alcoholics Anonymous said at once. Therefore, they suggested that we do the Fourth Step immediately after completing the Third Step because we must get rid of those things that have and are blocked us from our internal guidance system and a God of our understanding or a Power greater than us, namely our fears, inadequacies, inferiorities, and insecurities, as well as the Seven Deadly Sins—the misuses of pride.

And so, the Fourth Step is the beginning of a process of reconnecting to our internal guidance system and establishing a direct line of communication with a God of our understanding or a Power greater than us by eliminating resentment and fear, as well as eliminating those aspects of our personalities that kept us unsettled.

The forefathers and pioneers of Alcoholics Anonymous said that our addiction is but a symptom of our problems because although it was devastating and cut us off from our internal guidance system and a God of our understanding or a Power greater than you, we are still disconnected from our Creator because of selfish self is in the way and is producing our character defects and excesses, even though we had stopped acting out on our addiction of choice.

Likewise, we are going conduct the equivalent of a business inventory on our life, which implies that we are going to look at our assets and liabilities. It should be noted that the inventory is about examining our achievements and our failures, as well as promoting the positive and eliminating the negative. The forefathers and pioneers of Alcoholics Anonymous tell us exactly what we must do to complete a moral inventory.

They wrote that we did the same thing with our lives. We took stock honestly. First, we searched out our flaws in our make-up which caused our failure. Being convinced that self, manifested in various ways was what had defeated us, we considered its common manifestations.

Step Four is the first of the action steps that will set us free. You might have done some admitting in Step One, some believing in Step Two, and some deciding in Step Three, but now you are faced with taking some action in getting up to get a pencil and some paper, a computer, or a tablet or ipad, and start writing.

However, before getting into the details of completing this Step, a few things should be emphasized. A pamphlet written in 1944 called: *A.A.-An Interpretation of our Twelve Steps* gives us some specific instructions on working the Fourth Step. It states that some people, in error, think that the inventory is a lot of unpaid debts, plus a list of unmade apologies. Our trouble goes much deeper than that. We have found that the root of our troubles lies in: resentments, misuse of pride, selfishness, and many other things. In other words, we are making an inventory of our character, of our attitude toward others, and of our very way of living.

The character liabilities or defects mentioned above are our resentment, misuses of pride, and selfishness. To these, we add dishonesty and fear. It is important that you realize that there are many wrong ways to do a moral inventory, but only one right way. The ultimate determination whether your inventory has addressed all your defects and excesses is whether you stay sober, get well, and are at peace with yourself and the world.

The following inventory is like the one that many of the original members of Alcoholics Anonymous did in the early days of Alcoholics Anonymous. And so, many of the original members believed that newcomers should be guided through a simple form of the Steps, which kept with the "keep it simple" approach of the original fellowship, where the newcomer could grasp the life-saving message of the Steps, experience the miracle of recovery and discovery, and grow into the Fellowship as they worked with other addicts. Later, once the fog of early recovery lifted, they could go back and do a more comprehensive inventory.

Furthermore, the forefathers and pioneers of Alcoholics Anonymous believed that newcomers should be led from the problem of living a life based on selfishness and self-will into the solution of living in accordance to our own internal guidance system and the will a God of our understanding or a Power greater than us as quickly as possible.

In the early days of Alcoholics Anonymous, the forefathers and pioneers often did this during the newcomer's three to five day stay at St. Thomas Hospital in Akron, Ohio, and thousands of hopeless alcoholics recovered from alcoholism using this successful "keep it simple" approach. Dr. Bob and the original forefathers and pioneers of Alcoholics Anonymous strongly believed that the Steps should be taken quickly, as soon as the drunk was sober enough to tolerate the process.

Therefore, the long-held faulty notion that there is some officially endorsed time limit on when a person can or should work the Steps is a myth and should be dispelled. As stated above, the forefathers and pioneers of Alcoholics Anonymous stated emphatically that the Twelve Steps should be taken as quickly as possible. In fact, in the early days of Alcoholics Anonymous, the forefathers were taking people through the Steps in one month and setting them free.

It looked like this:

1. Newcomers were detoxed off alcohol for three to five days.
2. Newcomers were introduced to the concepts of recovery and were introduced to the idea that living a life based on selfishness and self-will was the problems and into solution was living in accordance to our own God-given internal guidance system.
3. After the newcomers were released from the hospital, they were taken through the Steps in a month.
4. Following this, they were taken to their first Alcoholics meeting and met the fellowship of ex-drunks.
5. They were assigned to another drunk at the hospital and repeated the process.

The forefathers and pioneers of Alcoholics Anonymous believed that by taking the Steps quickly, we could discover what was going within us in order to eliminate the behaviors that troubled us the most and that have cut us off from our own internal spirit and the Spirit of God. They stated that we went back through our lives. Nothing counted but thoroughness and honesty. When we were finished, we considered it carefully.

Since the forefathers and pioneers asked us to be thorough and honest and the next sentence tells us what to do when we are finished, it is assumed that they are asking us to complete the inventory in one sitting, given that these instructions are contained in one paragraph. Nevertheless, this is only a suggestion. You should spend as much time as you need on your inventory, so it is done thoroughly and honestly.

It is important that you are not misguided by one of the old erroneous doctrines of Alcoholics Anonymous that if you do not include the "bad stuff," you are not taking a moral inventory. The purpose of the moral inventory is to discover what is good about you and the principles you can run the rest of your life on. So, if you have given this notion weight, consider that there are no perfect people in this world and there are no perfect inventories—so just do it.

The forefathers and pioneers of Alcoholics Anonymous stated that resentment is the number one offender, and it destroys more addicts of all kinds than anything else. From it stems all forms soul sickness, for we have been not only mentally and physically ill, we have been soul sick. In dealing with resentments, we set them to paper.

Most of us came into the world of recovery and discovery because we wanted to stop something—our powerlessness over our obsessive compulsive learned helplessness. We probably did not put much thought into what we were starting, a program of recovery and discovery, by coming here. But if we have not looked at what we are getting out of this program, now might be a good time to pause and think about it.

First, you should ask yourself what you want out of wellness. Most of us answer this question by saying that we just want to be sober. But sobriety is the prerequisite for wellness. Wellness is much more than sobriety; it is being happy, content, comfortable, at peace, and living a meaningful existence. We just want to like ourselves. But how can we like ourselves when we did not even know who we are? The Fourth Step gives you the means to begin finding out who you are, the information you will need to begin to like yourself and get those other things you expect from the program—comfort, happiness, and serenity.

The Fourth Step heralds a new era in your discovery and wellness. Steps Four through Nine can be thought of as a process within a process. You will use the information you find in working the Fourth Step to work our Fifth, Sixth, Seventh, Eighth, and Ninth Steps. This process is meant to be done repeatedly in wellness.

There is an analogy for this process that is particularly fitting. If you can think of yourself as an onion, each time you begin a Fourth Step, you are peeling away a layer of the onion and getting closer to the core. Each layer of the onion represents another layer of denial, your character defects, and the harm you have caused. The core represents the pure and healthy spirit that lies at the center of you. It is our goal in discovery and wellness to have a spiritual awakening and a reemergence of our true healthy selves, and we get closer to that by beginning this process. Our spirits awaken a little more each time we go through it.

The Fourth Step is a method for learning about us, and it is as much about finding our character assets as it is about identifying the exact nature of our wrongs. The inventory process is also an avenue to freedom. We have been prohibited from being free for so long-probably all our lives. Many of us have discovered as we worked the Fourth Step that our problems did not begin the first time that we engaged in our obsessive compulsive learned helplessness, but long before, when the seeds of our powerlessness were planted. We might have felt isolated, different, like we did not fit in, inferior, and inadequate, long before we began engaging in our obsessive compulsive codependence or relationship addiction. In fact, the way we felt and the forces that drove us are completely enmeshed with our need to engage in our obsessive compulsive learned helplessness to feel better; thus, it was our desire to change the way we felt and to subdue these forces that led us to avoid or evade our first act of obsessive compulsive learned helplessness. Your inventory will lay bare the unresolved pain and conflicts in your past so that you are no longer at its mercy. You will have a choice, and you will have achieved a measure of freedom.

This portion of this twelve-step guide has two distinct sections. First, it will help you us prepare to work the Fourth Step by guiding you through an exploration of your motives for working this Step and what this Step means to you; and second, it is a guide for doing a thorough searching and fearless moral inventory.

Motivation

Although your motivation for working the Fourth Step is not as important as actually working the Fourth Step, you might find it helpful to examine and dispel any reservations you have about this step and think about some of the benefits you will get as a result of working this Step.

Answer the following questions:

- Do you have any reservations about working this step?
- What are they?
- What are some of the benefits that could come from making a searching and fearless moral inventory of you?
- Why should not you procrastinate about working this step?
- What are the benefits of not procrastinating?

Searching and Fearless

This is the phrase that has most puzzled many of us. You probably understand what "searching" means, but what about "fearless?" How can you get over all of your fear? That might take years, you think; but you need to work on this inventory right away.

Taking a fearless inventory means going ahead despite your fear. It means having the courage to take this action no matter how you feel about it. It means having the courage to be honest, even when you are cringing inside and swearing that you will take what you are writing to the grave. It means having the determination to be thorough, even when it seems that you have written enough. It means having the faith to trust this process and trust in a God of your understanding or a Power greater than you to give you whatever quality you need to walk through the process.

Let us face it, this Step does involve a lot of work. But we can take heart from the fact that there is rarely a deadline on completing this Step, other than how long we want to take to get well. We can do it in manageable sections, a little at a time, until we are done. The only thing that is important is that we work on it consistently.

There are times when your clean time can work against you such as when you fail to acknowledge your fear of taking an inventory. Many of us who have worked the Fourth Step numerous times and know it is ultimately one of the most loving things we can do for ourselves, but we might still find ourselves avoiding this task. You might think that since you know how good this process is, you should not have any fear of it. But you need to give yourself permission to be afraid, if that is what you feel.

You might also have fears that stem from your previous experiences with the Fourth Step. You know that an inventory means a change in your life. You know that if your inventory reveals destructive patterns, and that you cannot continue to practice the same behaviors without a great deal of pain. Sometimes this means having to let go of something in your life such as some behavior you think you cannot survive without or perhaps a resentment you have nursed so carefully that it has actually become, in a sick way, a source of reassurance and comfort. The fear of letting go of something you have come to depend on, no matter how much you have begun to suspect it is not good for you, is a valid fear. You just cannot let it stop you. You must face it and act with courage. So, which cases you more distress: holding or letting go?

You might also have to overcome a barrier that grows from an unwillingness to reveal more of your condition. Many of members of twelve-step programs with clean time have shared that an inventory taken in later recovery revealed that their addiction had spread its tentacles so completely throughout their lives that virtually no area was left untouched. This realization is often initially met with feelings of dismay and perplexity. We wonder how we could still be so sick. Has not all this effort in discovery and wellness resulted in more than surface healing? Of course, it has. We just need some time to remember that. After you have had time to accept what your inventory is revealing, you will feel a sense of hope rising to replace the feelings of dismay. After all, an inventory always initiates a process of change and freedom. Why should it not this time, too?

Answer the following questions:

- Are you afraid of working this Step?
- What is your fear?
- What does it mean to you to be searching and fearless?
- Are you working with a mentor and talking to other sugar addicts?
- What other action are you taking to reassure yourself that you can handle whatever is revealed in this inventory?

A Moral Inventory

Many of us have a multitude of unpleasant associations connected to the word "moral." It might conjure up memories of an overly rigid code of behavior we were expected to adhere to. It might make us think of people we consider "moral," people we think of as better than ourselves. Hearing this word might also awaken our tendency toward rebellion against society's morals and our resentment of authorities who were never satisfied with our morality. Whether any of this is true for us, as individuals, is a matter to be determined by us, as individuals. If any of the preceding seems to fit, we can alleviate our discomfort with the word "moral" by thinking about it in a different way.

In this Step, the word "moral" has nothing to do with specific codes of behavior, society's norms, or the judgment of some authority figure. A moral inventory is something we can use to discover our own individual morality, our own values, principles, and virtues. We do not have to relate them in any way to the values and principles of others.

Answer the following questions:

- Are you disturbed by the word "moral?"
- Why?
- Are you disturbed by thinking about society's expectations and afraid that you cannot or will not and will never be able to conform to them?
- What values and principles are important to you?

An Inventory of Ourselves

The Fourth Step asks us to take an inventory of ourselves, not of other people. Yet, when we begin writing and looking at our resentments, fears, behavior, beliefs, and secrets, we will find that most of these are connected to another person, or sometimes to an organization or institution. It is important to understand that we are free to write whatever we need to about others, if it leads us to finding our part in the situation. In fact, most of us cannot separate our part from their part at first. Your sponsor will help you with this.

Spiritual Principles

In the Fourth Step, you will call on all of the spiritual principles you began to practice in the first three Steps. First, you must be willing to complete a thorough and honest Fourth Step. You will need to be meticulously honest with yourself, thinking about everything you write down and asking yourself if it is true or not. You will need to be courageous enough to face your fear and walk through it. Last, but not least, your faith and trust will carry your through when you are facing a difficult moment and feel like giving up.

Answer the following question:

- How is your decision to work Step Four a demonstration of courage? Trust? Faith? Honesty? Willingness?

The Principles and Virtues of Wellness

Honesty

Step 1. We admitted that we were powerless over our obsessive compulsive codependence or relationship addiction; that our lives had become unmanageable.

Hope

Step 2. Came to believe that a power greater than ourselves could restore us to sanity.

Faith

Step 3. Made a decision to turn our will and our lives over to the care of God as we understood him.

Courage

Step 4. Made a searching and fearless moral inventory of ourselves.

Integrity

Step 5. Admitted to God, to ourselves, and to another human being the exact nature of our wrongs.

Willingness

Step 6. Were entirely ready to have God remove all these defects of character.

Humility

Step 7. Humbly asked Him to remove our shortcomings.

Brotherly Love

Step 8. Made a list of all persons we had harmed and became willing to make amends to them all.

Justice

Step 9. Made direct amends to such people wherever possible, except when to do so would injure them or others.

Perseverance

Step 10. Continued to take personal inventory and when we were wrong promptly admitted it.

Spirituality

Step 11. Sought through prayer and meditation to improve our conscious contact with God as we understood Him, praying only for knowledge of his will for us and the power to carry that out.

Service

Step 12. Having had a spiritual awakening as the result of these steps, we tried to carry this message to others, especially others suffering from obsessive compulsive leaned helplessness and to practice these principles in all our affairs.

Your Inventory

Get a notebook or whatever means of recording your inventory you wish. Get comfortable. Remove any distractions from the place where you plan to work on your inventory. Pray for the ability to be searching, fearless, and thorough. Do not forget to stay in touch with your mentor throughout this process. Finally, feel free to go beyond what is asked in the following questions. Anything you think of is inventory material.

Resentments

Resentment, also described as bitter displeasure at having been treated unfairly, is not classified among the six basic emotions of surprise, disgust, happiness, sadness, anger, and fear, but is a mixture of disappointment, anger, and fear. As the surprise of injustice becomes less frequent, so too does anger and fear fade, leaving disappointment as the predominant emotion. So, to the extent perceived disgust and sadness remain, so too does the level of disappointment remain. So, resentment is best described as felt state of ruminating, churning bitter indignation at having been unfairly fairly.

The word *resentment* originates from the French word "ressentir," where "re" is an intensive prefix, and "sentir "means "to feel," which means "to feel again, and which has become synonymous with anger or spite.

We have resentments when we re-feel old feelings; when we are unable to let go; and when we cannot forgive and forget something that has upset us. We list our resentments in the Fourth Step for several reasons. First, doing so will help you let go of old anger that is affecting your life today. Second, exploring your resentments will help you identify the ways in which you set yourself up to be disappointed in others, especially when your expectations are too high. Third, making a list of your resentments will reveal patterns of behavior that kept you trapped in a cycle of anger, self-pity, or both. Finally, it should be explained that resentments are not about other people, although we project them on to others, they are reflections of what we find unacceptable about ourselves. So, if you spot in someone else, you had it first. We often hold others accountable for the things they do, but usually we do not look at ourselves and what we contributed to the situation until we begin the process of introspection or looking within to see our fears, shortcomings, and our selfishness.

Page One—List of Resentments

Write a list of the people, places, things, rules, employers, schools, government institutions, religious organizations, and civic organizations you resent or have been brooding about, ruminated about, or have anger or bitterness toward. This can be for any reason—real or perceived. Note here: be thorough. You should have 35 to 50 entries here. Write about the following:

- What people do you resent (identify names)?
- What family members do you resent (identify, parents, siblings, grandparents, uncles, aunts, cousins, and in-laws)?
- What places and things do you resent (identify)?
- What institutions or organizations (school, government, religious, correctional, law enforcement, or civic) do you resent (identify)?
- What rules do you resent (identify)?
- What employers do you resent?

Page Two

For each entry listed on Page One, explain what the person, place, thing, rule, institution, school, government institution, organization, employer, or civic organization did that led you to resent them or have long-felt bitterness toward. Be sure to use complete sentences here.

Next write the statement: "How, where, and when have I done the same things listed above." Write what led you to act as you did in retaliation to, withdrawal from, or avoidance of these situations. Also explore how your fears, inferiorities, inadequacies, insecurities, and dishonesty, as well as your selfishness (pride), enviousness, gluttonous, lustfulness, anger, greediness, or laziness or slothfulness led to the situation. Be honest here. Explore how your inability or unwillingness to experience certain feelings led you to churn over these events or situations. Explore how your behavior contributed to your resentments. Additionally, explore how holding on to your resentments served you and what they did for you, not what they did to you

Also write about:

- What was your motivation, or what did you believe, that led you to act as you did in these situations?
- How has your dishonesty contributed to your resentments?
- How has your inability or unwillingness to experience certain feelings led you to develop resentments?
- How has your behavior contributed to your resentments?
- How have your resentments affected your relationships with yourself, with others, and with a Power greater than yourself?
- What recurring themes do you notice in your resentments?
- Are you afraid of looking at your part in the situations that caused your resentments?
- Why?

Remember: resentments are not about other people; they are about you. There is a wise saying in the fellowship: "If you spot; you got it!"

Page Three—The Exploration of Pride

Next, explore your misuses of pride. Pride is one of the main contributors to our situation. If you were raised to be powerless as child and were shamed throughout your childhood, you would naturally and normally come to believe that you were powerless, inferior, inadequate, and less than. Naturally, you would want to counter these feelings of inferiority, inadequacy, insecurity, and inferiority by going to an opposite extreme. These extremes would be selfishness (pride), enviousness, gluttonous, lustfulness, anger, greediness, or laziness or slothfulness. Therefore, we see that when even we had any significant life problem; pride in its seven forms would be right in the middle of our live situations.

These are known as the *Seven Deadly Sins*, and we must explore our most serious defects of character in regard to pride, self-esteem, ambitions, emotional security, financial security, sexual relationships, and personal relationships.

Perhaps in order to understand these most serious defects of character, an exploration of the Seven Deadly Sins as seen through the eyes medieval Christian church might be helpful.

The Seven Deadly Sins, also known as *Capital Vices* or *Cardinal Sins*, are a classification of vices that were originally used by early Christian theologians during medieval period, commonly known as the period from the sacking of Rome 476 CE by the Visigoths to the fall of Constantinople in 1517 CE, to educate and instruct the masses on man's tendency to sin. The medieval Roman Catholic Church divided sin into two principal categories: *Venial sins*, which are relatively minor sins that are forgiven through any sacrament of the Church, and more severe *Capital* or *Mortal Sins*, which, when committed, destroy the life of grace and create the threat of eternal damnation, unless either absolved through the sacrament of confession, or otherwise forgiven through contrition on the part of the penitent.

In 375, CE, the Greek monastic theologian Evagrius of Pontus drew up a list of eight offenses and wicked human passions, including gluttony, lust, avarice, sadness, anger, acedia, vainglory, and pride. Evagrius saw the escalating severity as representing increasing fixation with the self, with pride as the most egregious of the sins.

In the late sixth century CE, Pope Gregory the Great redefined Evagrius' wicked human passions and reduced the list to seven, folding vainglory into pride, acedia into sadness, and adding envy. These were later clarified by Dante in Part II of his epic poem: *The Divine Comedy*, known as *The Purgatorio*.

Pope Gregory and Dante listed the Seven Deadly Sins as:

Lust or extravagance

Gluttony

Greed

Sloth

Wrath

Envy

Pride

Lust is usually thought of as involving obsessive thoughts or desires of a sexual nature. Nevertheless, unfulfilled lust sometimes leads to sexual compulsions and/or transgressions including, but not limited to, sexual addiction, adultery, bestiality, child molesting, and rape. But Dante's description was more about the excessive love of others, which rendered the love and devotion to God as secondary.

However, lust and love are two different things. Whereas a genuine, selfless love could represent the highest degree of development and feelings of association with others in human relationships, lust could be described as the excessive desire for sexual release, fantasy, or power where the other person is often seen as a means to an end for the fulfillment of the subject's desires and becomes an object in the process.

Gluttony or over-consumption is derived from the Latin word: "guttire," which means to "gulp down" or "swallow." Gluttony is the over-indulgence and over-consumption of anything to the point of excess or waste. It should be noted that in the medieval Christian religion, it is considered a sin to desire to excessively use food or withhold food from the needy.

Depending on the culture, gluttony could be seen either as a vice or a sign of status. In situations where food is scare, being able to eat well might be something to take pride in, although this could also result in a moral backlash when confronted with the reality of those who have less and are less fortunate. But where food is plentiful, it might be considered a sign of over-consumption, extravagance, and waste self-control, and it might be considered proper to resist the temptation to over-indulge.

The leaders of the Medieval Church, such as Thomas Aquinas, took a more liberal view of gluttony, arguing that it could also include obsessive anticipation of meals and the constant eating of delicacies and excessively costly foods. Thomas Aquinas listed six ways to commit gluttony, including: eating too soon; eating too expensively; eating too much; eating too eagerly; eating too daintily; or eating too enthusiastically.

Greed or avarice, like lust and gluttony, is a sin of excess. However, greed, as seen by the medieval Church, is attached to the selfish acquisition of excessive wealth in particular. Thomas Aquinas wrote that greed is: "a sin against God, just as all mortal sins, in as much as man condemns things eternal for the sake of temporal things."

However, avarice is seen as more of a blanket term that describes many other examples of sinful behavior, including disloyalty, deliberate betrayal, or treason, especially for personal gain, such as bribery. Additionally, scavenging and/or keeping of scared materials or objects; theft and robbery, especially by means of violence, trickery, or manipulation of authority; and the trading of sacred things, where one profits from soliciting goods from the Church are all actions that might be inspired by greed.

Sloth, or laziness or apathy, more than any other sin has been redefined since its original inclusion among the seven deadly sins. In fact, it was originally called the *sin of sadness*. It has been characterized in early years of Christianity by what modern writers would now describe as melancholy, apathy, depression, and joylessness, which was seen in the early Church as a refusal to enjoy the goodness of God and the world He created.

Originally, its place was fulfilled by two other aspects, acedia or laziness in religious matters was described as a spiritual apathy that affected the faithful by discouraging them from their religious work, and sadness, which was described as a feeling of dissatisfaction of discontent caused by unhappiness with one's current situation. When Aquinas selected acedia or sloth for his list, he described it as uneasiness of the mind, being a direct ancestor of lesser sins such as restlessness and instability.

In the modern view of vice, highlighted by its opposite virtue, zeal or diligence, it represents the failure to utilize one's talents and gifts. For example, a student who does not work beyond what is required and fails to achieve his or her potential could be labeled as slothful.

Dante refined this definition further; describing sloth as being the failure to love God with all one's heart, mind and soul. He described sloth as the middle sin, and as such was the only sin characterized by an absence or insufficiency of love. In his understanding of Purgatory, which the Church believes to be an intermediate state after physical death for atonement or purification of sin, the slothful were made to run continuously at top speed.

Current interpretations are much less stringent and comprehensive that they were in medieval times and portray sloth as being more simply as a sin of laziness, an unwillingness to act, or an unwillingness to care, rather than a failure to love God and His works. For this reason, sloth is now often seen as being considerably less serious than other sins.

Wrath, anger, hatred, rage, or revenge might be described as an inordinate and uncontrolled feeling of hatred and anger. These feelings could manifest as vehement denial of the truth, both to others and in the form of self-denial, impatience with the procedure of law, and the desire to seek revenge outside the workings of the justice system, such as engaging in vigilantism, and generally wishing to do evil or harm to others.

The transgressions borne of vengeance are among the most serious, including murder, assault, and the extreme cases of genocide. Wrath is the only sin not necessarily associated with selfishness or self-interest, although one could be wrathful for selfish reasons, such as jealousy. Dante described vengeance as love of justice perverted to revenge and spite.

Envy or jealousy, like greed, is characterized as an insatiable desire. However, they differ for two main reasons. First, greed is largely associated with material goods, whereas envy might apply more generally to status. Second, those who commit the sin of envy desire something that someone else has which they perceive themselves as lacking.

Dante defined envy as love of one's own good perverted to a desire to deprive other men of theirs, whereas Thomas Aquinas described envy as sorrow for another's good.

Pride, vanity, arrogance, and narcissism are considered the original and most serious of the seven deadly sins, and indeed, the ultimate source from which all others arise. It is identified as a desire to be more important or attractive than others, failing to give compliments to others who deserve them, and excessive love of self, especially holding one's self out of proper position with God. Dante's definition was love of self that was perverted into hatred and contempt for one's neighbor. Pride is seen as the deadliest of all sins and leads directly to damnation.

In perhaps the most famous example, the story of Lucifer, pride was what caused his fall from Heaven, and his resultant transformation into Satan. Vanity and narcissism are prime examples of this sin.

And so, we must examine our extravagance or lust, gluttony, greed, sloth, wrath, envy, and pride, and how they affect those around us. Thoroughly and honestly explore these defects of character and put them to paper.

Page Four—Fears, Inferiorities, Inadequacies, and Insecurities

First, ask yourself this question: "What is the sum of all human fears for me?" Consider this carefully and write the answer at the top of Page Four. For instance, rejection and abandonment. What does this mean? It means that at the core of every wrong you have done to others lies real or perceived rejection and abandonment. Now, you know the exact nature of your wrongs which you will use in Step Five

Explore your fears of abandonment, intimacy, losing your freedom, the unknown, loneliness, fear of rejection, fear of success, and fear of failure. Explore and write down how you over or under-compensated for these. Understand that the most primal human fear is rejection or not being accepted.

Feelings

We want to examine our feelings for much the same reason that we want to examine our resentments—it will help us discover our part in our own lives. In addition, most of us have forgotten how to feel anything but anger and rage by the time we get clean. Even if we have been around awhile, we are still uncovering new information about the ways we have shut down our feelings. Unfortunately, we confuse the terms feelings and emotions. Emotions are defined as the natural instinctive state of mind deriving from our circumstances, mood, or relationships with others; whereas feelings are the felt state in the body experienced as tension, stress, or distress.

Make a timeline of significant life events in your life and explore and write about the following:

- How do you identify your individual feelings?
- What feelings do you have the most trouble allowing yourself to feel?
- Why have you tried to shut off your feelings?
- What means have you used to deny how you really felt?
- Who or what triggered a feeling?
- What was the feeling?
- What were the situations?
- What was your part in each situation?
- What was your motivation, or what did you believe, that led me to act as you did in these situations?

- What do you do with your feelings once you have identified them?

Guilt, Shame, and Remorse

There are two types of guilt, shame, and remorse—real or imagined. The first grows directly out of our conscience, where we feel guilty, ashamed, or remorseful because we have done something that goes against our principles, or we harmed someone and feel ashamed about it. On the other hand, imagined guilt, shame, and remorse results from any number of situations that are not our fault or situations we had no part in creating. We need to look at our guilt, shame, and remorse so that we can separate these situations. We need to own what is truly ours and let go of what is not.

Answer the following questions:

- Who or what do you feel guilty or ashamed about?
- Explain the situations that led to these feelings.
- Which of these situations have caused me to feel shame, although you had no part in creating them?
- In the situations you did have a part in, what was your motivation, or what did you believe, that led you to act as you did?
- How has your behavior contributed to your guilt and shame?

Fear

If we could look at the affliction of addiction stripped of its primary symptoms; that is, apart from any addictive behavior, and without its most obvious characteristics, we would find a swamp of self-centered fear. We are afraid of being hurt, or maybe of just having to feel too intensely, so we live a sort of half-life, where we go through the motions of living, but never become fully alive.

We are afraid of everything that might make us feel, so either we isolate and withdraw ourselves or we over-exaggerate ourselves determined to over-power, possess, or dominate.

We are afraid that people will not like us, so we use drugs to be more comfortable with other; or we have multiple affairs with people who we have no emotional attachment to; or we masturbate to Internet pornography, so we can fanaticize how superior we are; or we exercise to excess; our we engage in obsessive compulsive codependence or relationship addiction to find and keep people we can fix sos we have a sense of value and worth.

We are afraid we will get caught at something and have to pay a price, so we lie or cheat or hurt others to protect ourselves.

We are afraid of being alone, so we use and exploit others to avoid feeling lonely or rejected or abandoned.

We are afraid we will not have enough of anything, so we selfishly pursue what we want, taking it from other, becoming a taker, user, and a consumer, not caring about the harm we cause in the process. Sometimes, if we have gathered things or people we care about, but since we are afraid we will lose them, so we begin to control them and compromising our values and principles to protect them.

Why do we do this? We do this to discharge the pent up energy resulting from the internal conflict between what we want to be versus what we are allowed to be governed by our own fears, inadequacies, inferiorities, and insecurities, and so, we need to uproot our self-centered, self-seeking fear so it no longer has the power to destroy us or those around us.

Answer the following questions:

- Who or what do you fear?
- Why?
- What have you done to cover your fear?
- How have you responded negatively or destructively to your fear?
- What do you most fear looking at and exposing about yourself?

- What do you think will happen if you do?

- How have you cheated yourself because of your fear?

Page Five—All Relationships

What is a relationship? It is when two or more people get together and interact with each other. So, you need to write about all your relationships in the Fourth Step—all your relationships, not just the romantic ones, but all relationships with family, friends, work, and intimate relationships, so that you can find out where your choices, beliefs, and behaviors have resulted in unhealthy or destructive relationships. You need to look at your relationships with relatives; spouses or partners; friends and former friends; present and former co-workers; neighbors; people from school; people from clubs and civic organizations and the organizations themselves; authority figures such as the police, legal and government institutions; and anyone or anything else you can possibly think of. You should also examine your relationship with the God of your understanding as well.

You might be tempted to skip the relationships that did not last long, such as a one-night sexual involvements, or perhaps an argument with a teacher whose class you then dropped. But these relationships are important too. If you think of it or have feelings about it, it is inventory material.

Answer the following questions:

- What defects of character, shortcomings, fears, inadequacies, inferiorities, and insecurities make it difficult for you to maintain friendships and/or romantic relationships?
- How has your fear of being hurt, abandoned, or rejected affected your friendships and romantic relationships?
- How have you sacrificed platonic friendships in favor of romantic relationships?
- In what ways did you compulsively seek relationships?

- In your relationships with family, do you sometimes feel as though you are locked into repeating the same patterns over and over without any hope of change?

- What are those patterns?

- What is your part in perpetuating them?

- How have you avoided intimacy with my friends, partners or spouses, and family?

- Have you had problems making commitments?

- Describe.

- Have you ever destroyed a relationship because you believed you were going to get hurt anyway so you should get out before that could happen?

- Describe.

- To what degree do you consider the feelings for others in your relationships?

- Equal to your own?

- More important than your own?

- Of minor importance?

- Not at all?

- Have you felt like a victim in any of your relationships? (Note: This question is focused on uncovering how you set yourself up to be a victim or how too-high expectations contributed to your being disappointed in people, not on listing instances where you were actually abused).

- Describe.

- What have your relationships with your neighbors been like?

- Do you notice any patterns appearing that carried through no matter where you lived?

- How do you feel about the people with and for whom you have worked?

- How has your thinking, beliefs, and behavior caused problems for you at work?

- How do you feel about the people you went to school with (both in childhood and currently)?

- Did you feel less than or better than the other students?

- Did you believe that you had to compete for attention from the instructor?

- Did you respect authority figures or rebel against them?

- Have you ever joined any clubs or membership organizations?

- How did you feel about the other people in the club or organization?

- Have you made friends in these organizations?

- Have you joined clubs with high expectations, only to quit in a short time?

- What were your expectations, and why were they not fulfilled?

- What was your part in these situations?

- Have you ever been in a mental hospital or prison or otherwise been held against your will?

- What effect has that had on your personality?

- What were my interactions with the authorities like?

- Did you follow the rules?

- Did you ever break the rules and then resent the authorities when you got caught?

- Did early experiences with trust and intimacy hurt you and cause you to withdraw?

- Describe.

- Have you ever let a relationship go even when the potential existed to resolve conflicts and work through problems?

- Why?

- Did you become a different person depending on who was around you? Describe.

- Have you discovered things about your personality (perhaps in previous inventories) that you did not like, and then found yourself overcompensating for that behavior? (For instance, you might have uncovered a pattern of immature dependence on others and then overcompensated for this by becoming overly self-sufficient).

- Describe.

- What defects are most often at play in your relationships (dishonesty, selfishness, control, manipulation, etc.)?

- How can you change your behavior so that you can begin having healthy relationships?
- Have you had any kind of a relationship with a God of your understanding or a Power greater than you?
- How has this changed in my lifetime?
- What kind of a relationship do you have with the god of your understanding or a greater than you now?

All Relationships including Sexual Behavior

This is a very uncomfortable area for most of us. In fact, we might be tempted to stop here, thinking: "Okay, this has gone far enough! There is no way I'm talking about my sexual behavior!" There is an old saying: "Me thinks you protest too much." What are you hiding? You must get over such unwillingness quickly. Thinking about the reason why you need to do this should help: We want to be at peace with our own sexuality. That is why we need to include our sexual beliefs and behaviors in our inventories. It is important to remind ourselves at this point that we are not taking our inventory to compare ourselves with what we think is "normal" for others, but only to identify our own values, principles, virtues, and morals.

Answer the following questions:

- How was your sexual behavior based in selfishness?
- Have you confused sex with love?
- Have you traded sex to get love?
- Have you traded love to get sex?
- What were the results of acting on that confusion?
- How have you used sex to try to avoid loneliness or fill a spiritual void?
- In what ways did you compulsively seek or avoid sex?
- Have any of your sexual practices left you feeling ashamed and guilty?
- What were they?

- Why did you feel that way?

- Have any of your sexual practices hurt you or others?

- Are you comfortable with your sexuality?

- If not, why not?

- Are you comfortable with others' sexuality?

- If not, why not?

- Is sex a prerequisite in all or most of your relationships?

- What does a healthy relationship mean to you?

- Do have hate or prejudice toward others who have different beliefs than you regarding sex such as lesbian, gay, bisexual, transgender, queer, intersex or asexual people.

Also, as part of this part of Step Four, you should make a timeline of all of your sexual relationships, including sexual partners and affairs. It should have times, dates, and outcomes. This can be most helpful in understanding the patterns of your behavior.

Abuse, Neglect, and Family Violence

You must exercise extreme caution before beginning this section. In fact, you might need to postpone this section to a later time in your recovery after you some trauma work. You should utilize all the resources at hand to make the decision about whether to begin this section now: your own sense of whether you are ready to withstand the distress this work will cause you, discussion with our sponsor, and prayer. Perhaps you will need help through this, and so, you might need to seek professional help and clear these traumas before we explore this part of you. If you do decide to go ahead with this section, you should be aware that working on this area of your Fourth Step will probably be the most painful work you will do in discovery.

Recording the times when you were neglected or hurt by the people who were supposed to love and protect you is certain to cause some of the most distressful feelings you will ever have to go through. However, it is important to do so when you are ready. If you keep the pain wrapped up inside you, a secret, it might be causing us to act in ways you do not want, or it can contribute to a negative self-image or other destructive beliefs. Getting the truth out begins a process that can lead to the relief of your distress. You were not to blame. Nothing you did or said caused what happened to you.

Answer the following questions:

- Have you ever been abused, neglected, or witnessed family violence?
- By whom?
- Have you been bullied or teased in school?
- Have you ever been removed from your family, placed in a foster home, or an orphanage?
- Dis you move around a lot?
- Were you a "latch key kid" who spent a lot of time at home by yourself?
- What feelings did you or do you now have about it?
- Has being abused affected your relationships with others?
- How?
- If you have felt victimized for much of life because of being abused in childhood, what steps can you take to be restored to spiritual wholeness?
- Can a God of your understanding help you?
- How?

It is also possible that you have physically, mentally, or verbally abused others. Recounting these times is bound to cause you to feel a great deal of shame, but you cannot afford to let that shame become despair. It is important that you face your behavior, accept responsibility for it, and work to change it. Writing about it here is the first step toward doing that. Working the rest of the steps will help you make amends for what you have done to others.

Answer the following questions:

- Have you ever physically, emotionally, or verbally abused anyone?

- Who and how?

- What was you feeling and thinking right before you caused the harm?

- Did you blame your victim or make excuses for your behavior?

- Describe.

- Do you trust your Higher Power to work in your life and provide you with what you need so you do not have to harm anyone again?

- Are you willing to live with the painful feelings until they are changed through working the Steps?

Previously, we explored gaslighting. It must be pointed out that sociopaths, narcissists, and addicts of all kinds including codependent people or relationship addicts frequently use gaslighting tactics. These individuals consistently transgress social mores, break laws, and exploit others, but typically also are convincing liars, sometimes charming ones, who consistently deny wrongdoing. As a result, some who have been victimized by these individuals might doubt their own perceptions. Some physically abusive spouses might gaslight their partners by flatly denying that they have been violent. Gaslighting might occur in parent–child relationships, with either parent, child, or both, lying to each other and attempting to undermine perceptions.

The sociopath, narcissist, or addict's ultimate goal is to make their victim second guess their every choice and question their sanity, making them more dependent on these individuals. A tactic which further degrades a target's self-esteem is for the sociopath, narcissist, or addict to ignore, then attend to, then ignore the victim again, so the victim lowers their personal bar for what constitutes affection and perceives themselves as less worthy of affection.

Gaslighting might be experienced by victims of school bullying and teasing, and when combined with other psychological and physical terror tactics, the result can lead to long-lasting psychological disorders and even progress into illnesses such as depression or avoidant personality disorder.

Gaslighting describes a dynamic observed in some cases of marital infidelity where a therapist might contribute to the victim's distress by mislabeling the woman's reactions by describing the gaslighting behaviors of the spouse as a recipe for a "nervous breakdown" for some women and suicide in some of the worst situations.

Many argue that gaslighting involves the projection and introjection of psychic conflicts from the perpetrator to the victim, and this imposition is based on a very special kind of transfer of painful and potentially painful mental conflicts. There are a variety of reasons why the victim may have a tendency to incorporate and assimilate what others externalize and project onto them and concluded that gaslighting may be a very complex highly structured configuration which encompasses many elements of the psychic behavior.

With respect to women, scholars argued emphatically that in such cases, the victim's ability to resist the manipulation depends on her ability to trust her own perceptions and judgments, something many people from dysfunctional family systems have difficulty doing. Establishment of "counterstories" might help the victim reacquire ordinary levels of power and control.

In truth, the lies that addicts intentionally tell their loved ones so they can continue their addictive activity without interference are absolutely relentless, and they usually they are just plausible enough to possibly be true. But when these gaslighting behaviors continue over a long enough period, the victim might begin to doubt his or her own feelings and intuitions, eventually starting to believe the addict's lies and manipulative defenses. When this occurs, the victim often takes on responsibility for the problems in the relationship, even though the addict is causing the vast majority of these problems.

The truly unnerving part is that even emotionally healthy people are vulnerable to gaslighting, primarily because it occurs slowly and gradually over time. It is a bit like placing a frog in a pot of warm water that is then slowly heated to a boil. Because the temperature rises so gradually, the frog never even realizes it is being cooked. We see this exact scenario with spouses or significant others of addicts, where a relatively healthy individual could be slowly drawn into the addict's insanity as a way to keep their relationship intact.

Sometimes spouses and partners of addicts can become codependent with the addict, meaning they feel compelled to aid and abet the addict in their addiction, even when their "assistance" serves no positive purpose and in fact does damage. In essence, they become the addict's de facto caregiver and enabler. When this sort of unhealthy codependency is coupled with gaslighting, the result might be a *folie à deux*—a delusion shared by two or more people with close emotional ties. A minor version of this would be the spouse's belief that the alcohol she sometimes smells on the addict's breath is "all in her head," although the addict would also need to truly believe that lie for this to qualify as a true folie à deux.

Sadly, gaslighting behaviors are often more distressing than whatever it is that the addict is attempting to cover up. For instance with the spouse of an alcohol addict, the most painful part of addict's behavior is not that they drink too much on a regular basis and occasionally disappear on drinking binges, it is that he lied about it and made her feel crazy and mistaken for doubting his many semi-plausible excuses and even his outright fabrications.

Unfortunately, the spouses and partners of addicts, despite the hurt, anger, confusion, and betrayal they experience, often resent the idea that they might need help to deal with their feelings. And this resistance is perfectly natural. For those who have experienced the betrayal of addiction and the gaslighting that very often accompanies that betrayal, the obvious and overwhelming impulse is to assign blame to the addict. Nevertheless, many of these spouses and family members do need therapeutic assistance, especially to recognize and process the trauma of gaslighting. At the very least, these individuals need validation for their feelings, education, and support for moving forward; empathy for how their life has been disrupted by the addict's repeated betrayals; and help in processing the shame they feel about falling for all of the addict's now obvious lies and excuses.

When betrayed spouses and other loved ones choose to remain in their relationship with the addict, as they often do, it is usually quite some time before they are able to reestablish trust in anything the addict says or does. Rightfully so, after what they have been through. Happily, if the addict is committed to long-term sobriety, behavioral change, living honestly, and regaining their personal integrity, the redevelopment of relationship trust is indeed possible. And when the betrayed partner joins the addict is their efforts at growth by also engaging in a process of support, education, and self-examination, this renewal is even more likely.

Nevertheless, some loved ones do ultimately conclude that the violation they have experienced at the hands of an addict is greater than their desire to remain in the relationship. For these individuals, trust cannot be restored and ending the relationship may be the best they can do. Just as a betrayed loved one is not wrong to continue a relationship with an addict, he or she is also not wrong to end it. Ultimately, more important than whether a betrayed individual chooses to stay or go is how they go about growing beyond the loss. This sort of recovery places a powerful emphasis on developing and trusting instincts, finding a greater willingness to express emotions, engaging in self-care and self-nurture, and developing an ongoing and trustworthy peer support network. Oftentimes, this begins in therapy, including group therapy with other people who have experienced betrayal and gaslighting related to someone else's addiction. It might also include twelve step support groups like Overeaters Anonymous.

Answer the following question:

• Have you used Gaslighting tactics in your relationships with others?

Secrets

Before you finish your Fourth Step, you should stop and reflect: Is there anything you have missed, either intentionally or not? Is there something you think is so bad that you just cannot possibly include it in your inventory? If so, you should be reassured by the fact that a multitude of people in recovery who have worked this step, there has never yet been a situation in anyone's Fourth Step that was so unique that you had to create a new term to describe it.

Keeping secrets is threatening to your wellness. If you are keeping a secret, you are actually building a reservation in your program.

Answer the following questions:

• Are there any secrets that you have not written about yet?
• What are they?

Another question you should ask yourself now is, is there anything in this inventory that is either an exaggeration of what happened or something that is not true at all? Almost all of us came into wellness and had trouble separating fact from fiction in our own lives. We did not think we had anything to feel good about that was true, so we made up lies or exaggerations to build ourselves up. But you do not have to do that anymore. You are building true self-worth in the process of working Step Four, not false self-worth based on some phony image. Now is the time to tell the truth about you.

Answer the following question:

• Is there anything in this inventory that is not true, or are there any stories you have told repeatedly that are not true?

Page Six—Shortcomings

Now begins the magic of the Step Four. You begin by compiling a list of defects of character or shortcomings by going through your entire inventory and picking out all of the action words and compiling a list. Again, you should have 35 to 50 entries on this list. This list represents your shortcomings or what is wrong with you.

Page Seven—Definition of the True Self

Now write the exact opposites of every one of your shortcomings. This is your definition of your true self in wellness. The following list of shortcomings is an example the cause of your problems and is the root of our wrongs. Honestly identify any of the following that apply:

Shortcoming	Virtue
Aggressive, Belligerent	Good-natured, Gentle
Angry	Forgiving, Calm, Generous
Apathetic	Interested, Concerned, Alert
Apprehensive, Afraid	Calm, Courageous
Argumentative, Quarrelsome	Agreeable
Arrogant, Insolent	Unassuming, Humble
Attacking, critical	Fair, Self-restrained
Ambivalent	Faces Problems and Acts
Blocking	Honest, Intuitive
Boastful	Modest, Humble
Careless	Careful, Painstaking, Concerned
Cheating	Honest
Competitive (socially)	Cooperative
Compulsive	Free
Conceited, Self-important	Humble, Modest

Contradictory, Oppositional	Reasonable, Agreeable
Contrary, Intractable, Pigheaded	Reasonable
Controlling	Lets Go
Cowardly	Brave
Critical	Non-judgmental, Praising, Tolerant,
Cynical	Open-Minded
Deceitful	Guileless, Honest
Defensive	Open to Criticism
Defiant, Contemptuous	Respectful
Denying	Honest, Accepting
Dependent	Accepts help but is self-reliant
Depressed, morose	Hopeful, Optimistic, Cheerful
Dirty, Poor Hygiene	Clean
Dishonest	Honest
Disloyal, Treacherous	Faithful, Loyal
Disobedient	Obedient
Disrespectful, Insolent	Respectful, Reverent
Enabling	Setting Boundaries, Tough love
Envying	Empathetic, Generous, Admiring
Evasive, Deceitful	Candid, Straightforward
Exaggerating	Honest, Realistic
Faithless, Disloyal	Reliable, Faithful
Falsely Modest	Honest, Has self-esteem
Falsely prideful	Modest, Humble
Fantasizing, Unrealistic	Practical, Realistic
Fearful	Confidant, Courageous
Forgetful	Responsible

Gluttonous, Excessive	Moderate
Gossiping	Closed-mouth, Kind, Praising
Greedy	Moderate, Generous, Sharing
Hateful	Forgiving, Loving, Concerned for others
Hypersensitive	Tolerant, does not personalize
Ill-Tempered, Bitchy	Good-Tempered, Calm
Impatient	Patient
Impulsive, reckless	Consistent, Considered actions
Inconsiderate	Thoughtful, Considerate
Indecisive, Timid	Firm, Decisive
Indifferent, Apathetic, Aloof	Caring
Inflexible, Stubborn	Open-minded, Flexible
Insecure, Anxious	Self-confident, Secure
Insincere, Hypocritical	Sincere, Honest
Intolerant	Tolerant, Understanding, Patient
Irresponsible, Reckless	Responsible
Isolating, Solitary	Sociable, Outgoing
Jealous	Trusting, Generous, Admiring
Judgmental	Broadminded, Tolerant
Justifying one's own actions	Honest, Frank, Candid
Lack of Purpose	Purposeful
Lazy, Indolent	Industrious, Conscientious
Loud	Tasteful, Quiet
Lustful	Healthy Sexuality
Lying	Honest
Manipulative	Candid, Honest, Non-Controlling
Masked, Closed	Honest, Open, Candid

Nagging	Supportive
Narrow-Minded	Open-minded
Obscene, Crude	Modest, Courteous
Over-Emotional	Emotionally stable
Perfectionistic	Realistic goals
Pessimistic	Realistic, Hopeful, Optimistic, Trusting
Possessive	Generous
Prejudiced	Open-minded
Procrastinates	Disciplined, Acts promptly
Projecting (negative)	Clear-sighted, Optimistic
Rationalizing	Candid, Honest
Resentful, Bitter, Hateful	Forgiving
Resisting	Willing to grow
Rude, Discourteous	Polite, Courteous
Sarcastic	Praising, Tolerant
Self-important	Humble, Modest
Self-Centered	Caring of others
Self-Destructive, Self-Defeating	Self-fulfilling
Self-Hating	Self-accepting, Loving
Self-Justifying	Admitting wrongs, Humble
Self-Pitying	Grateful, Realistic, Accepting
Self-Righteous	Humble, Understanding
Self-Seeking	Selfless, Concerned for others
Selfish	Altruistic, Concerned with others
Shy	Outgoing
Slothful (lazy)	Industrious, Takes action
Spiteful, Malicious	Forgiving

Stealing	Honest
Stubborn	Open-minded, Willing
Sullen	Cheerful
Superior, Grandiose, Pretentious	Humble
Superstitious	Realistic, No magical thinking
Suspicious	Trusting
Tense	Calm, Serene
Thinking negatively	Thinking positive
Treacherous	Trustworthy
Undisciplined, Self-Indulgent	Disciplined
Unfair	Fair
Unfriendly, Hostile, Bitchy	Friendly
Ungrateful	Thankful, Grateful
Unkind, Mean, Malicious, Spiteful	Kind
Unsupportive of others	Supportive
Untrustworthy, Unreliable	Trustworthy
Useless, Destructive	Helpful
Vain	Modest, Humble
Vindictive	Forgiving
Violent	Gentle
Vulgar	Polite
Wasteful	Thrifty
Willful	Accepting of the inevitable
Withdrawn	Outgoing
Wordy, Verbose	Frank, to the point, Succinct

Another list of shortcomings and virtues include:

Shortcoming	Virtue
Resentment/Anger	Forgiveness
Fear/Judgmental	Love
Self-pity/Whining	Letting go
Self-Justification	Humility
Self-Importance/Egotism	Modesty
Self-Condemnation/Guilt	Self-Valuation
Lying/Evasion/Dishonesty	Honesty
Impatience	Patience
False Pride/Phoniness/Denial	Unpretentiousness
Uncertainty/Jealousy	Trust
Envy/Craving/Need/Want	Satisfaction
Laziness	Activity
Procrastination	Promptness
Insincerity	Straightforward
Negative Thinking	Positive thinking
Immoral Thinking	Spiritual thinking
Intolerance/Perfection	Tolerance
Criticism/Loose Talk/Gossip	Praise for others
Hyper-Active/Hyper-Talker	Calmness
Greed/faithlessness	Generousness

The wise men who founded the original twelve-step program, Alcoholics Anonymous, knew that we would never be happy, joyous, and prosperous unless we could saw our part in the problem. To get that awareness, you just looked at liabilities that often lead to the problem that makes your life unmanageable and insane.

Accordingly, let us look at another set of assets and liabilities, when manifested, could either bring you closer to your Creator, or separate you from your real self and from the God of your understanding, as well as cutting you off from others, which caused you to become isolated, alone, and abandoned. Honestly identify any of the following that apply:

Shortcoming	Virtue
Invulnerable	Vulnerable
Perfectionism	Fallible
False belief of immortality	Mortal
Cruel	Kind
Selfishness	Considerate
Violent	Gentle
Resentful and bitter	Forgiving
Stingy	Generous
Unsympathetic	Understanding
Disagreeable	Good-Natured
Unfeeling	Sensitive

Do you see something interesting here?   Are the items listed on this list what you have always wanted to be? Now, you can become this.

Most of the preceding questions have been directed at helping us identify the exact nature of our wrongs, information we will need for the Fifth Step. It is also important that you take a look at things that you have done right or that have had a positive impact on yourself and others. You want to do this for a couple of reasons. First, you want to have a complete picture of yourself from working the Fourth Step, not a one-sided picture. Second, you want to know what character traits and behaviors we want more of in your life.

Answer the following questions:

- What qualities do you have that you like?

- That others like?

- That work well for you?

- How have you shown concern for yourself and others?

- Which spiritual principles are you practicing in your life?

- How has doing so changed your life?

- How has your faith and trust in a God of your understanding grown?

- What is your relationship with your sponsor based on?

- How do you see that positive experience translating into other relationships?

- What goals have you accomplished?

- Do you have other goals you are taking action to reach?

- What are they, and what action are you taking?

- What are your values?

- Which ones are you committed to living by, and how?

- How are you showing your gratitude for your wellness?

Moving On

Finishing a Fourth Step can mean many things: maybe a letdown, maybe exhilarating, or maybe uncomfortable. However, you should definitely feel good about what you have accomplished. The work you have done in this step will provide the foundation for the work you will do in Steps Five through Nine. Now is the time to contact your sponsor and make arrangements to work Step Five.

Chapter Nine

Step Five

Admitted to God, to ourselves, and to another human being the exact nature of our wrongs.

This means that you must look over your inventory and admit to the God of your understanding or a Power greater than you; to your innermost self; and to another human being the exact nature of our wrongs, not what your wrongs were. This is not a reading of your Fourth Step, nor is it a confession. You must also discuss select parts of your inventory with another person. It should be noted that this person could be a member of a twelve-step program who is sponsoring you, but it does not have to be. The forefathers and pioneers of Alcoholics Anonymous provide us with some alternatives.

They give us directions on how to choose the person with whom we should share our inventory.

They wrote that we must be entirely honest with somebody if we expect to live long or happily in this world. Rightly and naturally, we think carefully before we choose the person or persons with whom we will share this intimate and confidential Step. Those of us belonging to a religious denomination that requires confession might want to go to the properly appointed authority whose duty it is to receive confessions and do our Fifth Step with this individual. Although Alcoholics Anonymous has no religious connection, the founders and pioneers of Alcoholics Anonymous maintained that we may still do well to talk with someone ordained by an established religion who will keep our confidentiality.

The forefathers and pioneers of Alcoholics Anonymous went on to say that if we cannot or will not want to do this, we can search our acquaintances for a close-mouthed, understanding friend. Perhaps our doctor, a psychologist; or a licensed mental health counselor; or a licensed social worker; or a priest, minister, rabbi, or imam could be the person because they are required to uphold our privacy by law.

In regard to sponsorship, please keep in mind that the book: *Alcoholics Anonymous* was written in 1939 before any type of formalized sponsorship process had been established, and it was never mentioned in the book.

The idea of sponsorship was not developed until the middle 1940s when the supply of recovered people exceeded the demand for the Fellowship's help. With the rapid growth of Alcoholics Anonymous, primarily in the Cleveland area, and its sudden emergence onto the national stage, the need for classes where new members could be taken quickly through the Steps became evident.

Regarding sponsorship, the authors of the book: *Alcoholics Anonymous Comes of Age,* written in 1957, wrote that it was soon evident that a scheme of personal sponsorship would have to be devised for the new people. Each prospect was assigned an older member of Alcoholics Anonymous who visited him at his home or in the hospital; instructed him on the principles of Alcoholics Anonymous and took him the Twelve Steps of recovery; and conducted him to his first meeting. But in the face of many hundreds of pleas for help, the supply of elders could not possibly match the demand, so a new plan was devised. So, brand-new members of Alcoholics Anonymous, sober only a month or even a week, were pressed into sponsoring alcoholics who were still dying in the hospitals.

The Beginners' Meetings of the 1940s, also known as the "A.A. Classes," were an integral part of the original Alcoholics Anonymous program that produced a 75% recovery rate from alcoholism. For a period, these meetings became a lost piece of history, but with the publication of the book: *Back to Basics-The Alcoholics Anonymous Beginners' Meetings* in 1997, these very effective and successful meetings have been reintroduced to the Alcoholics Anonymous fellowship.

In the 1940s and 1950s, the original Alcoholics Anonymous program of recovery consisted of:

- Three to five days of detox in a hospital
- Newcomers were taken the Twelve Steps in one month
- Three to six months of Beginners Meetings where newcomers took others through the Steps and led meetings
- Regular meetings consisted of Open Speakers Meetings and Closed Discussion Meetings where members discussed the Big Book and the Alcoholics Anonymous design for living

This plan of action produced a 75% recovery rate from alcoholism. As a result, the fellowship grew rapidly, with membership doubled every ten years from the 1950s through the 1970s.

By the 1980s, the recovery program had changed dramatically because treatment was now being done in treatment centers, using the Twelve Steps of Alcoholic Anonymous as the cornerstone for treatment; overseen by physicians; and funded by insurance companies and the federal government.

It consisted of:

- Three to five days of detox in a hospital
- Treatment for 21 to 28 days
- Open Discussion Meetings

By the 1980s, the recovery rate dropped from 75% to less than 5%, and the Alcoholics Anonymous rate of growth slowed dramatically. From 1992 to 1995, membership in the United States stopped growing altogether. In 1992, world-wide membership peaked, and by 1997, it had declined by 20%.

By 1997, dramatic changes were taking place. Insurance companies severely cut back on the amount of money they were willing to spend for treatment of alcoholism; treatment programs began to close; and the Beginners' Meetings were reintroduced to the fellowship:

By the early 2000s, the modified program of recovery consisted of:

- Five to eight days of detox in a hospital or designated detox facility.
- Working the Twelves Steps were suggested but not enforced.
- Three to six months of Beginners Meetings where they took others through the Steps and led meetings.
- Regular meetings consisted of Open Discussion Meetings, Big Book Studies, Speakers Meetings, and Eleventh Step Meetings

As a result, although membership in Alcoholics Anonymous began to rise again, the recovery rate remains less than 5%, most newcomers are not expected to work the Twelve Steps of Recovery and only do not act out other addiction of choice and go to meetings. Does this mean that your cause is hopeless? Certainly not. If you do the work necessary for recovery to happen, it does. Remember what the founders and pioneers of Alcoholics Anonymous said: "Rarely have we seen a person fail. Those who do not recover cannot or will not give themselves to this simple program. They are such unfortunates..."

Back to the 1940s. Because of its rapid growth, newcomers had to grasp the basic principles of the Alcoholics Anonymous program in a very short time or go back to drinking. They were then pressed into service helping other newcomers through the Steps.

This method became very successful as evidenced by the early recovery rates in Cleveland, which set the standard for the Alcoholics Anonymous' "Twelve Step Classes," which became the primary means of recovery and spreading the Fellowship until the late 1950s when it was discontinued.

The forefathers and pioneers of Alcoholics Anonymous said that records in Cleveland showed that 93% of those who came to Alcoholics Anonymous never had to drink again.

The role of the sponsor is to share their experience, strength, and hope with the people they sponsor. The sponsor's role is not of a legal advisor, a banker, a parent, a marriage counselor, a social worker, or an intimate companion. Nor is a sponsor a therapist, physician, psychologist, or psychiatrist offering any sort of professional advice. Nor is a sponsor a person who dominates a newcomer or makes them dependent on them. A sponsor is simply another addict in recovery who is willing to share their journey through the Twelve Steps of recovery with a willing newcomer. A sponsor is a more experienced person in recovery who guides the less experienced newcomer through the Twelve Steps.

Sponsors and the people they sponsor participate in activities that lead to spiritual and personal growth and enlightenment, such as literature study and discussion, meditation and writing. Completing the Twelve Steps of Recovery does not imply being competent to sponsor newcomers in recovery. It is the quality of program of recovery and the quality of the person's character, not the length of time in sobriety that defines a good sponsor, so there is no time in service requirements or any other prerequisites to be a sponsor. A person who acts as a sponsor typically guides a newcomer through the Twelve Steps of Recovery, hears the person's Fifth Step, and guides them through their Ninth Step.

The personal nature of the behavioral issues that lead to seeking help in twelve-step fellowships results in a strong relationship between the sponsor and the person they sponsor. Since this relationship is based on mentorship, it is not generally characterized as a "friendship." Fundamentally, the sponsor has a single purpose: helping the person they sponsor discover and overcome the behavioral problems that brought them into the fellowship by helping them work the Twelve Steps of Recovery, which reflexively helps the sponsor discover and recover as well. Once the newcomer completes the Steps, the relationship between the sponsor and the person they sponsor ends or is transformed to a relationship between equals.

Therefore, you could share select parts of your inventory with any number of people who you believe are safe and will keep your private stuff in confidence. Thus, the misleading modern idea that we *must* share our inventory and the exact nature of our wrongs with a member of Alcoholics Anonymous, a sponsor, should be dismissed. In fact, it probably is a good idea to burn your Fourth Step Inventory as symbolic closure to our old way of life once you are done with it.

The forefathers and pioneers of Alcoholics Anonymous explain why it is important that we admit our shortcomings to another person.

They wrote that the best reason is that if we skip this vital step, we may not overcome our addiction. Time after time, newcomers have tried to keep to themselves certain facts about their lives. Trying to avoid this humbling experience, they have turned to easier ways. Almost invariably, they got drunk. Having persevered with the rest of the program, they wondered why they failed. We think the reason is that they never completed their housecleaning. They took inventory all right but hung on to some of their worst character flaws. They only thought they had lost their pride and fear, and they only thought they had humbled themselves. But they had not learned enough humility, fearlessness, and honesty, in the sense we find it necessary, until they told someone else all the nature of their wrongs.

Therefore, since we are not good judges of character, especially our own, we must confide in another person, whom we trust. Nevertheless, by the same token, since we are poor judges of character, it is important that we carefully choose a person we can confide and trust in with great care. This task should not be taken lightly. Thus, it might be wise, as stated by the forefathers and pioneers of Alcoholics Anonymous, to confide in a priest, member of the clergy, psychologist, or therapist because these individuals are required to maintain confidentiality by state and federal law. The forefathers and pioneers stated that it is important that the person we share this with be able to keep a confidence; that he fully understands and approves what we are driving at; that he will not try to change our plan.

Furthermore, we share parts of our inventory because we are great at self-deception and denial. It should be pointed out that we are the ones who said that we did not have a problem, and often emphatically said that we would never engage in their addiction again. We also blamed others over and over, projecting our unacceptable thoughts and beliefs onto others, while sinking deeper and deeper into the darkness of addiction.

It is interesting, considering the way we have lived our lives thus far that we could even think that we could have the right or entitlement to criticize anyone, especially when we are now seeing the faults in ourselves that we once saw in others. Can you see where you have done some things to others that might need to be forgiven? What are the odds that these people are going to walk up to you and say that they forgive you? Now that you see some of your defects and excesses of character, you now know what led you to do the wrongs you have done, and what caused your life to become unmanageable and insane. These are the nature of your wrongs.

Step Five asks you to admit to God as you understand Him or a Power greater than you, yourself, and to another human being the exact nature of your wrongs. Remember, you cannot ask the God of your understanding or a Power greater than you to get rid of things you did in the past, but you can ask this Power to remove the fears, inadequacies, inferiorities, and insecurities that underlie your defects and excesses which in turn caused you to act in the way you did, and you can ask for forgiveness for those things you did in the past to harm others. In order to complete this Step, you must uncover the exact nature of your wrongs that led to your defects and excesses of character that lie within your unconscious mind before you ask the God of your understanding or a Power greater than you to remove your defects and excesses of character.

However, it should be noted that your unconscious mind does not like an honest inventory, and so, it will fight to protect the mind from harm with a variety of defense strategies. According to the forefathers and pioneers of Alcoholics Anonymous, working with addicts has shown that there are identifiable human wrongs that most addicts have in common that make up the defects and excesses, which led to our problems.

It should be noted that the inventory that you completed in Step Four addressed the conscious part of your mind and its subsequent behaviors and consequences, known as our defects of character. However, you still need to address the underlying causes of your behaviors seen in the Fourth Step located in your unconscious mind, known as the exact nature of our wrongs. These caused your subsequent defects of character.

The following exercise will help you bring these unconscious values, beliefs, rules, roles, drives, and attitudes into the consciousness, so you could see where they are causing your problems and afford you the opportunity to change them, as well as ask the God of your understanding or a Power greater than you to remove the resulting defects and excesses of character.

The forefathers and pioneers of Alcoholics Anonymous give us specific instructions on how to do this Step. The forefathers and pioneers wrote that when we decide who is to hear our story, waste no time. We have our written inventory handy and we prepare ourselves for a long talk. We explain to the person who will hear our Fifth Step what we are about to do and why we have to do it. He should realize that we are engaged upon a life-and-death errand. Most people approached this way will be glad to help; they will be honored by our confidence.

The forefathers and pioneers went on to say that we pocket our pride and go to it, illuminating every twist of character and dark cranny of the past.

The forefathers and pioneers of Alcoholics Anonymous tell us that after we have shared the exact nature of our wrongs, we will be rewarded, and provide a list of benefits that we will receive as a result of taking this Step.

The forefathers wrote that once we have taken this Step, withholding nothing, we are delighted. We can look the world in the eyes. We can be alone at perfect peace and ease. Our fears fall from us. We begin to feel the nearness of the God of our understanding or a Power greater than us. We may have had certain spiritual beliefs, but now we begin to have a spiritual experience. The feeling that our problem has disappeared will often come strongly. We feel we are on the road to wellness, walking hand in hand with the God of our understanding or Power greater than us.

In order to understand the exact nature of our wrongs, it is important to know and understand how our defects and excesses have influenced our behavior, thinking, and beliefs.

In order to understand the Fifth Step, you must understand the terms the forefathers and pioneers used in the Fourth and Fifth Steps because they are separate but inexorably tied together. The Fourth Step uses the term: "Defects of Character" and the Fifth Step uses the term: "Exact Nature of Our Wrongs." Are these the same? No, although they are commonly used interchangeably.

So, to complete Step Five, you must identify the exact nature of your wrongs. What is the exact nature of your wrongs? The exact nature of your wrongs is the Seven Deadly Sins you found on Page Three and the fears, inferiorities, inadequacies, and insecurities that you found on Page Four of your Fourth Step inventory. Therefore, to complete this vital step you must link your Seven Deadly Sins found on Page Three and your fears, inferiorities, inadequacies, and insecurities found on Page Four of your Forth Step to the list of behaviors or defects of character found on Page Six of your Fourth Step. For example, if you have a fear of rejection, you might have engaged in apprehensiveness, fear, argumentativeness, quarrelsomeness, arrogance, insolence, attacking, critical, controlling, and avoidance, which hurt others.

Therefore, to complete Step Five, you must complete three tasks. First, you must admit to your innermost self the exact nature of your wrongs, or your fears, inadequacies, inferiorities, and insecurities, as well as how you compensated for these with the Seven Deadly Sins, and how they caused the defects of character or behaviors you found in Step Four that caused harm to others.

Second, you must admit to another human being the exact nature of your wrongs, or your fears, inadequacies, inferiorities, and insecurities, and how they caused the defects of character or behaviors you found in Step Four that caused harm to others, preferable to someone who will respect your confidentiality such as a priest, clergy, psychologist, or therapist.

And third, you must admit to a God of your understanding or a Power greater than you the exact nature of your wrongs, or your fears, inadequacies, inferiorities, and insecurities, and how they caused the defects of character or behaviors you found in Step Four that caused harm to others. Are you willing to admit to your innermost self, another person, and to a God of your understanding or a Power greater than you the exact nature of your wrongs, or your fears, inadequacies, inferiorities, and insecurities, that led to your defects of character or behaviors that caused harm to others?

It should be noted that you are well on the way to recovering from your addiction. The forefathers and pioneers of Alcoholics Anonymous tell us that we are in the process of having a spiritual awakening and as a result, our obsession to drink alcohol to relieve our anxiety is being removed.

Furthermore, the forefathers give us specific directions on what to do after we have finished sharing our inventories and explored our unconscious motivations.

They wrote that when we return home, we find a place where we can be quiet for an hour, carefully reviewing what we have done. We thank the God of our understanding or a Power greater than us from the bottom of our heart that we know Him better. Taking this book down from our shelf, we turn to the page which contains the Twelve Steps of Recovery. Carefully reading the first five Steps, we ask if we have omitted anything, for we are building an arch through which we shall walk a free man at last. Is our work solid so far? Are the stones properly in place? Have we skimped on the cement put into our foundations? Have we tried to make mortar without sand? And so, we review Steps One through Five at this point to make sure that we have not omitted anything.

Now that you have thoroughly examined yourself and have admitted your faults to yourself, to a God of your understanding or a Power greater than you, and to another human being, you are ready to move to Step Six.

The operational principle of Step Five is Integrity. If we have truly done a thorough job of introspection and evaluation of our assets and shortcomings, do we have the integrity to own up to it? It could be very difficult to be open and honest about our behaviors. We accept the need for a dose of humility.

It must be strongly stated that Step Five is not simply a reading of your Step Four, and it is not a confession; it is an affirmation of the exact nature of our wrongs. It is the admission you make to a God of your understanding or a Power greater than you, to yourself, and to another human being that brings about the spiritual growth connected with this Step. You have had some experience with making admissions already. You have admitted you have an illness of escape; you have admitted you need help to overcome it; and you have admitted there is a Power greater than you that can help you. Drawing on your experience with these admissions will help you in Step Five.

Many of us finished our Fourth Step with a sense of relief, thinking that the really hard part was over, only to realize that we still had the Fifth Step to do. That is when the fear and panic set in again. Some of us were afraid that our sponsor would reject or judge us. Others hesitated because we did not want to bother another person with our burden, and we were not sure the hearer of our Fifth Step could keep our secrets.

You might have been concerned about what your inventory might reveal. There might be something hidden from you that your sponsor would spot immediately, and it probably would not be anything good. Some of us were afraid of having to re-feel old feelings and wondered if there was really any benefit to stirring up the past. Some of us felt that as long as we had not actually spoken our inventories out loud, the contents would not be quite real.

The Fourth and Fifth Steps are your tools for releasing and healing yourself. You wrote an inventory of what was bothering you, and then you verbalized your part and your responsibility to the a God of your understanding or a Power greater than you, yourself, and another person. You take responsibility for yourself and you accept situations and yourself the way you are.

You can do them formally, by writing an inventory and making an appointment to discuss it, or informally, whenever things arise in the course of your life that needs attention. These two steps give you the formula for healing from your past, from your old negative beliefs, from repressed feelings, from mistakes, from all that you are striving to be healed from. Likewise, you learn to connect with yourself honestly and emotionally, so you can do the same with others.

Be open to using the process and the tools defined in Fifth Step by initiating change and healing in yourself, trusting that it will bring positive results, harmony with others, and good feelings about yourself. When you are confused about your part in an incident or who to talk to about it, wait for guidance, but do not wait too long.

This Step gives you permission to be who you are, to forgive and love yourself, and to forgive and love others. Likewise, this Step gives you a formula for self-care in relationships: looking within, and honesty with self, a God of your understanding or a Power greater than you, and others. This Step give you permission to be human, vulnerable, and honest; and it gives you permission to have emotions. This is the telling-the-truth Step. You use it as often as necessary, and this is the Step that will set you free. These are cleansing and freeing Steps.

You need to tell the God of your understanding or a Power greater than you about you. Quietly, silently, during your morning meditation, your afternoon break, or your evening walk say to this Power who you are, what you did to harm others, what you think, what you want, what you need, what you are feeling, what you are going through, what you are worried about, and your fears and hopes. Speak of your old beliefs and what you think you cannot deal with and what need His help with.

You must be honest, open, and vulnerable with the God of your understanding. When you do this, you will achieve the highest form of spirituality. You are not burdening the God of your understanding or a Power greater than you by bringing yourself to Him. That is what this Power wants you to do.

Besides telling the God of your understanding or a Power greater than you, you must tell yourself who you are, what you want, what you have done, your wrongs, your secrets, your good points, and your beliefs. You need to admit to yourself what you are really feeling, what you fear, and who you are. You need to break through your own denial. You need to be honest with yourself.

Some call addiction a disease, some call it an illness; whereas others call it a problem, and some do not know what to call it. Some do not even like to call it alcoholism at all. But many, including some forefathers and pioneers of Alcoholics Anonymous called it a "soul-sickness." What we do in recovery is to practice the daily behaviors that we call "recovery." What are we recovering? We are recovering our healthy selves. What we are seeking are psychic and soul-level changes in ourselves; changes that can be manifested in our lives and our relationships, beginning with our primary relationships with ourselves.

To begin that process, it is imperative that you unearth, release, get rid of, and be done with shame, fear, guilt, secrets, and anything else inside you that bothers you, causes you to feel less than, weighted down by, burdened by, and bad about yourself. The way to do that is by opening your mouths and getting it out. It is a simple but effective way to begin healing yourself. You simply tell the truth about yourself to yourself, to another person, and to a God of your understanding or a Power greater than you in an attitude of self-responsibility, acceptance, and forgiveness.

If you have done the work called for in the Fourth Step and if you have sat down and inventoried yourself, you have started to shake up your soul. You have reached in with a Brillo pad and begun to scrub loose the debris and grunge within; those things blocking you from living the life you want to live. No matter what form of Fourth Step you use, no matter if you do a small, medium, or large one, you have loosened some things that need immediately to be washed away.

Once you start this process of loosening the "stuff" within, you will often notice it more. You might feel the weight of it all. You might begin to notice the feelings, needs, guilt, and burden of what you have carried around. You need to set up an appointment with your sponsor to talk about this soon. You need to move quickly on to this Step to do the washing away and cleansing of all that has been loosened.

It is important to take a Fifth Step soon after completing your Fourth Step inventory. They suggest beginning on deadline to do the Fourth and going immediately in for the "cleansing" part. However, you do it, you can do yourself a favor and move quickly to this Step. Just as it is important to do your Fifth Step soon after you write your inventory, it is also important to choose carefully the person who will hear your Fifth Step. Some people choose to do the Fifth Step work with a minister, priest, rabbi, or imam, whereas others prefer not to. Some people choose a trusted person to do this work with, whereas others search around until they find the right person. An important criterion is that you do your Fifth Step with someone experienced in hearing Fifth Steps, someone who has done it before, and knows what you are looking for, someone who can assist and lead you through the process.

Sometimes you find that the most troublesome things. For many of us, stealing something when we were younger. For others, it is our flaws about ourselves and our lives, but it does not seem so bad once we get them into the light. You quickly learn that nobody is perfect, and nobody needs to be. But when something bothers you, you need to get it out into the light to be healed from it. If it is bothering you, you need to talk about it. And the more it bothers you, the more shame and self-hatred it causes, the more it controls you and your life, the more important it is to bring it out. Maya Angelou, the former Poet Laureate of the United States, once said: "There is no greater agony than bearing an untold story inside you."

If you consider all your feelings about the Fifth Step, you might find that you are also motivated to continue this process by a desire for more discovery and wellness. Think about all the people you know who have worked this step. You maybe struck by their genuineness and by

316

their ability to connect well with others. They are not always talking about themselves. They are asking about others, and they are truly interested in knowing the answer. And if you ask them how they learned so much about relationships with others, they will probably tell you that they began learning when they worked Step Five.

Many of us, having worked the Fourth and Fifth Steps before, know that this process always results in change. In other words, you will have stop behaving in the same old ways, even though you might not have been entirely sure you wanted that. On the other hand, many of us knew we had to change, but were afraid we could not.

The two things you need to begin working Step Five are courage and a sense of trust in the process of recovery. If you have both these things, you will be able to work through more specific fears and go through with the admissions you need to make in this Step.

Facing Your Fears

Any of the fears you have talked about here might be yours, or you might have other fears that plague you. It is essential that you know what your fears are and move forward despite them so that you are able to continue with your wellness.

Answer the following questions:

- What reservations do you have about working the Fifth Step?
- Do you have any fears at this point?
- What are they?

No matter where our fears come from, in recovery, most of us have done pretty much the same things to deal with them: We pray for courage and willingness. Many of us have had the experience of going to twelve-step study meetings and finding that coincidentally the topic always seems to be on Step Four or Five. If you make the effort to share what you are going through, you are sure to get the support you need from other members. Calling upon the spiritual resources you have developed through working the previous Steps will allow you to proceed with your Fifth Step.

Answer the following questions:

- What are you doing to work through your fears about doing a Fifth Step?
- How has working the first four steps prepared you to work the Fifth Step?

What does Step Five ask you to do? It asks you to admit to the God of your understanding or a Power greater than you, to yourself, and another human being the exact nature of our wrongs. It does not ask you to confess all the wrongs you have ever done. So, take your inventory and look at your list of shortcomings or defects of character on Page Six and you see the behaviors that you have used to cause great harm to yourself and others. Step Five asks you what the nature of these wrongs are, which are listed on Page Six of your inventory. So, you look a little further up your inventory and you will see two pages that show that exact nature of your wrongs: Page Three, which show your misuses of pride, and Page Four, which show your fears, inadequacies, inferiorities, and insecurities.

Admit to a God of Your Understanding of a Power Greater Than You

Why must you admit the exact nature of your wrongs to the God of your understanding or a Power greater than you in addition to admitting them to yourself and another human being? In wellness, we experience a way of life where the spiritual meets the everyday, where the ordinary meets the extraordinary. When we admit the exact nature of our wrongs to the God of our understanding or a Power greater than us, our admission becomes more meaningful.

How you make your admission to the God of your understanding or a Power greater than you depends on the specifics of your understanding. Some of us make a formal admission to God of our understanding or a Power greater than us apart from the admissions we make to ourselves and another human being. Others acknowledge or invite the presence of a God of their understanding or a Power greater than them in some way before going over their inventory with the hearer of your Fifth Step. Those agnostics or atheists who use the spiritual principles of recovery or the power of a twelve-step fellowship as a Higher Power might have to explore a different method of working this portion of the Fifth Step because it would be inappropriate to make such disclosures to a group.

Answer the following questions:

- How will you include the God of your understanding in your Fifth Step

- How is your Third Step decision reaffirmed by working the Fifth Step?

To Ourselves

When we were active in our obsessive compulsive learned helplessness, most of us probably had people telling us we had a problem and should get some help. Their comments did not really matter to us. Or even if they did matter, it was not enough to stop us from acting out on our obsessive compulsive learned helplessness. Not until we admitted that we were powerless over our obsessive compulsive learned helplessness and surrendered our selfish self, were we able to stop acting out. It is just the same with the admission we make in the Fifth Step. You can have everyone from our spouse to our employer to your sponsor telling you what you are doing that is working against you, but until you admit to your own innermost self the exact nature of our wrongs and what is driving those wrongs, you are not likely to have the willingness or the ability to choose another way.

Answer the following questions:

- Can you acknowledge and accept the exact nature of your wrongs?

- How will making this admission change the direction of your life?

And to another Human Being

As people who are powerless over our obsessive compulsive learned helplessness, one of the biggest problems we have is telling the difference between our responsibility and the responsibilities of others. We often blame ourselves for catastrophes over which we have no control, or we blamed others. Conversely, we are often in complete denial about how we have hurt ourselves and others. We over-dramatize minor troubles, and we shrug off major problems we really should be looking at.

If you are not sure what the exact nature of your wrongs are when you begin your Fifth Step, you will know by the time you finish, because of your admissions to another human being. What you cannot see, the hearer of your Fifth Step can, and they will help you sort out what you need to accept as your responsibility and what you do not. So, you need a denial or deception detector who will gently confront you when you are denying your responsibility for your bad behavior or alert you when you are being deceptive.

Most of us asked someone to be our sponsor before we formally began working the Steps and have been developing a relationship with that person ever since. For most of us, our sponsor will be the "another human being" we choose to hear our Fifth Step, and they will help us separate the things that were not our responsibility from the things that were.

The relationship that you have been building with your sponsor or mentor will give you the trust you need to have in them. The therapeutic value of one person who is powerless over their obsessive compulsive learned helplessness helping another person with obsessive compulsive learned helplessness is often powerfully demonstrated when your sponsor shares parts of their their inventory as you share yours. This goes a long way toward reassuring you that you are not unique.

As was stated previously, the trust you must have in the person who is to hear our Fifth Step goes beyond simply being assured that they will keep your confidences. You need to trust that your listener can respond appropriately to what you are sharing. One of the primary reasons that so many of us find ourselves choosing our sponsor or as the person who will hear our Fifth Step is because they understand what we are doing, and therefore, knows just what kind of support we need during this process. Also, if your sponsor is the person who will hear your Fifth Step, it will help promote continuity when you work the following Steps.

Still, if for any reason you choose someone else to hear your Fifth Step admission, their "qualifications" are the same ones that you would look at for in your sponsor: an ability to be supportive without minimizing your responsibility; someone who can provide a steadying influence if you begin to feel overwhelmed during your Fifth Step; and someone with compassion, integrity, insight, and an ability to hold your confidence.

As was said above, it should be noted that many people who work this Step do so with some kind of professional who is obligated by law to keep our confidence, such as a therapist or a member of the clergy. This is highly suggested.

Answer the following questions:

- What qualities does your listener have that are attractive to you?
- How will his or her possession of these qualities help you make your admissions more effective?

For most of us, developing an honest relationship is something new. We are very good at running away from relationships the first time someone tells us a painful truth. We are also good at having polite, distant interactions with no real depth. The Fifth Step helps you to develop honest in-depth relationships. You tell the truth about who you are; then, the hard part: you listen to the response. Most of us have been terrified of having a relationship like this.

The Fifth Step gives you a unique opportunity to try such a relationship in a safe context. You can be pretty much assured that you would not be judged.

Answer the following questions:

- Are you willing to trust the person who is to hear your Fifth Step?

- What do you expect from that person?

- How will working the Fifth Step help you begin to develop new ways of having relationships?

The Exact Nature of Our Wrongs

Another way to ensure that your Fifth Step is not simply a reading of your Fourth Step or a confession is to focus on what you are supposed to be admitting: the exact nature of your wrongs. There is a diversity of experience in what precisely the term: "the exact nature of our wrongs" means. Most of us agree that in working Step Five, we should be focusing our attention on what underlies the patterns of our obsessive compulsive learned helplessness and the reasons we acted out in the ways that we did.

Identifying the exact nature of your wrongs is the purpose of this important Step. Sometimes the repetition of the same type of situation will reveal the exact nature of that situation. For example, why do you keep engaging in your obsessive compulsive learned helplessness when in the face of all evidence, it is doing serious damage to you and those around you? Why do you keep putting your obsessive compulsive learned helplessness before those you love? Why do you feel threatened by people who are more powerful than you and either try to overpower them through coercion or manipulation of try to avoid them? Why do you undo every success you have with a catastrophic failure?

Finding the common thread in your own patterns of codependence or relationship addiction will lead you right to the exact nature of your wrongs. At some point in this process, you will probably begin identifying certain patterns of behavior as your character defects or shortcomings. It is here that you begin an in-depth examination of how each one of your defects of character play a role in keeping you tied to your obsessive compulsive learned helplessness.

Answer the following questions:

- How does the exact nature of your wrongs differ from your actions?
- Why do you need to admit the exact nature of your wrongs, and not just the wrongs themselves?

So, how do you do this important step. Keep in mind that this not a confession and you are not confessing your sins. Save that for your priest. Here is the process of admitting your wrongs: Go to Page Six of your inventory and identify the first defect written there such as: "I have been selfish." Next, go to Page Four of your Inventory and identify which fear, inferiority, inadequacy, or security is responsible and how you compensated for these and your real or perceived feelings of rejection or abandonment. Additionally, go to Page Three of your Inventory and identify which of the Seven Deadly Sins or misuses of pride lie at core of your selfness. Explore how your selfishness worked for you, not what it did to you. Do, this same process for each of the defects of character you listed on Page Six of your inventory.

Spiritual Principles

In the Fifth Step, you will focus on trust, courage, self-honesty, and commitment.

Practicing the spiritual principle of trust is essential if you are to get through the Fifth Step. As mentioned above, you will probably have some experience with your sponsor that allows you to trust them enough to go ahead with this step; but what about the more profound issues that arise when you wonder if working this step will really do any good? You have to trust a process as well as another person.

The connection between the Fifth Step and your spiritual development is not always clear. This does not mean that the connection is any less real, but it may make it harder for you to trust the process.

Answer the following questions:

- Do you believe that working the Fifth Step will somehow make your life better?
- How?

Courage is one principle you will have to practice just to get started on this Step. You will probably need to continue drawing on your courage periodically throughout your work on this Step. When you call your sponsor for an appointment to make your Fifth Step admissions, you will likely feel fear, so you need to practice courage. It should be noted again that you are not sharing your whole inventory; only the parts that relate to the exact nature of your wrongs, so you need not fear that you just cannot tell anyone about those many embarrassing and excruciatingly painful things you did to harm others.

Each time you feel fear, you must remind yourself that giving in to it has rarely had anything but negative consequences in your lives and doing so this time would not be any different. Such a reminder should be enough to motivate us to gather your courage.

Answer the following questions:

- What are some of the ways in which you can find the courage you need to work this step?
- How does practicing the principle of courage in working this step affect you whole Journey to wellness?
- Have you set a time and place for my Fifth Step?
- When and where?

Practicing the principle of self-honesty is essential when you admit to yourself the exact nature of your wrongs. Just as you must not disassociate yourself from your emotions simply because you are afraid of your listener's response, so you cannot afford to shut down your own reactions. You must allow yourself to experience the natural and human reaction to the subject under discussion: your obsessive compulsive learned helplessness. You have missed out on a lot because of your obsessive compulsive learned helplessness and your own unresolved childhood fears, inferiorities, inadequacies, and insecurities. These realizations are painful. However, if you pay close attention, you will probably recognize another feeling that is beginning to form in the wake of the pain—hope.

You have finally stopped running away from our feelings and shutting down because of your feelings. Remember your condition is an illness of escape. Now, for the first time, you have a chance to walk through your feelings, even the painful ones, with courage, and doing so, these will, in the long run, make you feel better about yourself. This is one of the paradoxes that you often find in recovery and wellness. What begins in pain; ends in joy and serenity.

Answer the following questions:

- How have you avoided self-honesty in the past?
- What are you doing to practice it now?
- How is a more realistic view of you connected to humility?
- How does practicing the principle of self-honesty help you accept yourself?

The principle of commitment is demonstrated by the action you take in this Step. Many of us have made so-called "commitments" in our lives, commitments that we had no intention of sticking to in tough times; and so, our "commitments" were made solely for the sake of convenience. With each Step we have taken, we have deepened our real, practical commitment to our wellness.

Answer the following question:

- How does sharing the exact nature of your wrongs with your sponsor further your commitment to your twelve-step program of discovery and wellness?

Moving On

One of the many benefits we get from working Step Five is a sense of self-acceptance. We clearly recognize who we are today and accept ourselves without reservation. Just because we are lacking in certain areas does not mean we are worthless. We begin to see that we have both assets and liabilities. We are capable of doing great good and we are equally capable of inflicting great evil. There are aspects of our personalities that make us very good and some that make us very bad. Nevertheless, our experiences, even the negative ones, have often contributed to the development of the very best parts of us.

For the first time, we can acknowledge that we are okay just as we are, right at this moment. But accepting ourselves as we are today does not mean we can relax and stop striving for improvement and excellence in everything we do. True self-acceptance includes accepting what we are lacking as well. It would not be self-acceptance if we believed we had no further growing to do—it would be denial. So, we acknowledge what we are lacking, and we make a commitment to work on those shortcomings. If we want to be more compassionate, we work on it by practicing the principle of compassion. If we want to be better educated, we take the time to learn. If we want to have more friends, we take the time to develop our relationships.

Answer the following question:

• How has working Step Five increased your humility and self-acceptance?

As you finish your Step Five, you might feel a sense of relief. You have unburdened yourself by sharing what you previously had put a lot of energy into hiding or suppressing. It is true that your defects die in the light of exposure. Exposure to the light of truth brings a sense of freedom that you feel no matter what the outer circumstances of your life might be like.

All our relationships begin to change as a result of working this Step. We especially need to acknowledge how much our relationship with ourselves, with a Higher Power, and with other people have changed.

Answer the following questions:

- How has your relationship with a God of your understanding or a Power greater than you changed as a result of working the Fifth Step?
- How has your relationship with your sponsor changed as a result of working the Fifth Step?
- How has your view of yourself changed as a result of working this step?
- To what extent have you developed love and compassion for yourself and others?

Chapter Ten

Step Six

We were entirely ready to have God remove all these defects of character.

In Step Six, the forefathers and pioneers of Alcoholics Anonymous ask us to answer a simple question. They asked us if we are we now entirely ready to let the God of our understanding or a Power greater than us remove from us all the things which we have found and admitted that are objectionable? Can this Power now take them all away? Yes, but only if we get out of the way and let these things go. If we still cling onto something, and we will not let it go, we can ask this Power to remove these things, but nothing is likely to happen until we get out of the way and we are willing to let these things go. We can ask ourselves: How important is it hold on to these things? What is holding on to things doing for you, not to you? Is the pain of holding on to these things worse than the pain of letting them go?

So, according to the forefathers and pioneers of Alcoholics Anonymous, it is decision time again. In the Fifth Step, you identified and admitted the exact nature of your wrongs, or your fears, inadequacies, inferiorities, and insecurities, that led to your defects and excesses of character or behaviors that harmed others around you, but in Step Six, you make the preparations necessary to let go of these defects and excesses or bad behaviors, and do the work necessary to rid yourself of these behaviors.

Begin with a moment of silence or meditation. We ask the God of our understanding or Power greater than us for the willingness to do whatever is necessary to ready ourselves to have Him remove the defects of character and the nature of your wrongs, namely, your fears, inadequacies, inferiorities, and insecurities we discovered in Step Four. Have the person who heard your Fifth Step ask you the following question: "Are you now ready to do whatever is necessary make yourself ready to have this Power remove all the things which you have admitted are objectionable from you." If you answered "yes," you have completed Step Six and are ready to move on to Step Seven, right? Well, not quite.

We begin working Step Six full of the hope that we have developed in the first five Steps. If we have been thorough, we have also developed some humility. In Step Six, "humility" means that we can see ourselves more clearly. We have seen the exact nature of our wrongs. We have seen how we have harmed ourselves and others by acting on our defects of character. We have seen the patterns of our behavior, and we have come to understand how we are likely to act on the same defects over and over. Now, we have to become entirely ready to have our defects of character removed.

Becoming entirely ready to have these defects of character removed will not happen in an instant—it is a process that often takes place over the first 12 to 18 months of wellness. Immediately following your inventory, you might feel very ready indeed to have your defects removed. If you have been around awhile and are generally pretty well aware of what your defects are, you are likely aware that you still act on them from time to time. But you will naturally find that your level of willingness still rises. Awareness alone will never be enough to ensure your readiness, but it is the necessary first step on the path to readiness. The inventory process itself has raised your awareness about your character defects; and working the Sixth Step will do so even more because it is the introspection or look within that is crucial to wellness. To be entirely ready is to reach a spiritual state where you are not just aware of your defects; not just tired of them; not just confident that the God of your understanding will remove them; but all these things.

In order to become entirely ready, you will need to address your fears about the Sixth Step. You will also need to take a look at how your defects will be removed. The Sixth Step says that only a God of your understanding can remove them, but what does that mean in practical terms? What is your responsibility in the Sixth Step? These questions, when reviewed with your sponsor or mentor, will help give you direction in working this Step.

Entirely Ready for What?

If you are new in recovery and this is your first experience with the Sixth Step, many of your character defects will be so blatant that your immediate reaction will likely be one of overwhelming willingness to get rid of them. Perhaps, you are seeing them for the first time in all their glory, so to speak, and you want them gone today. Once you have gotten past your initial reaction, you will find that you probably have at least some measure of fear or uncertainty about changing.

The unknown is terrifying for almost everyone. You have had the defects you are about to let go of for a long time, probably most of your life. You probably have some fears about what your life will be like without these defects. Some of them might seem more like vital survival skills than defects of character. You might wonder if the removal of your defects will inhibit your ability to earn a living. Many of us are strongly attached to our image and our power, but these are merely over-compensations or misuses of pride. You might be afraid that by working the Sixth Step you will be changed into dull conformity. Some of us might think that we are nothing but our defects and wonder what will be left of us if our defects are removed. Your fears are probably vague and unformed. If you pursue them to their logical conclusion, you are sure to find that they are unfounded. In other words, if you say them out loud, you can see them for what they are.

Answer the following questions:

- Are there parts of you that you like that might be defects?
- Are you afraid you will turn into someone you do not like if those parts of your character are removed?
- What do you think will be removed?

If you have had some previous experience with the Sixth Step, your character defects are nothing new. In fact, you might be feeling dismayed right now that you still have a certain defect, or you might be upset because you are looking at the same old defect in a new manifestation. For instance, if you are still insecure, you might no longer run around indulging in a series of transparent attempts to convince others that you are better than everyone, but you still have the defect.

The way you have been acting on it lately is far subtler and far more insidious. You might have been unconsciously sabotaging the efforts of others so that you can look better by comparison or trampling on someone else's desires because they do not directly serve your own needs. What is especially painful about realizations such as this in later recovery, is that you have thought of yourself in a better light, and so, you are deeply ashamed of harming others. You might feel a dull fear that you are incapable of change and that one character defect or another is here to stay.

But you can draw some measure of comfort from the fact that you are now aware of what you have been doing and are willing to work on it. You need to maintain a sense of hope and trust that the process of recovery works even on the most firmly entrenched defects.

Answer the following questions:

- Do you still believe in the process of discovery and wellness?

- Do you believe you can change?

- How have you changed so far?

- What defects do you no longer have to act on?

- Do you have any defects that you think cannot be removed?

- What are they?

- Why do you think they cannot be removed?

To Have a God of Your Understanding or a Power greater than you remove...

Yes, the Sixth Step specifies that only a God of your understanding or a Power greater than you can remove your defects of character. However, the extent to which most of us grasp what this actually means is directly influenced by how much experience we have with the up-and-down, on-again off-again struggle and surrender associated with Step Six.

The first thing most of us do about our character defects is decide not to practice them. Unfortunately, this is futile, and is about as effective as attempting to control your obsessive compulsive learned helplessness or perhaps nailing Jello to a tree. We might have some apparent success for a time, but our defects will eventually resurface. The problem is that your defects are part of you. You will always be subject to reverting to your worst character defects in stressful situations. Thus, you cannot think yourself into a new of acting; you must act yourself into a new way of thinking.

What you need to do in the Sixth Step is much like what you had to do in the first two Steps. You must admit that you have been defeated by an internal force that has brought you nothing but pain and degradation. Then, you have to admit you need help in dealing with that force. You must completely accept the fact that you cannot remove your own shortcomings, and you must prepare yourself to ask for the courage, faith, and determination in the Seventh Step from a God of your understanding or a Power greater than you to help you remove them. But just asking this Power to remove these shortcomings is not enough; you have to do something.

What is that something? You must practice a new set of values principles, and virtues in every aspect of your life; then these shortcomings will be miraculously and mercifully removed. Remember that this Power will not help you unless you get out of the way first and do your work.

Answer the following questions:

- How are you trying to remove or control your character defects?
- What have your attempts resulted in?
- What is the difference between being entirely ready to have the God of your understanding or a Power greater the you remove your defects of character and suppressing them yourself?
- How are you increasing your trust in the God of your understanding or a Power greater than you by working this step?
- How does your surrender deepen in this step?
- What action can you take that shows that you are entirely ready?

Our Defects of Character

Even after all the work you have done in the Fourth and Fifth Steps, you are likely still not entirely clear at this point about the nature of your defects of character until you do something. You are probably wondering where precisely your character defects end and your character assets begin within the complex structure of your personality.

Answer the following questions:

- Why do you do the things you do?
- Is it someone else's fault?
- When did you first feel this way?
- Why? How? Where?

If you are not careful, you can become so obsessed with this that you lose sight of why you are working a Sixth Step, so you need to focus your efforts. Your goal is to raise your awareness of your character defects so that you can become entirely ready to have them removed, not being indulging in bouts of selfishness.

Our character defects are indicators of our basic primitive nature, and we are likely to find that we have the same basic nature as anyone else. Thus, we have needs, and we try to get them met. For instance, we need love. How you go about getting love is where your defects come into play. If you lie, cheat, or harm others and degrade yourself to get love, you are acting on your defects. Your defects are basic human traits that have been distorted by your selfishness. With your sponsor's help, you need to list each defect you have, describe the ways in which you act on it, look at how it affects your life, and very importantly, find out what you are feeling when you practice it.

Imagining what your life would be like without your defects will help you see that you can live without them. Some of us take practical action by finding out what the opposite spiritual principle would be for each of our character defects. List each defect and give a brief definition of it.

Answer the following questions:

- In what ways do you act on this defect?
- When you act on this defect, what effect does it have on yourself and others?
- What feelings do you associate with this defect?
- Are you trying to suppress certain feelings by acting on certain defects
- What would your life be like without this behavior?
- Which spiritual principle can you apply instead?

Spiritual Principles

In the Sixth Step, you will focus on commitment and perseverance, willingness, faith, trust, and self-acceptance. At this point in your Sixth Step work, you should be acutely aware of your shortcomings. In fact, you are probably so aware of them that in the course of your daily life, you can see them coming and even stop yourself from acting on them much of the time.

At times, your awareness might fade, and you might no longer be as vigilant in watching for your religious addiction to rise again. It takes an incredible amount of energy to monitor ourselves every second and curb every impulse to engage in your obsessive compulsive codependence or relationship addiction. You will relax into everyday life until suddenly, you will be left feeling sick and ashamed and wondering how, after all the work you have done, you could have possibly did it again.

However, do not give up. Instead, make a commitment to recovery and wellness. Maintain your newly emerging values, principles, and virtues despite your setbacks. Keep taking steps forward even though you have just taken one or more backward. You are looking for gradual improvement, not instant faultlessness.

Answer the following questions:

- How are you demonstrating your commitment discovery and wellness today?
- By working the first five steps, you have persevered in your recovery.
- Why is this quality so vital to the Sixth Step?

Applying the spiritual principle of willingness means, very simply, that you are willing to act differently. It does not necessarily mean that you will act differently or even that you can do so. We can perhaps best illustrate this attitude by an example. Suppose you have been dishonest with your family, your employer, or your friends in many ways, ranging from the minor to severe. Even though it might seem better to become willing in "layers," focusing your willingness on the worst and most destructive forms of dishonesty first, this Step says that you were entirely ready to have all your defects removed. That means being willing never to be dishonest again, even in a minor way, to the best of your ability and we practice this in every part of our lives. This might seem like more than you can expect of yourself, but you only must do it for today.

It is hard to have this kind of willingness, especially when the apparent consequences for mild dishonesty are not so severe. You might be aware that you are not being entirely honest, but you think you are not hurting anyone, and you were getting away with it, so why be concerned about it? But it is this kind of thinking that has perhaps the most severe spiritual consequences. It might turn out that no one is obviously harmed by your dishonesty, and that no one ever finds out, but the dishonesty reverberates in your spirit from then on. Even if you are not consciously aware of it, even if you sleep just fine at night, the result of acting on a defect when you have the ability not to is an impairment of your spiritual growth. If you continue being unwilling, you will eventually paralyze your spiritual growth. Remember that integrity and honesty are most meaningful when no one is watching.

Answer the following questions:

- Are you willing to have all your defects of character removed at this time?
- If not, why not?
- What have you done to show your willingness today?

The amount of willingness you must develop in this Step requires a corresponding amount of faith and trust. You must believe that a God of your understanding or a Power greater than you is going to work in your life to the exact degree that is necessary. Continuing with the example of dishonesty, you must trust that a God of your understanding or a Power greater than you is not going to remove the defect of dishonesty from your life to such a degree that you become brutally honest, incapable of remaining silent even when speaking a truth that might hurt someone. As long as you get out of the way so that the God of your understanding or a Power greater than you can work in your life, you will experience the exact degree of spiritual growth that you need.

Answer the following questions:

- To what degree is your fear of what you will become still present?
- Has it diminished since you began working this step?
- How are you increasing your trust in the God of your understanding or a Power greater than you by working this Step?

With words like "entirely" and "all" playing such a prominent role in this Step, it is easy to become overly self-critical and perfectionistic. You need to remember that even though your willingness must be complete, you are not going to become perfect—not today, not ever. When you act out on a defect against your will, you need to practice the principle of self-acceptance. You need to accept that although you are still capable of acting out on your defects of character, you are also still willing to change, and with that acknowledgment, you renew your commitment to be changed. You have grown exactly as much as you were supposed to for today, and if you were perfect, you would have no further need to grow.

Answer the following questions:

- Do you accept yourself today?
- What do you like about yourself?
- What has changed since you have been working the steps?

Moving On

You might have had fleeting glimpses in the past of what you could become, maybe during childhood, or maybe during your obsessive compulsive learned helplessness. You probably thought either that life did not put you in a place where you could become what you dreamed of, or that you were just innately incapable of rising to a higher place. You might once have dreamed of money, status, or position. In a program of soul or self development, you will become more concerned with your soul or self growth. You will begin thinking about qualities you wish you had, or about the qualities other people you know in recovery you wish to emulate. This is called healthy envy.

As we work this Step, we begin developing a vision of the person we would like to become. If we have been selfish, we probably have a vision of becoming selfless, maybe by helping another addict find wellness or by some other act of selfless giving. If we have been lazy, we might see ourselves becoming productive and reaping the rewards of our efforts. If we have been dishonest, and we might have a dream of the freedom that can be ours when we no longer have to spend so much time worrying about being found out. We want to get from this step is a vision of ourselves and a sense of hope that we can attain that vision.

Answer the following questions:

- What do you see yourself doing with the qualities you wish to attain?
- What will you do with your career?
- What will you do in your spare time?
- What kind of parent, partner, or friend will you be? Be specific.

This vision can be your inspiration. Recalling it during the times when you feel despair, or when it seems to be taking a long time to reach your goals, will sustain you and help you renew your willingness. Your vision is your springboard into Step Seven, where you will ask the God of your understanding or a Power greater than you to remove your shortcomings.

The operational principle of Step Six is Willingness. Now that we have accomplished an inventory of the good and not so good aspects of our character and behavior, are we willing to change them? All of them? The important part of this principle is the willingness to let go of our old behaviors.

Chapter Eleven

Step Seven

Humbly asked Him to remove our shortcomings.

Since we are doing the Steps the way they were originally done by the forefathers and pioneers of Alcoholics Anonymous, we will do Step Seven the way it was written in the original manuscripts of the "Big Book:" "Humbly, on our knees, asked God to remove our shortcomings, holding nothing back." Have your inventory ready, get on your knees, and read the original Seventh Step Prayer:

My Creator, I am now willing that You should have all of me, good and bad. I pray that You now remove from me every single defect of character which stands in the way of my usefulness to You and my fellows. Grant me strength, as I go out from here, to do Your bidding.
Amen.

In Step Four, Five, and Six, you completed your moral inventory; admitted to yourself, to a God of your understanding or a Power greater than you, and another person the exact nature of your wrongs; and did deep introspection or look within. You are now entirely ready to ask and pray that the God of your understanding or a Power greater than you to remove every defect of character you find objectionable. Specifically, you ask this Power to remove the the shortcomings listed in your Fourth Step moral inventory and read these defects aloud.

Then thank this Power for this opportunity for a new beginning in your life and a chance to be a part of the solutions in life instead of the problems. Ask this Power to please grant you wisdom, knowledge, and strength as you go out from here to do His work and live the victorious life that this Power has designed for you, and thank this Power for the steps which will make His plan for your life clear to you. Now, you are done with Step Seven, right? Well, not quite—there is more.

Now comes the most misunderstood part of the Twelve Steps. Why is this? Because to truly understand this Step, you must understand how this Step was originally written in the first drafts of the "Big Book" by Bill Wilson back in 1938, before he altered it as part of a compromise with some of the early pioneer members in the original New York Alcoholics Anonymous program by taking out much of the "God" language that a certain few found offensive, but unfortunately, he also took out the principle purpose of this Step—action.

In Step Seven, you are asked to humbly ask the God of our understanding or a Power greater than you to remove your shortcomings, but many people who do not know the parts that were deleted become frustrated and disillusioned when they soon realize that the behaviors that they asked this Power to remove are still with them, causing the same misery and havoc as before, or perhaps worse, perhaps in a different form, because all they did was ask this Power to remove their defects of character and shortcomings, but they did nothing else, and so, nothing happened.

Therefore, many uninformed members of Alcoholics Anonymous and many other twelve-step programs continue engage in the same corrupted behaviors they engaged in while they were acting out on their addictions living under the mantle of sobriety, erroneously thinking that this Power had removed them simply because they asked this Power to do so. Remember faith without work is meaningless and purposeless. So, what did they miss?

They did not take the actions necessary to ensure that they were living a life in accordance with a higher moral excellence demanded to live a good life free of sin and corruption. They just asked the God of their understanding or a Power greater than them to remove their defects of character and shortcomings, but did not take the actions necessary to make that happen. In other words, you can ask this Power for anything you wish, like removing your shortcomings, but if you do nothing, you will get nothing.

Here are the moral values which are upheld as moral excellence:

Humility	Justice
Generosity	Strength
Love of self and others	Determination
Kindness	Obedience
Self-control	Wisdom
Faith	Knowledge
Temperance	Understanding
Enthusiasm	Counsel or service to others
Hope	Gentleness
Charity	Modesty
Discretion	

These are the higher moral standards you should subscribe to, adopt, and live up to the best your ability. And so, to work the Seventh Step, you must ask a God of your understanding or a Power Greater than you to remove the defects of character and shortcomings you discovered in your Fourth Step, and then adopt the list of virtues you discovered on Page Seven of your inventory as well as the aforementioned standards and perform them everyone, every day, every where, to the best of your ability.

It should be noted here that once you complete this Step in its entirety, you are probably the cleanest, purest person on earth right now. Why? Because you have not had a chance to harm anyone or practice your defects of character or excesses following their removal a few seconds ago and because you have not even had a chance for even milder forms of your defects to show up.

However, for many people who work Step Six and Seven honestly, it seems that their lives often take a real downhill turn for a brief period. This is the backlash of emotional catharsis, or the process of releasing, and thereby providing relief from, strong or repressed emotions, and the expression and consequent release of a previously repressed emotion, achieved through reliving the experience that caused it. This is known as the "Sixth Step Funk." Uninformed people in early recovery often complain that that the Steps do not work. Watch for this. Unfortunately, many people stumble here and go back to using.

In fact, it should be noted that if you see that things in your life are not going well at this point, it means that the Steps are working. Why? Your defects of character, excesses, and shortcomings that allowed your selfish self to run amok have been removed, but your unconscious motivations are not completely gone yet because your unconscious mind, which controls a lot of what you do, still contains a lot of old ideas and beliefs. It takes some time for the spiritual adjustment to happen. Be patient.

Unfortunately, you have not yet developed the skills to cope with your unconscious motivations. Read your list of higher moral standards you discovered in Step Four and affirmed in Step Seven every morning and commit to moral excellence every day. Every evening before you sleep, read the list again and ask yourself: "Have I lived my life in accordance with these moral standards and have I treated all people will justice and fairness today." If you have, sleep well knowing you are well on the way to wellness. If, on the other hand, you have fallen short, identify those areas you need to work on, forgive yourself for being human, and commit to doing better in those areas tomorrow. Be patient, you will develop the necessary skills to reconnect with your internal guidance system that will guide your future endeavors, which comes when you get all your stuff out of the way and reconnect to power of a God of your understanding or a Power greater than you. Remember: practice, practice, practice everyone, everywhere, every day. What you practice at, you will get better at.

It should be noted that your selfish self will remain intact within your unconscious for some time. Therefore, it is not unusual that you might catch yourself engaging in some of your old behaviors. As a result, it is not uncommon that you will feel tension, stress, and anxiety. This internal conflict manifests itself within you because your unconscious mind with its need to avoid tension and stress often fights with your conscious mind with its new moral standards in order to avoid stress or tension from the conflict within, since your conscious, subconscious, and unconscious mind is not yet aligned with the will of a God of your understanding or a Power greater than you.

To help explain this, let us look art an iceberg. We can see only about 10% of the mass of the iceberg above the surface, but 90% of the mass of the iceberg still lies below the surface. According to Freud's structural model, the personality is divided into the id, ego, and superego. The smaller portion of an iceberg that is seen above the water signifies the conscious mind; whereas the portion of the iceberg we can from the surface down maybe 30 to 50 feet represents the subconscious or the dream state; and the much larger portion below the water illustrates the unconscious mind composed of the id, ego, and superego. But with any iceberg, the currents that move the iceberg are not on the surface, they are the currents that lie deep below the surface. The same is true with us humans. We must know these currents.

Although each of the Twelve Steps of Recovery is a separate process onto itself, they all blend together to some degree as their parts interact with one another, where aspects of Step One fuse into Step Two, and components of Step Four mesh into the following Steps. Perhaps the finest line between two Steps is the one between Steps Six and Seven. At first glance, Step Seven might seem almost an afterthought to Step Six. You spent a great deal of time and effort raising your awareness of your character defects in Step Six and getting to the point where you are entirely ready to have them removed. Now, all you need to do is ask, right? Well, not exactly.

As was said previously, there is much more to this Step than just filing a request with the God of your understanding or a Power greater than you and waiting for a response. There is spiritual preparation. Remember the God of your understanding or Power greater than you will not do anything for you until you do something first. Sadly, many people misunderstand this Step and simply stand around waiting for this Power to remove their shortcoming, but realize, much to their dismay, that they still have all the defects and shortcomings they have always had, and they were not removed.

There is the need to develop an understanding about what "humbly" means in this context. Remember, you have to get your selfish self out of the way. There is the need to find a way of asking to have your shortcomings removed that fits into your individual spiritual path, and there is the need to practice of your newfound values, principles, and virtues in all your interactions with everyone, everywhere, every day in the place of your character defects so that our selfish self can be pushed aside.

Preparing to Work Step Seven

You have already done much of the spiritual preparation work you will need to begin Step Seven. It is important that you draw the connection between the work you have done and the results that work has produced so far.

The previous Steps have all served to sow the seeds of humility in your spirit. In this Step, those seeds now take root and grow. Many of us have difficulty with the concept of humility, and even though we began addressing this issue in Step Six, and so, it merits attention in Step Seven. You need to understand what humility is for, and how its presence is revealed in your life.

You should not confuse humility with humiliation. When you are humiliated, you are ashamed and you feel worthless. Humility is almost the opposite of this feeling. Humility is defined as the quality of not being proud because you are aware of your bad qualities or the feeling or attitude that you have no special importance that makes you better than others--lack of pride. Through working the Steps, you have been stripping away layers of denial, ego, pride, and selfishness. You have also been building a more positive self-image and practicing your spiritual principles, as well as your new values and virtues. Before, you could not see your strengths because the good, healthy part of you was hidden behind your defects of character. Now you can. This is humility.

Some examples of how humility are often revealed might help you understand this concept. You started out in recovery with fixed ideas. Since you have been in the world of recovery, discovery, and wellness, everything you believed in the past has been challenged. You have been barraged with new ideas.

For instance, if you believed you were in control, just the fact that you have wound up here admitting your powerlessness is probably enough to change your outlook. Because of powerlessness over your sugar addiction, you likely failed to learn the lessons that life itself would have taught you about how much control you have. Through your journey to wellness and the working of the first six Steps, you have learned a great deal about how to live and a healthy life.

Many of us came into recovery with a certain "street" mentality. The only way we knew to get what we wanted was by taking it or manipulating people to get our selfish needs met. We did not realize that we could just be forthright and ask fro our needs to be met and have the same chance, if not a better chance, of fulfilling our needs. You spent years learning to blank your facial expressions, hide your compassion, and harden yourself. By the time you arrived here, you were very good at the game of powerlessness.

Removing yourself from the arena in which such games are played is exposing you to new ideas. You will learn that it is okay to have feelings and to show them. You will find out that the rules of unhealthy religious activities only make sense in unhealthy religious places; but in the real world, they do not fit. You become softer and more vulnerable, and you will no longer mistake kindness for weakness. Changing these attitudes will have a dramatic effect on you and everyone around you. Oftentimes, it even changes your physical appearance, where knotted brows and jaws relax into smiles, and tears flow freely out, uncovering your hidden spirit.

Many of us arrived here convinced that we were victims of bad luck, unfavorable circumstances, and conspiracies to thwarted what we thought were our good intentions. We believed we were good people, but profoundly flawed and misunderstood. We justified any harm we caused as self-defense or protection, if we could realize that we caused harm at all. Feelings of self-pity went together with that attitude. We reveled it in our suffering, and we secretly knew that the payoff for our pain was never having to look at our part in anything.

But the first six Steps gets us to begin to do just that—we look at our part in things, all things. Once we thought that certain situations happened to us; now we see how those situations were really created by us. We become aware of all the opportunities we have wasted. We stop blaming other people for our lot in life. We begin to see that where we ended up has been determined mostly by the choices we have made and mostly of our own doing.

Humility is a sense of your own humanness. If this is your first experience with the Seventh Step, this might be the point when you first feel a sense of compassion for yourself. It is deeply moving to realize that for the first time, you are truly just human and trying your best. You make decisions, both good and bad, and hope things will turn out okay. With this knowledge about who you are, you will realize that just as you are doing your best, but so are other people. You feel a real connection with others, knowing that we are all subject to the same fears, inadequacies, inferiorities, insecurities, and failings as everyone else; and that we all have the same wants, needs, and dreams for the future as everyone else. Now, you need to acknowledge your own humility and explore how it makes it known in your everyday life.

Answer the following questions:

- Which of your attitudes have changed since you have been in the world of recovery and discovery?

- Where has the overblown been deflated, and where has the healthy part of you been uncovered?
- How does humility affect your wellness?
- How does being aware of your own humility help when working this step?

Your work in the previous Steps has helped you build a relationship with a God of your understanding or a Power greater than you. That work will now pay off in a big way as you proceed with Step Seven. In Step Two, you first began to think about a God of your understanding or a Power greater than you that could help you find recovery from your powerlessness over your sugar addiction and restore you to wellness. From there, you went on to make your Third Step decision to trust the God of your understanding or a Power greater than you in a joining of His will and your human will. You called upon this Power many times to get you through Step Four, and then in the Fifth Step you shared with the God of your understanding, your innermost self, and another human being the most intimate details of your life. In Step Six, you discovered that the God of your understanding or a Power greater than you could do more for you than just keep you free of your religious addiction.

Answer the following questions:

- How has your comprehension of a God of your understanding or a Power greater than you grown in the previous steps?
- How has your relationship with that Power developed?
- How has your work on the previous steps made you ready to work the Seventh Step?

Asking to Have Your Shortcomings Removed

So, how do you ask the God of your understanding or a Power greater than you to remove your shortcomings? The answer is likely depends a great deal on what kind of understanding you have with this Power. There are many, many ways to understand the God of your understanding or a Power greater than you; so many that I could not possibly provide examples in this book of how each person's individual spiritual path would influence their Seventh Step work. Suffice it to say, your recovery work should reflect your own spiritual path.

As an individual, you might pick a particular personal routine or ritual as your way of asking your this Power to remove your shortcomings. For the purposes of this guide, we will call this prayer.

Prayer is an invocation or act that seeks to activate a rapport with an object of worship through deliberate communication. In the narrow sense, the term refers to an act of supplication or intercession directed towards a deity or a deified ancestor. More generally, prayer can also have the purpose of thanksgiving or praise, and in comparative religion is closely associated with more abstract forms of meditation and with charms or spells.

Prayer can take a variety of forms. It can be part of a set liturgy or ritual, or it can be performed alone or in groups. Prayer may take the form of a hymn, incantation, formal creedal statement, or a spontaneous utterance from the praying person.

In twelve-step programs, prayer is commonly a way we communicate with the God of our understanding or Power greater than us. The tone of asking is captured in the word "humbly." Coming from the place in ourselves that is most honest, the place that is closest to our spiritual center, we ask to have our shortcomings removed.

Answer the following questions:

- How will you ask the God of your understanding or a Power greater than you to remove your shortcomings?
- Can other recovering sugar addicts help you figure out how you are going to ask?
- Have you asked them to share their experience, strength, and hope with you?
- Have you asked your mentor for guidance?

As with any other aspect of your program of recovery and wellness, you are not going to ask just once to have your shortcomings removed. You will ask again and again throughout your life. The way you ask is certain to change as your understanding of a God of your understanding or a Power greater than you changes. Nothing you do at this point locks you into one way of working the Seventh Step forever.

Getting Out of the Way

Most of us realize that we probably need to do something more in this Step than just pray for our shortcomings to be removed. You need to take some action that will invite the God of your understanding or Power greater than you to work in your life. You cannot ask this Power to remove your shortcomings and then hang on to them with all your might. The more distance you keep between yourself and the God of your understanding or a Power greater than you, the less you will feel His presence. You have to maintain the awareness of yourself that you gained in the Sixth Step and add to it an awareness of this Power working in your life.

Answer the following questions:

- How does the spiritual principle of surrender apply to getting out of the way so the God of your Understanding or a Power greater than you can work in your life?
- What might be the benefits of allowing a God of your understanding or a Power greater than you to work in your life?
- How do you feel, knowing that a God of your understanding or Power greater than you is caring for you and working in your life?

Spiritual Principles

In the Seventh Step, you will focus on surrender, trust, faith, patience, and humility. Likewise, in the Seventh Step, you take your surrender to a deeper level. What began in Step One with an acknowledgment of your powerlessness over your obsessive compulsive learned helplessness now includes an acknowledgment of the shortcomings that go along with your powerlessness. You also take your Second Step surrender to a deeper level. You come to believe that a God of your understanding or a Power greater than you can do more than help you live a rich joyous life free of the endless torment of your obsessive compulsive learned helplessness. You look to a God of your understanding or a Power greater than you to relieve you of your shortcomings as well. As time goes by, you place more and more of your trust in this Power and in the process of recovery.

Answer the following questions:

- Have you accepted your powerlessness over your shortcomings as well as your powerlessness over your obsessive compulsive learned helplessness? Expand on this.
- How has your surrender deepened?

The spiritual principles of trust and faith are central to the Seventh Step. You must be sure enough of a God of your understanding or a Power greater than you to trust Him to remove your shortcomings when you do your work and get out of the way. You have to believe the God of your understanding or a Power greater than you is going to do something with them, or how can you ask this Power with any faith at all that they will be removed? You must avoid any tendency to keep score of how you think God is doing on removing your defects. It is not too hard to see where this kind of thinking can lead if you find that you still have certain character defects after some arbitrary amount of time has passed.

Instead, you focus on the action you must take in this Step: humbly asking, practicing spiritual principles, and getting out of the way the God of your understanding or a Power greater than you. The results of the Seventh Step might not materialize immediately, but they will in time.

Answer the following questions:

- Do you believe that a God of your understanding or a Power greater than you will remove your shortcomings or grant you freedom from the compulsion to act on them?

- Do you believe that you will be a better person as a result of working this step?

- How does your faith in the God of your understanding or a Power greater than you become stronger as a result of working this step?

Trust and faith alone can never carry you through a lifetime of working this Step. You need to practice patience as well. Even if it has been a long time since you started asking for the removal of a shortcoming, you still must be patient. Maybe, in fact, impatience is one of your shortcomings. You can look at the times when you have to wait as gifts; the times when you most need to practice the principle of patience. After all, one of the surest ways you progress is by rising up over the barriers you run into on your spiritual path.

Answer the following questions:

- Where have you had opportunities for growth lately?
- What did you make of them?

Finally, you need to maintain your awareness of the principle of humility, more than any other, as you work this Step. It is easy to see if you are approaching this step with humility by asking ourselves a few questions:

- Do you believe that a God of your understanding or a Power greater than you can remove your shortcomings?
- Or have you been trying to do it myself?

- Have you become impatient that your shortcomings have not been removed right away, as soon as you asked?

- Are you confident that they will be removed in the time a God of your understanding or a Power greater than you?

- Has your sense of perspective been out of proportion lately?

- Have you begun thinking of yourself as more significant or more powerful than you really are?

Moving On

At this point, you might wonder how you are supposed to be feeling right now. You have asked the God of your understanding or a Power greater than you to remove your shortcomings; and even though you have faithfully practiced the principles of your program to the best of your ability, you might still find yourself acting out on your your obsessive compulsive learned helplessness before you have had a chance to think. Sure, you are no longer acting out on your obsessive compulsive learned helplessness, and many of the outside circumstances of your life have probably gotten better, your relationships are more stable, perhaps, but have you changed? Have you become a better person?

In time, you will find that the God of your understanding or Power greater than you is worked in your life. You might even be startled by the level of maturity or spirituality you have demonstrated in handling a situation that in years past would have had us acting very unspiritual. One day, you will realize that some of the ways you used to act have become as alien to you as your new spiritual principles once were when you first started practicing them.

After such a revelation, you might begin thinking about the person you were when you first came into recovery and how little you resemble that person now.

Answer the following questions:

- Have there been times when you have been able to refrain from acting on a character defects and practice a spiritual principle instead?

- Do you recognize this as the God of your understanding or a Power greater than you working in your life?

- Which shortcomings have been removed from your life or diminished in their power over you?

- Why does the Seventh Step foster a sense of serenity in you?

You will begin to live a more spiritual life and you will stop thinking so much about what you are going to get, even from your recovery, and you will start looking about how you can contribute to the welfare of others. The things you do to sustain and nourish your spirit become habit and you might even look forward to them. You find that you are free to choose how you want to look at any situation in your life. You will stop grumbling about small inconveniences as if they were major tragedies. You will become able to hold up your heads with dignity and maintain our integrity, no matter what life presents to you. As you begin to get more comfortable with your spiritual self, your desire to heal your relationships will grow. You begin that process in Step Eight.

The operative principle of Step Seven is Humility. Here we move further into action. In Step Six, we became willing to let go of our old behaviors, and now we ask for help in actually letting go of these things. Could we learn to forgive ourselves?

Chapter Twelve

Step Eight

Made a list of all people we had harmed, and became willing to make amends to them all.

The forefathers and pioneer of Alcoholics Anonymous tell us to make a list. Do we need to make another list? Yes. Although we made a list of people we had harmed in the Fourth Step, we now we need more action, without which we find that our faith in recovery without works is meaningless and we will get nothing in return.

Let us look at Steps Eight. We are instructed to make a list of all persons we have harmed to whom we are willing to make amends. We began this list when we did our inventory, but now we have to make it more precise. Therefore, we hang onto our Fourth Step inventory because it lays the foundation for our Eighth Step amends list.

Many of us realized, maybe for the first time, the real harm we caused to ourselves and others. As a result, many of us are plagued with guilt, shame, remorse, anxiety, and depression. However, if you look at the asset-side of your inventory, you will see the goodness within you that is blocked off by your selfish self with its defects and excesses. These assets can manifest themselves in your daily interactions with others and you can become a healthy, useful, and prosperous person again if you will get out of the way.

It should be noted that everything that you have done up until now has worked, and you have done the best you could at surviving, considering your situation because although your behavior might have been destructive, it was adaptive, proper, and correct because you are still here.

You should also realize that you did not understand the internal forces that drove your obsessive compulsive learned helplessness and phenomenon of craving and your obsessive mind until now. Consequently, you had no other choice but to engage in your obsessive compulsive learned helplessness to relieve your anxiety or tension caused by your hurt, pain, anger, and shame. Remember, we are not saints. We are spiritual creatures living a human experience, so accept your humanness and stop beating yourself up. You have done enough of that.

Are you willing to admit to your inner most self that you have harmed yourself and others; you have taken things that were not yours; you have deprived others of attention and affection; and you have broken relationships with loved ones that need mending in order for you to have any peace and serenity? Then it is time to clear away the wreckage of your past by making amends and restitution, which is defined as the giving back of something that was taken away. Sometimes we took money and sometimes we took peace of mind.

Step Eight is much like the Fourth Step, in that you are making a list. With this list as your guide, you are to go to the people you harmed and repair the damage that you have done. A face-to-face approach is always best, but sometimes this not possible, so another means will be necessary.

Next, you are going to repair the damage. What repairs are necessary? You cannot know what repairs are necessary until you know what harm you did. In many cases, the harm you did seems obvious, but the full impact cannot be realized until you walk in the other person's shoes. Do you see that people were turned off by your actions and rejected you? Do you see that their hearts and minds are closed to you because they were deprived of the fullness and richness, which they had turned to you for? Do you realize that all the people you harmed could go to a thousand therapists and still not have the door opened to their pain and suffering you caused because only you have the key? Are you willing to go to whatever length needed to make amends by going to each person, opening the doors to their hearts, and setting them free.

Take out your Fourth Step and look at the list of the people you wrote down on Page One. Consider the people you have harmed directly or indirectly and make a list of who you harmed; how did you harm them; and what amends will be done to set things right. Review it carefully and add anyone else you can think of. This is your Step Eight list. Are you willing to go on to Step Nine and begin the process of making amends to these people in order to allow your selfish self to pass; to join your will with the God of your understanding or a Power greater than you; and to return to happiness, joyousness, prosperity, and wellness?

The operative principles of Step Eight are Discipline and Action. We continue to remove the barriers that can block our growth in sobriety. We are getting ready to sweep our side of the street clean.

To this point, the Steps have focused mostly on repairing yourself and your relationship with a God of your understanding or a Power greater than you. Beginning with the Eighth Step, you will bring other people into your healing process, such as people you had harmed in the depth of your obsessive compulsive learned helplessness; the people you harmed on the way to wellness; people you meant to harm; people you hurt by accident; people who are no longer in your life; and people you expect to be close to for the rest of your life.

The Eighth Step is about identifying the damage you caused. It does not matter whether you caused it because you were overtaken by rage, carelessness, or because you were afraid. It does not matter whether your actions were based in selfishness, arrogance, dishonesty, or any other defect of character. It does not even matter that you did not intend to cause someone harm. All the damage you caused is material for the Eighth Step.

It might turn out that some of the harm you did cannot be repaired. It might turn out that you cannot directly make the repairs necessary. It might even turn out that you are not responsible for something you have placed on your Eighth Step list. Your sponsor will help you sort that out before you go on to the Ninth Step. For now, your task is only to identify who you harmed; what the harm was; determining how to make amends; and become willing to make amends.

It is natural to wonder about the Ninth Step and how you will make your amends while you are working the Eighth Step. What you think about your amends is bound to influence your work on this Step. You might need to get some common misconceptions out of your way before you can make your list.

It is wonderful that you have already begun repairing your relationships with some of the people your life. Your family is probably delighted that you are no longer engaging in your obsessive compulsive learned helplessness. Some of the more overt damage you inflicted on others ceased as soon as you stopped your behaviors related to your obsessive compulsive learned helplessness. If you managed to keep your job or remain in your family, you are probably already performing better in those places. You are no longer harming your family, loved ones, co-workers, employers, or others. But is that enough?

You might have heard people in meetings emphasizing that "amends" means to change, not just to say: "I'm sorry." What really counts is the way you are treating people now. But this does not mean that formal apologies have gone out of fashion in recovery. Direct, face-to-face verbal amends are extremely powerful, both as a means of spiritual growth for you and as a long-awaited comfort for the people to whom you make them. What members of twelve-step programs emphasize is that we cannot just offer people lame apologies and then go right back to what we were doing that caused them harm in the first place.

Some of us might be feeling a bit weary at this point, especially if our sponsor had us do extensive writing on the first seven Steps. You have inventoried your behavior in Step Four and catalogued your character defects in Step Six. Now, you must examine the same situations from yet another angle. It might seem as if you have examined your life and your obsessive compulsive learned helplessness in every possible way by the time you are done with these Steps. Is all of this really necessary? Are we not just punishing ourselves by going over and over the same thing?

Not so. The Eighth Step is the beginning of a process that lets you feel equal to others. Instead of feeling shame and guilt or feeling forever "less than," you become able to look people in the eye. You will not have to avoid anyone anymore. You will not have to be afraid that you will be caught and punished for some neglected responsibility. You will be free.

Answer the following questions:

- Are you hesitating in any way about working the Eighth Step?
- Why?

Some of us go to the other extreme with this Step, where we cannot wait to get right out there and make everything okay, unaware that we might cause more harm. We blunder forward, confessing our wrongs to our spouses and our friends. We sit our families down and make them listen to every detail of our misadventures in our endless bouts of obsessive compulsive learned helplessness, confirming some of their worst fears about what we were doing out there and filling in some blanks that, until then, had been left mercifully empty. In a state of excitement, we give our children a speech about how we have a "disease" for which we are not responsible, how we love our recovery, and how wonderful life is going to be from now on, forgetting all the times before when we had made these same empty promises and betrayed all those around us.

Although your own experience with rushing out to make amends is probably not this extreme, you can surely grasp the point: If you try to make amends without your sponsor's guidance and without a plan, you can end up causing even more harm.

Answer the following questions:

- Do you realize the need to slow down and consult your sponsor before making amends?

- Have you created more harm in any situation by rushing out to make amends before you were ready?
- What was the situation?

Some of us might still believe that we are just basically nice people who have never truly harmed anyone, except ourselves, that is. If you are truly stumped about who belongs on your amends list or you have a vague idea that your family belongs there, but you are not sure why, it could be that you are overlooking something or that your denial is still pretty thick.

Sometimes, you are just not able to see the truth about certain situations, even after many years in the world of recovery and wellness. A suggestion that many of us have followed is that if we think of someone to whom we think we owe amends, but we cannot think of the situation that resulted in our owing amends to them, we put the name on the list anyway.

Sometimes, we will think of the "why" later on. You should do the best you can with this Step for now, contact your sponsor, and keep working on your recovery and discovery. As the saying goes: "more will be revealed." You just need to keep an open mind, so that when the knowledge comes, you will be prepared to accept it.

Finally, many of us delay starting this Step because we are not willing to make amends to certain people. We either resent them, or we feel too afraid to ever imagine ourselves approaching them. We need to start this Step and list these people even if we are not sure we will ever be able to make the amends. If it is truly unsafe to make the amends, our sponsor will help us figure out how to handle the situation.

Answer the following questions:

- List the resentments that are in the way of your willingness to make amends.
- Can you let these resentments go now?
- If not, can you muster the willingness to add these names to your list anyway, and worry about becoming willing later?

- Are there any people to whom you owe amends that might be a threat to your safety or about whom you are truly concerned in some other way?
- What are your fears?

The People we Harmed and How we Harmed Them

Before you begin making your list, there is one final concept with which you must familiarize yourself with: the meaning of "harm" in this Step. You need to strive to understand all the ways in which it is possible to cause harm, so that your list can be thorough.

Certain types of harm are obvious. For instance, if you stole money or property from a person or a business. That is quite obviously a form of harm. In addition, most of us have no trouble recognizing physical or emotional abuse as a type of harm.

Then, there are situations where you will have no problem recognizing what you did as harmful, but might have difficulty identifying who, in particular, you harmed. For instance, what if you had cheated on a test in school? Did this cause harm to the instructor? Your fellow students? Yourself? The students who came after you and had to pay the price of your instructor's mistrust because of your dishonesty? The answer to this example is that all of these people were harmed, even if only indirectly. They belong on our Eighth Step list.

Finally, we get to the deeper types of harm. These types of harm might be the most damaging, for they strike at the most vulnerable places in the human heart. For instance, you had a friend, perhaps an old one, spanning many years. Emotions, trust, and even personal identity were part of the friendship you shared. This relationship really mattered to your friend and to you as well. Then, without explanation, because of some real or imagined slight, you withdrew from the friendship, never talked to the person again, and never tried to renew the friendship.

Losing a friend is painful enough without the added burden of not knowing why, but many of us inflicted just this kind of harm on someone. We damaged that person's sense of trust, and it might have taken many years to heal. A variation on this is that we might have allowed someone to take the blame for a relationship ending, making the person feel unlovable, when we had just grown tired of the relationship and were too lazy to maintain it.

There are many ways we can inflict deep emotional harm: neglect, withdrawal, exploitation, manipulation, and humiliation, just to name a few. The "victims" and "nice people" among us might find that we made others feel inferior when we passed ourselves off as better than everyone else, projecting an attitude of moral superiority. The competent and self-sufficient among us may find names to add to our Eighth Step list by thinking about the people whose offers of help and gestures of support we rejected.

An additional struggle that many of us face when we identify types of harm arises from an automatic tendency to focus only on the time before we stopped our obsessive compulsive learned helplessness, and so, it is an easier for you to be rigorously honest about the harm you already caused by your obsessive compulsive learned helplessness because when you were active in it, you were a different person. However, some of us have caused harm on our path to wellness as well. Remember, whether you intended to do harm or not does not matter.

In fact, you have probably caused more harm to people with whom you share your world, and in some cases, the people in your twelve-step community as well. You might have gossiped about them, withdrew from them, responded with insensitivity to their pain, interfered in their relationships with others, tried to control another person's behavior, behaved in an ungrateful way with others, stolen or misappropriated money, manipulated people by using your clean time as a source of credibility, or sexually exploited a newcomer to name a few common examples.

Most of us have an extremely hard time placing these situations on our Eighth Step list because the thought of making the amends makes us so uncomfortable. We hold ourselves accountable to a higher standard of behavior in wellness, and we are sure that others expect more from us, as well. The fact is that our fellows in recovery are likely to be especially forgiving because they know what we are trying to do, but again, we should avoid worrying about the Ninth Step now.

Making Our List

The first thing to know is that this is not a list that you can keep in your head. You need to put down each name, what you did to harm the person, and how you intend to set things right with them down on paper. Once it is on paper, it is hard to forget anyone or go back into denial about an amends you would rather avoid. If for some reason, you cannot use paper, we can use any other method recording you wish.

When you are ready to begin your list, sit down and recall all you have learned about harm and start writing. Some names are going to spring to mind immediately. Others might come to mind as you think about the types of harm you have caused. You absolutely need to go back through your Fourth Step inventory and search out any information you can extract from it.

You should include every name and situation you can think of even if you are relatively, but not entirely, sure that your sponsor is going to tell you that you do not owe any amends in that situation. It is almost always better to delete names than to try to recall names you should have added, but did not, when you are going over the list with your sponsor.

In addition, there might be times when you remember an incident in which you caused harm, but not the names of the people involved. You can at least list the incident. You should also list harms that you believe you have set right or forgiven because we often give blanket indulgences but still harbor bitterness and resentment which may be projected as passive-aggressive anger the person or on others.

Putting yourself on the list might seem awkward. You might have been informed in your early discovery that making amends to yourself was a self-centered idea, and that you needed to stop thinking about yourself all the time and start thinking about the people you had harmed. Then, the whole notion of making amends to yourself would be made more confusing. Some of us probably thought that making amends should involve "rewarding" ourselves for staying clean or some other accomplishment. You might have tried to do this by buying yourself things you could not afford, or by indulging other obsessions or compulsions.

In reality, the way you make amends to yourself is by stopping irresponsible or destructive behavior. You need to identify the ways you have created your own problems; that is, harmed yourself through your inability to accept personal responsibility. Then, when you add yourself to the list, you can list the harm you caused to your finances, your self-image, or to your health.

There is also a delicate situation that many of us have faced: What if we have harmed someone, and they do not know about the harm. In this situation, you should consult your sponsor and seek guidance on to deal with this issue. Remember: do no harm!

What about people we have harmed that have passed away or that we do not where they are? We still owe these people amends. We can do ritual amends to these people by writing them a letter detailing our wrongs and asking them forgiveness; burning the letter, praying for forgiveness as the smoke from the burins rises; and collecting the ashes of the burning and scattering them n some meaningful way.

Answer the following question:

- List the people you have harmed and the specific ways you harmed each one.

Becoming Willing

Now that you have your list or have added new names to the list you have been keeping since your first time through the Eighth Step, it is time to get willing to make amends. In order to become willing, you must know at least a little about what "making amends" involves. Earlier in this guide, we talked about the need to do more than just change your behavior, but some of us may be afraid that we just are not capable of changing. We are sincere. You want to refrain from ever repeating the same behaviors again, but you think about the times when you have made promises before. Are you not subject to doing the same thing again? This is when you have to really believe in your wellness. No matter how long you have been clean and the wrongs for which you are making amends, you have to have faith that the God of your understanding will give you the strength and the ability to change.

Answer the following questions:

- Why is saying "I'm sorry" alone not sufficient to repair the damage you have caused?
- Why is only changing your behavior not sufficient to repair the damage you have caused?

For some of the amends you owe, you will find that you are willing as soon as you put the name on your list. For others, the willingness might not come so easily. It is very rare that you do not owe at least some financial amends, whether they are to people from whom you stole, people who lent you money but never paid back, businesses, or lending institutions, student loans, unpaid taxes, or unpaid child support. You know that making the amends is going to deprive you of money you would rather keep for yourself. It might take time for you to appreciate the profound internal freedom that comes from discharging such debts, and thus gain the willingness to make these amends. It might help to ask the God of your understanding to give you the willingness to make these amends.

Answer the following questions:

- Do you have financial amends that you do not want to make?
- What would your life be like if you had already made these amends?

Some of our amends might be to people who have also harmed us. These are usually the amends we have the most difficulty becoming willing to make. It seems like every time we think about these amends; we get so angry thinking about what they did to us that we forget all about making amends. But your wellness calls on you to practice the spiritual principle of forgiveness.

Forgiveness

All of us have been hurt by the actions or words of another person. Psychologists generally define forgiveness as a conscious, deliberate decision to release feelings of resentment or vengeance toward a person or group who has harmed you, regardless of whether they actually deserve your forgiveness or not. In the Bible, the word "forgive" is used 109 times.

According to the Bible, forgiveness means ceasing to feel resentment for wrongs and offenses done toward us. It includes pardon and the restoration of broken relationships. Forgiveness is the act of renouncing anger and ill feelings against others.

Perhaps it was your mother criticized your parenting skills, or a colleague sabotaged a project, or your partner had an affair. These wounds can leave us with lasting feelings of anger, bitterness, or even vengeance, but if we do not practice forgiveness, we might be the one who pays a price. By embracing forgiveness, we can also embrace peace, hope, gratitude, and joy. Consider how forgiveness can lead you down the path of physical, emotional, and spiritual well-being.

What is Forgiveness?

Generally, forgiveness is a decision to let go of grudges, resentments, and thoughts of revenge. The act that hurt you or offended you might always remain in your memory, but forgiveness can lessen its grip on you and help you focus on other, positive parts of your life. Forgiveness can even lead to feelings of understanding, empathy, and compassion for the person who harmed you. Forgiveness does not mean that you deny or ignore the other person's responsibility for hurting you, and it does not minimize or justify the wrong they committed. You hold them accountable for their actions, and they are still responsible to make amends for their wrongs, but that is not your concern. You can forgive the person without excusing the act. Forgiveness brings a kind of peace that helps you go on with life.

What are the Benefits of Forgiving Someone?

Letting go of resentment, grudges, and bitterness can make way for compassion, kindness, and peace, but forgiveness can also lead to:

- Healthier, happier, more content relationships with others

- Greater spiritual, psychological, and physical well-being

- Less anxiety, stress, and stress-related health problems

- Lower risk of alcohol or substance abuse

Why is it so Easy to Hold a Grudge or Resentment?

When you are hurt by someone you love and trust, you might become angry, sad, or confused. If you dwell on hurtful events or situations, grudges filled with resentment, vengeance, and hostility can get internalized and begin causing external and internal problems. The mind is a problem-solver that always wants resolution on unfinished life challenges, the unconscious mind keeps grinding away at these unfinished life challenges in a relentless drive to resolves the unresolvable—why. If you allow negative feelings to push aside positive feelings, you could be swallowed up or consumed by your own bitterness and resentment

What are the Effects of Holding a Grudge or Resentment?

If you do not forgive those who have harmed you, you might pay a bitter emotional, physical, and spiritual price by repeatedly by bringing up pent up anger and bitterness into every relationship and new experience, thus poisoning them. You could become so wrapped up in the wrong committed against you that you cannot enjoy the present. You might become depressed or anxious. You might become consumed with the resentment making vengeance the only meaning or purpose of your life. You might lose valuable and enriching connectedness with others.

How do we Forgive?

Forgiveness is a process of change. To begin with, you might consider the value of forgiveness and its importance in your life. Reflect on the facts of the situation, how you reacted, and how this combination has affected your life, health, and well-being. When you are ready, actively choose to forgive the person who has offended you by moving away from your role as victim and release the control and power the offending person and situation has over you. As you let go of your grudges and resentments, you will no longer define your life by how you have been hurt. Instead, you might even find compassion and understanding.

In summary, forgiveness is a choice and a decision you make. However, as you do this, you discover that it is for your own good and you receive a reward of your forgiveness—freedom.

Through prayer and any additional help you need to seek, you can find it within yourself to forgive the people who have also harmed you.

Answer the following questions:

* Do you owe amends to people who have also harmed you?
* What have you done to become willing to make these amends?

Amends that you cannot ever see yourself making should also be on your list. Maybe you are so unwilling tp make these amends that you do not even want to try praying for willingness; and you cannot imagine even having any compassion for the person to whom you owe these amends. In this case, you just need to leave these amends on your list. You do not have to make all your amends in one day or in any set amount of time. It might take some time to become willing to make some amends. Every time you look at your Eighth Step list, you should ask yourself if you have become willing to make this amends yet. If not, you can keep checking periodically.

It should be noted that making amends is a four-step process:

1. A sincere apology for wronging the person.
2. A complete accounting of the wrongs done to the person.
3. Acts of atonement or restitution.
4. Plea for forgiveness.

Sincere Apology

To begin the process of amends, you must apologize for the wrongs you did to the person in question. It must be sincere. Superficial apologies will often be met with disbelief or even an angry response.

Complete Accounting

Second, you must make a complete accounting of what you did to wrong the person in question. It must be thorough and detailed. No half measures here.

Acts of Atonement

Third, you must demonstrate acts of atonement for wrongs and harm done related to your sugar misuse. This could be emotional restitution, such as showing the injured person that you are living to a new set of values, principle, and virtues; financial restitution, such as paying back debts, paying back money stolen or misappropriated, or replacing stolen or pawned items; or spiritual restitution, such as going to confession and confessing your sins to a priest, making restitution on the Jewish Day of Atonement, Yon Kippur, or make restitution on the Islamic Holy Day of Atonement, Ashura.

Plea for Forgiveness

Finally, you must ask the injured party for forgiveness in a very real and authentic way.

Spiritual Principles

In the Eighth Step, you will focus on honesty, courage, willingness, and compassion. To practice the principle of honesty in the Eighth Step, you need to draw on your experience in the previous Steps. You have admitted the nature of your problem, namely your obsessive compulsive learned helplessness, and what lies beneath it, and affirmed the solution to that problem. This was an act of honesty. You have taken a searching and fearless moral inventory of yourself, and so, doing so exercised your newfound honesty. Extracting the nature of your wrongs from within the fabric of your personality takes your honesty to an even higher level. So you have some experience separating your part in things from what others may have done. That is the level of honesty you will need to call on in Step Eight. You have to forget about resentments, blaming others, believing you were somehow an innocent victim, and any other justification for the harm you caused. You simply need to put it on the list!

Answer the following questions:

- How is determining the exact nature of your wrongs valuable in the Eighth Step?
- Why is it so essential that you are clear about your responsibility?
- What are some examples of your experience with honesty from the previous steps?
- How will you translate that experience into this step?

To practice the principle of courage in the Eighth Step, you have to put yourself in the care of a God of your understanding or a Power greater than you. You cannot restrict your list to only those amends that you think will turn out okay. You have to believe that a God of your understanding will provide you with the fortitude, the humility, the inner strength, or whatever you need to get through any amends. Whether you need to face someone, and you are afraid of how you will feel, or you need to accept the consequences of a crime for which you are sought, you will be able to handle it with the help of the God of your understanding.

Answer the following questions:

- What are some examples of your experience with courage from the previous steps?
- How will you translate that experience into this step?

We have already talked a great deal about willingness in this Step, especially becoming willing to make amends. But you will need a certain amount of willingness to work this Step that has nothing to do with making amends. First, you need the willingness to make your list. No matter what you are feeling about adding a certain name to your list, you need to become willing to add it. You also need the willingness to practice the other spiritual principles connected to this step.

Answer the following questions:

- Are there any names you have not yet added to your list?
- Are you willing to add them now?
- Have you completed your list?
- What are some of the things you have done to increase your willingness?
- How do you feel about having to pray for willingness?

Developing a compassionate spirit becomes possible at this stage in your recovery. Before you did the work involved in the previous Steps, you were too caught up in resentment, blame, and self-pity to think about others. Along with your ability to think of yourself as ordinary human beings, you begin to see that others are doing the best they can with their humanness, too. As human beings, we know that we are subject to periodic doubts and insecurities about ourselves, and so are others. We know that we are likely to speak before thinking, and so are others. We realize that they regret it as much as we do. We know we are prone to misreading situations and over or under reacting to them. As a result, when you see others act on a character defect today, you feel empathy rather than annoyance or anger, because you know what caused them to act as they do. Our hearts feel full when we think about how we share the same dreams, fears, passions, and faults as everyone else.

Answer the following questions:

- Are you beginning to feel connected with others? Describe.
- Are you beginning to feel compassion and empathy for others? Describe.

Moving On

Discussing every single one of the amends on your list with your sponsor is essential. It does not matter how long you have been clean or how much experience with making amends you have. Every one of us is liable to misjudge a situation when working alone, but we often find that we can see things more clearly when we look at situations from another point of view. You need insight on these matters from a trusted other such as a sponsor, as well as their encouragement and their vision and hope. It is amazing how much a simple discussion with your mentor can do to help you tap into the quiet strength that lives in each one of us. When you have stripped away the distracting influences and have exposed that solid core of serenity, humility, and forgiveness, you are ready for Step Nine—making amends to those we have harmed.

Chapter Thirteen

Step Nine

Made direct amends to such people, wherever possible, except to do so would injure them or others.

The forefathers and pioneers of Alcoholics Anonymous tell us that, we must sweep away the debris of the past, which has accumulated out of our effort to live on self-will run amok and running the show ourselves. At the end of this Step, you should experience a profound sense of freedom. In order to begin this Step, you need to determine what action you will need to take to clear up any harm you have done to the people you listed in Step Eight. It is a good idea to get input on each from others who understand the Fourth Step and the amend-making process.

Why should we make these amends? Perhaps the following example might help to make it clear. If you are making a cake with a twelve-step recipe and you stop at Step seven, you probably will not have a cake; you will likely have a mess.

It should be noted that the forefathers and pioneers of Alcoholics Anonymous claim that 90% of those who went back out and drank again stopped their recovery process at the Third Step, and of those who made it past Step Three, 90% of those relapsed after Step Eight. This is true of all addiction, including obsessive compulsive learned helplessness.

So, why make these amends? If you want to experience a spiritual awakening and live a sane life free of the ravages of your obsessive compulsive learned helplessness, taking this Step is vital. Remember, there is a price for everything you do in recovery, and there is a price for everything you do not do, as well.

As was said previously, the process of making amends is straightforward. It is as clear-cut as one human being going to another and doing four things: (1) make a humble apology for your wrong doing accepting full responsibility for your actions, (2) make a complete accounting of what you did to harm the other person, again taking full responsibility for your actions, (3) do at least one act of atonement or compensation to demonstrate your desire to set things right, and (4) a humble plea for forgiveness.

Why would we do this, you might ask? You might think: "Why open up a new can of worms?" The fact is, if we do not bring this up and set right the wrongs we committed on others, the guilt, shame, and remorse will sit within us and fester and manifest itself in some other way that will be troublesome later on. It is not uncommon for people who unfinished work in the area to launch sex addiction, love addiction, work addictions, gambling addictions, spending addictions, hoarding or collecting addictions, and strangely enough, twelve-step meeting addictions. What do all these addictions have in common—they are illnesses of escape.

It should be noted that if we have normal moral development, when we harm another person through our selfishness or defects of character, we usually feel strong feelings of guilt, remorse, shame, and regret, or resentment toward the self. These strong emotions, as with all emotions, are energy, and are stored within us in the form of tension until they are released. How are these emotions released? They can be projected outward in the form of aggression or passive-aggressive behavior, or inward in the form of depression, anxiety disorders, and a host of health problems, such as headaches, Migraine headaches; all kinds of digestive disorders like ulcer disease, irritable bowel disease, and gastritis; musculoskeletal disorders; genitourinary disorders; skin disorders; cardiovascular disorder like heart disease; and many forms of cancer.

If this energy is not discharged safely and in a healthy way, it could drive you back to your obsessive compulsive codependence or relationship addiction, or any number of other forms of addictions used to escape, because the body will not tolerate this tension for very long before it finds a way to discharge this energy as self-preservation because this is seen by the body as a threat to the self.

It should be noted that how a person reacts to our amends is irrelevant because we are not responsible for their reactions. Besides, it should be pointed out that the only time Dr. Bob went back out and got drunk after starting the Steps was when he stopped working the Steps at at Step Eight   Once he sobered up after his binge, he made all of his amends and arranged for payments of all his debts he owed to others in one day.   He never drank again.

The forefathers and pioneers of Alcoholics Anonymous explained the amends process. They wrote that now we go out to those we have harmed and repair the damage done in the past. We attempt to sweep away the debris that has accumulated out of our effort to live on self-will and run the show ourselves. If we do not have the will to do this, we ask for it until it comes. Remember it was agreed at the beginning we would go to any lengths for victory over our obsessive compulsive need to get into relationships with abusers.

The forefathers and pioneers went on to provide us with some insight into how to approach a person we owe amends. They wrote that you probably still have some misgivings. As we look over the list of family members, business acquaintances, and friends we have hurt, we may feel different about going to some of them on a spiritual basis. Let us be reassured. To some people we need not, and probably should not emphasize the spiritual feature on our first approach. We might prejudice them. Now, we are trying to put our lives in order. But this is not an end. Our real purpose is to fit ourselves to be of maximum service the God of our understanding or a Power greater than us and the people about us.

The forefathers and pioneers of Alcoholics Anonymous clearly stated that our purpose for living is to serve the God of our understanding or a Power greater than us and our fellow man. The forefathers and pioneers of Alcoholics Anonymous tell us that our actions demonstrate that we have changed, not our words.

They wrote that it is seldom wise to approach an individual, who still smarts from our injustices to them, and announce that we have gone religious. In the world of boxing, this would be called leading with the chin. Why lay ourselves open to being branded fanatics or religious bores? We may kill a future opportunity to carry a beneficial message. But those we approach are sure to be impressed with a sincere desire to set right the wrong. They are going to be more interested in our demonstration of good will than our talk of spiritual discoveries.

The forefathers and pioneers went on to describe how to make amends to someone we genuinely dislike. They wrote that nevertheless, with a person we dislike, we take the bit in our teeth. It is harder to go to an enemy than a friend, but we find it much more beneficial to us. We go to him in helpful and forgiving spirit, confessing or former ill feeling and expressing our regret.

In addition, the forefathers and pioneers of Alcoholics Anonymous gave us instructions on what to say. They wrote that under no condition do we criticize such a person or argue. Simply, we tell them that they will never get over their addiction until we have done our utmost to straighten out the past. We are there to sweep of our side of the street, realizing that nothing worthwhile could be accomplished until we do so, never trying to tell him what he should do. His faults are not discussed. We stick to our own. If our manner is calm, frank, and open, we will be gratified with the result.

Furthermore, the forefathers and pioneers went on to explain how to deal with our debts. We might not like the sacrifice required to make good on our debts, but we must sacrifice. This process forces us to rely on a God of our understanding or a Power greater than us for guidance, which takes us out of self-will and into will of this Power. Under direction of this Power, we find it easier to make restitution than we ever thought possible.

They wrote that most addicts owe money. We do not dodge our creditors. Telling them what we are trying to do, we make no bones about our actions. Likely, they usually know it anyway, whether we think so or not. Nor are we afraid of disclosing our misbehavior on the belief that it may cause us financial harm.

Approached in this way, the most ruthless creditor will sometimes surprise us. Arranging the best deal we can, we let these people know we are sorry. Our addiction has made us slow to pay. We must lose our fear of creditors no matter how far we have to go, for we are liable to relapse if we are afraid to face them.

Keep in mind that courage is not the absence of fear; courage is facing our fears and walking through them. The Forefathers and pioneers of Alcoholics Anonymous go on to give instructions on how to ask a God of our understanding or a Power greater than us for guidance. The forefathers and pioneers tell us that a reliance on a God of our understanding or a Power greater than us is essential it we are to outgrow our fears that have separated us from the sunshine of the spirit.

They wrote that although these reparations take innumerable forms, there are some general principles which we find guiding. Reminding ourselves that we have decided to go to any lengths to find a spiritual experience, we ask that we be given strength and direction to do the right thing, no matter what the personal consequences may be. We may lose our position or reputation or face jail, but we are willing. We have to be. We must not shrink from anything.

The forefathers and pioneers of Alcoholics Anonymous went on to say that we should seek help from others, preferable from someone who understands the Fourth Step Inventory and the restitution process, before we make our most difficult amends because we usually need direction, so we do not cause more harm as we clean the wreckage of our past.

They wrote that before taking drastic action which might implicate other people, we secure their consent. If we have obtained permission, have consulted with others, asked the God of our understanding or a Power greater than us to help, and we do not shy from this drastic Step.

The forefathers and pioneers of Alcoholic Anonymous reminded us yet again to ask God for guidance as we make amends for our past misdeeds. They wrote that perhaps there are some cases where the utmost frankness is demanded. No outsider could appraise such an intimate situation. It may be that both will decide that the way of good sense and loving kindness is to let by-gones be by-gones. Each might pray about it, having the other one's happiness uppermost in mind.

It should be noted that above-mentioned is an example of how we must be tactful and considerate of others, as we make our amends. The forefathers and pioneers of Alcoholics Anonymous also give us directions on what to do if we could not make amends to someone face-to face.

They wrote that there might be some wrongs we could never fully right. We do not worry about them if we could honestly say to ourselves that we right them if we could. Some people cannot be reached, so we send them an honest letter if we know where they are, and we do not know where they are or if they have passed away, we write a sincere heart-felt letter asking for forgiveness, burn the letter, and scatter the ashes in a meaningful way.

The forefathers and pioneers of Alcoholics Anonymous tell us that Dr. Bob Smith, co-founder of Alcoholics Anonymous, found that he could not stay sober until he made amends to those he had harmed. They tell us he accomplished this in one day.

They wrote that one morning Smith took the bull by the horns and set out to tell those he feared what his trouble had been. He found himself surprisingly well received and learned that knew of his drinking. Stepping into his car and made the rounds of people he had hurt. He trembled as he went, fearing that might mean ruin, particularly to a person in his line of business.

The forefathers and pioneers went on to tell us that at midnight, Smith came home exhausted, but very happy. He has not had a drink since. Yet, in many cases, you do not have the power or the courage to do what you must do to achieve these promises in your life, namely making amends. Consequently, pray for the strength and the willingness, and remember that doing wrong is breaking your relationships with others, and amends are making your relationship.

This Step is one of atonement; that is, being at one with the God of your understanding or a Power greater than you, yourself, and others. It also should be noted that addicts are impatient people, who want everything done right now. Could you finish all your amends in one day like Smith did? Probably not, but it should not take long, if you are conscientious.

Finally, the forefathers and pioneers of Alcoholics Anonymous close the Ninth Step with a list of benefits. They tell us precisely what is going to happen once we begin the process of clearing away the wreckage of the past. They describe these benefits as: "The Promises."

They wrote if we are painstaking about this phase of our development, we will be amazed before we are half way through. We are going to know a new freedom and a new happiness. We will not regret the past nor wish to shut the door on it. We will comprehend the word serenity and we will know peace. No matter how far down the scale we have gone, we will see how our experience could benefit others. That feeling of uselessness and self-pity will disappear. We will lose interest in selfish things and gain interest in our fellows. Self-seeking will slip away. Our whole attitude and outlook upon life will change. Fear of people and of economic insecurity will leave us. We will intuitively know how to handle situations which used to baffle us. We suddenly realize that the God of our understanding or a Power greater than us is doing for us what we could not do for ourselves. Are these extravagant promises? We think not. They are being fulfilled among us—sometimes quickly, sometimes slowly. They will always materialize if we work for them.

What a message of great hope! For many of us this is beyond comprehension. How could all these promises come true if we clean up the wreckage of the past and make amends to those we have harmed? But the promises do happen—guaranteed!

The forefathers and pioneers of Alcoholics Anonymous state emphatically that stopping engaging obsessive compulsive learned helplessness is just the beginning because our addiction is not the problem; it is the symptom of a deeper problem. We must take additional action if we are to achieve recovery from obsessive compulsive learned helplessness.

They wrote that sometimes we hear an addict say that the only thing they need to do is to keep sober. Certainly, they must keep sober, for there will be no home if they do not. But there is a long way from making good to those whom for years they have so treated so shockingly.

The forefathers and pioneers went on to say that the addict is like a tornado roaring their way through the lives of others, breaking hearts, shattering relationships, and uprooting affections. Our selfish and inconsiderate habits have kept our home in turmoil. We feel that they are unthinking when they say that sobriety is enough.

They also wrote that there is a long period of reconstruction ahead. We must take the lead. A remorseful mumbling that we are sorry will not do at all. We must sit down with the family and other we have harmed and frankly analyze the past as now we now see it, being very careful not to criticize them. Their defects may be glaring, but the chances are that our own actions are partly responsible. So, we clean house with the family and others, asking each morning in meditation that our Creator show us the way of patience, tolerance, kindness, and love.

Furthermore, the forefathers and pioneers stated that the spiritual life is not a theory. We have to live it. They tell us that in order to recover from addiction, we must live a program of recover and wellness. So, we do not just take the Steps, we live the Steps daily, everyone, everywhere, every day.

The operational principle of Step Nine is Forgiveness. Asking for the forgiveness of those we have intentionally or unintentionally injured is the order the day here. A key point here is to try to correct those injuries through action, not just words. It is highly recommended that guidance and help is sought here. Asking forgiveness is not a gift to the other person, but rather an act of kindness to you.

We hear over and over that the Steps are written in order for a reason: Each Step provides the spiritual preparation we will need for the following steps. Nowhere is this more evident than in the Ninth Step. We would never in a million years have been able to sit down with the people we had harmed and make direct amends to them without the spiritual preparation we got from the previous Steps.

If we had not done the work of admitting our own limitations, we would not now have a foundation on which to stand while we make our amends. If we had not developed a relationship with a God of our understanding or a Power greater than us, we would not now have the faith and trust we need to work Step Nine. If we had not done our Fourth and Fifth Steps, we would probably still be so confused about our personal responsibility, and we might not even know for what we were making amends. If we had not developed humility in the Sixth and Seventh Step, we would probably approach our amends with self-righteousness or anger and wind up doing more damage. The willingness we gained through our acceptance of personal responsibility made it possible for us to make our Eighth Step list. That list was our practical preparation for working the Ninth Step.

The final preparations you are about to do before you make your amends are mostly to strengthen what is already a part of you. The level at which you can practice the principle of forgiveness, the depth of insight you have, and the amount of self-awareness you are able to maintain throughout the amends process will depend on your previous experience with the steps and how much effort you are willing to put into your wellness.

Answer the following questions:

- How has your work on the previous eight steps prepared you to work the Ninth Step?
- How does honesty help you in working this step?
- How does humility help you in working this step?

Amends

The Ninth Step is not a step that can be neatly contained within a particular time frame. We do not write our Eighth Step list and then resolutely start making amends, crossing off completed ones like we would items on a shopping list. In fact, many of our amends will never be "finished" and our efforts will go on throughout our recovery and our journey to wellness. For instance, if you owe your family amends, you will spend the rest of your life practicing the spiritual principles that will bring real change to the way you treat people. There might be one day when you sit your family down and make a commitment to treat them differently than you have in the past, but that would not be the end of your amends. Each day that you try to refrain from hurting your family and try to practice loving behavior with them is a day when you have continued your amends to your family.

Even such relatively concrete amends such as paying a past-due debt is not likely to be done once the debt is paid off. Living your Ninth Step requires that you try not to incur new debts that you cannot pay in the future. On a deeper level, you might need to look at the debts you have incurred. For instance, taking out loans from banks or from friends but not paying them off or defaulting on the loans would certainly overextend the patience of people or institutions you borrowed money from. Avoiding such liabilities in the future is just as much a part of your amends process as making regular payments on past-due debts.

Answer the following questions:

- What does "making amends" mean?
- Why does making amends mean that you have to do more than say "I'm sorry?"
- How is making amends a commitment to a continuous process of change?

Fears and Expectations

Making amends is not always a nerve-wracking, joyless experience. Often, we will feel excited about the prospect of healing a relationship. We might find that we are happily anticipating the relief of having made an amends. However, for most of us, we will feel fearful about at least some of our amends. You might be afraid that if you make financial amends, you would not have enough for yourself. You might be afraid that you will have to go jail or prison. You might be afraid of rejection, retaliation, or something else.

If you have never had any experience with the Ninth Step before, you are really venturing into the unknown. You are not sure how you are going to feel immediately before the amends, during the amends, and after the amends. You might feel wildly overconfident at one moment and then, the next moment feels totally unable to go on with the Ninth Step. This is a time when it is very important to understand that the ways things feel is not necessarily the way things are. Just because you feel afraid does not mean there is truly something to fear. On the other hand, feeling excited and happy would not necessarily reflect the reality of making your amends. It is best to let go of all your expectations about how your amends will be received.

Answer the following questions:

- What fears do you have about making amends?
- Are you worried that someone will take revenge or reject you?
- How does the Ninth Step require a new level of surrender to the program?
- What about financial amends?
- Do you have faith that the God of your understanding or a Power greater than you will ensure you have what you need even though you are sacrificing to make amends?

No matter how long you have been free of your obsessive compulsive learned helplessness or how many times you have been through the Steps, you are bound to have some fears and expectations as you begin a new Step. This might be especially true if you have previous experience with a Step. The Ninth Step is likely to produce some ambivalence. For instance, many of us might find ourselves thinking about our past experiences with making amends at this point. Some have probably been very positive. If you made amends to a loved one who was open to your gesture of conciliation, you probably came away with a wonderful feeling of hope and gratitude. You were hopeful that the relationship would keep on getting better, and you were grateful to be forgiven and have your amends accepted.

Believe it or not, such experiences might work against us in later amends. They can set us up to believe that all our amends should turn out so well, and then be crushed when they do not. Or we might recognize that such amends are not going to be the norm, and dread to the point of delay making amends whose outcome we are not sure will be so good. If you find yourself hung up on projecting how your amends will turn out, you need to re-focus on the purpose of the Ninth Step.

The Ninth Step is meant to give a way to set right the damage you have caused in the past. Some of us keep in mind that three primary concepts are associated with making amends: resolution, restoration, and restitution. Resolution implies that to find an answer to the problem; you must lay to rest what was previously plaguing or disturbing you in some way. Restoration means to bring back to its former state something that had been damaged. This can be a relationship or a quality that used to exist in a relationship, such as trust. You can perhaps restore your reputation if you were good moral character at some point in the past.

Restitution is very similar to restoration, but in relating it to the Ninth Step, you can think of it as the act of returning something, material or more abstract, to its rightful owner. Your mentor can help you explore each of these concepts so that you can gain perspective on the nature of making amends and stay focused on what you are supposed to be doing.

It is only through the process that you realize many of the benefits associated with the Ninth Step. The ones that you might be aware of first are a sense of freedom, or an absence of guilt and shame. It might take some time in or search for wellness for you to appreciate some of the spiritual rewards of the Ninth Step: a more consistent awareness of the feelings of others and the effect of your behavior on others, a sense of joy that you were able to heal a long-standing hurt, an ability to be more loving and accepting of the people around us.

Answer the following questions:

- What other fears or expectations do you have about your amends?
- Why does it not matter how your amends are received?

- What does this have to do with the spiritual purpose of the Ninth Step?

- How can you use other people with obsessive compulsive learned helplessness, your sponsor, and these as sources of strength in this process?

Amends—Direct and Indirect

In recovery, we tend to think it is best to make direct, face-to-face amends, and indeed, this step says we should do so wherever possible. But direct amends are not the only way to make amends, and in some cases, they might be the worst way.

Before I provide some examples, it is very important to note that these are only examples. This guide is not meant to take the place of a mentor and working together to decide what is best.

Some situations are more complicated than they appear at first glance. You might think the solution is obvious, but you should always take the time for further reflection. For instance, there might be a situation where the person or people you harmed are not aware of what you did and learning what you did might possibly harm them more. You might have some friends, relatives, or an employer who were unaware of your obsessive compulsive learned helplessness. To tell them might harm them. Your sponsor will help you look at your motives for wanting to tell people about your obsessive compulsive learned helplessness. Do they need to know? What good purpose will be served by sharing such information? What damage could such information do?

But what if this same situation was complicated by you borrowing money from your friends and not paying it back? Would you need to tell them about your obsessive compulsive learned helplessness, along with admitting not paying off the loan and then paying the money back? Possibly, but perhaps not. Each of these kinds of situations needs to be taken on an individual basis. People need to know only what the really need to know. Vomiting all of your torrid history on people really works out well.

Again, your sponsor will help you decide how best to handle each one. In your discussions with your sponsor, if you are open-minded, you are sure to think about these kinds of situations in ways you have not thought about them before. You might see how what you first thought the obvious method was of making amends might not be right after all. It is very helpful to prepare for this discussion by listing all the circumstances for these difficult amends so that it will be right in front of you when you talk to your mentor.

Answer the following questions:

- Which names on your Eighth Step list are complicated by circumstances like the ones above?

- What were the specific circumstances?

A problem that presents difficulty for many of us is that we owe amends that might likely result in serious consequence. For instance, if you turn yourself into law enforcement for a crime you committed, you might indeed go to jail. So, what effect would that have on your life? Would you lose your job? Would that compromise anyone's security besides your own, say that of your family? On the other hand, if you are a fugitive from justice, what effect might a sudden arrest have on your life and your family? It is probably best in such a situation to seek legal counsel and explore your legal options. No matter what, you need to somehow accept the consequences of your behavior, but you should bear in mind that your family might very well be represented in the part of this Step that says: "except when to do so would injure them or others." You will have to evaluate these situations very carefully. With guidance from wise others, you can explore how to make amends.

Answer the following questions:

- Do you owe any amends that might have serious consequences if you made them?

- What are they?

Another circumstance when you would not be able to make direct amends, although not because of the possibility of further injury, would be when a person to whom you owe an amends has passed away. This is very common. So much so, that people in the world of wellness have developed a variety of creative ways of dealing with such situations.

You must make sure that amends of this nature do more than discharge your own sense of shame. Some have made financial donations in the name of the person to whom they owed amends. Others have taken on a task that was something that person cared about. Some have made restitution to the person's children, who might have their own spot on your Eighth Step list.

The ways you might deal with such a situation are only limited by your imagination and level of willingness. You might be surprised at how effective an "indirect" amends can be in situations like this. Many of us strive to make the amends as directly as possible by visiting the person's grave or other meaningful place and perhaps reading a letter or simply speaking to the person's memory or spirit. Again, your response to these situations will be determined by the nature of the harm you inflicted, your spiritual beliefs, and of course, your sponsor's guidance.

Answer the following questions:

- Do you owe amends to anyone who has passed away?
- What was special about that person that you might be able to use in planning your amends?

I have been emphasizing the need to check each and every amends with your sponsor before proceeding. Although important, there is no need for you to become a mindless robot, afraid to think for yourself or act without asking your sponsor about it. Many of us have had the experience of running into a person from our past who we had not put on our Eighth Step list but might belong there. Sometimes the amends owed are so clear, you would be foolish not to avail yourself of such a lucky coincidence. Other times, you might run into a person and experience very uncomfortable feelings but not know what is causing them. If this happens, it is better to take the relationship through the Fourth and Fifth Step process in order to gain more clarity about it. In any event, you should never consider your Eighth Step list closed. Chances are you will be adding new names to it throughout your lives.

What about people you cannot find? Should you go ahead and make indirect amends to them, too? Perhaps, although many of us have had the experience of running across someone we thought we would never be able to find, usually in a location in which we would never expect to find them. You can certainly draw the conclusion a God of your understanding or a Power greater than you is at work when such coincidences happen, but even if not; you certainly should not ignore the opportunity to make direct amends.

If you cannot find someone on your amends list, you might want to wait. You should continue making every effort to find the person; you should try not to cause the same type of harm to someone else; and you should remain willing. A spirit of willingness can often serve the purpose of the amends when you cannot make the actual amends.

After considering the complications involved in making indirect amends, it might seem as though making direct amends is easy, or at least more straightforward. You did something that hurt someone. You need to apologize and repair the harm. That is it, right? Not very often, if ever. As mentioned earlier, the amends process is not one that has a distinct beginning and end. We often begin making amends, in one sense, as soon as we get cease our obsessive compulsive learned helplessness. Most of the time, we immediately make amends for our behavior. This part of the amends process, the one in which we change ourselves, goes on long after we have spoken directly to someone we harmed.

Answer the following question:

• What behavior do you need to make amends for?

What about those direct amends, the ones you make when you sit someone down, acknowledge and accept responsibility for the harm you caused, and accept whatever response you get? These are the amends that might strike fear into your heart. Imagine yourself sitting before one of the people on your amends list, humbly and sincerely admitting your wrongs, then just as humbly and sincerely offering to repair the wrongs done, only to have the person respond: "It can never be repaired. What you did was too awful," or, "Forget it. I'll never forgive you."

In truth, a situation like the one above is exactly what you most fear, because you are afraid of having your faith in the process destroyed. We have taken an incredible risk by allowing yourself to believe in a God of your understanding or a Power greater than you, in yourself, and in the possibility of wellness. Your worst nightmare is that the damage cannot be repaired and you come to believe that you are such horrible person that you cannot be forgiven.

It might comfort you to know that many recovering addicts have received a negative reaction from someone they were making amends to, and not only have they not let it get them down, they have received the same spiritual benefits from making the amends as they would have if it had been received with love and forgiveness. Remember: making amends is not for the people you are making amends to—they are for you. They get you out of the meat grinder of guilt, shame, and remorse that grinds on you, but the person you are making amends get something out it; well, that is good too.

Sometimes, when your attempts at making amends are received negatively, you find that you need to take additional steps so that you can feel that you have attained some resolution. Contacting someone who is still hurting from your misdeeds can be risky. It can also be unproductive, especially in the case of family members and close friends. Contacting people you have harmed before they have had the chance to cool off might cause them to respond very angrily to you, when after a bit more time, they might react quite differently. If you have approached such a person too soon, you might want to wait until some time has passed and try again.

However, sometimes no matter how well you have prepared or how sincere your amends are, the person simply will not accept your amends. If you encounter such a situation, you need to realize that there is a point at which your responsibility ends. If someone is determined to nurse a grudge against you for the rest of their life, it might be that the best you can do is wish the person well and consider the amends made and move on.

If you have difficulty coping with feelings that arise in the wake of such an amends, your mentor will help you find a way of coming to terms with the amends. Perhaps, in certain situations, you might be better off making indirect amends, or it might feel that your amends are more complete if you take some other action that restores or repairs a situation. Perhaps, you can donate the money to a worthy cause or put in the church donation basket.

We need to remember that making amends is part of your personal recovery program. It is true that you make amends because you owe them, but you also need to recognize the spiritual growth inherent in the process of making amends.

First, recognize and accept the harm you caused. This action shocks you out of your tendency to blame others to defend your own bad behavior. Because selfishness and fear are the parts of your disorder that most strongly affect your spirituality, alleviating and diminishing those parts of your affliction will surely cause your recovery to flourish.

Second, approaching the person you harmed directly and acknowledging the harm you caused is an enormous step on your spiritual journey no matter how the amends are received. The fact that you went ahead with something that required such a great deal of humility was proof, in fact, that you had attained some measure of humility.

Finally, after making your amends, you will be left with a sense of peace and freedom. You are no longer burdened with the weight of unfinished business and a sense of shame about the harm you caused. It is gone and your spirit soar.

Answer the following questions:

- Are you spiritually prepared for making any difficult amends and dealing with the results?

- What have you done to prepare yourself?

What About People who Have Harmed You?

The spiritual growth you get from making direct amends often depends on how much you put into your spiritual preparation. You start with getting rid of any beliefs you have that might be causing you to hesitate or that might inhibit your ability to approach your amends with courage, humility, acceptance, and faith.

Something that seems to be a problem for many of us is that we often owe amends to people who have also harmed us. This might be a parent or other relative who abused you, a friend who let you down somehow, an employer who did not treat you fairly, and so on. You have done a lot of work in the previous Steps to separate what they did to you from what you did to them. You know exactly what your part in these situations were, and you know why you are making amends. You need to remember that it is you who are rising to a higher moral level, and perhaps the most meaningful thing you can is to forgive those who have wronged you.

As you prepare to make direct, face-to-face amends, you need to be perfectly clear that you are making amends for your part in these conflicts. You are not making amends to coerce or manipulate a reciprocal amends. You are not responsible for cleaning up anything not on your side of the street. Keeping this in mind throughout your amends will help you keep focused on your purpose no matter how your amends are received and whether or not we receive amends in return for harm done to you.

But sometimes the wrong done to you was so extreme that it is better to postpone making your amends until a later time. For instance, many of us were emotionally, physically, or sexually abused as children by others. Although you had no part in that situation and owe no amends because of it, you might have caused harm to this individual or individuals by somehow retaliating against them. So, you owe amends for the wrongs you did them.

The question that arises in this situation is not whether to make amends, but when and how. It might take time before you are ready to make an appropriate amends, but that is okay. It is strongly advised to seek professional services from a high trained clinician who can help you clear your traumas before you attempt this. Nevertheless, it is important that you this as soon as you can, so you can be at peace.

You need to try to forgive the people who have harmed you before you make amends to them. You do not want to sit down with someone with whom you are furious and try to make an amends. Your attitude will be apparent, no matter how much you try to hide it. Amends are a time when it is not usually very productive to "act as if."

There is a big difference between situations when you were harmed against your will and situations in which your behavior contributed to the way you were treated. For many of your amends, when you were angry with someone who treated you badly, you need to ask yourself if anything you did could have caused them to treat you as they did.

For instance, you might be enraged at your parents for not trusting you to go out on a weekend to a dance, but when you think about how many times you lied to them before about where you were going and what you are doing, it might help you see that your parents could not help but treating you with mistrust, and so, that you might have to spend more time earning their trust.

Or you might have been selfish and withdrawn with some of your friends day after day, week after week. Then when you needed them, they were not available, and so, you became angry and resentful. Reminding yourself that you engineered much of your own misery might help you forgive those who hurt you.

Another way you might find forgiveness for those who hurt you is by getting out of your own head and thinking about what other people's lives are like. Maybe the people who hurt you did so because they had problems that made them less sensitive to the needs of others. Maybe your sponsor or mentor did not return your phone calls for a week because his youngest child was in jail. Maybe your best friend told you that your relationship was unhealthy, and you should get out of it, immediately following their own divorce. Maybe your employer did not praise your work because they were worried about being able to meet payroll that week. We usually feel petty and small when we find out that a person we resented had some painful problem as well. Maybe you can be more forgiving and loving if you just assume from the start that most people's intentions are good and that if someone is unkind to you, it might be because he or she is in a lot of pain and very distracted by it.

Remember that resentments are not about what the other person did to you; they are about you and your response to the situation. Ask yourself the question: "Why does this bother me so?"

First and foremost, preparing yourself spiritually to make amends requires that you tap into the strength and love of a Power greater than yourself. Contemplating a loving this Power's forgiveness of the times when you hurt people will help you approach people with an attitude of love and forgiveness. Using the God of your understanding as a sort of protective force will ensure that negative reactions to your amends do not cause you to lose hope. You can center yourself by praying and meditating before each amends.

Answer the following questions:

- Do you owe amends to people who have also harmed you?
- Have you forgiven them all?
- Which ones have you not forgiven yet?
- Have you tried all of the above ways of generating a spirit of forgiveness?
- What does your sponsor say about it?

Making Amends

Now you are ready to make your amends. You have discussed each person, place, thing, organization, or institution on your Eighth Step list with your sponsor and made a plan for how you would go about making each amends. You have talked to the God of your understanding or a Power greater than you, and you have prayed for the willingness, serenity, courage, and wisdom to go through with your amends.

Now, you need to follow through with your amends. You need to continue changing your behavior, and you need to keep whatever commitments you have made to the people on your amends list. But this is where it can get difficult. When you first make an amends, you are usually feeling as if you could float away on a cloud of freedom. You feel a heightened sense of self-respect and the initial euphoria that comes along with the disappearance of a large chunk of guilt, shame, and remorse. You feel like a good person, like you are on equal footing with the rest of humanity. This feeling is extremely powerful, and if it is your first time feeling it, it might seem like more than you can handle.

You should not worry. The feelings will not be so intense for long, although there will be some permanent change in your feelings about yourself. After the glow of making an amends fades, you will face the truly challenging part of making amends: the follow-through. For instance, a year after you approach a lending institution to which you owe money and promise to pay back a certain amount every month, you might not find it "spiritually inspiring" to hand over a portion of every hard-earned paycheck, especially if you are going to be making the same payment for several more years. Asking yourself one simple question should help you continue with your amends: How free do you want to be?

To continue with all aspects of your wellness, making amends included, makes your freedom grow day by day.

Answer the following questions:

- Are there amends with which you are having trouble following through?
- What are you doing to recommit yourself to making these amends?

It is not necessarily a comforting and comfortable process to make amends. The Steps are not designed to make you happy and comfortable without also making you grow. The fear, the risk, and the feeling of vulnerability that comes with making amends might be so uncomfortable for you that the memory keeps you from repeating the behavior that led to you having to make amends in the first place. We hear that "it gets better." The "It" is us; we get better. We become better people. We become less willing to engage in destructive behavior because we are aware of the cost in human misery, both our own and those around us. Your self-centeredness is replaced by an awareness of other people and concern about their lives. Where you were indifferent, you begin to care. Where you were selfish, you begin to be selfless. Where you were angry, you begin to be tolerant.

Your love and tolerance also extends to yourself. You explored some of the issues surrounding making amends to yourself in Step Eight. Now, it is time to recognize how you have already begun making amends to yourself and perhaps make some plans to continue or take on some new things. You began making amends to yourself for your sugar misuse when you stopped acting out and started working the Steps. Just these two acts alone will go a long way toward healing the damage you did to your spirit.

You might have to do some other things to heal the damage you did to your body and mind. There are many ways you can begin taking care of your physical health, from diet to exercise to medical treatment. Whatever ways you choose will need to fit your personal needs and desires. The damage you did to your mind might be healed in some measure by pursuing knowledge in the future. A return to school, or just learning something new, will help you repair years of mental neglect.

Answer the following questions:

- What are your immediate plans for making amends to yourself?
- Do you have any long-range goals that might also fit as amends to yourself?
- What are they?

- What can you do to follow through?

Spiritual Principles

In the Ninth Step, you will focus on humility, love, and forgiveness. The humility you have gained in this Step has resulted from getting a good look at the damage you did to others and accepting responsibility for it. You acknowledge to yourself: "Yes, this is what I've done. I'm responsible for the harm I caused and for making it right." You might have been led to this awareness by the experience of having someone tearfully tell you how much you hurt them. You have found yourself on the receiving end of some hurt you inflicted on someone else and been so jarred by such an experience that you were able to see on a deeper level how you hurt people. Then again, it might have been only the process of the previous steps, coupled with the experience of making amends that led you to experience increased humility.

Answer the following questions:

- Have you accepted responsibility for the harm you caused and for repairing that harm?
- What experiences have you had that led you to see the harm you caused more clearly?
- How has that contributed to an increase in your humility?

It becomes much easier to practice the spiritual principle of love in Step Nine, although you have probably been working on practicing it throughout your recovery. By this time, you have eliminated many of the destructive views and feelings you had, making room for love in your life. As you become filled with love, you find yourself compelled to share it by nurturing your relationships and building new ones and by selflessly sharing your recovery, your time, your resources, and above all, yourself with those in need.

Answer the following question:

- How are you giving to yourself or being of service to others?

As you experience being forgiven, you begin to see the value in extending that to others. This motivates you to practice the spiritual principle of forgiveness as much as possible. Recognizing your own humanness gives you the capacity to forgive others and not be as judgmental as you have been in the past. It becomes second nature for you to give other people the benefit of the doubt. You no longer suspect vile motives and sneaky conspiracies are at play in every situation over which you do not have full control. You are aware that you usually mean well, and so extend that belief to others. When someone does harm you, you are aware that holding resentments only serves to rob your own peace and serenity, so you tend to forgive sooner rather than later.

Answer the following questions:

- What are the benefits to you of practicing the principle of forgiveness?
- What are some situations in which you have been able to practice this principle?
- What you have forgiven yourself for?

Moving On

Many of us find it helpful to reflect on our amends after making each one. Some of us do this by writing about how it felt to make the amends and what we learned from the experience.

Answer the following questions:

- How did it feel to make this amends?
- What did you learn from it?

"Freedom" seems to be the word that most clearly describes the essence of Step Nine. It seems to sum up the relief from guilt and shame, the lessening of your obsession with yourself, and the increased ability to appreciate what is going on around you as it is happening. You start being less consumed with yourself, abler to be fully present in all your relationships. You begin to be able to just be in a roomful of people without trying to control the room or dominate every conversation. You start thinking of your past, specifically your obsessive compulsive learned helplessness, as a gold mine of experience to share with people you are trying to help in recovery, instead of as a period of darkness you want to forget about. You stop thinking about your lives in terms of what you do not have and begin to appreciate the gifts you receive every day. You know that to keep this feeling of freedom, you will need to keep applying what you have learned in the previous steps. Step Ten gives you the means to do that.

Chapter Fourteen

Step Ten

Continued to take personal inventory and when we were wrong promptly admitted it.

In Steps One through Three, you made a decision that put you on the spiritual path. In Steps Four through Nine, you took the actions necessary to remove those things, which had separated you from the God of your understanding or a Power greater than you and from the direction of your spirit and your own internal guidance system.

Now, you are ready for the promised spiritual awakening or epiphany. Step Ten is the first of the maintenance Steps. Step Ten is a summary of Steps Four through Nine. Step Eleven, gives you instructions on how to establish and maintain your conscious contact with a God of your understanding or a Power greater than you. Step Twelve, tells you how to carry your life-changing message to others.

The key to Step Ten is: Continuing to take personal inventory. The forefathers and pioneers of Alcoholics Anonymous emphasized the importance of continuing to take the Steps.

They wrote that this thought brings us to Step Ten, which suggests that we continue to take personal inventory and continue to set right any new mistakes we make as we go along. We vigorously commenced this way of living as we cleaned up the past. We have entered the world of the Spirit. Our next function is to grow in understanding and effectiveness. This is not an overnight matter. It should continue for our lifetime.

The forefathers and pioneers of Alcoholics Anonymous went on to tell us how to live one day at a time. This is known as the "Twenty-Four Hour Plan." We continue to take inventory, continue to make amends wherever necessary, and we continue to help others every day.

Let us look at the sentence: "We have entered the world of the Spirit." This sentence contains an amazing revelation. The forefathers of Alcoholics Anonymous informed us that our lives have already changed as a result of taking Steps One through Nine. We have had a spiritual awakening. How could this be?

The answer is simple. It should be noted that there is no way that a person driven by self-will, such as us, could have worked through the Steps alone because our devious minds would have misled us long ago. You have not only developed a belief in a God of your understanding or a Power greater than you, you have reconnected to your integral internal guidance system. You have also come to rely on upon this Power and direction to help you through the inventory and the restitution process. You are now living in the solution. Some of us might not have realized that the psychic change has already occurred.

The forefathers and pioneers Alcoholics Anonymous tell us precisely how to do Step Ten. They wrote that we continue to watch for selfishness, dishonesty, resentment, and fear. When these occur, you ask the God of your understanding or a Power greater than you at once to remove them. You also discuss them with someone immediately and make amends quickly if you have harmed anyone. Then you resolutely turn your thoughts to someone you can help. Love and tolerance of others is our code.

The forefathers and pioneers of Alcoholics Anonymous provide us with specific instructions on how to rid ourselves of self-centered behaviors, such as selfishness, dishonesty, self-seeking, fear, and resentment.

First, these behaviors are not consistent with the plan the God of your understanding or a Power greater than you for you, nor are they consistent with your own integral guidance system. Therefore, you must take actions necessary to move from your selfishness to the will of God of our understanding or a Power greater than you. You ask the God of your understanding or a Power greater than you to remove your shortcomings, discuss them with someone who understands this process, and if necessary, you make restitution.

The forefathers and pioneers went on to say that if we test for selfishness on a daily basis, the God of our understanding or a Power greater than us will remove the obsession to engage in your obsessive compulsive learned helplessness. This will be discussed in the next chapter. This is another one of the many promises of Alcoholics Anonymous.

They wrote that we have ceased fighting anything or anyone—even our obsessive compulsive learned helplessness. For by this time, sanity will have returned. You will seldom be interested in a codependent relationship with a wounded soul to maintain your learned helplessness, and if tempted, you recoil from it as if it was a hot flame. You will react sanely and normally, and you will find that this happens automatically. You will see that your new attitude toward engaging in your obsessive compulsive learned helplessness has been given to you without any thought or effort on your part. It just happens when you get out of the way. That is the miracle of it. You are no longer fighting it, and neither are you avoiding temptation. You feel as though you have been placed in a position of neutrality—safe and protected. The problem has been removed and it exists is no longer. You are neither arrogant nor are you afraid. This is your experience and this is how you will react so long as you keep in fit spiritual condition.

How can you keep in a fit spiritual condition? The answer lies in taking a daily inventory. So, what is your reward? It is a daily reprieve from the insanity and unmanageability of obsessive compulsive learned helplessness.

The forefathers and pioneers of Alcoholics Anonymous describe this daily reprieve by saying that it is easy to let up on the spiritual program of action and rest on your laurels. You are headed for trouble if you do, for your obsessive compulsive learned helplessness is a subtle foe. Even though you are cured of your obsessive compulsive learned helplessness, you do not tempt your addiction by playing with it. You are just neutral to it where you neither embrace it or reject it. What you really have is a daily reprieve contingent on the maintenance of your spiritual condition. Every day is a day when you must carry the will of the God of your understanding or a Power greater than you in all your activities by continuing to join your will with that of this Power on a united mission to wellness.

Another reward is what is known as "God Consciousness," which is the direct contact with the God of your understanding or a Power greater than you and your internal guidance system.

The forefathers and pioneers of Alcoholics Anonymous said that much has already been said about receiving strength, inspiration, and direction from this Power who has all knowledge and power. If you have carefully followed the directions, you have begun to sense the flow of this Power into you. To some extent you have developed a "God-conscious." And so, you have begun to develop this vital sixth sense. But you must go further and that means more action.

The forefathers and pioneers went on to say that we have already had the spiritual wakening because we have become conscious of the God of our understanding or a Power greater than us and we are now receiving strength, inspiration, and direction from this Power and from our soul or self and our own internal guidance. The forefathers and pioneers of

Alcoholics Anonymous give us the directions for taking Step Ten. They wrote that we continue to take personal inventory and continue to set right any new mistakes as we go along.

Therefore, you see in Step Ten that you were powerless over our obsessive compulsive learned helplessness; your behavior was insane whether you engaged in it or not; and only a power greater than you could save you from yourself. You must find truth through a daily inventory. You should discuss any problems you have with a spiritual advisor daily; you must stay close to the God of your understanding or a Power greater than you; and you help others by doing random acts of kindness.

Consequently, it is important to do all the Steps daily. Interestingly, Bill Wilson, co-founder of Alcoholics Anonymous, referred to a troublesome setback that many recovering addicts run into during this time. He called it: "reconstruction of the ego."

"Reconstruction of the ego" causes the destructive, insane parts of our self to come back and wreck our lives, along with our resulting in insanity and unmanageability. This might be called a relapse. It is likely to occur if we do not work the Steps thoroughly and honestly, and if we do not continue to work them.

The forefathers and pioneers of Alcoholics Anonymous realized that they had to cease fighting anything or anyone, including our addiction, if they were going to remain sober. Therefore, in order to remain sober, we should be neutral toward our addiction and seldom be interested in it, although we might think of it occasionally or have a periodic "drunk dream."

However, if you are tempted to engage in an obsessive compulsive learned helplessness, you should back away from it, after all, you allergic to it. Consequently, you begin to automatically react normally and sanely to situations where you might have to consume sugar or sugar products, neither being fearful of them, nor shunning those who have healthy normal appetites for sugar.

By practicing Step Ten as it is written in the "Big Book," not as it is written on wall signs in twelve-step rooms, and by doing Steps Eleven and Twelve on a daily basis, we can keep spiritually fit. So, what is the difference between the way Step Ten is written on wall signs of twelve-step rooms and the way it was revealed in the "Big Book?" The forefathers and pioneers of Alcoholics Anonymous tell us that Step Ten involves touching the truth of all twelve steps daily.

Furthermore, you can get a better sense of this by observing that you have entered the world of the spirit [Step Eleven]. Continue to watch for selfishness, dishonesty, resentment, and fear [Step Four]. When these occur, you quickly evaluate the situation and observe your part in it and set things right [Steps Four and Ten]. You discuss them with someone immediately [Step Five] and make amends quickly if you have harmed anyone [Steps Eight and Nine]. Then you resolutely turn your thoughts to someone we can help [Step Twelve]. We cease fighting anything and anyone—even our obsessive compulsive learned helplessness [Step One]. Sanity will have returned [Step Two]. Every day is a day when you must see and act on the vision of the will of the God of our understanding or a Power than you for you in all of your activities [Step Eleven], and you begin to see how to best serve humanity [Step Three].

Finally, Step Ten gives you some tools to use daily. Watch for the return of your selfish self, ask the God of your understanding or a Power greater than you to remove it, and turn from the selfishness toward the will of the God of your understanding or a Power greater than you as this enlightenment becomes your internal guidance system. You must continue to take daily personal inventory; continue to set right any new mistakes as you proceed through your new life; and rework the Steps when you become restless, irritable, or discontented because selfish self has returned?

It should be noted that once you have cleaned up the wreckage of your past, and you are living in accordance with your new moral principles, you are at peace with yourself and the world around you. However, in the course of human events, you will inevitably harm others with your defects of character and selfishness. We are not saints, so it would be unreasonable to think that we could live a life free of harming others.

The Tenth Step permits you to set right wrongs that you do on to others by promptly admitting your wrongs and making amends to those you have harmed. As was said previously, making an amends is a four-step process:

1. Make a humble apology for your wrong doing taking full responsibility for your actions.
2. Make a full accounting of your wrong doing.
3. Doing at least one act of atonement or compensation to demonstrate your desire to set things right.
4. A plea for forgiveness.

Another major benefit of the Tenth Step is to relieve you of your pent-up guilt, shame, remorse, and regret you experience when you harm those around you. If you hold on to these emotions, which are internalized energy, it would likely send you back to drinking, using drugs, engaging in stimulating activities, or acting out on your obsessive compulsive learned helplessness to relieve your burden of guilt, shame, remorse, and regret.

The operational principle of Step Ten is Acceptance. To be human is to make mistakes. Hopefully, your journey has led you to the point where you can readily admit your mistakes and accept yourself for being imperfect. For the best we can ever hope to become is to be perfectly imperfect. You must also learn not to judge others, but accept them for who they are, not your vision of who they should be.

Through working the first nine Steps, your life has changed dramatically, way beyond what you expected when you first came into the world of recovery. You have become more honest, humble, and concerned about others, less fearful, selfish, and resentful. But even such profound changes are not guaranteed to be permanent. Because you have the affliction of alcohol addiction, you can always return to what you were before.

But wellness has a price; it demands vigilance. You must continue doing all the things you have been doing for your wellness so far. You must continue to be honest; to have trust and faith; to pay attention to your actions and reactions; and to assess how these are working for you or against you. You also have to pay attention to how your actions affect others, and when the effects are negative or harmful, promptly step forward and take responsibility for the harm caused and for repairing it. In short, you have to continue to take personal inventory and promptly admit your are wrongs. Now, you begin the maintenance Steps ten, eleven, and twelve.

As you can see, the Tenth Step has you repeat much of the work you did in Steps Four through Nine, although in a much shortened format. The format suggested in this guide is one that covers in a general way the elements of a personal inventory. Some of us might find that we need to add questions that focus on specific areas that are affecting our individual recovery to the questions already in this guide. You might find some additional areas upon which to focus. Your mentor might have specific direction for you on this point. As noted before, this guide is meant to be a starting point, not the final word on any of the Steps.

Answer the following questions:

- Why is a Tenth Step necessary?
- What is the purpose of continuing to take personal inventory?

Feeling versus Doing

You will use Step Ten to create and maintain a continuous awareness of what you are feeling, thinking, and, even more importantly, what you are doing. Before you begin a regular pattern of personal inventory, it is imperative that you understand what you are assessing. It will not do much good to make a list of your feelings without tying them to the actions that they generate or fail to generate. You might often be feeling very badly though behaving very well, or vice versa.

For instance, a young woman in recovery walks into her home group. "How are you?," someone asks." Terrible," she replies. Of course, this member is referring to the way she feels. She cannot possibly be referring to what she is doing, because she is behaving very well indeed: She is going to a meeting, honestly expressing how she feels, and reaching out to another member who will be supportive.

On the other hand, you might be busy indulging your impulses and acting on character defects. On the surface, you might feel very good. It usually takes a while before you notice the emptiness that goes along with living this way. You are avoiding the work that will help you stay free of your obsessive compulsive learned helplessness. You are indulging your impulses and taking the easy way out. And you know where this will take you! This is a relapse. There are 11 stages and 48 different parts of relapse, most of which you will not be even aware of until it is too late.

The Tenth Step will keep you aware of yourself, so you do not end up going to either extreme. You do not have to beat yourself up because you feel badly. You can instead focus on the positive action you are taking. It might even turn out that by shifting your focus this way, you will wind up feeling better as well. Staying aware of what you are doing helps you see patterns of destruction long before they become entrenched, so you do not wind up feeling good at the cost of what is good for you.

As people who are powerless over our obsessive compulsive need to engage in codependent relationships with wounded souls to maintain our learned helplessness, we tend to make judgments about what we are feeling. When anything that feels bad, you immediately want it to go away. This is a natural process. After all, feeling bad was why you began the path down the dark road of obsessive compulsive learned helplessness in the first place. You often do not consider that the way you are feeling makes perfect sense and normal in the context of what happened to you when you consider the circumstances.

For instance, many of us have problems with anger. You do not like the way it feels. You judge it, concluding you have no right to feel that way, and then you do your very best to suppress your angry feelings. Yet, you might be experiencing a situation that would make anyone else angry.

Perhaps you are in a relationship with someone who constantly mistreats you and shows you disrespect. Perhaps you have been passed over for several well-deserved promotions at work. Your response to these situations is anger. You have been treated poorly, so of course you are angry. Now comes the moment when your recovery can propel you forward into greater self-respect or your affliction can drag you down into a thick fog of depression and resentment.

It all has to do with how you respond to your anger. Anger is energy; it cannot be created or destroyed; it just changes forms. If you scream and curse and throw things, you will feel better for a moment, but it will destroy any possibility of making your relationship or job situation better. If you do nothing and bury your feelings of anger, you will push the energy inside and you will become depressed, anxious, resentful, or you will begin suffering from health problems like migraine headaches; digestive disorders like ulcer disease, Irritable Bowel syndrome, Ulcerative Colitis, Crohn's disease; heart disease; cancer; neurological disorders like Fibromyalgia or Chronic Fatigue Disorder; or skin problems like Psoriasis; and that will not improve your situation either. Additionally, you could launch another addiction or escape.

But if you take positive action aimed at improving the situation, it might get better, and at the very least, you will know when it is time to leave and be able to do so without regrets.

Sometimes the only thing you need to do with your feelings is feel them. You do not need to react to them. For instance, if you have lost someone, you are going to feel sorrow. Your sorrow might go on for a long time. It will lift when you have grieved sufficiently. You cannot afford to let your sorrow drag you down to the point where you cannot go on with your life, but you should expect to be affected.

You might be easily distracted or have a hard time participating in activities that are supposed to be enjoyable. You need to strike a balance between being in denial of your feelings and letting them overwhelm you, and so, you do not want to go to either extreme. This seems like a simple concept, almost as if it could go without saying, but many of many members of twelve step programs share that it takes years of recovery before we are able to achieve a balance most of the time.

So, the Tenth Step grants you the freedom to feel your feelings by helping you see the difference between feeling and doing.

Answer the following question:

- Are there times in your life when you are confused about the difference between your feelings and your actions? Expand on this.

Right and Wrong

The Tenth Step tells us that we have to promptly admit when we are wrong. This Step seems to assume that you know when you are wrong, but the fact is that most of us do not, at least not right away. It takes a consistent practice of taking a personal inventory for you to become proficient at figuring out when you are wrong.

Let us face it. When you were new in recovery, you were at odds with the rest of the world for some time. Your living skills were reduced to an animal level. You did not know how to communicate with others well. You began to learn in recovery, but in the process, you made a lot of mistakes. Many of us went through a period when we became very rigid about the values we had developed in recovery. We applied that rigidity not only to ourselves, but to everyone around us. We thought it was principled and correct to confront those whose behavior was "unacceptable." In truth, it was our behavior that was unacceptable. We were self-righteous and overbearing. We were wrong.

But some of us, after years of serving as a doormat for everyone to walk on, decided our recovery required that we become assertive, or in most cases, aggressive. But we went too far. We demanded that everyone treat us perfectly all the time. No one could have a bad day and fail to return our phone call. No one could be emotionally unavailable to us for any length of time. We angrily demanded perfect service at the places we did business. We were not being assertive; we were being immature and belligerent. We were wrong.

You can even end up being wrong if someone hurts you. How? Say your sponsor says something very hurtful to you. Instead of taking it up with them, you talk to ten or twelve of your closest friends at the next three meetings you go to, and before the week is out, half of your local recovery community is talking about what the rotten so-and-so said to one of his sponsees. So, the situation started out with you having done no wrong but ended up with you being responsible for damaging your sponsor's reputation in the program; a place where he needs to be, as much as you do, and to be allowed to make mistakes and recover at his own pace.

Answer the following questions:

- Have there been times in your recovery when you have been wrong and not been aware of it until later?
- What were they?
- How do your wrongs affect your own life?
- Other peoples' lives?

It is hard enough to figure out when you are wrong; admitting your wrongs can be even more challenging. Just like in the Ninth Step, you must be careful that you are not doing more damage by making the admission.

For instance, many of us realize we have hurt someone close to us, perhaps because the person stopped speaking to us, but are not quite sure what we said or did wrong. Rather than taking the time to reflect on what you might have done, or ask the person, you decide you will just cover all eventualities and make a blanket admission. You might approach the person and say: "Please forgive me for anything I have ever done to offend you or hurt you, in all the time we have known each other." This kind of blanket apology seldom gets a good response.

The Tenth Step requires that you take the time for personal reflection for instances just like this. Chances are that if you think about when the person's attitude toward you changed, and think about your behavior immediately preceding that change, you will know what you did wrong.

It might be painful or embarrassing to think about; however, it definitely takes effort, but so do all the Steps. Laziness is a character defect like any other, and you cannot afford to act on it. Then again, if you are truly stumped, if you just cannot pinpoint anything you might have said or done that was harmful, there is nothing wrong with approaching the person and saying you have noticed that they seem to be angry or upset with you, that you care about your relationship with that person, and want to hear what they have to say. Most of us are afraid of what we will hear in a situation like this, but we cannot let our fear stop us from working Step Ten.

There is another way you can render your admission of wrong completely ineffective: admit you are wrong and then immediately point out what the other person did first that made you act as you did. For instance, say one of your children used poor manners, so you yelled at her and called her a name. Now when you admit you were wrong, if you tell your child that her behavior made you act the way you did, you have just delivered a message that justified your first wrong, thus making yourself doubly wrong.

Unlike the process contained in Steps Four through Nine, when you go through events from the past, Step Ten is designed to keep you current. You do not want to let unresolved wrongs pile up. You need to try your very best to stay abreast of what you are doing in the now. Most of your work will be done by making constant adjustments to your outlook.

If you find yourself becoming negative and complaining all the time, you might want to spend some time thinking about the things for which you are grateful. You need to pay attention to the way you react when you have done something wrong. It is usually our first impulse to make an excuse or claim to be victims of someone's negative influence or of our affliction.

All excuses aside, you are responsible for what you do. It might very well be that your character defects got the better of you, but that does not excuse your behavior. You need to accept responsibility and continue to be willing to have your shortcomings removed.

Answer the following questions:

- What does "When we were wrong promptly admitted it" mean to you
- Have there been times in your recovery when you have made situations worse by talking to someone before you should have or blaming your behavior on someone else?
- What were they?
- How does promptly admitting your wrongs help you change your behavior?

Step Ten points out the need to continue taking personal inventory and seems to assert that you do this solely to find out when you are wrong. But how can you identify the times you are wrong unless you also look at the times you are right as a basis for comparison. Identifying the times you do things right and forming personal values are as much a part of personal inventory as identifying your liabilities.

Most of us have a very difficult time with the concept of being right. We think of the times we vigorously defended an opinion because we just knew we were right, but in light of our recovery, we have come to understand that trampling over others in a discussion makes us wrong. Or we think of our personal values. We know they are right for us, but if we began insisting that others live them, we would no longer be right, but self-righteous.

So, how do you get comfortable with being right? First and foremost, by working the Sixth and Seventh Steps so that your character defects do not turn your positive acts into negative acts. Then, you have to realize that it will probably take some time, and some trial and error, before you are completely comfortable in your new life in wellness.

Answer the following question:

- Have there been situations in your recovery in which you felt uncomfortable about acknowledging something you had done well? Describe.

How Often Should we Take a Personal Inventory?

Although our goal is to maintain continuous awareness of ourselves throughout each day, it is very helpful to sit down at the end of each day and do this Step. We need the consistency of doing something every day for it to become a habit and to internalize the spiritual principles of the activity.

As you stay clean and your days in healthy recovery and wellness turn into weeks, months, and years, you will find that taking a personal inventory will become second nature. You will find that keeping track of your spiritual fitness comes naturally, without having to think about it too much. You will notice right away when you are headed in a direction you do not want to go or about to engage in a behavior that is sure to cause harm. You will become able to correct it. So, the frequency of your formal efforts to take personal inventory might depend on your experience with recovery. A wise man once said living the good life is never having to apologize for anything you say or do.

In the beginning, some of us sat down at the beginning of our day, the end of our day, or even both times and went through our day and took our spiritual temperature. The point is that you want to keep at it until it becomes a habit, until it is second nature to continuously monitor your recovery and your spiritual state, notice when you are going off-course right away, and work to change it.

Answer the following question:

- Why is it important to continue to take personal inventory until it becomes second nature?

A Personal Inventory

The following questions address the general areas you want to look at in a personal inventory. There might be times when your sponsor wants you to do an inventory on a specific area of your lives, such as romantic relationships or your patterns at work, or your sponsor might have specific questions to add to this. You should always consult your sponsor on any step work you are doing.

Answer the following questions:

- Have you reaffirmed your faith in a loving, caring God of your understanding or a Power greater than you today?
- Have you sought out the guidance from the God of your understanding or a Power greater than you today?
- How?
- What have you done to be of service to the God of your understanding or a Power greater than you and the people around you?
- Has the God of your understanding or a Power greater than you given you anything to be grateful for today?
- Do you believe that a God of your understanding or a Power greater than you can show you how to live and better align yourself with the will of that power?
- Do you see any "old patterns" in your life today?
- If so, which ones?
- Have you been resentful, selfish, dishonest, or afraid?

- Have you set yourself up for disappointment?

- Have you been kind and loving toward all?

- Have you been worrying about yesterday or tomorrow?

- Did you allow yourself to become obsessed about anything?

- Have you allowed yourself to become too hungry, angry, lonely, or tired?

- Are you taking yourself too seriously in any area of your life?

- Do you suffer from any physical, mental, or spiritual problems?

- Have you kept something to yourself that you should have discussed with your mentor?

- Did you have any extreme feelings today?

- What were they and why did you have them?

- What are the problem areas in your life today?

- Which defects played a part in your life today?   How?

- Was there fear in your life today?

- What did you do today that you wish you had not done?

- What did you do today that you wish you had done?

- Are you willing to change?

- Has there been conflict in any of your relationships today?   What?

- Are you maintaining personal integrity in your relations with others?

- Have you harmed yourself or others, either directly or indirectly, today?

- How?

- Do you owe any apologies or amends?

- Where were you wrong?

- If you could do it over again, what would you do differently?

- How might you do better next time?

- Did you act out on your addict behavior today?

- Were you good to yourself today?

- What were the feelings you had today?

- How did you use them to choose principle-centered action?

- What did you do to be of service to others today?

- What have you done today about feeling positive?

- What has given you satisfaction today?

- What did you do today that you want to be sure you repeat?

- Did you go to a meeting or talk to another recovering addict today?

- What do you have to be grateful for today?

Spiritual Principles

In the Tenth Step, you focus on self-discipline, honesty, and integrity. Self-discipline is essential to your recovery. When you were acting out on your obsessive compulsive learned helplessness, you were self-seeking and selfish. You always took the easy way out, giving in to your impulses, ignoring any opportunity for personal growth. If there was anything in your lives that required a regular commitment, chances are that you only followed through if it was not too hard, if it did not get in the way of your self-indulgence, or if you happened to feel like it.

The self-discipline of recovery calls on you to do certain things regardless of how you feel. You need to go to meetings regularly even if you are tired, busy at work, having fun, or filled with despair; you need to go regularly even when, especially when you are feeling hostile toward the demands that recovery makes on you. You go to meetings, call your sponsor, and work with other suffering people suffering from obsessive compulsive learned helplessness because you have decided that you want recovery, and those things are the actions that will help assure your continued recovery.

Sometimes we are enthusiastic about these activities. Sometimes it takes every bit of willingness we possess to continue with them. Sometimes they become so woven into our daily existence, we are hardly aware that we are doing them.

Answer the following questions:

- Why is the principle of self-discipline necessary in this step?
- How can practicing the principle of self-discipline in this step affect your entire recovery?

The principle of honesty originates in Step One and is brought to fruition in Step Ten. We are usually nothing less than amazed at the range and depth of our honesty by this point in our recovery. Where before, you might have had honest hindsight, where you able to see your true motives long after a situation was over, you will now able to be honest with yourself, about yourself, while the situation is still occurring.

Answer the following question:

- How does being aware of your wrongs help you change your behavior?

The principle of integrity can be quite complex, but it is integrity, more than anything else, that commands your ability to practice other principles. In fact, integrity is knowing which principles you need to practice in a given situation, and in what measure. So, what is integrity? Integrity is defined as an adherence to moral and ethical principles ad a soundness of moral character.

In ethics, when discussing behavior and morality, an individual is said to possess the virtue of integrity if the individual's actions are based upon an internally consistent framework of principles—an internal guidance system. These principles should uniformly adhere to sound logical and moral principles. You can describe a person as having ethical integrity to the extent that an individual's actions, beliefs, methods, measures, and principles all derive from a single core group of wholesome values. You must therefore be flexible and willing to adjust these values in order to maintain consistency when these values are challenged. Because such flexibility is a form of accountability, it is regarded as a moral responsibility as well as a virtue.

Your value system provides a framework within which we acts in ways that are consistent and expected. Integrity is the state or condition of having such a framework and acting congruently within the given framework.

One essential aspect of a consistent framework is its avoidance of any unwarranted or arbitrary exceptions for a person or group, especially the person or group that holds to the framework. In law, this principle of universal application requires that even those in positions of power be subject to the same laws that pertain to their fellow citizens.

In personal ethics, this principle requires that you should not act according to any rule that you would not wish to see universally followed. For example, you should not steal unless you would want to live in a world in which everyone was a thief. In other words, you engage in a right manner even when others are not looking.

The concept of integrity implies a wholeness, a comprehensive body of beliefs, often referred to as a worldview. This concept of wholeness emphasizes honesty and authenticity, requiring that one act at all times in accordance with the individual's chosen worldview.

For instance, you hear a person gossiping about someone you know. Let us say they are discussing an affair your best friend's spouse is having, and you know it to be true because you heard it from your best friend the previous night. Knowing what to do in this situation will probably take every ounce of integrity you possess.

So, which spiritual principles do you need in this situation? Honesty? Tolerance? Respect? Restraint? It is probably your first impulse to rush in, condemning the gossip because you know how much it would hurt your friend to have such private matters discussed publicly. But by doing so, you might confirm the gossip's truth and so hurt your friend even more, or you might end up self-righteously humiliating the people involved in the gossip. Most of the time, it is not necessary to prove you have integrity by confronting a situation you do not approve of. There are a couple of things you could do in this situation. You could either change the subject, or you could excuse yourself and walk away. Either of these choices would send a subtle message about your feelings, and at the same time, allow you to be true to your own principles and spare your friend as much as possible.

Answer the following questions:

- What situations in your recovery have called on you to practice the principle of integrity?
- How have you responded?
- Which times have you felt good about your response, and which times have you not?

Moving On

One of the most wonderful things about the Tenth Step is that the more you work it, the less you will need the second half of it. In other words, you will not find yourself in the wrong as often. When we come to recovery, most of us have never been able to have any kind of long-term relationship, certainly not any in which we resolved our conflicts in a healthy and mutually respectful way. Some of us had fights with people, and once they were over, we never spoke of the underlying problems that caused the fights, so nothing ever got resolved. Some of us went to the other extreme, never disagreeing at all with the people who were supposed to be our closest friends and relatives. It seemed easier to keep our distance than to risk creating a conflict that we might then have had to deal with. Finally, some of us just walked away from any relationship in which conflict arose. It did not matter how much we were hurting the other person; it just seemed easier than working through a problem and building a stronger relationship.

The Tenth Step makes it possible for you to have long-term relationships, and you need to have long-term relationships with people in healthy recovery. After all, we depend on each other for our very lives. Many of us feel deeply connected to the people who came into recovery when we did and have stayed around. We have done service work with one another, shared apartments with one another, married one another, and sometimes divorced one another. We have celebrated milestones in each other's lives: births, graduations, buying homes, promotions, and recovery anniversaries, we have mourned losses together, We have comforted one another through the painful times in life, and we have touched each other's lives and formed a shared history. We are a community.

Along with learning to admit when you are wrong, comes a freedom that is unlike any you have ever experienced before. It becomes so much more natural for you to admit when you are wrong that you might wonder why you ever found it so terrifying. Perhaps because you felt so "less than" in so many ways, an admission of a mistake felt like you were revealing your deepest secret: your inferiority. But when you found out through working the steps that you were not inferior at all, that you had just as much value as anyone else, it no longer seemed so crushing to admit you were wrong. You began to feel whole again.

Answer the following questions:

- How does the Tenth Step help you live in the present?
- What are you doing differently as a result of working Step Ten?

Working the Tenth Step makes it possible for you to achieve more balance and harmony in your life. You find that you are happy and serene much more often than not. Feeling out of sorts becomes so rare that, when it does happen, it is a signal that something is wrong. You can readily identify the cause of your discomfort by taking a personal inventory.

The personal freedom that has been building since you began working the Steps yields an increase in your choices and options. You have total freedom to create any kind of life you want for yourself. You begin to look for the meaning and purpose in your lives. You ask yourself if the lifestyle you have chosen helps the still-suffering obsessive compulsive codependent person or relationship addict or help makes the world a better place in some other way. What you are searching for, you will find in the Eleventh Step.

❧

Chapter Fifteen

Step Eleven

Sought through prayer and meditation to improve our conscious contact with God, praying only for knowledge of God's will for us and the power to carry that out.

This idea of a "conscious contact" with a God of your understanding of a Power greater than you is a difficult concept to grasp for the uninitiated. Perhaps a little known concept of this idea might be helpful. The endowment of imperfect beings with a freedom of choice can often lead to tragedy. So, our Creator has endowed us with what is known as a "Thought Adjuster." The Thought Adjuster should not be thought of as living in the material brains of human beings. They are not organic parts of the physical being of its hosts. The Thought Adjuster may be more properly seen as indwelling the mortal mind of its host rather than than existing in it. Nor should it be thought of as part of the spirit or the soul.

The Thought Adjuster is unrecognized but is constantly indirectly communicating with the mind and soul of the being they dwell in. When a Thought Adjuster indwells a human mind, they bring with them from the Creator a model life preordained by the Creator. They begin with a definite and preordained plan for their human host, but humans, because they are blessed by the Creator with a freedom of choice, are not forced to accept this model life sent forth by their Creator, and has the liberty to reject it, but at their own peril. If they rect this preordained plan they become self-willed beings and are at the mercy of their excesses and their resulting consequences. In other words, they are on their own cut off from their Creator.

We have seen that the forefathers and pioneers of Alcoholics Anonymous have been writing about the importance of prayer and meditation throughout the "Big Book," but it is discussed specifically in this Step.

They wrote that Step Eleven suggests prayer and meditation. You should not be shy on this matter of prayer. Better people than us are using it constantly. It works, if you have the proper attitude and work at it.

What do the forefathers and pioneers mean when they said: "it works?" They are telling us that prayer and meditation puts us in contact with a God of our understanding or a Power greater than us.

Furthermore, the forefathers and pioneers of Alcoholics Anonymous make some valuable suggestions. They wrote that it would be easy to be vague about this matter. Yet, we believe we could make some definite and valuable suggestions.

They went on to tell us that when we retire at night, we constructively review our day. Were we resentful, selfish, dishonest or afraid? Do we owe an apology? Have we kept something to ourselves which should be discussed with another person at once? Were we kind and loving toward all? What could we have done better? Were we thinking of ourselves most of the time? Or were we thinking of what we could do for others, of what we could pack into the stream of life?

Regarding the beginning of our day, the forefathers and pioneers of Alcoholics Anonymous tell us that upon awakening, we are to practice the equivalent of the Oxford Group's technique of "Quiet Time" and "Guidance."

It should be noted that since Bill Wilson and Dr. Robert Smith, the co-founders of Alcoholics Anonymous, as well as many of the forefathers and pioneers of Alcoholics Anonymous, were members of the Oxford Group, much of the material in this section comes directly from the text book the Oxford Group, titled: *What is the Oxford Group?* This book was written in 1933, six years before the "Big Book" was written.

In the book: *What is the Oxford Group?* published in 1933, there is an entire chapter devoted to "guidance." Oxford Group members were asked to conduct a morning meditation as part of their daily routine.

They stated that a Quiet Time with the Holy Spirit every morning before the daily toil of the world commences will put us in the right key for the day. These early morning Quiet Times in which God impresses on our minds His counsel become living spots in the daily routine of ordinary life.

Similarly, the forefathers and pioneers of Alcoholics Anonymous tell us precisely the same thing. They wrote that upon awakening let us think about the twenty-four hours ahead. We consider our plans for the day. Before we begin, we ask the God of our understanding or a Power greater than us to direct our thinking, especially asking that it be divorced from self-pity, dishonest or self-seeking motives.

Let us look at the sentence: *"Before we begin, we ask God to direct our thinking..."* Before we begin what? Before we begin listening to the God of our understanding or a Power greater than us. How do we know that we are supposed to listen to this Power? Because the next sentence states we ask this Power to direct our thinking. If we ask the God of our understanding or a Power greater than us to direct our thinking, does it not stand to reason that our next thoughts should come from our soul or spirit that was placed in us by this Power? These thoughts from our soul or spirit are called guidance are experienced through our internal guidance system and represent Will of the God of our understanding or a Power greater than us, or His plan for us.

The Oxford Group tells us to write these thoughts or ideas down in our daily meditation. Although this section is not specifically mentioned in the book: *Alcoholics Anonymous*, it is an essential part of the meditation process.

The Oxford Group advocates our use of a pencil and note-book so that we may record every God-given thought and idea that comes to us during our time alone with Him, that no, however small, may be lost to us and that we may not shirk the truth about ourselves or any problem, when it comes to us.

Likewise, the forefathers and pioneers of Alcoholics Anonymous tell us to test our thoughts and ideas because not all of them come from our soul or spirit. With time and practice, we begin to rely upon these thoughts.

They wrote that what used to be a hunch, or the occasional inspiration, gradually becomes a working part of the mind. Being still inexperienced and having just made conscious contact with the God of your understanding or a power greater than you, it is not probable that you are always going to be inspired. We might pay for this presumption in all sorts of absurd actions and ideas. Nevertheless, we find that our thinking will, as time passes, be more and more on the plane of inspiration. We come to rely upon it.

In order to protect ourselves from absurd actions and ideas, the forefathers and pioneers of Alcoholics Anonymous tell us we need to test our thoughts and ideas. Bill Wilson, co-founder of Alcoholics Anonymous, tested his thoughts and actions using the principles of the Oxford Group. Wilson tells us that we were to test our thinking by the new God-consciousness within us. Common sense would thus become uncommon sense.

The forefathers and pioneers went on to say that we need to test our thoughts and actions to separate our selfish self from the Will of the God of our understanding or a Power greater than us.

They wrote that we subjected each relation to this test—was it selfish or not? We asked God to mold our ideas and help us live up to them.

Furthermore, the forefathers and pioneers of Alcoholics Anonymous described the "Alcoholics Anonymous Test for Self-Will," which tests for selfishness, dishonesty, self-seeking, and fear, as well as resentment, and uses the opposites of the Four Absolutes—honesty, purity, unselfishness, and love used by the Oxford Group.

The Alcoholics Anonymous Test for Self-Will includes testing for:

Selfishness

Dishonesty

Self-Seeking

Fear

Resentment

Whereas, the Oxford Group Test for God's Will tests for:

Unselfishness

Honesty

Purity

Love

Although you can choose either the Alcoholics Anonymous Test for Self-Will or the Oxford Group Test for God's Will to check your guidance, the forefathers and pioneers of Alcoholics Anonymous recommend the Alcoholics Anonymous Test for God's Will since none of us can ever be so perfect to live anywhere close these absolute standards.

Nevertheless, regarding the Oxford Group Test for God's Will, the Oxford Group wrote that God will tell you all that you need to know. He will not always tell you all that you want to know. These are a few simple suggestions for people who are willing to make an experiment. You could discover for yourself the most important and practical thing any human being could ever learn—how to be in touch with God. All that is needed is the willingness to try it honestly. Every person who has done this consistently and sincerely has found that it really works. Before you begin, look over these fundamental points. They are true and are based on the experiences of thousands of people.

They write that anyone could be in touch with God, anywhere and at any time, if the conditions are obeyed.

The conditions of meditation are:

- Be quiet and still.

- Listen.

- Be honest about every thought that come into your mind.

- Test your thoughts to be sure they come from God.

- Obey.

The Oxford Group went on to give additional insight into getting in touch with God and our spirit through meditation. They wrote:

1. Take Time

Find some place and time where you can be alone, quiet, and undisturbed. Most people have found that the early morning is the best time. Have with you some paper and a pen or pencil.

2. Relax

Sit in a comfortable position. Consciously relax all your muscles. Be loose. There is no hurry. There needs to be no strain during these minutes. God cannot get through to us if we are tense and anxious about later responsibilities.

3. Tune In

Open your heart to God. Either silently or aloud, just say to God in a natural way that you would like to find His plan for your life—you want His answer to the problem or situation that you are facing just now. Be definite and specific in your request.

4. Listen

Just be still, quiet, relaxed and open. Let your mind go "loose." Let God do the talking. Thoughts, ideas, and impressions will begin to come into your mind and heart. Be alert and aware and open to everyone.

5. Write

Here is the important key to the whole process. Write down everything that comes into your mind. Everything. Writing is simply a means of recording so that you could remember later. Do not sort your thoughts at this point. Do not say to yourself: "This thought isn't important;" "This is just an ordinary thought;" "This couldn't be guidance;" "This isn't nice;" "This couldn't be from God;" or "This is just me thinking." Write down everything that passes through your mind. Names of people; things to do; things to say; and things that are wrong and need to be made right. Write down everything: good thoughts, bad thoughts, comfortable thoughts, uncomfortable thoughts, "Holy" thoughts, "unholy" thoughts, sensible thoughts, or "crazy" thoughts. Be honest and write down everything. A thought comes quickly, and it escapes even more quickly unless it is captured and put down.

6. Test

Just be still, quiet, relaxed and open. Let your mind go "loose." Let God do the talking. Thoughts, ideas, and impressions will begin to come into your mind and heart. Be alert and aware and open to everyone.

a)   Are these thoughts completely honest, pure, unselfish, and loving?

b)   Are these thoughts in line with our duties to our family, our country?

c)   Are these thoughts in line with our understanding of the teachings found in our spiritual literature?

The Oxford Group tells us to test our guidance using the Oxford Group Four Absolutes of honest, purity, unselfishness, and love. If what we have written is selfish, dishonest, self-seeking, or frightened, we could be assured that it is based on our self-will, and therefore, is not from God or our spirit.

7. Check

The Oxford Group asks us to check the source of our guidance. Advice from a spiritual advice could be helpful. They say that when in doubt and when it is important, what does another person who is living two-way prayer think about this thought or action? More light come in through two windows than one. Someone else who also wants God's plan for our lives may help us see more clearly. Talk over what you have written. Many people do this. They tell each other what guidance has come. This is the secret of unity. There are always three sides to every question—your side, my side, and the right side. Guidance shows us which is the right side, not which side is right, but what is right.

8. Obey

The Oxford Group explains that obeying is the most difficult part of all. They say that carry out thoughts that have come. You will only be sure of guidance as you go through it. A rudder will not guide a boat until the boat is moving. As you obey, very often the results will convince you that you are on the right track.

Remember, God gave us free will, but we are free to not listen to God's guidance. However, we must be prepared to accept the consequences if we are not willing to follow our Creator's plan or our internal guidance system.

9. Blocks

The Oxford Group goes on to tell us what we need to do if we do not hear any definite thoughts during our meditation. They state that it is a sign that we have not completely cleared the wreckage of the past. The essay states that we need to make additional amends. They state that if we are not receiving thoughts when we listen, the fault is not God's. Usually it is because there is something you will not do:

- Something wrong in my life that I will not face and make it right.
- A habit or indulgence I will give up.
- A person I will not forgive.
- A wrong relationship in my life I will not give up.
- A restitution I will not make.
- Something God has already told me to do that I will not obey.

If we do not receive any guidance, it means we have work to do. Maybe we have taken back our will in some area of our lives, or maybe we have not made a necessary amends. If this is the case, we need to take the action necessary to re-establish our connection with our creator.

The forefathers and pioneers of Alcoholics Anonymous wrote that we alcoholics are undisciplined. So, we let God discipline us in a simple way we have just outlined. But this is not all. There is action and more action. Faith without works is dead.

10. Mistakes

The Oxford Group went on to say that suppose you make a mistake and do something in the name of God that is not right? Of course, we make mistakes. We are humans with many faults. However, God will always honor our sincerity. He will work around and through every honest mistake we make. He will help us make it right. But remember this—sometimes when we obey God, someone else may not like it or agree with it. So, when there is opposition, it does not always mean you have made a mistake. It could mean that the other person does not want to know or to do what is right. Suppose you fail to do something that you have been told and the opposition to do it passes? There is only one thing to do. Put it right with God. Tell Him you are sorry. Ask Him to forgive you, then accept His forgiveness and begin again. God is our Father—He is not an impersonal calculator. He understands us far better than we do.

11. Results

The Oxford Group tells us that we never know what swimming is like until we get into the water and try. We will never know what this is like until we sincerely try it. Every person who has tried this honestly finds that a wisdom, not their own, comes into their minds and that Power greater than human power begins to operate in their lives. It is an endless adventure. Regarding results, they say states that there is a way of life, for everyone, everywhere. Anyone could be in touch with the living God, anywhere, anytime, if we fulfill His conditions: When man listens, God speaks—When man obeys, God acts. This is the law of prayer.

It should be noted that most of these items are described in the book: *Alcoholics Anonymous* as part of your inventory and restitution process. If you have been thorough and honest in Steps Four through Nine, you will have removed the blocks that have prevented or are preventing you from establishing a two-way communication with the God of your understanding or a Power greater than you. In other words, as was stated earlier, you are consciously communicating with your "Thought Adjuster" which has been indwelled with you.

Therefore, whether you use the Oxford Group Test for God's will, which is honesty, purity, unselfishness, and love, or the Alcoholics Anonymous Test for Self-Will, which is selfishness, dishonesty, resentment, and fear, you need to analyze what you have written during your morning meditation. When you finish your morning meditation or Quiet Time, check what you have written. If what you have written is honest, pure, unselfish, and loving, you can be assured those thoughts have come from the God of your understanding or a Power greater than you through your "Thought Adjuster." On the other hand, if what you have written is selfish, dishonest, resentful, or fearful, you can be equally assured those thoughts have come your selfish self.

The forefathers and pioneers of Alcoholics Anonymous insist that the God of your understanding or a Power greater than you will provide you with the answers to all of your questions if you get out of the way and listen quietly. They even disclose how the Spirit of the Universe is going to answer your requests for help. They write that in thinking about your day, you may face indecision. You may not be able to determine which course to take. Here, you ask the God of your understanding or a Power greater than you for inspiration, an intuitive thought or decision. Relax and take it easy and do not struggle. You will often be surprised how the right answers come after you have tried this for a while.

Therefore, the God of your understanding or a Power greater than you is going to tell you His plan for you in the form of inspiration, an intuitive thought or decision. If the God of your understanding or a Power greater than you is going to provide you with directions on how to live, it is a good idea to write down the directions, so you do not forget them.

The forefathers and pioneers of Alcoholics Anonymous tell us that we must get out of selfish self in order to get out of the way and learn the of plan of the God of our understanding or a Power greater than us has for us.

They wrote that we constantly remind ourselves we are no longer running the show, humbly saying to ourselves many times a day "Thy will be done." We are then in much less in danger of excitement, fear, anger, worry, self-pity, or foolish decisions. You become much more efficient. You do not tire so easily, for you are not burning up energy foolishly as you did when you were trying to arrange life to suit yourself.

This really does work. From firsthand experience, we can say with confidence that guidance has been working in our lives ever since we cleaned out the wreckage of the past and began our journey to wellness. But what if you do not receive any God-given thoughts or guidance? Remember, this can happen at any time, because you are human after all, fallible, prone to making mistakes, and prone to distraction.

All you really have is a daily reprieve from your insanity contingent upon the maintenance of your spiritual condition. Prayer and meditation take dedication and practice. If you do the work, you will receive the rewards—a life filled with health, happiness, and serenity beyond your wildest dreams.

Furthermore, we are told how the forefathers and pioneers of Alcoholics Anonymous did their prayers and meditation. We are told that they did their prayers and meditations in guidance sessions in accordance with the principles of the Oxford Group of which they were members.

The forefathers and pioneers met each morning in the living room of Dr. Bob Smith's home and a held guidance session. Here is the format they followed:

1. They took a few minutes of quiet time.
2. They read inspirational readings.
3. Next, they got pen and paper, and went to separate rooms.
4. They had a few minutes of silence, and they wrote whatever thoughts came to mind.
5. They reconvened and shared, one at a time, the guidance that came to them. Sometime, the guidance was for the writer, and sometimes it was for someone else.
6. Then, they closed, after which all had the opportunity to go to a quiet place in the house for individual prayers on their knees.
7. They then shared coffee and donuts together in fellowship.

Such was the way the forefathers and pioneers of Alcoholics Anonymous did their morning prayers, meditation, and received guidance from God of their understanding, when the program of Alcoholics Anonymous was enjoying a 93% recovery rate. It should be noted that you should spend more time listening quietly for the inner guidance of the God of your understanding or a Power greater than you to come forth, than saying prayers that tell God what you need or want. This Power already knows this.

Those who have truly recovered from this disorder use daily prayer and meditation in order to know the new vision that is promised in the chapter of the "Big Book:" entitled: "A Vision for You," which states there is a new vision that is giving you sane guidance, and that is circumventing the negative influences of your unconscious mind that was inspiring your previously insane thoughts and behaviors.

Furthermore, there is a reward for the "God-consciousness" or communication with your Thought Adjuster which results from doing the routine mentioned above every day. Nevertheless, for many of us, our first thought could still be a totally wrong one because our thoughts are filtered through our flawed unconscious belief system, which contains the corrupted values, beliefs, attitudes, virtues, and rules that were placed in us by our parents through rewards and punishments.

Therefore, it is vital to know what is in your unconscious belief system and clean out these distortions when you work the Steps, so your thoughts and actions are more often sane, rational, and spiritually-based which are more in concert with your aligned spirit or soul. This is your internal guidance system. In addition, for many of us, our history of decision-making, both under the influence of our addiction and sober, has been disastrous. Therefore, we ask the God of our understanding or a Power greater than us for guidance and thereby freeing ourselves from running our lives in accordance with a belief system that simply does not work as evidenced by our histories.

Why do you need to do this daily? In order to remain spiritually connected, you must have a daily contact or relationship with a God of your understanding or a Power greater than you. Keep in mind that your obsessive compulsive learned helplessness is the symptom of your problem, not the problem itself. The real problem lies in the conflict between the belief system that your parents, schools, churches, and society imposed on you in childhood and your own integral guidance system. This conflict caused us to try to find peace by any means you could.

As a result, you became selfish, dishonest, self-seeking, and insatiable in your self-driven desire to avoid or reduce your anxiety and tension produced by your internal conflict between what you wanted to be versus what your flawed internalized beliefs allowed to be, which not only caused you to fear others and resentment others, it caused others to do the same to you in retaliation. Consequently, you used your selfishness run amok in the form of alcohol, using various mood-altering drugs, or engaging in various addictive behaviors like our obsessive compulsive need to engage in codependence relationships with wounded souls or relationship addiction.

Consequently, you abandoned the will of the God of your understanding or a Power greater than you and became driven by your selfish self, which resulted in your soul sickness. Therefore, if you are not conscientious in your efforts in cleaning out the wreckage of your pasts, reclaiming your aligned soul, and opening your mind to the good orderly direction of through the Steps, you might delude yourself, as well as others, that you have been set free from the insanity of obsessive compulsive learned helplessness, when in fact, you are still driven by self-will and remain soul sick. As a result, you might engage in another bout of obsessive compulsive learned helplessness, or you might live in a chronic state of misery known as "white-knuckle sobriety" because you did not do the necessary preliminary work of working the Steps thoroughly and honestly.

In addition to morning prayers and meditation, you should spend a few minutes at night in reviewing your day. The forefathers and pioneers of Alcoholics Anonymous tell us that when we retire at night, we constructively review our day. Have we been resentful, selfish, dishonest, or afraid? The forefathers and pioneers of Alcoholics Anonymous tell us to answer these questions every evening. As a result, this technique becomes yet another form of an Asset and Liabilities Checklist, as well as another form of quiet time, meditation, and guidance.

Therefore, just as you had a negative daily routine when you were engaging in your obsessive compulsive learned helplessness that maintained your unmanageable life, a positive daily routine in which you spend time in the morning and evening reading, praying, meditating, and writing down the guidance you receive could help you maintain a happy, prosperous life. Are you willing to commit to spending a few minutes each morning and evening praying, mediating, and reviewing your day?

In order to help you get started with this vital step, the following is a guide to Step Eleven that should be repeated daily each morning following your Step Four inventory, or until change occurs. Realize that the people who wronged you are perhaps unhealthy people who have their own unfinished work. Ask the God of your understanding or a Power greater than you whatever you conceive that to be to help you show them the same tolerance, pity, and patience that you would cheerfully grant a sick friend. Ask the God of your understanding or a Power greater than you to show you how to be helpful to those you resent, and help you moderate your anger. Ask this Power to show you where you have been selfish, self-seeking, dishonest, or fear-based which has causing your own trouble and relieve you of the notion that you have to retaliate or that you are a victim.

Ask the God of your understanding or a Power greater than you to relieve you of all your fears, worries, and doubts. Pray for the willingness to get out of way of this Power and start make decisions together on a joined journey to wellness. Until your pain and suffering leave, keep asking the God of your understanding or a Power greater than you to help you realize that both are leading you to a positive change in your life.

In all your relations with others, ask for the God of your understanding or a Power greater than you for guidance. Ask the God of your understanding or a Power greater than you to give you a vision of a sane and sound ideal in all of your relationships with others, and allow you imagine what might happen in your life would be if you were able to move closer to the ideal.

Dr. Bob Smith, co-founder of Alcoholics Anonymous, recommended daily readings of what he called "Power Phrases." These include:

- What I resist persists.

- I will cease fighting.

- I could resist nothing today while still standing up for my own highest good.

- I do not have the power to drive anyone crazy or make anyone sane. Each individual is responsible for his own peace of mind.

- It is none of my business what anyone thinks about me or about anything else.

- I do not have the power to make anyone stay in my life.

- I do not have the power to drive anyone away.

- I do not have the power to make anyone miserable.

- I do not have the power to make anyone happy

- I will love all.

- My goal is peace of mind.

- The only way I could forgive someone today is to think I am God; I and the world will be better off if I do not judge in the first place.

- Not being God, I do not know what is good or bad, and since God knows all and does not only good, everything is ultimately for the good.

- God will take charge when I let go.

- I do not need to know anything or understand anything, but I shall instead only seek God's guidance, which I receive intuitively if I become still and quiet.

- I will not wish, hope, want, desire, nor crave today.

- I will not seek love—I will simply give love.

- I will receive human love, should God send it; however, I could only be content if I am attached to God.

- I could not be content in a human relationship with anyone until I am content without any human relationship.

- I will seek nothing God does not send.

- I will accept all that is sent be God.

- I will think less and employ intuition more.

- The past is gone—it is an image in my mind.

- The future could be no more than an image in my mind.

- Therefore, the present moment is the only real moment. I shall not allow false images to affect the way I feel.

- Everything really is going to be okay.

- I must get rid of any belief that was wrong by unlearning it.

- I will ask myself: "How important is it that I...?"

The operative principle of Step Eleven is Knowledge and Awareness. Here we search and become aware of following our path being aware of our purpose in life and actively pursuing it. This principle could be viewed as just being aware, not being caught up the rush of life, making conscious efforts to do the right thing and to be at peace.

Step Eleven suggests that you already have a conscious contact with the God of your understanding or a Power greater than you, and that the task before us now is to improve that contact. You began to develop your conscious awareness of the God of your understanding in Step Two, learned to trust this Power for guidance in Step Three, and relied on it many times for many other reasons in the process of working through the Steps. Each time you called upon the God of your understanding or a Power greater than you for help, you improved your relationship with Him. Step Eleven recognizes that reaching out to the God of your understanding or a Power greater than you, referred to most simply as prayer, is one of the most effective means for building a relationship with God of your understanding or a Power greater than you.

As was noted previously, the other means put forth in this Step is meditation. In this step, you will need to explore your own concepts of prayer and meditation, and make sure they reflect your spiritual path.

Your Own Spiritual Path

The Eleventh Step allows you the opportunity to find your own spiritual path, or further refine your path if you have already embarked on one. The steps you take toward finding or refining your path, and the way you walk down it, will depend to a large degree on the culture in which you live, previous experiences with spirituality, and what best suits your personal nature.

Your spirituality has been developing since you first came to recovery. You are constantly changing, and so is your spirituality. New territory, new people, and new situations have their effect on you, and your spirituality needs to respond.

Exploring your spirituality in the Eleventh Step is a wonderful and illuminating experience. You will be exposed to many new ideas, and you will find that many of these new ideas come directly from your own knowledge of spiritual matters. Because you have developed a frame of reference about spirituality in the previous ten Steps, you find that your insight has grown along with your capacity to comprehend new information about yourself and your world. Spiritual exploration is wide open, and you will learn and find personal truths both in your concentrated efforts to understand more and in the most mundane details of your lives.

Many of us find that when we get into wellness, we really need to "change Gods." Some of us believed in something we vaguely referred to as "God," but we did not really understand anything about it, except that it seemed to be out to get us. You probably did some work in Steps Two and Three aimed at uncovering unhealthy ideas about a God of your understanding or a Power greater than you, and then you tried to form some new ideas that allowed for a loving, caring Power. For many of us, simply believing that we had a God of our understanding or a Power greater than us that cared about us as individuals was enough to get us through the following Steps. We did not feel any need to develop our ideas any further.

But our ideas were developing anyway, even without our conscious effort. Each specific experience with working the Steps provided us with clues about the nature of the God of our understanding or a Power greater than us. We sensed truths about the God of our understanding or a Power greater than us rather than understanding them intellectually. The moment you sat down with your sponsor to share your Fifth Step, you were likely filled with a quiet certainty that you could trust your sponsor, trust this process, and could go forward. This was a moment in which you likely felt the presence of the God of your understanding or a Power greater than you for the first time. This, along with the work you did in Steps Eight and Nine, implanted in you a growing awareness of the will of a God of your understanding for you.

Answer the following questions:

- What experiences have you had with the previous Steps or elsewhere in life that gave you some inkling of what the God of your understanding is like?
- What did you come to understand about the God of your understanding from those experiences?
- What qualities does the God of your understanding have?
- Can you use those qualities for yourself?
- Can you experience their transformative power in your life?
- How has your understanding of a God changed since coming into recovery?

These clues about the nature of a God of your understanding or a Power greater than you are perhaps the primary factor in determining your spiritual path. Many of us have found that the spiritual path of our childhood does not mesh with the truths we are finding within the steps. For instance, if you sense that God is vast and open, and the spirituality that you have been exposed to in the past suggested that God was confined and confining, you are probably not going to return to your earlier path. If you sense that the God of your understanding or a Power greater than you cares in a very personal and individual way about you, a belief system that presents a distant, unknowable, alien force might not work for you.

Although some us need to take a new path, others have found that just the opposite is true, where what we are discovering in the Steps can be explored in more depth through the spiritual path of our childhood. It is possible that through your Step work you have healed resentments you might have held against religious institutions, and as a result are able to return to those institutions with an open mind. For others, the religion of your childhood was little more than a place to hang out, a community to which you only have a sentimental connection. In wellness, you begin to see how you can use your religion as your personal spiritual path.

It bears emphasizing that you should never confuse religion with spirituality. In the world of recovery, they are not the same thing at all. Twelve-step programs offer a set of spiritual principles, and use a concept referred to as "God," "Higher Power," or "Power greater than ourselves" for their members to use as a path out of active addiction. What are spiritual principles? It is the virtues that all major religions define and uphold as moral excellence.

The spiritual principles and the concept of a God of our understanding or a Power greater than us can go along with our personal spiritual path that we follow outside of a program of wellness, or those principles and the concept of a God of our understanding or a Power greater than us can serve as a spiritual path all by themselves. It is up to each of us to decide.

What about those who are agnostic and are unsure of the presence of an all-knowing, wise, loving power of the universe; or those who are atheist who do not believe in a "higher power" because they believe that a "higher power" really means a supernatural force capable of affecting outcomes in the material world. Atheists do not believe in the supernatural or things that do not exist in nature or that are not subject to explanation according to natural laws. How do these people manage Step Eleven that requires an understanding of a Power greater than themselves? The agnostic can believe in any power greater than themselves, whereas the atheist can stay in touch with their own inner wisdom through meditation and calm contemplation.

Some of us get to this point, and we just do not know. The institutions we have been involved with in the past hold no answers, but we cannot think of anything that sounds like a better idea. For those with this experience, this is the point at which we embark on one of the most important journeys in your life: the search for a way to understand a God of your understanding.

In this process, you are likely to visit every place that has anything to do with spirituality that is available in your community. You are also likely to read a great number of books concerned with spirituality and personal growth and talk to a great number of people. You might commit for a time to any number of practices before settling on one, or you might never really settle on any one practice permanently. Many adopt an "eclectic approach" to spirituality. If this applies to us, it is important to know that doing this is okay and will serve the spiritual needs of recovery just fine.

Answer the following questions:

* Do you have a specific spiritual path?
* What are the differences between religion and spirituality?
* What have you done to explore your own spirituality?

As we explore our spiritual path, and perhaps pick up and discard various moral practices, some of us are troubled by what seems to be an inherent bias in Alcoholics Anonymous' *Twelve Steps and Traditions* published in 1953 when "God" is referred to as having a male gender. Even more painful, some of us might feel that we do not have much support within our local community because of our spiritual and religious beliefs. It is important for us to understand that the language of twelve-step literature is not meant to determine a member's spirituality or religious beliefs. It is also important for us to understand that as people addicts, we have character defects, and sometimes some of our us will act on ours by ridiculing someone else's spiritual path. They might even quote Twelve Step recovery literature to "support" such ridicule.

Again, twelve-step programs themselves have no official or approved spiritual path, and any member who claims otherwise is quite simply wrong. I mention this here because I believe it is very important for all to know what is true and not true about Twelve Step programs when working the Eleventh Step. It can be a dangerous time. If we follow a spiritual path and feel unwelcome in Twelve Step programs because of it; their recovery can be in jeopardy. We all have a duty to encourage the spiritual explorations of other people, and we who are exploring need to know that we can look wherever we want for our spirituality without threatening our membership in a Twelve Step program.

Answer the following questions:

- Have you encountered any prejudice in Twelve Step programs while exploring your spirituality?
- How did that make you feel?
- What have you done to adhere to your beliefs?

It is essential that you do not let your spiritual path take you away from the fellowship. It is easy to float back out the door on a cloud of religious zeal and forget that you are powerless over your obsessive compulsive codependence or relationship addiction. We need to always remember that we need twelve-step programs to help us overcome our obsessive compulsive codependence or relationship addiction.

Anything else you add to your life can enhance its quality, but nothing can take the place of healthy recovery. If you continue practicing the basics of recovery such as going to meetings regularly, staying in contact with your sponsor, and working with newcomers, you should not have to worry about drifting away.

Answer the following questions:

- No matter what spiritual path you are following, are you still keeping up your involvement with Twelve Step programs?
- How does your involvement in Twelve Step programs complement your spiritual journey?
- How does your spiritual path contribute to your wellness?

Prayer and Meditation

Members of twelve-step programs often describe prayer as talking a God of our understanding or a Power greater than us, and meditation as listening to a God God of your understanding or a Power greater than you. This description has been part of the collective wisdom of twelve-step programs for a long time because it captures the distinct meanings of prayer and meditation so well. You are building a relationship with the God of your understanding or a Power greater than you, and you need to have a dialogue with that God, not merely a monologue aimed in its direction. Prayer is talking to the God of your understanding or a Power greater than you, although not always in the form of actual speech.

You worked on developing a form of prayer that felt right to you in the Second Step. You might find by now that you have further refined your approach to prayer to fit with your spiritual path. One of the forms of prayer in which virtually every member of twelve-step programs engages is the closing or opening prayer said at most twelve-step meetings. Ultimately, the way you pray is up to you as an individual.

How often should you pray? Many of us set aside a specific time in our day. The beginning of the day is common. These prayers usually involve asking the God or your understanding or a Power greater than you for another day free of acting out or, as we will explore more fully later in this chapter, knowledge of the will of the God of your understanding or a Power greater than you for you. When you communicate with the God of your understanding or a Power greater than you at the end of your day, it is usually to express gratitude. Many of us try to incorporate prayer throughout our day. It is very good practice to pray regularly. It helps us form a habit of communicating with the God of your understanding or a Power greater than you that might save our recovery someday.

Answer the following questions:

- How do you pray?
- How do you feel about praying?

- When do you usually pray?

- When you are hurting?

- When you want something?

- How is it helpful to use spontaneous prayer throughout the day?

- How does prayer help you put things in perspective?

If this is your first experience with the Eleventh Step, you might be surprised to learn you have already been meditating and doing so on a regular basis. Each time you stand as a community at a meeting and observe a moment of silence, you are meditating. It is from such beginnings that you go on to build a pattern of regular meditation.

There are many ways you can go about meditating, but its usual goal is to quiet the mind so that you can gain understanding and knowledge from the God of your understanding or a Power greater than you. You try to minimize distractions so that you can concentrate on knowledge arising from your own spiritual connection. You try to be open to receiving this knowledge. It is essential that you understand that such knowledge is not necessarily, or even usually, immediate. It builds in us gradually as we continue to practice regular prayer and meditation. It comes to us as a quiet sureness of our decisions and a lessening of the chaos that used to accompany all our thoughts.

Answer the following questions:

- How do you meditate?

- When do you meditate?

- How do you feel about meditating?

- If you have been meditating consistently for some time, in what ways have you seen changes in yourself or your life as a result of meditating?

Conscious Contact

Many of us think "conscious contact" sounds like something very mysterious, implying a cosmic union with a God of our understanding or a Power greater than us. But it is really very simple. It just means that you have a conscious awareness of your link to a God of your understanding or a Power greater than you. You notice the presence of this Power and see some of the ways it works in your life. There are so many ways people in recovery have experienced the presence of a loving God of your understanding or a Power greater than you: when we experience something in nature, such as a forest or an ocean; through the unconditional love of our sponsor or other members of twelve-step programs; through the feeling of being anchored during difficult times; through feelings of peace and warmth; through a coincidence that later on we see having led to some great good; through the simple fact of our recovery; through our ability to listen to others at a meeting; and countless other means. The point is that we are looking, and we are willing to acknowledge that the God of our understanding is active in our lives.

Answer the following questions:

- In what circumstances do you notice the presence of a God of your understanding?
- What do you feel?
- What are you doing to improve your conscious contact with the God of your understanding?

God's Will as You Understand It

The knowledge that has been building in you as you have prayed and meditated is the essence of the will of the God of your understanding or a Power greater than you for you. The whole purpose of praying and meditating is to seek knowledge of the will the God of your understanding or a Power greater than you for you, and, of course, the power to carry it out. But the first thing to do is to identify purpose of the God of your understanding or a Power greater than you for your life.

It takes a large amount of open-mindedness to begin to understand the will of the God of your understanding or a Power greater than you for you. Many of us find that it is easier to identify what is not the will of the God of our understanding or a Power greater than us for us than what is. This is okay. In fact, this is a great starting point that can lead us to more specific knowledge of the will God of your understanding or a Power greater than you for you. First, and most obvious, it is not the will of the God of your understanding or a Power greater than you for you to relapse. You can extend this simple fact to conclude that acting in way that might lead you to relapse is also not the will of the God of your understanding or a Power greater than you for you. You do not need to become overly analytical about this and start questioning whether your daily routines could possibly lead to you relapse; it is really much easier than that.

You will use all the knowledge about yourself and the patterns that you gained from the work you did in Steps Four through Nine, and you try your very best to avoid destructive patterns. You will discover that you no longer have the luxury of consciously acting out. You cannot deal with a situation by thinking: "Oh, I'll just be manipulative this one time, and then I'll write about it later, work with my sponsor, and make amends." If you do such a thing, you are not only on very dangerous ground, you are making a conscious and deliberate decision to go against the will of the God of your understanding or a Power greater than you. There will be many, many times when you will act on defects unconsciously. It is your consciousness and willingness to be deliberately destructive in this situation that is the real cause for concern.

In the Third Step, you explored the fine line that divides humble and honest pursuit of your goals from subtle manipulation and forced results. Now, with the experience you have gained in the intervening steps, you are much better equipped to spot that line and stay on the right side of it. As you go after the things you want, you need to continuously gauge your distance from that line. For instance, you might decide you want to be in a romantic relationship. There is nothing wrong with that, provided that you are mentally, physically, and spiritually motivated and keep track of the line between the will of the God of your understanding or a Power greater than you and your selfish self. If you lie to make yourself seem more attractive, or become a chameleon where you try to become anything your partner wants you to be, you are acting on your selfish self. If you honestly express who we you are, you are more likely to be pursuing the will of the God of your understanding or a Power greater than you. If you are trying to change your potential partner in a relationship into something they are not, you are acting on selfish self.

If, on the other hand, you have already determined what you want in a partner and the person you are seeing seems to be matching that vision without your intervention, you are probably living in the will of the God of your understanding or a Power greater than you. That is how you tell whether a relationship is the will of the God of your understanding or a Power greater than you or not. Or say you want a college education. Are you willing to cheat on a test to get it? Doing such a thing would turn an otherwise worthy goal into an act of self-will. The act of acting on selfish self is the primary reason you pray only for the knowledge of the will of the God of your understanding or a Power greater than you for you and the power to carry that out.

Answer the following questions:

- What are some situations you can identify from your own life where you acted on self-will?
- What were the results?
- What are some situations you can identify from your own life where you tried to align your will with that of the will of the God of your understanding or a Power greater than you?
- What were the results?

The will of the God of your understanding or a Power greater than you for you is the ability to live with dignity, to love yourself and others, to laugh, and to find great joy and beauty in your surroundings. Your most heartfelt longings and dreams for your life are coming true. These priceless gifts are no longer beyond your reach. They are, in fact, the very essence of the will God of your understanding or a Power greater than you for you. Your personal vision of the will the God of your understanding or a Power greater than you for you is revealed in how your life might be if you were consistently living with purpose and dignity. For instance, it is a good expression of purpose to help others stay clean and find recovery. The individual ways you go about doing that, such as sponsorship, sharing with newcomers at meetings, carrying the message into institutions, and working with professionals to develop programs that will lead religiously addicted people into the world of wellness, are your choice.

Answer the following questions:

- What are some examples of how you live with purpose and dignity?
- What is your vision of God's will for you?

The Power to Carry That Out

In addition to praying for knowledge of the will the God of our understanding or a Power greater than us for us, we are also asking for this Power to carry out that will. In this context, power does not refer only to forceful qualities. There are many different qualities you might need to carry out the will of the God of your understanding or a Power greater than you: humility, a sense of compassion, honesty, integrity, or an ability to persevere and the patience to wait for results over a long period. A strong sense of justice and an ability to be assertive might be what is called for in a certain situation. Sometimes eagerness is required, and other times only a sense of caution will do. Courage and fortitude are qualities that you will often be called upon to display. Sometimes, the best quality to promote the will of the God of your understanding or a Power greater than you is a sense of humor.

Most likely you will need all these qualities at various times in your life. When you pray for the power to carry out the will of the God of your understanding or a Power greater than you for you, you probably would not know exactly what qualities you need. You must trust that the ones you believe will be provided. It might be tempting for you to demand from the God of your understanding or a Power greater than you the things you think you need, but you usually cannot see the "big picture" or the long-term effects of something that seems very reasonable now.

Answer the following questions:

- Why do you pray only for knowledge of the will of the God of your understanding or a Power greater than you for you and the power to carry that out?
- How does humility apply to this?

Spiritual Principles

In the Eleventh Step, you will focus on commitment, humility, courage, and faith. You need to make a commitment to the practice of regular prayer and meditation. Many of us find that our first experiences with prayer and meditation makes us feeling kind of silly. You glance around the room to see if anyone is looking and wonder just what you are supposed to be feeling, anyway. As you continue with your commitment, this feeling will pass, as will the consuming feelings of frustration when the results are not what you expect, and the boredom that sets in when the things you are doing become routine. The point is that you need to continue, no matter how you feel about it. The long-term results of peace of mind and a deeper relationship with the God of your understanding are worth waiting for.

Answer the following questions:

- How do you show your commitment to working the Eleventh Step and to your recovery?

- Have you prayed and meditated today

The often-heard warning: "Be careful what you pray for!" captures the kind of humility you need to practice in this Step. You simply need to acknowledge that you do not always know what is best for you, or for anyone else. That is why you ask for knowledge of the will God of your understanding or a Power greater than you for you.

Answer the following question:

- Have you ever prayed for a specific thing and then wished you did not have it after all? Expand on this.

There is nothing that requires as much courage as trying to live according to the will of the God of your understanding or a Power greater than you when there is frequent pressure not to. Not everyone in your life will be delighted that you have chosen to live your life in a spiritual way. You might have family members who are used to you living according to their will and want you to continue. Your growth threatens them. Or say you are with some friends who are gossiping. Your efforts to live the program have resulted in you becoming uncomfortable with participating in gossip, yet you do not want to be self-righteous and start moralizing when you are with friends. Merely refraining from participating in something like this requires courage. You might lose some friends as you grow spiritually.

Almost all of us face some situation in life where we are either being asked to participate in something that is morally reprehensible or just keep quiet about it and allow it to happen. It might be that the truly courageous course of action is to protest loudly and doing so might have severe consequences for us. What we do at such a time is a defining moment and might very well affect the choices we make for the rest of our lives.

Answer the following questions:

- Have you ever been faced with a situation that required you to stand up for your beliefs at some personal cost?
- How did you respond?
- What were the results?

The principle of faith will help us to practice the principle of courage and live our lives with integrity. Faith is defined as confidence in what we hope for and the evidence of things not seen. You need not be so afraid of losing friends or having relationships change or even having your life profoundly affected because you know that you are being cared for. You have faith that if you have to let go of old friends because what they are doing is unhealthy for your spiritual development, you will form new relationships with people whose values you share. Basically, you need to have faith that you will be given the power to carry out the will of the God of your understanding or a Power greater than you.

Answer the following questions:

- Have you been given what you needed so far?
- What have you received?

Moving On

Your practices in this Step show up in every area of your lives. From the regular practice of meditation, you might notice that you are able to listen more attentively to what others have to say in meetings. You have some experience with quieting your mind and so are able to do so in many places. You no longer find yourself so consumed with planning what you will say when it is your turn that you are unable to listen to others.

You begin to be satisfied with your life. You no longer feel such an urgency to control things. You are focused on a higher purpose instead of on yourself. Your regrets begin to disappear. Your active religious addiction no longer seems like such a tragedy and a waste as you see how you can use that experience to serve a higher purpose: carrying the message to the addict who still suffers. In Step Twelve, you will explore some ways of doing that, and see how practicing the principles of recovery are essential to such an effort.

❧

Chapter Sixteen

Step Twelve

Having had a spiritual awakening as the result of the steps, we tried to carry this message to other addicts, and to practice these principles in all our affairs.

Now that you have made a conscious contact with God, as we understand Him, you have received the greatest gift of this simple program—a spiritual awakening. The God of your understanding or a Power greater than you is now guiding you in such a way that it is indeed miraculous. You will become sensitive to the needs of others and want to be helpful and loving to all. In order to be happy and prosperous, you must try to love everyone, even if we do not like their behavior or their words. You stop judging others and getting angry at their insane, selfish behavior because we have seen it in ourselves. You stop hating others in your actions and your speech because you do not like their politics or their religion. What you say and do is a mirror that magnifies your own defects and flaws for everyone to see. So, when you condemn others for their flaws and defects, you are shining a light on your own. Nevertheless, the spiritual awakening is only part of Step Twelve.

Let us look at what we must do to sustain our spiritual transformation, and therefore sustain our sanity and sobriety. In the first printing of the "Big Book," Step Twelve read: "Having had a spiritual experience as the result of these steps…" In the 16 years between the first edition of the "Big Book" written in 1939 and second printing written 1955, the forefathers and pioneers of Alcoholics Anonymous discussed the word: "experience" at length. Eventually, the word "experience" was replaced with the word "awakening." Alcoholics Anonymous World Services made this change in order to include those whose lives had truly been changed, but more slowly.

For many of us, our lives have changed, but gradually, rather than suddenly. We might not be able to point to a specific experience that brought about the change, but the spiritual awakening has occurred, nonetheless.

In the second edition of the "Big Book" published in 1955, Alcoholics Anonymous World Services wrote in Appendix II that the terms "spiritual experience" and "spiritual awakening" were used many times in this book which, upon careful reading, shows that the personality change enough to bring about recovery from addiction has manifested itself among us in many different forms. Yet, it is true that the first printing gave many readers the impression that these personality changes, or religious experiences, must be in the nature of sudden and spectacular upheavals. Happily, for everyone, this conclusion is erroneous.

Therefore, the spiritual awakening is nothing more than a psychic change that, among other things, eliminates our obsession to drink. So, Bill Wilson's rapid conversion experience is the exception, rather than the rule. The forefathers and pioneers of Alcoholics Anonymous describe a more gradual spiritual experience.

They wrote that among the membership of thousands of alcoholics such transformations, although frequent, are by no means the rule. Most of our experiences are what the psychologist William James called an "educational variety" because they develop slowly over time. Quite often friends and loved ones of the newcomer are aware of the differences long before the addict is aware of them. The addict finally realizes that they have undergone a profound alteration and transformation in their reaction to life and that such a change could hardly have been brought about by themselves alone. What often takes place in a few months could seldom have been accomplished by years of reading self-help books or self-discipline. With few exceptions, recovering addicts find that they have tapped into an unsuspected inner resource which they identify as their own conception of a Power greater than themselves.

The forefathers of Alcoholics Anonymous tell us how easy it is to experience a spiritual awakening. They wrote that most of us think that this awareness of a Power greater than ourselves is the essence of spiritual experience. More religious members call it "God-consciousness."

That is all there is to it. If you have developed a relationship with the God of your understanding or a Power greater than you and have started to listen for guidance, you have, in fact, already had the spiritual awakening. Congratulations! You are now living in the sunshine of the Spirit.

However, a spiritual awakening is just the first part of Step Twelve. Let us look at what we must do to sustain this spiritual transformation. Chapter Seven of the Big "Book," "Working with Others," is entirely devoted to carrying the message of Alcoholics Anonymous to others. The forefathers and pioneers of Alcoholics Anonymous tell us what we must do to enhance our awareness of the God of our understanding or a Power greater than us.

They wrote that practical experience shows that nothing will so much insure immunity from our addiction than intensive work with other addicts. It works when other activities seem to fail. This is our twelfth suggestion: Carry this message of recovery and wellness to other suffering addicts. You can help when no one else can. You can secure their confidence when others fail to do so.

So, what is the message we are to carry to the still suffering addict? The message is: This what we used to be like; what happened to us; and what we are like now.

The forefathers and pioneers went on to say that when we work others, our lives change, and life takes on a new meaning. By watching others recover, we see them help others. We see loneliness vanish. We see a fellowship grow up about us and to have a host of friends is an experience we must not miss. We know you will not want to miss it. Frequent contact with newcomers and with each other is the bright spot of our lives.

In this chapter, the forefathers and pioneers of Alcoholics Anonymous provided us with specific instructions on how to carry our lifesaving message of recovery to others.

They wrote that when you discover a prospect for recovery, find out all you could about them. If they do not want to stop drinking, using drugs, engaging in stimulating activities, or stop engaging in their obsessive compulsive learned helplessness, do not waste time trying to persuade them into recovery. You may spoil a later opportunity to bring them to wellness. Remember that recovery is receiving the healthy self, not abstinence.

The forefathers and pioneers of Alcoholics Anonymous provided us with specifics on what to say and what not to say. They wrote that you see your prospect alone, if possible. At first engage in general conversation. After a while, turn the talk to some phase of addiction. Tell them enough about your addiction habits, symptoms, and experiences to encourage them to speak of themselves. If they wish to talk, let them do so. You will get a better idea of how you ought to proceed.

Furthermore, the forefathers and pioneers wrote that you should not be discouraged if your prospect does not respond at once. Search out another addict and try again. You are sure to find someone desperate enough to accept with eagerness what you offer. We find it a waste of time to keep chasing someone who cannot or will not work with you. If you leave such a person alone, they may soon become convinced that they cannot recover by themselves. To spend too much time on any one situation is to deny some other addict an opportunity to live and be happy.

Regarding the person who makes one excuse after another, claiming they cannot stop their addiction until their material needs are cared for. The forefather and pioneers said nonsense. They wrote that some of us have taken very hard knocks to learn this truth: Job or no job, wife or no wife, home or no home, we simply do not stop acting out on our addiction so long as we place dependence upon people and things ahead of dependence on the God of our understanding or a Power greater than us.

They also said that we should lose the idea that we can get well regardless of others. The only condition is that you trust in the God of your understanding or a Power greater than you and come to, come to believe, clean house, make restitution for past wrongs, and serve humanity.

The forefathers and pioneers of Alcoholics Anonymous tell us how grow spiritually when we work with others. They wrote that both you and the newcomer must walk day by day on a path of spiritual progress. If you persist, remarkable things will happen. When you looked back, you will realize that the things which came to you when you put yourself in the hands of the God of your understanding or a Power greater than you were better than anything you could have planned or done. Follow the dictates of the God of your understanding or a Power greater than you and you will presently live in a new and wonderful world, no matter what your present circumstances are.

The forefather and pioneers of Alcoholics Anonymous believed that the God of your understanding or a Power greater than you is your new employer and He or It gave you a new job description. They wrote that your job now is to be at the place where you may be of maximum helpfulness to others, so never hesitate to go anywhere if you could be helpful. You should not hesitate to visit the most sordid spot on earth on such an errand.

Being of service to others is critical to the continued growth and the maintenance of your sobriety. Keep in mind that one of the primary services you can perform is to take prospective members through the Twelve Steps of Recovery and set them free. Each time you do this, you learn more about this lifesaving program and gain additional insight into the Divine inspiration that is the heart of your new way of life.

After completing the Twelve Steps of Recovery, it is vital that you not cling to and become dependent on others because you are beyond human guidance at this point in your development because guidance is now internally guided by the God of your understanding or a Power greater than you. It should be noted that after taking the Steps, you are not just in the Spirit of the Fellowship of Recovery, you in the Fellowship of the Spirit. Bill Wilson., co-founder of Alcoholics Anonymous, once said in an essay, you must practice the "principle of absolute dependence on God." Therefore, instead of clinging to others, you will immediately become a person who guides others through the Steps and works with still suffering people addicts.

Remember that Ebby Thacher, one of the forefathers of Alcoholics Anonymous, carried the message of recovery to Bill Wilson after only sixty days of sobriety. It should also be noted that the average length of sobriety of the 40 men who helped wrote the "Big Book" was 18 months, and the person with the most sobriety was a little over four years–Bill Wilson.

In the early days of Alcoholics Anonymous, a commitment to work with a newcomer did not go on more than a month or so because the forefathers and pioneers discovered that everyone had too much work to do to cling to one person, or to be clung onto by a newcomer. In addition, the forefathers and pioneers of the Alcoholics Anonymous intended that those who had recovered from addiction would help all those who needed help, but the goal was to get people to become independent of human guidance, and dependent on the guidance of the God of their understanding or a Power greater than them. Furthermore, being of service to others is critical to your continued growth and to the maintenance of your sobriety. Keep in mind that if you do not help other addicts through working with others and guiding them through the Steps or serving humanity in some way, you will likely regress back into your selfish insanity.

Now, the only task left is practicing these principles in all your activities. What principles? They are the Twelve Steps of Recovery. They are the principles you practice daily for the rest of your life. The forefathers and pioneers of Alcoholics Anonymous concluded with yet another statement on the importance of Divine guidance and the necessity of working with others.

They Wrote that the "Big Book" is meant to be a guide, not a rule. They realized that they knew only a little but the God of their understanding or a Power greater than them would constantly disclose more to them, just as this Power will do for you. Ask the God of your understanding or a Power greater than you in your morning meditation what you could do each day for the person who is suffering. The answer will come, if your own house is in order. But obviously you cannot transmit something you have not got. See to it that your relationship with the God of your understanding or a Power greater than you is right, and great events will come to pass for you and countless others. This is the great fact for us.

The forefathers and pioneers went on to say that you should abandon or selfish self and seek the guidance of the God of your understanding or a Power greater than you. Admit your faults to this Power and to your fellows. Clear away the wreckage of your past. Give freely of what you find and join others in recovery. You shall be loved and cared about within the Fellowship of Recovery, and you will surely meet some of us as you trudge the road of happy destiny.

Therefore, since you have had a spiritual awakening as a result of these Steps, the most important task is to carry this message to other addicts and practice these principles in all our activities to the best of our ability. However, it is important that you not just take the Steps just once. You should make continual trips through the Steps, as Step Ten suggests. If this is your first trip through the Steps, hopefully it will not be your last. Will you practice these principles in all of your affairs and carry this message to other alcoholics?

In short, here is how to stay sober:

1. Get someone to guide you through the Twelve Steps of Recovery. The first three Steps are the "Coming to Believe Steps." Steps Four through Nine are the "Cleaning House Steps," and Steps Ten through Twelve are the "Maintenance Steps." It should

be pointed out that Step Four is essential because it is the opening of the "Golden Door" to wellness and prosperity.

2. Recovery is an inside job, so it is essential to the inside work; that is, to explore, resolve, or let go past hurts and unsolved bitterness.

3. Help others by taking them through the Steps as quickly as possible. Then, you will see that a sane, spiritual life has a paradox--you have to give it away to keep it. We do not need to seek guidance from other people any longer because our guidance should be coming from God, not other people. We try to do the will God of your understanding or a Power greater than you, as He or It gives you the vision to do that will.

4. Seek guidance from the God of your understanding or a Power greater than you every morning, abandoning dependence on your conscious mind, your unconscious mind, and human guidance, and seek guidance from the God of your understanding or a Power greater than you to remain happy and prosperous.

5. All your life, you were in a fight or flight mode. Now, you do not have to fight anyone or anything, including you addiction. Trying to flee the past with your addiction did not serve you well, so when you want to get out of a bad space, you must go to a place of peace and serenity, which is called the Realm of the Spirit.

6. Take an inventory at the end of every day, and assess where you were resentful, fearful, selfish, or dishonest in any relationships with others, and right any wrongs before retiring.

7. Note that your selfish self will come back if you let it, so you must subdue it again and again because it often comes back in a form that may be different from that which you uncovered in Steps Four and Five.

The operative principle of Step Twelve is Service and Gratitude. Having brought about a personality change enough to remain in recovery; you are empowered to demonstrate the new principles by which you live your daily life through example. And so, you seek help when needed and are available to help others in need.

If you have made it to this point, you most likely have had a spiritual awakening. Although the nature of your awakening is as individual and personal as your spiritual path, the similarities in your experiences are striking. Almost without exception, those in recovery speak of feeling free, of feeling more light-hearted more of the time, of caring more about others, and of the ever-increasing ability to step outside yourself and participate fully in life. The way this looks to others is astonishing. People who knew you when you were in your active religious acting out, often appearing withdrawn and angry, tell you that you are different people. Indeed, many of us feel as if we have begun a second life.

You know the importance of remembering where you came from, so you try not to forget, but the way you lived and the things that motivated you seem increasingly bizarre the longer you stay clean. The change in you did not happen overnight. It happened slowly and gradually as you worked the Steps in every aspect of your life. Your spirit awoke a bit at a time. It became increasingly more natural for you to practice spiritual principles and increasingly more uncomfortable to act out on your character defects. Notwithstanding the powerful, one-of-a-kind experiences some of us have had, we have all slowly and painstakingly built a relationship with the God of our understanding or a Power greater than us. That Power, whether it is your own best and highest nature or a force outside yourself, has become yours to tap into whenever you want. It guides your actions and provides inspiration for your continued growth.

Answer the following questions:

- What is your overall experience as a result of working the steps?

- What has your spiritual awakening been like?

- What lasting changes have resulted from your spiritual awakening?

Each time you work through the Twelve Steps of Recovery, you will have a different experience.

Subtleties of meaning for each of the spiritual principles will become apparent, and you will find that as your understanding grows, you are also growing in new ways and in new areas. The ways in which you can be honest, for instance, will expand along with your basic understanding of what it means to be honest. You will see how practicing the principle of honesty must first be applied to yourself before you are able to be honest with others. You will see that honesty can be an expression of your personal integrity. As your understanding of the spiritual principles grows, so will the depth of our spiritual awakening.

Answer the following question:

- What does the phrase "spiritual awakening" mean to you?

We Tried to Carry This Message

Many of us recall the first time we heard the words: "You never have to act out again if you don't want to." For many of us, hearing this message was shocking. Perhaps you had never thought in terms of "having" to act out before and were surprised to find out just how much truth that statement held. Of course, you thought, acting out ceased to be a choice for you a long time ago. Although just hearing this message might or might not have resulted in you immediately getting clean, you still heard the message. Someone carried it to you.

Some of us had the experience of believing that we could stay well in twelve-step recovery programs, but when it came to wellness, it seemed beyond us. Without the inner work necessary for wellness, wellness will not happen no matter how many books you read, recovery meetings you attend, or churches you attend. Gaining a sense of self-respect, making friends, being able to carry ourselves out in the "real world" without it being obvious that we were addicted people all seemed like more than we could expect from twelve-step programs.

The day you began to believe that wellness can do more for you than just help you from engaging in your obsessive compulsive codependence or relationship addiction is a time you remember as a turning point in your discovery and wellness. What happened to give you that sense of hope was that someone gave you a reason to believe? Maybe it was someone sharing at a meeting with whom you identified in a very personal way. Maybe it was the cumulative effects of hearing many former addicts share that recovery was possible. Maybe it was the unconditional love and quiet insistence of your sponsor that you could get well. In whichever way you heard it, it was the message, and someone carried that message to you.

Some of us have the experience of staying free of our addiction for a long time and finding joy in recovery, but then we experience a tragedy of some kind. Maybe it was the breakup of a long-term committed relationship or the death of a loved one. Maybe it was a loss of a job or financial problems. Maybe it was that you found yourself lonely. Maybe it is simply that you have realized that other people you care about are not perfect, and are capable of hurting you.

But because of whatever crisis you experienced, you find that you have lost your faith. You no longer believe that discovery and wellness hold the answer for you. The bargain you thought you had made to get well and try to do the right thing, and consequently, live a life of happiness had been breached and you were left wondering about your purpose in life all over again. At some point, you began to believe again. Maybe someone who had been through the same crisis reached out to you and helped you through in a way no one else could have. Again, someone carried the message to you.

Answer the following question:

- What are the different ways in which you have experienced the message?

So, the message can be broken down very simply. It is that you can stay clean, that you can recover, and that there is hope. Recalling the times when you heard the message personally will provide part of the answer to why you should now carry the message, but there is more. We can only keep what we have by giving it away. This statement is perhaps the most powerful reason you can present for carrying the message. Many of us wonder exactly how this concept works. It is simple. You reinforce your recovery by sharing it with others. When you tell someone that people who go to meetings regularly stay clean, you are more likely to apply that practice to your own recovery. When you tell someone that the answer is in the Twelve Steps of Recovery, you are more likely to look there yourself. When you tell newcomers to get and use a mentor, you are more likely to stay in touch with your own.

There are probably at least as many ways to carry the message as there are people with obsessive compulsive codependence or relationship addiction. Greeting a newcomer that you meet and remembering his or her name is powerful and extraordinarily welcoming to another people addict who feels angry, betrayed, and alone. Fellowship with others makes sure there is a place for the message to be carried. You can do a great deal of good if you approach your service to others in a caring, loving, and humble way. Sponsoring another who suffers from obsessive compulsive misuse of sugar brings to your life a therapeutic value of one person helping another.

Answer the following question:

• What kind of service work are you doing to carry the message?

Sometimes it is challenging to carry the message. The person with whom you have decided to share the message seems unable to hear it. This can range from someone who keeps returning to the insane world of obsessive compulsive learned helplessness and the destruction that accompanies it. It is tempting to think that your efforts are being wasted and you should just give up on such a person. Before you make such a decision, you should think about all the mitigating circumstances. Say you are mentoring someone who just is not following your direction. You have suggested a writing assignment, and you do not hear from the person again until a fresh crisis is brewing. You have shared, with all the enthusiasm you can summon, about your own experience with the situation the person is facing, explaining in detail how your condition was present and how you used the Steps to find wellness, but your sponsee keeps doing the same destructive thing over and over again. This can be very frustrating, but before you give up, you need to remember that your choice is not whether to carry the message, but how?

We need to get your own ego and selfish self out of the way. You do not get to take credit or blame for someone else's discovery and wellness. You simply present the message as positively as you can and remain available to help when you are asked. You also need to remember that you cannot possibly know what is going on in another person's mind or spirit. Your message might seem to be missing its mark, but perhaps the person just is not ready to hear it today. It might be that the words you spoke will stay with a person for a long time and might resurface at exactly the right moment.

If you think about it, you can recall all the things you heard people in twelve-step programs say when you were new that you did not understand at the time, but which rose up in your mind years later and gave you reason to hope or a solution to a problem you were experiencing. You carry the message, and you share it freely, but you cannot ever force another person to get the message. The principle that applies to our fellowship's public relations policy, attraction, not promotion, applies very well to your personal efforts to carry the message too.

It might also be the case that you are not the best person to sponsor someone. Individuals have different needs and learn in different ways. Some people might thrive with one sponsor, but not do well with someone who has a different sponsorship style. Some sponsors give a lot of writing assignments. Some are very insistent about their sponsees going to a certain number of meetings. Some are very "proactive," whereas others might simply respond to a sponsee's stated needs. No one is better or worse than any other. They are just different.

Another time you might find it very hard to carry the message is when you are not feeling very positive about life or recovery. It is probably your first impulse to go to a twelve step meeting or someone and dump all your problems out, so you can purge them from your own mind. But twelve-step meetings exist to provide a place to carry the message of recovery and wellness, not a place dump your stuff. Dumping your problems without trying to overcome them does not further the primary purpose why these groups exist. You can carry the message even if you just point out that you are having terrible problems, but are not returning to your old behaviors and that you are attending a meeting and reaching out to work on your recovery.

In most cases, the best way to carry the message is to focus on the person who still suffers from powerlessness over their sugar addiction and tell them what is good about the world of recovery and wellness. You should also keep in mind that sometimes, no matter how long you have been out of the insanity of your obsessive compulsive learned helplessness, you need to hear the message, and if you sit quietly, you have a good chance of doing so.

Answer the following questions:

- What are some different ways of carrying the message?
- Which ones do you personally participate in?
- What is your personal style of mentorship?
- What is the difference between attraction and promotion?
- What does it do for you to carry the message?
- How are the Fifth Tradition and the Twelfth Step tied together?
- What keeps you coming back and trusting in the journey to wellness
- What is selfless service?
- How do you practice it?

Practicing These Principles in All Our Activities

When we talk about practicing the principles of wellness in all our activities, the key word is "practice." What you practice at, you will get better at. You just need to keep trying to apply spiritual principles to your lives, not be able to do it perfectly in every situation. The spiritual benefits you derive from working this Step depend on your effort, not your success.

For instance, you try to practice the principle of compassion in every situation in your life. It is probably relatively easy to practice the principle of compassion with a person who are powerless over their learned helplessness who has been abstinent for a while, no matter how belligerent or needy they are, but what about someone who has returned after another bout of destructive obsessive compulsive learned helplessness? What if they walk in blaming others for their situation? What if they casually project an attitude that seems to take recovery and wellness for granted? What if it is someone you sponsored? You might find that practicing the principle of compassion does not come as easily as it used to. You might not feel compassionate toward the person, but you can still practice the principle of compassion. All you have to do is continue to carry the message without condition. Your sponsor can help you learn how to be compassionate without giving the impression that you think that returning to active sugar addiction is okay. You can pray and meditate, asking the God of your understanding to help you be compassionate.

This Step calls upon you to practice principles in all your activities. Many of us would like to separate our careers, our romantic relationships, or other areas of our lives from this requirement because we are not sure we can get what we want if we have to practice spiritual principles. For instance, it might very well lead to apparent success and financial reward if you practice these principles at work. You might be asked to meet a production deadline that results in profits for the company but produces an inferior product that could compromise the safety of the people who purchase it. So, what do you do? You practice the spiritual principles of your recovery. There are probably many different choices about the specific action to take in response to your principles; the important thing is that you respond guided by your own values, principles, and virtues.

What about service to others? Strangely enough, some of us reserve service as the one place where we forget our principles. We cease giving people the benefit of the doubt in a service setting. We openly accuse others of hatching plots, and we say cruel things because we are not practicing the principle of kindness. We set up impossible processes for those we elect to do a job because we are not practicing the principle of trust. We become self-righteous, belligerent, and sarcastic. It is ironic that we seem to want to attack those whom we trust with our very lives in recovery meetings. We need to remember to practice spiritual principles in any meeting, whether service, recovery, or every aspect of our lives. Service gives us many opportunities to practice spiritual principles.

Knowing which spiritual principle to practice in any given situation is difficult, especially early in recovery, but it is usually the opposite of the character defect you would normally be acting out on. For instance, if you feel compelled to exert absolute control over a situation, you can practice the principle of trust. If you would usually be self-righteous in a certain situation, you can practice the principle of humility. If your first impulse is to withdraw and isolate, you can reach out instead. The work you did in the Seventh Step on finding the opposites of your character defects and the work you did at the beginning of this step on identifying the spiritual principles in the previous steps will give you some additional ideas about the principles you need to practice. Although most of us will wind up with very similar lists of spiritual principles, the attention we devote to certain ones will reflect our individual needs.

Answer the following questions:

- How can you practice principles in the different areas of your life?
- When do you find it difficult to practice principles?
- Which spiritual principles do you have a particularly hard time practicing?

Spiritual Principles

Even in the Step that asks you to practice spiritual principles, there are specific principles connected to the Step itself. Nevertheless, you focus on unconditional love, selflessness, and steadfastness.

Practicing the principle of unconditional love in the Twelfth Step is essential. Nobody needs love without condition more than a still suffering addict. You do not ask anything of the people to whom you are trying to carry the message. You do not ask for money. You do not ask for gratitude. You do not even ask that they stay out of situation that might trigger their religious addiction. You simply extend yourself. This does not mean you should not take reasonable precautions. If you believe it is not safe to bring someone into your home, you should not do so. Twelfth Step calls should always be done with another person. Nor does practicing the principle of unconditional love require that you allow yourself to be walked over or abused. Sometimes the best way of loving and helping is to stop enabling someone else to use.

Answer the following question:

* How are you practicing the principle of unconditional love with the addicts you are trying to help?

Why do you carry the message? Not to serve yourself, even though you will benefit from it. You carry the message to help others, to help them find freedom from their obsessive compulsive codependence or relationship addiction and grow as individuals. If you have an attitude that the people you sponsor are somehow your possessions, that their lives would fall apart if you were not directing their every move that most likely they would not even be clean without us, then you have missed the point of the Twelfth Step.

We do not expect recognition from those around us. We do not expect recognition for being of service. We do these things to accomplish something good. It is a great paradox that selfless service becomes an expression of your deepest self.

Through your work in the previous Steps, you have uncovered a self that cares more about allowing the God of your understanding to work through you than it cares about recognition and glory. You have uncovered a self that cares more about principles than the exercise of your individual personalities. Just as your affliction is often expressed in self-centeredness, your recovery is expressed beautifully as selfless service.

Answer the following questions:

- What is your attitude about sponsorship?
- Do you encourage others to make their own decisions and grow as a result?
- Do you give advice, or do you share your experience?
- What is your attitude about service?
- Could your wellness program survive without you?
- How are you practicing the principle of selflessness in your efforts to be of service?

Practicing the principle of steadfastness means you need to keep on trying to do your best. Even if you have had a setback and fallen short of your own expectations, you need to recommit yourself to wellness. Steadfastness keeps a bad morning or a bad day from turning into a pattern that can lead to bad results. This commitment ensures that you will keep practicing the principles of your program despite how you feel. Whether you are happy about it, bored with it, disgusted by it, or completely frustrated over it, you keep on trying to work a program.

Answer the following questions:

- Are you committed to your wellness?

- What are you doing to maintain it?

- Do you practice spiritual principles regardless of how you feel?

Moving On

Before you get too excited about the prospect of being finished with the Twelve Steps of Recovery, you should realize that you are not finished. Not only will you continue trying to practice the spiritual principles of all twelve steps, which many of us call "living the program," but you will formally revisit each of the Steps, probably many times, throughout your life.

Some of us might immediately begin working through the Steps again with the perspective that we have gained from our journey thus far. Others wait for a time or concentrate on certain aspects of the Steps. However, you do it, the point is that whenever you find yourself powerless over your sugar addiction, whenever more has been revealed about your shortcomings or people you have harmed, the Steps are available as your path to wellness.

You should feel good about what you have done. You have, in many cases for the first time, followed a process all the way through. This is an amazing accomplishment, something about which you should be very proud. In fact, one of the rewards of working a wellness program is finding that your self-esteem has grown a great deal. You will rejoin your society. You can do things that seemed beyond you before: exchanging greetings with a neighbor or the clerk at your local market, taking on positions of leadership in your communities, joining in social events with people who do not know you were powerless over power and not feeling "less than." In fact, you might have looked with contempt upon such things in the past because you felt we would never be able to fit in, but now you know you can.

You become approachable. People might even seek your advice and counsel on professional matters. When you think about where you have come from and what your recovery has brought to your lives; you can only be overwhelmed with gratitude. Gratitude becomes the underlying force in all that you do. Your very lives can be an expression of your gratitude; it all depends on how you choose to live. Each one of us has something very special and unique to offer in gratitude.

Answer the following question:

- How will you express your gratitude?

Chapter Seventeen

Conclusion

In conclusion, those who have worked the Steps should take another alcoholic through them. What has worked in the past and brought the early fellowship a 75% to 93% recovery rate and gave countless thousands of suffering alcoholics a chance at a new way of life, could work again. But there is nothing else that will so much insure your sobriety and mental health as working with others. Our illness is three-part problem with a one-step solution, and our goal in this new way of life is two-fold: (1) we want to stay sober and sane, and (2) we want to be useful to others who are still suffering.

I will close this book with *Desiderata*, which is Latin for: "Something desired as essential:"

Desiderata

Go placidly amid the noise and haste, and remember what peace there may be in silence. As far as possible, without surrender, be on good terms with all persons. Speak your truth quietly and clearly; and listen to others, even to the dull and ignorant; they too have their story. Avoid loud and aggressive persons; they are vexations to the spirit.

If you compare yourself with others, you may become vain and bitter, for always there will be greater and lesser persons than yourself. Enjoy your achievements as well as your plans. Keep interested in your own career, however humble, it is a real possession in the changing fortunes of time.

Exercise caution in your business affairs, for the world is full of trickery. But let this not blind you to what virtue there is; many persons strive for high ideals, and everywhere life is full of heroism. Be yourself. Especially do not feign affection. Neither be cynical about love; for in the face of all aridity and disenchantment, it is as perennial as the grass.

Take kindly the counsel of the years, gracefully surrendering the things of youth. Nurture strength of spirit to shield you in sudden misfortune. But do not distress yourself with dark imaginings. Many fears are born of fatigue and loneliness. Beyond a wholesome discipline, be gentle with yourself.

You are a child of the universe no less than the trees and the stars; you have a right to be here. And whether or not it is clear to you, no doubt the universe is unfolding as it should. Therefore be of peace with God, whatever you conceive him to be.

And whatever your labors and aspirations, in the noisy confusion of life, keep peace in your soul. With all its sham, drudgery and broken dreams, it is still a beautiful world. Be cheerful. Strive to be happy (Ehrmann, 1927).

References

12 Steps from the original manuscript. Retrieved June 2016 from http://members.aol.com/-
     _ht_a/transitionsdaily/originalsteps.html.

A guide for working the steps with alcoholics. (2000).

Alcoholics Anonymous Comes of Age. (1957). New York: Alcoholics Anonymous World Services,
     Inc.

Alcoholics Anonymous, (1955). 2nd ed. New York: Alcoholics Anonymous World Services, Inc.

Alcoholics Anonymous. (1939). 1st Ed. New Jersey: Works Publishing.

Alcoholics Anonymous. (1976). 3rd ed. New York: Alcoholics Anonymous World Services, Inc.

Alcoholics Anonymous. (2001). 4th ed. New York: Alcoholics Anonymous World Services, Inc.

Alcoholics Anonymous—An interpretation of our Twelve Steps. (1944). Washington, DC:
     Paragon Creative Printers.

Anonymous. (1934). *What is the Oxford Group?*

Batterson, J. E. (2001). *How to Listen to God,* Reprint of Oxford Group Pamphlet. Retrieved
     June 2016 from http://www.aabibliography.com.

Dr. Bob and the Good Old Timers. (1980). New York: Alcoholics Anonymous World Services,
     Inc.

Ehrmann, M. (1927). *Desiderata,* Retrieved June 2016 from http://webpages.charter.net/
     rfhale/desiderata.html.

P., W. (1998), *Back to Basics: The Alcoholics Anonymous Beginner' Meetings,* Second Edition.
     Tucson, AZ: Faith with Works Publishing Company.

Step 4, (2002). Retrieved June 2016 from http://webpages.charter.net/rfhale/step4.htm.

The Little Red Book. (1954). Minneapolis, MN: Coll-Webb Company.

എ

About the Author

The author is an ordained minister, certified chaplain, a Licensed Clinical Social Worker who has over 35 years of healthy sobriety and wellness who has sponsored many people throughout the years, taking them through the Twelve Steps of Recovery and setting them free. The author's sponsor was one of the first 100 alcoholics in the early days of Alcoholics Anonymous who taught this writer and many others what the forefathers and pioneers of Alcoholics Anonymous knew and what healthy recovery and living a good life in wellness really means. Now, the author passes along the knowledge and wisdom of the forefathers of Alcoholics Anonymous to those who read this book.

Printed in Poland
by Amazon Fulfillment
Poland Sp. z o.o., Wrocław